(HETEROSEXUALITY)

A Feminism & Psychology Reader

edited by

SUE WILKINSON and CELIA KITZINGER

SAGE Publications
London • Newbury Park • New Delhi

This Collection first published 1993

Items by the contributors listed below appear in print for the first time in this Collection:

Victoria Robinson (pp. 80–2); Alison M. Thomas (pp. 83–5); Elizabeth Mapstone (pp. 86–9); Loulou Brown (pp. 90–2); Pauline B. Bart (246–52); Cindy Patton (pp. 257–60); Julia Penelope (pp. 261–5); Helen (charles) (pp. 270–2).

All other items appeared first either in *Feminism & Psychology* 2(3) 1992, the Special Issue on Heterosexuality, or as listed below:

Feminism & Psychology 2(2) 1992: Jackie Gilfoyle, Jonathan Wilson and Brown, 'Sex, Organs and Audiotape: A Discourse Analytic Approach to Talking About Heterosexual Sex and Relationships'.

Feminism & Psychology 3(1) 1993: Mary Boyle, 'Sexual Dysfunction or Heterosexual Dysfunction'; S.P. Schacht and Patricia H. Atchison, 'Heterosexual Instrumentalism: Past and Future Directions'.

SAGE Publications Ltd
6 Bonhill Street
London EC2A 4PU

SAGE Publications Inc
2455 Teller Road
Newbury Park, California 91320

SAGE Publications India Pvt Ltd
32, M-Block Market
Greater Kailash – I
New Delhi 110 048

British Library Cataloguing in Publication data

ISBN 0–8039–8822–2
     0–8039–8823–0 (paper)

Library of Congress catalog card number 00–0000

Typeset by Mayhew Typesetting, Rhayader, Powys
Printed in Great Britain by J.W. Arrowsmith, Bristol.

HETEROSEXUALITY

A Feminism & Psychology Reader

Edited by Sue WILKINSON and Celia KITZINGER

CONTENTS

———————————————————————————— ABOUT THE EDITORS

Sue WILKINSON is Senior Lecturer in Health Studies Research at the University of Hull. She is the founding and current editor of *Feminism & Psychology: An International Journal*, and edits the international feminist book series *Gender & Psychology* (both published by Sage). She has published extensively in the areas of feminist research and methodology.

Celia KITZINGER teaches social psychology and women's studies in the Department of Social Sciences at Loughborough University. She is the author of *The Social Construction of Lesbianism* (Sage, 1987) and co-author of *Changing Our Minds: Lesbian Feminism and Psychology* (London and New York: Onlywomen and NYU Press, 1993).

Celia KITZINGER and Sue WILKINSON[1]

Theorizing Heterosexuality

Heterosexuality has been largely untheorized within both feminism and psychology. Feminist theory tends to assume heterosexuality as a given, developing analyses with women's (and men's) heterosexuality as a taken-for-granted, but never explicitly addressed, substrate. Psychology similarly assumes heterosexuality, with lesbianism (and male homosexuality) as 'alternative lifestyles' at best, 'pathological perversions' at worst. In both feminism and psychology, heterosexuality disappears into the background, leaving lesbianism as the interrogative focus. In this *Reader* (an expanded version of the Special Issue of *Feminism & Psychology* 2(3), 1992), we foreground heterosexuality as requiring analytic attention. The set of questions we asked in our 'Call for Contributions' was a deliberate reversal of those which psychology has traditionally addressed to the topic of lesbianism: 'What is heterosexuality and why is it so common? Why is it so hard for heterosexuals to change their "sexual orientation"? What is the nature of heterosexual sex? How does heterosexual activity affect the whole of a woman's life, her sense of herself, her relationships with other women, and her political engagements?'

When we told people we were working on a Special Issue on heterosexuality, one common reaction was delighted laughter. What delights is recognition of the implicit politics which inspires the reversal of all those Special Issues on lesbians (e.g. *Feminist Review* 34, 1990; *Signs: Journal of Women in Culture and Society* 9(6), 1984; *Feminist Arts News* 3(5), 1990; *Jump Cut* 24/25, 1981; *Textual Practice* 4(2), 1990; *Sinister Wisdom* 2 and 42). Another response, which came mostly from heterosexuals, was fear and hostility: what would we lesbians have to say about heterosexuality, and what would *we* know about it, anyway? Finally, there was blank incomprehension: *why*? When the whole of psychology, literature, art and the popular media present virtually nothing *but* heterosexuality, and images of lesbians are so rare, why would we, as lesbians, want to add to the heterosexual deluge? This response is similar to that received by feminist psychologist Halla Beloff when she announced her intention to research men: 'the whole of psychology is about men — they have had their day'. This she describes as 'a terrible falsity', because psychology has not been about men *qua* men — merely men as generic people. 'The idea that you would actually look at . . . male self-presentations, male meanings, male perspectives was something that had been absolutely absent' (quoted in Wetherell and Griffin, 1992). As Julia Penelope's contribution shows, the same is true of research on heterosexuality. Woman *qua* woman is heterosexual and belongs in Special Issues rather than as part of the normal business of a journal. To know who the Generic Woman of feminist theory is, look at the topics of Special Issues (lesbians, black women, old women, working-class women, disabled women) — all 'word ghettos' (Brown, 1990) for those who do not conform to the white-heterosexual-middleclass-ablebodied-young-western woman who passes for Generic Woman in so much feminist theorizing.

It is more than a decade since Adrienne Rich wrote her classic article 'Compulsory Heterosexuality and Lesbian Existence' (Rich, 1980). This

> . . . was written in part to challenge the erasure of lesbian existence from so much of scholarly feminist literature, an erasure which I felt (and feel) to be not just antilesbian but antifeminist in its consequences, and to distort the experience of heterosexual women as well. It was not written to widen divisions but to encourage heterosexual feminists to examine heterosexuality as a political institution which disempowers women — and to change it. . . . I wanted, at the very least, for feminists to find it less possible to read, write or teach from a perspective of unexamined heterocentricity (Rich, 1989).

The 'unexamined heterocentricity' of psychology was one of her concerns. Of the four books (then just recently published) which prompted her analysis, three have been enormously influential in feminist psychology: Jean Baker Miller's (1976) *Toward a New Psychology of Women*, Dorothy Dinnerstein's (1976) *The Mermaid and the Minotaur* (published in the UK as *The Rocking of the Cradle and the Ruling of the World*), and Nancy Chodorow's (1978) *The Reproduction of Mothering*. (The fourth is Barbara Ehrenreich's and Deirdre English's [1978] *For Her Own Good*.) Adrienne Rich points out that in these books female heterosexuality is simply assumed as the natural, taken-for-granted way to be for most women, obscuring the overt and covert violence with which 'compulsory heterosexuality' is forced upon us, through, to cite only a fraction of her catalogue: the socialization of women to feel that male sexual 'drive' amounts to a right, the idealization of heterosexual romance, rape, pornography, seizure of children from lesbian mothers in the courts, sexual harassment, enforced economic dependence of wives and the erasure of lesbian existence from history and culture.

The assumption that 'most women are innately heterosexual' stands as a theoretical and political stumbling block for feminism. It remains a tenable assumption partly because . . . to acknowledge that for women heterosexuality may not be a 'preference' at all but something that has had to be imposed, managed, organized, propagandized, and maintained by force is an immense step to take if you consider yourself freely and 'innately' heterosexual. . . . To take the step of questioning heterosexuality as a 'preference' or 'choice' for women — and to do the intellectual and emotional work that follows — will call for a special quality of courage in heterosexually identified feminists . . . (Rich, 1980).

So far, feminists (within and beyond psychology) have failed sufficiently to address the issues raised by Adrienne Rich, or to theorize heterosexuality *qua* heterosexuality. It remains true that feminist scholarly writing generally, and feminist psychology in particular, perpetuates the myth of heterosexuality as an innate and unquestioned 'given' for most women (see, for example, Dorothy Smith's [1992] identification of the 'heterosexist . . . prejudices' of Cynthia Fuchs Epstein's *Deceptive Distinctions*).

Despite the critiques levelled by Adrienne Rich and other lesbian writers (e.g. Bart, 1977, 1983), feminist psychologists routinely cite the work of Baker Miller, Chodorow and Dinnerstein without any reference to the heterocentrism of these theories (nor, indeed, their cultural specificity and racist implications: cf. Rich, 1980; Brown, 1990). 'Heterosexual' (like 'white', 'male' or 'ablebodied') is always a silent term. Although most feminist social science books index a few pages (at most) on lesbians, few feature 'heterosexuality' (or any variant thereof) in their indices because women's heterosexuality is the assumed, taken-for-granted topic of the remainder of the book (for example, Oakley, 1981; Whitelegg et al., 1982; Midgely and Hughes, 1983; Bernay and Cantor, 1986; Matlin, 1987; Phillips, 1987; Walsh, 1987; Williams, 1987; Chaplin, 1988; Doyle and Paludi, 1991; Basow, 1992). Ironically, although almost all of these books cite Rich's 'compulsory heterosexuality' article, in what appears to be routine obeisance to a classic text, her analysis is ignored, and the relentless tyranny of the heterosexual assumption continues unabated.

In the same year that Rich's 'compulsory heterosexuality' article was published, Bea Campbell (1980), writing in *Feminist Review*, regretted that 'no doubt many heterosexual women talked to one another about what they were doing, but there was and still is, no culture within the women's liberation movement that represented or legitimated their struggles'. More than a decade later, heterosexual women have still not produced any sustained theory about heterosexuality per se (cf. Victoria Robinson),[2] and we are aware of the irony that lesbians should be creating the space that heterosexual women have, apparently, been unable or unwilling to create for themselves.

To our role as editors we bring, despite our similarities (we are both white, middle class, thirtysomething and British) entirely different experiences of heterosexuality. One of us (CK) has always been lesbian, came out aged 16, has never had, or wanted to have, sex with men, and developed a feminist awareness through the experience of living as a lesbian under heteropatriarchy. The other (SW) was happily and exuberantly heterosexual, married for 15 years, becoming lesbian only relatively recently through the impact of feminism on her emotional and sexual experience. Out of our different pasts, we (along with many other lesbians) have theorized and debated the relationship between our lesbianism, the institution of heterosexuality and our feminist theories. This discussion has, for the most part, taken place outside the psychological arena, and its relevance for psychology is left unstated. So we are especially pleased to offer a forum for this debate. Our contributors come from many disciplines in addition to psychology — including sociology, social anthropology, women's studies, history, African and Asian studies, English literature, law, media and cultural studies, plus contributions from outside academia — but all are reflecting on questions of identity, sexuality and relationships, fundamental to psychology.

We are delighted by the interest this project has generated. It is very much a collaborative effort. In addition to the forty-three named authors (including the eleven writers of peer-reviewed articles), there were seventy-plus reviewers, and many people in the authors' (and editors') lives who discussed ideas, read drafts and gave feedback. We would like to thank everyone who has been involved and we hope that the ideas put forward here will be further explored within both feminism and psychology. We are particularly grateful to Rachel Perkins for her help in editing the Special Issue of *Feminism & Psychology* (on which this *Reader* is based), and in which she took special responsibility for the book review section (not reproduced here).

We are very pleased to be publishing a collection of writing from such varied theoretical and political approaches. It would be difficult to find anything upon which all contributors were in agreement — except, perhaps, the importance of theorizing heterosexuality. The crucial criterion for inclusion was not whether we thought the arguments were 'true', nor whether we happened to agree with them, but whether publication of them could advance the development of feminist theory on heterosexuality. Our disagreement with some authors is profound, but we thought it right to keep editorial interventions to a minimum in order not to impose our own (lesbian) perspectives on the material. This necessitated the difficult decision that for the Special Issue, and for that issue only, *Feminism & Psychology* should suspend its editorial policy against heterosexist language. Nonetheless, we think that the range and diversity of material included is an important strength, and we hope that it will speak to readers with a wide variety of perspectives. In the remainder of this editorial introduction, we identify some of the core themes raised by the contributors, and suggest how they might be developed.

WHAT IS HETEROSEXUALITY?: ON CATEGORIES AND CONTINUA

'How does your heterosexuality contribute to your feminist politics (and/or your feminist psychology)?'[3] We sent a letter asking for 1000 words in response to this question to feminists (including feminist psychologists), none of whom had ever, so far as we knew, made public statements identifying themselves as anything other than heterosexual. Two replied saying they were lesbian and had written publicly as such (we apologized). One wrote back saying she was lesbian but we weren't to tell anyone. And many many women wrote wanting to know how we *knew* they were heterosexual, and, indeed, how *they* could tell whether they were heterosexual or not, and just what *is* a 'heterosexual' anyway? 'Why address me so categorically as a heterosexual?', writes Mary Gergen.

> Why was anyone so sure? Because I am married? Or because my husband seems 'straight'? Is it about my hairdo or my shoes or the things I have said, or not said?. . . How did the heteros get picked out? (p. 62).

Only when we started to compile a list of heterosexual feminists as potential recipients of our letter did we realize how rare such a public identification is. It would have been much easier to compile a list of self-identified lesbian feminists. 'Heterosexual' is not a popular label, and many feminists express their concern about it. Where they had thought of themselves as 'women' or 'feminists', our invitation positioned them as 'heterosexual feminists' — making explicit the silent term, qualifying (as do labels like 'white', 'western', 'ablebodied') the presumed universality of their perspective as Generic Women. A couple of women we had known for years in professional contexts, who had never given us any reason to suspect that they were anything other than heterosexual — who had talked freely of their husbands and never (ever) spoken out on lesbian issues — wrote angrily in response to our letter, 'How dare you assume I'm heterosexual?' and 'Don't you think you are making one hell of an assumption?' We hope that those women who found our assumption of heterosexuality offensive will challenge that assumption when others make it about them too. We were making explicit an assumption they allow to be implicit in their everyday lives: we would welcome their public and professional rebuttal of it. Unwilling to accept the label 'heterosexual', several decided against participating, saying, 'I have a strong ambivalence about accepting the label "heterosexual"', or:

> While I do identify as a feminist, I don't have any sense of identity as a 'heterosexual feminist' and indeed would reject that label. For me feminist politics is inspired by a sense of solidarity with other women and I would find it difficult to set myself apart from other women by applying such a label to myself.

Discomfort with the label 'heterosexual' is common among many of those who did contribute (though not all: see, in particular, Bartky and Hunter). 'None of the labels seems adequate for who I am', writes Mary Crawford, describing how her love for, and sexual attraction to, women exists in conjunction with a long-term monogamous marriage. 'Saying "I am heterosexual" implies that my sexual preference is an unchanging and essential personal attribute. . . . No one should be limited by this or any other label', says Carol Nagy Jacklin. More forcefully still, Sandra Bem states: 'although I have lived monogamously with a man I love for over 26 years, I am not now and never have been a "heterosexual" '.

Overall, women felt that the label 'heterosexual' limited and constrained them, and that it was an inaccurate definition of their (albeit apparently heterosexual) lifestyles. In a particularly telling analysis, Alison Young, who (unusually) has previously written of herself as heterosexual in another context, contrasts that self-naming with the experience of being labelled: 'To be invited to write *in the name of heterosexuality* by another is to experience the force of being positioned as Other. In this context, the name "heterosexual" seems far more permanent and concrete than in my own use of it. Now my identity feels out of control.'

Here lies an important distinction. For many lesbian feminists, accepting the label 'lesbian' is a defiant act of self-naming, in which we assert our refusal of the heteropatriarchal order, and our commitment to women and lesbians. It is claiming for ourselves, and as political, the identity they taught us to despise. As Denise Thompson says: 'lesbianism is not only genital sexual desire and/or activity, but also a redefining by women for women'. In a heteropatriarchal world, lesbianism is never simply something a woman becomes by chance, without thinking, by default. Questions like 'What causes it?', 'Can I change it?', 'How will it affect my children?' are among those that virtually every lesbian has pondered at some time in her life. For heterosexual feminists, they are entirely new:

> I have given some thought to what if anything I would like to write, but in the end have come to the conclusion that heterosexuality has become such a submerged and taken-for-granted part of my identity that I would be dredging around for something interesting to say. You can take me as evidence that the Special Issue is indeed needed, but I'm afraid I don't have anything to contribute to it.
>
> I don't have time to contribute. I'd need to put an icepack on my head and think about nothing else for a couple of weeks.
>
> It scares me, not so much because of the fact that it will expose my gross ignorance, but because, for perhaps the first time, I will have to try to wrestle with a subject which is beginning to look like a 'black hole' for me and for which I have no vehicle or protection.

In sum, heterosexuality is not a *political* identity for heterosexual feminists in the way that lesbianism is a political identity for lesbian feminists. Several of the contributors recognize the apolitical nature of their heterosexualities. 'We feel guilty about our heterosexuality', say Ros Gill and Rebecca Walker, 'which is not "lived" as a political identity. . . . Who would want to mobilize around being straight?!' Or, as Caroline Ramazanoglu laments, 'there is no "politically correct" feminist way of bringing the men out of our closets'.

Perhaps because heterosexuality is so rarely 'a purposeful political stance' (Kadiatu Kanneh) heterosexual feminists' discomfort with the label leads often to a call for dissolution of the exclusive and dichotomous categories 'lesbian' and 'heterosexual' in favour of recognizing individual diversity, and the common bonds that unite all women. Shulamit Reinharz finds the idea of 'fixed positions' unappealing: 'I prefer to think that we move around, perhaps on a continuum, in different stages of our lives'; Alison Young rejects the notion of 'sides' in favour of the analogy of the colour spectrum; while Mary Gergen makes a passionate plea to all of us to 'spring beyond the dilemmas of binary oppositions'. Many identify feminism as their inspiration: 'One of the exciting discoveries that feminism has brought to us', says Nira Yuval-Davis, 'has been the social construction of sexuality and the realization that we all have, to a lesser or greater extent, bisexual desires'. Similarly, Mary Crawford points out:

> One thing that feminism has taught me is to question oppositional categories. 'Heterosexuals' can't exist without the corresponding category of 'homosexuals'. . . . [This opposition] obscures the many dimensions along which an individual might choose to place herself as a sexual, sensual and social being (p. 43).

Of course, many lesbians share this sense that the categories into which they are expected to slot their sexuality are limiting or inappropriate — especially those who, like heterosexual feminists, do not politicize their sexual identity (see the discussion in Kitzinger, 1987: 109–12). But there *is* a politicized lesbian feminist identity — or, rather, a range of such identities, within all of which lesbianism per se is constructed as political. By contrast, there have been no corresponding heterosexual feminist identities, political *by virtue of* their heterosexuality.[4]

In a perhaps understandable desire to dissolve their (unpoliticized) 'heterosexual' identities, choosing continua over categories, heterosexual feminists sometimes fail to appreciate the importance of the label 'lesbian' to those who claim it. It may be liberating for heterosexual feminists to know that they can be other than heterosexual, to cast off that label and to escape from the 'prison' of categorical heterosexual identity (to borrow a metaphor used by both Tamsin Wilton and Patricia Duncker), but for lesbian feminists, things are different. Every lesbian *knows* that she should be, is expected to be, and perhaps has been, or could be, other than lesbian. Affirming our lesbianism is a liberatory feminist act. When we say we are lesbian, it is not (necessarily) because we never enjoyed sex with men (although some of us didn't); not (necessarily) because we are never sexually attracted to men (although some of us aren't); not because we experience our sexuality as a 'rigid', 'fixed', 'essential personal attribute';

not because we cannot appreciate 'fluidity', 'flux' or 'change' in our lives; but because, while acknowledging the contradictions, we are making a political statement. The terms 'heterosexual' and 'lesbian' are not symmetrical; the consequences of accepting them are different, as are the consequences of letting them go. Safe and uncontested labels and dominant group membership can readily be shrugged off as unimportant; membership of an oppressed group needs to be claimed, and tenaciously too, despite the contradictions.

'Heterosexual' and 'lesbian' are *not* opposite ends of the same continuum. Because 'lesbian' is an intrinsically politicized identity, and heterosexuality is not, the two terms are not commensurate, do not belong in the same conceptual space. Lesbian feminists have available a whole set of explicitly political meanings — and in assimilating the term 'lesbian' into a heterosexual–lesbian continuum, these meanings are lost. We would suggest that what is needed is not the depoliticization of lesbianism (through the adoption of continua), but the politicization of the category 'heterosexual'. The problem for heterosexual feminists is, to quote Kadiatu Kanneh's question, 'How is it possible to inscribe a safe, uncontested identity as a purposeful political stance?'

THERE'S NOBODY HERE BUT US WOMEN: DIFFERENCE, SIMILARITY, AND THE 'LESBIAN/HETEROSEXUAL SPLIT'

Although many feminists describe their understanding of lesbian similarity and their preference for 'continua' rather than 'categories' as deriving from their feminist analysis, in fact, the dissolution of the categories of 'lesbian' and 'heterosexual' started long before second-wave feminism began to address these issues. It was Kinsey et al. (1948, 1953) who invented the 'heterosexual–homosexual continuum', and initiated the recognition of everyone's 'bisexual potential'. Far from polarizing 'lesbians' and 'heterosexual women' into two dichotomous and exclusive categories, mainstream sexologists, sociologists and psychologists emphasize the essential similarities between them. Lesbians are supposedly characterized by 'A Conformity Greater than Deviance' (Gagnon and Simon, 1973: 176), and are 'Not So Different' (headline reporting Bell and Weinberg's [1978] research, *Sunday Telegraph*, 15 October 1978). Both Jenny Kitzinger and Pam Alldred (1992) draw attention to the contemporary fashion for 'gender-neutral' approaches to sex, in which the gender of sexual partners is left unspecified, terms such as 'lover' or 'partner' are used, women's sexuality is dealt with as a homogeneous mass, and 'lesbians are simply . . . added into a book which is primarily about heterosexuality' (Alldred, 1992: 483) — in pretty much the same way that women were added into books about male psychology. Indeed, the belief that heterosexual women *are* different from lesbians is now treated as symptomatic of pathology ('homophobia'; Kitzinger, 1987, 1993a). The denial of lesbianism as a distinct state of being, and the characterization of lesbians as basically just the same as heterosexual women, is one of the most pervasive themes of liberal discourse on lesbianism (cf. Kitzinger, 1987). Parallel claims that women are 'just like' men or that blacks are 'just like' whites reveal the extent to which, in a hierarchically structured world, 'sameness' is conflated with equality, while differences serve as vehicles through which to enact and justify inequality (cf. Irvine, 1990). The refusal to see that race, class, culture, nationality, age and (dis)ability are core to women's experience of the world — that, in Kadiatu Kanneh's phrase, they all 'go deeper than the skin', results in a homogenizing of 'women's experience' and an obliteration of the full range of oppressions to which we are subject, the diversity of communities from which we draw our strengths. Nira Yuval-Davis comments that 'the differences among women are as important and significant as the differences between women and men . . . national, racial, class, place in the life cycle, and other social divisions are interrelated and enmeshed with gender divisions . . .', so that, as Chris Griffin shows, the experience of compulsory heterosexuality 'is racialized and class specific as well as gendered'. As Yvon Appleby's contribution makes clear, compulsory heterosexuality operates differently in constructing the experience of ablebodied women and disabled women. In saying, 'there's nobody here but us women', we lose sight of what else we are *beside* being women.

Early second-wave feminism was marked by a widespread refusal to notice that some of us are not (just) women, but are lesbians. Denise Thompson's paper points to the exclusion of lesbians from the politics of such key feminist writers as Germaine Greer and Betty Friedan (see also the critique by Uszkurat, 1990). Some feminists suggest that lesbians are also rendered invisible by Adrienne Rich's phrase 'lesbian continuum', a concept which is intended to 'include a range — throughout each woman's life and throughout history — of woman-identified experience . . . including the sharing of a rich inner life, the bonding against male tyranny, the giving and receiving of practical and political support' (Rich, 1980). Adrienne Rich has herself subsequently expressed regret at some of its applications. It can be, and is, she says:

> . . . used by women who have not yet begun to examine the privileges and solipsisms of heterosexuality, as a safe way to describe their felt connections with women, without having to share in the risks and threats of lesbian existence. What I had thought to delineate rather complexly as a continuum has begun to sound more like 'life style' shopping (Rich, 1989: 324).

In a controversial analysis, Tamsin Wilton suggests that women's bonding in the face of oppression (part of Rich's 'lesbian continuum') in fact plays a key role 'in *supporting and sustaining* the power differential between heterosexual women and men'. She argues that in heterosexual women's friendships:

> Men come in for much criticism, and sympathetic sisterly reassurance when a particular man has treated a particular woman badly typically depicts the man as an unfeeling or selfish bastard, and as representative of his sex. What

conspicuously does *not* come in for criticism, true to its ubiquitous 'elemental' status, is heterosexuality. The motivation for heterosexual woman-bonding is analogous to that of a battlefield hospital: to get the casualties fit and well so that they may be sent straight back to fight — not to rescue combatants from the horror of war or to protest at war itself . . . Thus the oppressed collude with the oppressor . . .' (p. 274).

In arguing that 'homosocial relations are organized in the ways they are *precisely in order to produce the gender differences heterosexuality requires*', Deborah Cameron (1992) implies a similar analysis. Both these authors point not just to the fact of 'difference' between women and men, and between lesbians and heterosexual women, but to the power dynamics which generate that 'difference'.

Recent uses of 'diversity' and 'difference' (with or without a French accent) often legitimize oppression by obscuring the operation of power. Some of our contributors point out that 'to be heterosexual is to be privileged over other forms of sexuality' (Alison Young), that as heterosexuals they 'have many of the privileges and rewards of the establishment' (Carol Nagy Jacklin) and that, as members of a dominant group, they have 'an obligation not to abuse their position' (Halla Beloff). 'No matter how marginal or alienated from the culture's categories I may feel subjectively,' says Sandra Bem, 'the outward pattern of my life is so completely in harmony with the culture's heterosexist institutions that I experience little or none of the flak that I would if I were living my life as anyone other than a heterosexual'. As Mary Crawford puts it:

> No one hassles me at my child's school, at the doctor's office or at work. No one tells me I'm an unfit mother. Because I am legally married, my job provides health care benefits for my partner and family (an urgent necessity in the USA, where health care is a privilege of the wealthy). Wills and mortgages, taxes and auto insurance, retirement pensions and school enrollment for the children — all the ways that individuals ordinarily interface with social structures — are designed to fit people like me and my partner (p. 44).

These privileges mean that heterosexual women may need to explore their own stake in the continuation of male supremacy: 'For example, if you are receiving heterosexual benefits through a man (or through his social, cultural or political system), are you clear about what those benefits are doing to you, both personally and in terms of other women?' asks Charlotte Bunch (1975), citing examples from her own experience (in the USA) of feminists who abandoned their political positions when their husbands' jobs were threatened by feminist hiring demands. In the UK a few years ago, we watched women channelling money to men *in the name of feminism*, when heterosexual women successfully lobbied the Universities Superannuation Scheme to enable widowers to inherit their wives' pensions, while our lesbian partners cannot.

But the power dynamic at work is more than simply a 'civil rights for lesbians' issue. Power does not simply operate to discriminate against or oppress lesbians; it also actively constructs woman-as-heterosexual. In political opposition to the hidden (heterosexual) specificity of the seemingly generic term 'woman', French radical lesbians (see Hoagland and Penelope, 1988: 429–500) argue that 'to be a lesbian, whether politically aware or not, is to be outside the concept of "woman"' (Brunet and Turcotte, 1988: 454). Monique Wittig's statement that 'lesbians are not women', calls into question the whole institution of heterosexuality. 'Woman', she says, 'has meaning only in heterosexual systems of thought':

> If we as lesbians and gay men, continue to speak of ourselves and to conceive of ourselves as women and as men, we are instrumental in maintaining heterosexuality. I am sure that an economic and political transformation will not dedramatize these categories of language. Can we redeem *slave*? Can we redeem *nigger, negress*? How is *woman* different? (Wittig, 1992: 30).

As Denise Thompson points out, the so-called 'lesbian/heterosexual split' is not so much a split between women of different sexual identities, but rather between those with differing political commitments. In Sydney, she says, 'It was a lesbian/lesbian split, with radical feminist lesbians on one side insisting that lesbianism was necessary for the feminist revolution, and socialist feminist lesbians on the other worrying about being too threatening to heterosexual women, often referred to as "most women", or "the women out there" . . .'. (See also Alderson, 1981, for a similar analysis of the UK 'split'.) Lesbians (and, to a lesser extent, heterosexual women) take up positions on both sides of the divide. The debate is about the extent to which lesbianism is an identity worth organizing around politically (as opposed to a sexual preference or choice of lifestyles); and about the extent to which it is possible to create specifically lesbian theories and politics (as opposed to generic 'woman's'). It is not simply an argument about whether or not all women should be lesbians (although this has certainly been part of it; cf. Onlywomen Press, 1981), but also an analysis of the meanings of lesbianism and heterosexuality under patriarchy.

> The lesbian/straight split is a metaphor for the life of every lesbian as she has been split off from the rest of the world by virtue of her lesbianism. She is split off from people close to her — family, friends, she is split off from women at work and in the neighborhood, she is split off from the communities that she may identify with as a black, Jewish, or working-class woman, she is split off from any validating images of herself in both the commercial and 'progressive' cultures. She is also split off from working openly in homophobic sectors of the women's movement. . . .
> Unless the feminist movement is able to accept an understanding of lesbianism that fully believes that lesbian oppression and compulsory heterosexuality hurt all women by limiting their possible visions for their own lives, then we will not survive (Sarah Shulman, 1982: 42).

Although, by the mid-1970s, feminists were optimistically describing the 'lesbian/straight split' as history, they also warned that unless we learned from it, we would be doomed to repeat it (cf. Bunch, 1975). Recent events within UK psychology (cf. Comely et al., 1992) represent a grim prophecy come true: a group calling itself 'lesbian' was told by a group calling itself 'women' (including, of course, some lesbians) that there was no need for lesbians to organize autonomously — that our aims could be 'accommodated and facilitated within the present structure of the Psychology of Women Section [of the British Psychological Society]' (Ussher, 1991). 'Woman' embraces 'lesbian', and the resulting inclusivity is as illusory, and as destructive, as 'man's' embrace of 'woman'.

It is sometimes suggested that only an acknowledgement of *similarity* between lesbian and heterosexual, only the 'continuum' model, can ensure the visibility of lesbians within feminism. Conversely, it has also been argued that only by stating categorical *differences* can lesbian existence be truly honoured. The frightening truth is that the erasure of lesbians can be effected irrespective of whether lesbians are considered to be 'the same as' or 'different from' heterosexual women. Both 'inclusion' and 'exclusion' have been used within the mental health disciplines, and within feminism, to obliterate lesbianism and to reinforce the institution of compulsory heterosexuality. Lesbians will become visible within feminism only when the institution of compulsory heterosexuality becomes a serious target for analysis and political action.

'A LONG GREY STREAM OF HETEROSEXUAL MISERY': EGO-DYSTONIC HETEROSEXUALITY UNVEILED?

A 'long grey stream of heterosexual misery' — that's how Patricia Duncker describes Margaret Atwood's novels. It's not a bad description of the material collected here either. Although criticism of heterosexuality is (it seems) less acceptable when it comes from lesbians, 'heterosexual women generally make no bones whatever about criticizing heterosexual relationships, in depth, in detail, and with considerable passion and bitterness' (Onlywomen Press, 1981: 56). Topics covered include coercive heterosexual sex (Nicola Gavey), the sexual abuse of girls (Jenny Kitzinger and Kelly, 1992), prostitution (Shameem, 1992), battered women (Mayne, 1992), sexual harassment (Hollway, 1992) and AIDS (Cindy Patton). We would like to have included more on the benefits and rewards of heterosexuality for feminists — but little of this was submitted.

We didn't ask for misery — in fact, we deliberately posed a 'positive' question about the contribution of heterosexuality to feminism, and we are aware that the contents of this collection stand in bleak contrast to the celebratory tone of journal Special Issues on lesbianism. Lesbians under pressure to 'justify' lesbianism frequently resort to protestations of happiness (the 'personal fulfilment account'; Kitzinger, 1987), having been 'pushed into years of shouting almost banal slogans such as "Glad to be Gay"' (Parker, 1987: 141). By contrast, it seems that on the rare occasions when heterosexual feminists are challenged about their heterosexuality, they tend to describe how miserable they are, compared with the (presumed) happiness of lesbians. Contributors to this volume write of 'unrelenting' tension (Hilary Lips and Susan Freedman), 'unbalanced struggles and compromises' (Caroline Ramazanoglu), 'painful' contradictions (Ros Gill and Rebecca Walker) and the 'toll on my self-esteem' (Carol Nagy Jacklin).

We shouldn't really have been surprised. The reasons for heterosexual women's misery have been well documented far more bleakly than in these pages. For example, despite pioneering studies on the politics of housework going all the way back to Charlotte Perkins Gilman (1898) in first-wave feminism, and developed by Pat Mainardi (1970) and Ann Oakley (1974) in early second-wave feminism, a 1985 survey found that while *un*married women in the USA do an average of 14.9 hours' housework per week, the burden of housework is half as much again for married women (22.4 hours), while married men average only 8.8 hours per week (cited in French, 1992: 187–8). In an earlier issue of *Feminism & Psychology*, Rose Croghan (1991) documented the huge discrepancies between male and female labour in the home after the birth of the first child, and here she reflects on its implications for heterosexual feminists, while Carol Nagy Jacklin points out the financial benefits that accrue to men as a consequence of their wives' labour. Not only is heterosexuality exhausting for women, it is also dangerous. Many feminists (lesbian *and* heterosexual) have pointed out that a great deal of violence against women takes place within or is associated with heterosexual institutions (see S.P. Schacht and Patricia Atchison for a review). Women who date men, voluntarily have sex with them and marry them, are disproportionately at risk of violence, rape and murder from those men. Each year in the USA, 30 percent of all women murdered are killed by their husbands or male lovers — about 1500 women each year — and male violence against their wives is well documented (see Mayne, 1992). More than 40 percent of all battered wives report having been raped by their husbands (Russell, 1990); and about half of these are subjected to anal rape, and are hit, kicked or burned as part of the rape (Campbell and Alford, 1989). According to a survey of a random sample of nearly 1000 women in the USA, 14 percent of all married women have been raped by their husbands (Russell, 1990), and date rape is increasingly coming to the fore as a serious problem for women (Muehlenhard and Linton, 1987; Johnson et al., 1992). When male college students are asked if they would rape if assured they would not be caught and punished, more than a third say they would (34 percent, Briere and Mulamuth, 1983; 37 percent, Tieger, 1981). Add to this the problems of dangerous contraception and unwanted pregnancies, and the rape of children by their mothers' husbands or male lovers — from all of which heterosexual women are disproportionately at risk.

No wonder, then, that psychologists have repeatedly found that heterosexuality is not very good for women. The classic study by Gove (1972) revealed that marriage is good for men's psychological health and bad for women's: there are much higher rates of mental illness among married women than among married men, but no significant sex differences in mental illness rates for the divorced, widowed or never married. Standard psychological tests administered to both heterosexual women and lesbians reveal that, compared with lesbians, heterosexual women score *higher* on neuroticism (Wilson and Green, 1971; Siegelman, 1972), tension (Hopkins, 1969), anxiety (Ohlson and Wilson, 1974) and depression (Siegelman, 1972); and that they score *lower* than lesbians on scales designed to measure 'capacity for status', 'good impression', 'intellectual efficiency', 'endurance' (Wilson and Green, 1971), 'goal-direction', 'self-acceptance' (Siegelman, 1972), 'alertness', 'responsibility' and 'self-confidence' (Ohlson and Wilson, 1974).[5]

'Lesbians might be oppressed in the public domain, but heterosexual women . . . enter unequal partnerships in which sexist norms and power relations prevail', says Nira Yuval-Davis, adding that lesbians enjoy 'the comforts of the ghetto experience' and the 'luxury' of 'doing away with men' (would it were that easy!). For Rose Croghan, whose research arises out of the 'stress [she] experienced as a mother within a heterosexual relationship', it is to lesbian mothers 'that heterosexual feminists look in the hope of finding a model of equality, which can eventually be applied to our relationships with men'. Hilary Lips and Susan Freedman write of 'luxuriating' in the space afforded them at feminist gatherings: 'Despite our sidestepping our (hetero)sexuality on these occasions, it sometimes seems, paradoxically, that the tone of these gatherings, the sense that this is *our* time, is set by the lesbians who attend'. Attributing comfort, luxury, equality and happiness to lesbians, heterosexual women write of the painful conflicts and compromises with the men in their lives. Most poignant is Sandra Lee Bartky, who has 'often wished that I could love women erotically'. In what is, perhaps, the first ever case of 'ego-dystonic heterosexuality'[6] reported in a professional psychology journal, she appeals to feminist psychologists to 'invent a therapeutic technique for releasing the heterosexual woman . . . from the prisonhouse of necessity into the free space of choice'.

For some heterosexual feminists, the contradictions between political ideology and lived personal experience are acute, painful and involve constant compromise. As Carol Nagy Jacklin puts it, 'heterosexual feminists live, work and may be in love relationships with the "enemy"', experiencing feminism as 'something that threatens our closest relationships' (Hilary Lips and Susan Freedman) and developing a feminist consciousness which is 'critical of our most intimate being and entails at least some resistance to close relationships with our nearest and dearest men' (Caroline Ramazanoglu). Understanding these personal contradictions is a political exercise. That old slogan, 'the personal is political' (Hanisch, 1971) means, amongst other things, that the personal, including love, sexuality and our erotic responses, is part of the political order we strive to change, part of our political agenda. As Lidstone (1992: 479) puts it, 'the personal does not precede the political, it *is* the political; the political does not simply "affect" our personal lives, the choices and actions which constitute our personal lives also have political meaning'. Heterosexual feminists in this collection are doing more than simply romanticizing lesbianism and wallowing in misery: they are beginning to theorize some of the contradictions inherent in feminist heterosexuality.

THE POLITICS OF THE EROTIC: RHETT BUTLER AND THE SISSY MAN[7]

Although many feminists describe heterosexual women's disappointment or disgust with heterosexual sex, none of our contributors write of their personal experience with the agonized revulsion of this anonymous author in a national British newspaper:

> Sometimes I lie in bed and think of all the women who might be crying tonight. Crying because they know they'll have to 'do it' tomorrow, crying because they can 'feel him' coming towards them, crying because he is grunting there on top of them, crying because their bodies aren't their own any more because they promised them away 20 years ago and it doesn't seem possible to get them back (Anon, 1989).

Over the following weeks, the newspaper was deluged with letters, two-thirds written anonymously, by women who clearly identified with her despair. Marriage guidance counsellor, Renate Olins (1989), who read through all the letters, says that most of the writers 'seem to find sex with their husbands anything along the scale from boring to repugnant, clenching their teeth or digging their nails into their palms to get them through the whole horrible process'.

In addition to many heterosexual women's distaste for sex with men, a sizeable percentage of women report submitting to unwanted sexual intercourse because of male pressure, social status or physical force. In survey studies about half of all women report such experiences (50 percent Koss et al., 1987; 47 percent, Johnson et al., 1992), although most do not apply the label 'rape'. In this collection, Nicola Gavey documents instances of coercive sex that avoid the label 'rape' only because women enduring them do not actually say 'no'; there is no 'rape' because, faced with no alternative, women acquiesce. As one of her interviewees puts it, 'if I'd resisted, then he might rape me'. The ultimate pragmatic reason for apparently 'consenting' to sex is to avoid being raped. According to feminist legal theorist, Catherine MacKinnon:

> If women did not resist male sexual aggression anymore, the confounding of sex with aggression would be so epistemologically complete that it would, indeed, be eliminated. No woman would ever be sexually violated, because sexual violation would be sex. The situation might resemble that evoked by a society Sanday (1981) characterised as 'rape-free' in part because the men assert there is no rape there: 'our women never resist'. Such pacification also occurs in 'rape-prone' societies like the United States, where some force may be perceived as force, but only above certain threshold standards (MacKinnon, 1987: 73).

Patricia Duncker quotes Margaret Atwood: 'He's got her jeans worked halfway down her thighs before it occurs to her that William is trying to rape her': the contrast between the reality of 'acquaintance rape' and stereotypes of strange rapists in dark alleys delays the recognition, and the naming. Dislike of the 'coital imperative' — the male equation of 'sex' with intercourse (Nicola Gavey) — is also a feature of several contributions. Remembering her own heterosexual experience, Tamsin Wilton describes her 'recognition that I would have to train myself to reach orgasm as rapidly as possible, because "sex" ended with male ejaculation'. For Ros Gill and Rebecca Walker, who are 'constantly struggling to persuade partners to see sex as more than simply penetration', the price is that 'We've both lain there feeling not pleasure but guilt that we're putting our "nice" men through this, and anger that they have no idea what makes us feel good'.

Women's *pleasure* in sex with men is generally less well theorized. It has become customary, as Catherine MacKinnon (1987: 70) points out, to affirm that sexual pleasure is socially constructed, but 'seldom specified is what, socially, it is constructed of'. A particular feature of this volume is its focus on the specific and peculiar nature of the social construction of (hetero)sexual pleasure, and one of the clearest arguments to emerge from many of the contributions is the equation of heterosexual sex with the expression of power and powerlessness — 'sex' as male domination and female submission (cf. Mary Boyle). Allan Hunter, who describes himself as a 'sissy man', makes explicit the link between the masculinity of the 'real man' — 'the huntin', shootin', fishin' type who has mastered the wilderness' (Patricia Duncker) — and the patriarchal construction of heterosexual sex:

> . . . sex would lose its sexiness if it no longer included the element of the 'hunt', the attempt to seduce, and the thrill of the chase . . . it has often been asserted that [sissy] men have too much in common with women for either of them to feel much excitement. There is no gap for the spark to jump. You get two sweet, nice people together, and nobody's going to do anything except with the permission of the other, assuming that anyone has the 'balls' to bring the subject up. Nobody getting turned on, chased down and *had* by someone who knows how to arouse the traitor body. Nobody feeling the triumph of coming in for the 'kill', gleefully and sardonically taking and *having* the teasing sexy someone they'd been wanting so long . . . opposites attract. . . . Women want real men, and that's all there is to it (p. 159).

One of Jackie Gilfoyle et al.'s interviewees extends this analysis of male sexual power to orgasm-production: 'pressing the right buttons is important, but . . . if a woman has an orgasm you probably feel more of a man. You know . . . it was because of you and your penis, you gave her that, you gave her one.'

Many feminist theorists have analysed the extent to which 'sex' is eroticized power difference, and have critiqued the phenomenon that Sheila Jeffreys (1990) labels 'heterosexual desire' — by which she means not just desire between women and men, but the eroticizing of dominance and submission. The problem, for feminists, is not just *men's* eroticizing of power — the therapist sexually aroused by a young woman's story of sexual abuse is a good example (see Kelly, 1992); the problem is also *women's* eroticizing of power*lessness*. A politics of the erotic requires *not* the grounding of our politics in our erotic responses ('whatever is right is what turns you on'), but the problematizing of the erotic within the context of our feminism (Denise Thompson). As Patricia Duncker says, 'any sexual act is as much about politics as it is about feelings. The urge to perform one particular sexual act rather than another doesn't rise up mysteriously from the gulf of our inward natures. . . . There is *always* a script.'

This 'script', identified by several contributors, revolves around power and powerlessness. Sadomasochistic themes surface repeatedly in descriptions of heterosexual women's eroticism. Read any book describing women's sexual fantasies, and you will find many devoted to sexual activities rooted in the eroticizing of powerlessness. The chapter headings of one of Nancy Friday's books include: 'Pain and Masochism: Ouch, Don't Stop', 'Rape: Don't Just Stand There, Force Me', 'Domination, or How Humiliating, Thankyou!' and 'The Sexuality of Terror' (Friday, 1973). These are sexual fantasies women use during masturbation or sexual activities with others to give them pleasure — fantasies of bestiality, rape, passivity, being looked at, tied up, beaten. Heterosexual feminist Barbara Sichterman (1986) writes of her desire to be 'taken violently by a man'; ex-heterosexual lesbian Justine Jones (1981) describes her CR group's hated masochistic fantasies: 'how in order to come they had to think of the man in the raincoat who'd flashed at them in the woods when they were fifteen; how images of rape, beating, bondage came to their minds when masturbating'; and Lynne Segal (1983: 42) describes 'the fantasies which I have always needed to come to orgasm, by any methods. . . . In them I am always passive, objectified, humiliated and whatever abuse I can imagine to be happening at the time also contains the threat of even worse to follow' (see Kitzinger, 1993b, for a more detailed analysis). As Sheila Jeffreys (1990) has said, 'If your oppression turns you on you have a much harder time fighting your oppression'.

Several contributors to this volume express political concerns in relation to their own erotic responses. In such instances it is not their *lack* of pleasure in heterosexual sex which is the problem, but rather the nature of heterosexual pleasure itself. Ros Gill and Rebecca Walker describe their 'deeply unsound' fantasies in which 'men "sweep us off our feet", wrap us in their "strong tanned arms" and, of course, adore us'. 'We live these desires', they say, 'through the discourse of patriarchal romances, not feminism. And the irony is that *we know it* — but that does not make the desires go away'. Jenny Kitzinger quotes a woman's description of her pleasure when a man looks at her with desire in his eyes 'like the look Rhett Butler gives Scarlett', and her colleague's fear of 'the look' because it 'communicates . . . power imbalance'. Two other contributors describe their attraction to powerful men, of the type Sandra Lee Bartky describes as 'fathers':

> . . . my first lover was the double, at least in my eyes, of my father — the
> Aryan Adonis my barely adult Jewish mother had 15 years previously taken to
> be her spouse (Janet Sayers, p. 73).

> I began to see that I was attracted only to certain kinds of men — men who were
> older than I, who were somewhat arrogant and occasionally tyrannical, men to
> whom I needed to ascribe, whether they really had them or not, qualities of
> talent and intelligence far superior to my own. . . . Continuities began to sug-
> gest themselves between these men and the heroes of film and fiction that had
> most excited me in adolesence: the arrogant and sarcastic Rochester of *Jane
> Eyre*; the distant and melancholy Max de Winter of *Rebecca*; the cold and harsh
> combination guardian and piano-coach of *The Seventh Veil* and, of course,
> Rhett Butler (Sandra Lee Bartky, p. 41).

Nice guys, 'new men', are apparently not attractive to many heterosexual
women: 'women may demand a more sensitive man, but aren't sure of what to
do with one when they find one' (Allan Hunter). In an article called, 'Can a
Good Man be Sexy?', Jane Finch (1990) poses the question 'Can husbands push
a supermarket trolley in the morning and turn us on 12 hours later?' — and concludes that they cannot: 'new men' are 'emasculated', 'feminized'. One of
Nicola Gavey's respondents describes a sissy man, 'quite cute and pathetic . . .
with these big sort of puppy dog eyes' and says 'that's what used to turn me off'.
There is, as Allan Hunter suggests, a strong link between heterosexuality and
masculinity such that 'heterosexuality is largely conceptualized, *unthinkingly*, as
a relationship between women and *masculine* males' — that is, between subor-
dinated and dominator:

> Erotic excitement, according to patriarchal ideology, depends on the tension
> created by setting men against women in a power struggle, setting them at
> cross-purposes with conflicting interests that create the possibilities of
> vulnerability and domination (Allan Hunter, p. 163).

Erotic excitement is constructed around power difference — the 'romantic
bromide that opposites attract' (Pogrebin, 1980). When (as in lesbian or gay
male sex) the gender hierarchy is missing, other social stratifications (race,
class) or specially constructed power differentials (as in sadomasochism) can
sometimes be eroticized (cf. Nichols, 1987). White ex-lesbian Jan Clausen
(1991) writes that her new relationship with a man is an 'exquisite relief', in
part because it 'affords an exhilarating sensation of risk-taking': her lover is
unlike her not just because he is male but also because he is black and 'the racial
difference is at least as charged with tension, fascination, promise and difficulty
as is the sexual one'.

Debate about (hetero)sexual activity is often conducted as though sexual
pleasure — or the lack of it — were the sole criterion on which a feminist assessment could be made. Yet, for many women, the problem is not (only) lack of
sexual 'pleasure', but serious political concern about the form that pleasure
takes. Lynne Segal (1983) points out that 'it does not feel like personal liberation

to be able to orgasm to intensely masochistic fantasies', and Sandra Lee Bartky's decision to change her 'sexual orientation', consciously substituting 'brothers' for 'fathers', choosing 'not to pursue men whose sadism excited me', was made at the cost of sexual 'pleasure': 'I have been, if not passionately sexual, then passionately political. . . . My narrow escape has, of course, been purchased at a price, that price a certain fracturing of myself.' This is a price worth paying, according to many feminist theorists. Sheila Jeffreys (1990: 314), for example, recommends that we seek to shut down those sexual responses which eroticize our subordination. She says: 'The question we have to ask ourselves is whether we want our freedom or whether we want to retain heterosexual desire. Feminists will choose freedom.'

TOWARDS A RECONSTRUCTION OF HETEROSEXUALITY?

'Most women are heterosexual. . .' (Sheila Kitzinger) — this is an apparent statement of fact to which heterosexual feminists often return: 'I assume the vast majority of the world's women live in heterosexual relationships' (Shulamit Reinharz); 'Most women are willingly enmeshed in more or less oppressive relationships with men' (Caroline Ramazanoglu, 1989: 163). In contrast to this assumption of near-universal heterosexuality, lesbian slogans have emphasized a different perspective: '*Any* woman can be a lesbian', or 'All women are lesbians but some of them don't know it yet'. The observable fact of most women's involvement in heterosexual relationships can operate *either* as a taken-for-granted assumption in feminist theory *or* it can be problematized — as can the 'naturalness' of many other activities in which 'most people' engage (e.g. in the West, eating meat: 'anyone can be a vegetarian'). Lesbian feminist Anna Wilson demands that heterosexual women:

> . . . question the assumption that heterosexuality is yours, a free gift with every chromosomal pack and that i'm not like that because i was either born missing or grew up missing. if you want to go on being heterosexual, that's ok. but i want you to think about the fact that you're doing it because you want to. you are responsible for being heterosexual — it's not like the colour of your eyes (Wilson, 1981: 61).

Understanding the role of heteropatriarchal compulsion in the construction of heterosexuality ('A child of patriarchy, I was shaped by it', Sheila Kitzinger) means questioning not just one's own heterosexuality ('am I heterosexual only because it is compulsory?', Shulamit Reinharz) but also the presumed heterosexuality of all the world's women.

Reconstructing heterosexuality is not, then, a political imperative in so far as an alternative strategy exists: the radical challenge to heterosexuality per se. Nor is it obvious to everyone that heterosexuality is open to reconstruction. Patricia Duncker describes how 'heterosexuality doesn't evolve, doesn't change, doesn't develop. The way in which women and men, in the hopeless attempt to love one another, slink helplessly, miserably, into ruts.' According to feminist therapist Doris DeHardt, feminist heterosexual relationships are, 'like military intelligence, an oxymoron'. And, writing of her celibacy, Loulou Brown says: 'I live a lonely life, but I prefer this to the nonsense of a heterosexual existence'. Others think differently. 'Heterosexual relations do not *have* to be expressions of male power over women', says Caroline Ramazanoglu (1989: 165); 'It seems possible to me', writes Shulamit Reinharz, 'to envision a heterosexuality that does not originate in the male standpoint and that does not transform women into sexual objects' and Robyn Rowland writes of her own 'radical feminist heterosexuality'.

Heterosexual sexual activity is a central focus for reconstructive efforts. Although, as we have seen, feminist reconstructions are not necessarily synonymous with increased pleasure in heterosexual sex, some theorists have argued that the feminist movement 'has enriched and added new dimensions to lesbian sexuality and there is no reason it cannot do the same for heterosexuality' (bell hooks, 1984: 154). Although, according to Robyn Rowland, 'intercourse does take place which is *not* degrading', in so far as 'having sex' is defined in heterosexist terms as 'male-dominant-female-subordinate-copulation-whose-completion-and-purpose-is-the-male's-ejaculation' (Frye, 1990a: 308), it is not difficult to see how feminist redefinitions can indeed enhance pleasure. As Ros Gill and Rebecca Walker say:

> It is not just that penetration can feel like one more invasion, or simply that we find it less pleasurable than other forms of sexual contact, or only that it has always held particular dangers for women — and never more so than today. It is all of these things, but it is also that it feels such an impoverished view of our sexual potential (p. 70).

John Stoltenberg (1990: 46), who describes himself as 'an erotic traitor to male supremacy', and defines sex as good 'to the extent that it empowers both partners equally, and to the extent that they succeed together in keeping their intimacy untainted by the cultural context of sexualized inequality' (1990: 105) says:

> Like others born with a penis, I was born into a sex–class system that requires my collaboration every day, even in how I have sex. Nobody told me, when I was younger, that I could have non-coital sex and that it would be fine. Actually, much better than fine. Nobody told me about an incredible range of other erotic possibilities for mutual love making. . . (Stoltenberg, 1990: 46).

Like John Stoltenberg, Allan Hunter rejoices in his 'refusal to be a man' which implies 'not having penetration in mind as the goal of erotic expression — or for that matter any goal other than intimacy and sharing and pleasure'.

Singling out the act of penile–vaginal penetration as a particular problem for women, early heterosexual feminist arguments (e.g. Atkinson, 1970) rested upon the notion of the insensitive vagina — we don't want sexual intercourse because we 'haven't got any nerve endings down there'. Many women reacted with incredulity, especially when this argument was used by male doctors to deny that we actually *feel* anything when cold blunt metal instruments are inserted into us in routine gynaecological examinations or during childbirth. Tamsin Wilton describes painful conflicts with a male lover 'who flatly refused to accept that I had any sensation whatsoever inside my vagina', insisting that her physical responsiveness was the result of 'hysterical delusion'. Jill Johnston (1972: 168–9) writes of her amazement that heterosexual feminists' 'stubborn refusal to submit to conventional intercourse' should be justified with reference to such arguments, 'as though the case for an insensitive vagina provided women with their first legal brief for the indictment of phallic imperialism'. There are plenty of reasons other than (presumed) lack of 'pleasure' to protest against 'the dominant assumption that heterosexual intercourse [coitus] is synonymous with "real" sex' (Nicola Gavey). As feminists we might rather hinge our arguments on the particular set of cultural and political meanings attached to penile penetration of women (being 'had', 'possessed', 'taken', 'fucked') which are 'oppressive, humiliating and destructive' (Patricia Duncker). Even though many women sometimes take pleasure in the sensation of a full vagina, it can be argued that:

> . . . no act of penetration takes place in isolation. Each takes place in a system of relationships that is male supremacy. As no individual woman can be 'liberated' under male supremacy, so no act of penetration can escape its function and its symbolic power (Leeds Revolutionary Feminist Group, 1981: 7).

The linguistic sleight proposed by some feminists in renaming penetration 'enclosure' (Ramazanoglu, 1989: 164) or 'penile covering' (Hite, 1989) simply serves to obscure the problem of the *institutionalization* of penile penetration under heteropatriarchy. Such terms are eagerly adopted by male sex therapists encouraging women to participate in penetration, now renamed 'vaginal containment' (Jehu, 1988, cited in J. Kitzinger). Mary Boyle chronicles this institutionalization in sex therapy, beginning with Masters and Johnson's 'granting of volition to male and female genitals (erections which demanded intromission, vaginas which invited penetration)'. As Nicola Gavey points out, as long as 'sex' is defined in male terms as synonymous with penetration, the question of women's 'consent' is problematic. 'For several years of my life I was raped', says Amanda Sebestyen (1982: 235): 'I was penetrated against my will because I didn't dare insist on any other kind of sex. And I *still* have a fight any time I start a sexual relationship with a man.'

Many heterosexual women are committed, in Caroline Ramazanoglu's words, 'to educating and encouraging men to resist the construction of patriarchal relationships'. They want 'to influence our brothers or our sons (who, after all, will become tomorrow's men), our male friends or lovers' (Hamblin, 1983: 120). Sometimes this takes the form of arguing that heterosexual women are 'on the frontline' in the feminist battle, 'fighting the "real" battle because you are "out there'' dealing with men, boys, the real world' (Wilson, 1981: 61). In bringing up children, they (along with lesbian mothers) are 'participating in the construction of new masculinities and femininities' (Susie Orbach). 'I firmly believe', says Alison Thomas, 'that educating the next generation is still the most productive way to achieve long-term change.' Several contributors point out how difficult it is for men and boys to change: 'while feminism gives women and daughters a basis for political solidarity in empowering themselves, our partners and sons have no comparable political platform for their own disempowerment' (Caroline Ramazanoglu). Whatever the personal damage inflicted on boys and men by (hetero)sexism, the price of challenging that oppression is high: 'one of my sons complained bitterly that I had no idea what it was like trying to be anti-sexist and anti-racist in the playground', says Caroline Ramazanoglu, while Susie Orbach's seven-year-old son, 'at present deeply enamoured of the World Wrestling Federation', reported to his father after his first few days at school: 'I'd like to be a gentle boy, Dad, but I just don't think I can manage it'. What is at stake here is far more than differential socialization patterns and problems in communication. As Cameron (1992: 467) says, 'conflicts between women and men are often political conflicts . . . they have material causes . . . they express something more profound than casual misunderstanding'. Moreover, it is often not in men's interests to change. Caroline Ramazanoglu points out that 'Men have much less reason to struggle and go on struggling than women', adding, 'very few men have really grasped the meaning of shared responsibilities'. For others, making women responsible for men's consciousness is 'another patriarchal plot for robbing women of even more resources' (Spender, 1984: 213). As Julie Burchill comments caustically:

> Helping a man get his 'head' together seems to have become the respectable post-feminist replacement for making him a cup of tea; personally, I'd rather make the tea. It's quicker, and leaves more time for oneself (Burchill, 1990: 17).

On the other hand, several contributors talk about their relationships with men in positive terms, and — as Pauline Bart shows — even some 'lesbians' choose men as their partners. The strategy advocated by Elizabeth Mapstone is to 'make a clear distinction between a man as an individual human being, whom I can love, and men as a social group against whom I must struggle'. Robyn Rowland celebrates her male partner's 'goodness, his kindness, his gentleness, his strength, his values and his humour. He himself: a decent non-oppressing man.' Others write of equally shared childcare (Susie Orbach) and 'egalitarian' relationships (Carol Nagy Jacklin). Reflecting on the relative infrequency with which heterosexual feminists publicly express positive feelings towards the men in their lives, Shulamit Reinharz comments: 'Having a good husband seems to be many feminists' well-guarded secret'. In particular, shared values and cultural identification are valued: 'loving men', says Kadiatu Kanneh, 'is not an accident, a problem for feminist identification, but a valid move towards cultural or racial self-determination'. Writing of the 'fundamental values' she shares with her husband, Sheila Kitzinger says:

> He knew what it was to be a Jew as a child in Nazi Germany. We first en-
> countered each other (briefly) at a meeting exploring the problems and
> challenges of building a better society . . . we committed ourselves not only
> to each other, but to work for political and social change, as equals, 'flying
> wing to wing' (p. 54).

Less explored is the extent to which, and the mechanisms whereby, 'equality'
with men can be freely chosen in a heteropatriarchal world. Living separately
from one's male partner appears to be helpful (see Robyn Rowland), while
Marilyn Frye (1990b) writes — somewhat mystically — of 'Virgins', imagined
as 'females who are willing to engage in chosen connections with males, who
are wild females, undomesticated females, thoroughly defiant of patriarchal
female heterosexuality. . .'.

One of the clearest arguments which emerges from this volume, as well as
from the Special Issue on heterosexuality, is that the institution of compulsory
heterosexuality is damaging not just for lesbians, but also for heterosexuals and
for children. Heterosexuality embodies distinctive codes of conduct, which are
'stereotypes in themselves', and heterosexuals seek 'respectability in the production and exposure of non-"pretended", always-happy couples and their
families' (Helen (charles)). As Ross Balzaretti (1992) comments: '"compulsory
heterosexuality" is not very sympathetic to those who do not conform (including
reformist heterosexuals)'. Reviewing a standard book on child sexual abuse,
Kelly (1992: 475) points to the way in which 'the ideology of the heterosexual
family' is protected by arguments against prosecuting men who have assaulted
members of their own family. Heterosexism is used to enforce children's conformity with gender roles: childcare 'experts' still write about the need for
'limits' on non-sexist child-rearing, claiming (for example) that 'the path along
which effeminate boys and masculine girls have come is often a bruising one.
Their futures may well be homosexuality' (Stein, 1984: 130). Terms like
'faggot', 'lessie' and 'queer' are hurled as insults in the playground (see Allan
Hunter) and parents' heterosexist fears for their children's futures ensure that
they do not deviate too far from traditional sexist child-rearing patterns (cf.
Pogrebin, 1980). In adulthood, the term 'lesbian' (as Denise Thompson points
out), is used to keep women subservient to and serving men: 'any strong-minded
independent woman can be labelled a lesbian and punished for it'.

Writing in the British journal of lesbian ethics, *Gossip*, Paula Jennings (1986)
points out that too often lesbians have asked feminists 'to support us in being visible, despite the disadvantages to themselves, because it's morally right for them
to do so'. She suggests instead that we 'look at the *benefits* for all the women involved if lesbians were visible in an ordinary, casual, taken-for-granted way',
arguing that the heterosexual assumption is damaging to heterosexual women as
well as to lesbians. Charlotte Bunch reinforces the point that analysis of
heterosexuality is, as the title of her article puts it, 'not for lesbians only':

> Analysis of the function of heterosexuality in women's oppression is available to any woman, lesbian or straight. . . . Since lesbians are materially oppressed by heterosexuality daily, it is not surprising that we have seen and understood its impact first — not because we are more moral, but because our reality is different — and it is a *materially* different reality. We are trying to convey this fact of our oppression to you because, whether you feel it directly or not, it also oppresses you; and because if we are going to change society and survive, we must all attack heterosexual domination (Bunch, 1975).

In describing their feminist ideals, many contributors express a shared hope for future abolition of the divisive patriarchal categories, 'male' and 'female', 'heterosexual' and 'lesbian'. Some draw on postmodernist theories in wanting to 'unbundle our binaries' (Mary Gergen) and deconstruct oppositional categories (Mary Crawford). Others evoke the 'androgynous' vision of which Patricia Duncker speaks: 'Can we imagine a world without sexual difference? A world in which gender was abolished? A world in which it had ceased to matter if your lover was a man or a woman?' In struggling to make real a world in which labels do *not* matter, it is a mistake to behave as though those labels are already meaningless. Their current meanings are sufficiently potent to infuse the legal system, national traditions, religion, the tax system, work patterns, art and culture, etc. (cf. Patricia Duncker, p. 148; Carabine, 1992). We cannot afford to ignore this; rather, we need to interrogate their meanings, and use them politically. Even radical deconstructionists, such as Kristeva, who believe that '*Woman as such* [i.e. as a philosophical category] does not exist', also argue that 'woman' is a viable *political* category; and that in order to achieve political goals (freedom of abortion and contraception, daycare centres for women, equality in the workplace), 'we must use "we are women" as an advertisement or slogan for our demands' (Kristeva, cited in Tong, 1989: 230). Sandra Bem makes a similar point, albeit from a very different perspective:

> On the one hand there's this Utopian ideal, by which I mean, yes, let's stop thinking about our maleness and femaleness, let's stop organising our lives around our gender, including the gender of the people we're attracted to. On the other hand, I can think about what we as political activists need to be doing right now . . . here in the real world, the last thing women need to do is to forget about being female, in the same way that I think the last thing lesbians and gays need to do is forget about sexual orientation. We have to use these cultural constructions for purposes of liberation and protest. . . . The culture says, 'we are going to oppress you on that basis'. So it doesn't seem problematic to turn around and say, 'well, we are going to take this category and transform its meaning and fight for its being privileged or at least not discriminated against', even while at the same time we are saying, 'this category doesn't need to last for ever, and by the time we get to Utopia it won't exist anymore, but we can't get from here to there without taking your category, damn you, and transforming its meaning, and using it for our own politics' (quoted in Kitzinger, 1992a).

ENDNOTE

Editing this collection has been a difficult and sometimes painful task. We have been accused by some feminists of 'oppressing' heterosexuals simply by raising the questions posed in our 'Call for Contributions', while others have charged us with giving space to heterosexist values and contributing to the silencing of lesbians. Theorizing heterosexuality is often distressing for both lesbians and heterosexual women. For heterosexual feminists, there is awareness of painful contradictions and conflicting loyalties, as well as apologetic defensiveness about the men in their lives: 'What will Martin think?'; 'I don't intend to set my husband up as a laughing stock'; or (from a woman who decided against participating) 'I decided to let my old man off the hook'. For lesbians, as Gillian Hanscombe (1987: 7–8) found when she invited contributions to her edited book on heterosexuality, there is pain caused by affection or loyalty to ex-husbands and boyfriends, to current male friends, and to sons; hurt and anger at the heterosexual privileges from which we are excluded; and distress caused by some ex-heterosexual lesbians' unhappy pasts — one would-be contributor tried several times to write something for Hanscombe's anthology, abandoning the attempt when distressing nightmares brought her raw anguish to the surface.

Part of this pain, for both lesbians *and* heterosexuals, lies in recognition of the chasm that sometimes opens up between us — 'all too often [lesbians and heterosexual women] feel enormously apart, even on "opposite" sides of the fence' (Alison Young) or 'wall' (Hilary Lips and Susan Freedman). Heterosexual feminists Ros Gill and Rebecca Walker write of their anger at having lost their closest friend because 'she has "fallen in love" with us and feels unable to remain friends knowing that her sexual feelings are not reciprocated'; on the 'other side', lesbian writer Tamsin Wilton writes of *her* pain and loss when her heterosexual women friends seem no longer to understand her life and her world (cf. Sheila Shulman, 1982). We set out to produce this volume in the belief that theorizing heterosexuality is a necessary part of developing both 'personal' and 'political' understandings of this gulf.

Most of all, we are acutely aware of the need for the continued development of more rigorous and sophisticated analyses of heterosexuality. Arguments first introduced in the early 1970s and 1980s (and, it seems, so readily forgotten or overlooked) require continually to be updated and their applicability to new social contexts and political situations re-examined. Sustained analysis is needed in order to arrive at new insights and develop and extend feminist and psychological theory on heterosexuality. We are glad to have (re)created the opportunity for this to happen.

Neither this *Reader* nor the Special Issue which preceded it (Kitzinger et al., 1992) represents a definitive statement on heterosexuality: we hope that many readers of *Feminism & Psychology* will want to respond and contribute further to the debates introduced here, and we draw your attention to the Observations

& Commentaries section of the journal for that purpose. We would like this to be the beginning of fruitful and politically engaged discussion.

ACKNOWLEDGEMENTS

We would particularly like to thank Barbara Rowland for her splendid secretarial assistance. Her calm efficiency and competence were invaluable in the preparation of the typescript. We would also like to thank Margaret Wetherell, Jenny Kitzinger and Sheila Kitzinger for their helpful comments on an earlier version of this introduction.

NOTES

1. This is a slightly revised and expanded version of the Editorial Introduction to the Special Issue of *Feminism & Psychology* (2(3)1992) on Heterosexuality. In that issue Celia Kitzinger took particular responsibility for the Special Feature on Heterosexual Feminist Identities and the Observations & Commentaries; Sue Wilkinson for the articles; and Rachel Perkins for the book reviews.
2. Throughout this Editorial Introduction, quotations from contributors to this volume are referenced by author name only, with the exception of longer 'displayed' extracts which carry a page reference.
3. See Editorial Introduction to the Special Feature for details.
4. Of course, many women become feminists as a direct result of their heterosexuality, becoming conscious of patriarchal oppression through the minute and particular details of their male partners' behaviour. Similarly, many women become feminists as a direct result of their lesbianism, becoming conscious of heteropatriarchal oppression through the experience of anti-lesbianism. In stating that there are no intrinsically politicized heterosexual identities, we do not mean to discount these experiences. Rather, we mean to refer to the fact that feminists have for decades consciously chosen lesbianism as an identity in accordance with feminist politics, and have at our disposal a theoretical framework for analysing the importance of lesbianism in achieving feminist goals. By contrast, few feminists have stated publicly that they choose heterosexuality as an identity most in accordance with their feminist politics, nor have they produced the theoretical writings which might support such a choice.
5. Heterosexual women were, of course, the 'control' groups in these studies, and this tongue-in-cheek reversal says more about the male bias of the tests than about the mental health of either lesbian or heterosexual women.
6. 'Ego-dystonic *homo*sexuality' is defined in the *Diagnostic and Statistical Manual of Mental Disorders (DSM III-R*, American Psychiatric Association, 1987) as 'persistent and marked distress about one's sexual orientation' and classified as a 'Sexual Disorder Not Otherwise Specified'. This distress refers only to homosexuality: there is no entry in the index for '*Hetero*sexuality, Ego-dystonic' to parallel that for '*Homo*sexuality, Ego-dystonic' (p. 561). (See Mary Boyle for a more detailed critique of *DSM-III*.)
7. This section is based on C. Kitzinger (1993) 'Problematizing Pleasure: Radical Lesbian Feminist Reconstructions of Sex and Power', in H.L. Radtke and H. Stam (eds) *Power and Gender*. London: Sage.

REFERENCES

Alderson, Lynn (1981) 'Statements from Individual Members of the Collective', in Onlywomen Press (ed.) *Love Your Enemy? The Debate Between Heterosexual Feminism and Political Lesbianism*. London: Onlywomen Press.

Alldred, Pam (1992) 'Review of Anne Dickson's *The Mirror Within*', in C. Kitzinger, S. Wilkinson and R. Perkins (eds) *Heterosexuality*, a Special Issue of *Feminism & Psychology* 2(3): 483–4.

American Psychiatric Association (1987) *Diagnostic and Statistical Manual of Mental Disorders-III-R*. Washington, DC: APA.

Anon (1989) 'Love Hurts', *The Guardian* 22 November.

Arcana, Judith (1983) *Every Mother's Son: The Role of Mothers in the Making of Men*. London: The Women's Press.

Atkinson, Ti-Grace (1970) 'The Institution of Sexual Intercourse', in Shulamith Firestone (ed.) *Notes from the Third Year*. New York: Random House.

Balzaretti, Ross (1992) 'Review of Jeffrey Weeks' *Against Nature*', in C. Kitzinger, S. Wilkinson and R. Perkins (eds) *Heterosexuality*, a Special Issue of *Feminism & Psychology* 2(3): 487–9.

Bart, Pauline (1977) 'The Mermaid and the Minotaur: A Fishy Story That's Part Bull' (Review of Dorothy Dinnerstein's *The Mermaid and the Minotaur: Sexual Arrangements and Human Malaise*, New York: Harper and Row, 1976), *Contemporary Psychology* 22(11): 834–5.

Bart, Pauline (1983) 'Review of Chodorow's *The Reproduction of Mothering*', in Joyce Trebilcot (ed.) *Mothering: Essays in Feminist Theory*. New York: Rowman and Allanheld.

Basow, Susan (1992) *Gender: Stereotypes and Roles*, 3rd edn. Pacific Grove, CA: Brooks/Cole

Bell, Alan P. and Weinberg, Martin S. (1978) *Homosexualities: A Study of Diversity Among Men and Women*. London: Mitchell Beazley.

Bem, Sandra Lipsitz (1983) 'Gender Schema Theory and Its Implications for Child Development: Raising Gender-aschematic Children in a Gender-schematic Society', *Signs: Journal of Women in Culture and Society* 8(4): 598–616.

Bernay, Toni and Cantor, Dorothy W. (1986) *The Psychology of Today's Woman: New Psychoanalytic Visions*. Cambridge, MA: Harvard University Press.

Briere, John and Mulamuth, Neil (1983) 'Self-reported Likelihood of Sexually Aggressive Behavior: Attitudinal versus Sexual Explanations', *Journal of Research in Personality* 17: 315–23.

Brown, Laura (1990) 'The Meaning of a Multicultural Perspective for Theory-building in Feminist Therapy', in L. Brown and M. Root (eds) *Diversity and Complexity in Feminist Therapy, Part 1*. Special Issue of *Women and Therapy* 9(1/2): 1–21.

Brunet, Ariane and Turcotte, Louise (1988) 'Separatism and Radicalism', in Sarah Hoagland and Julia Penelope (eds) *For Lesbians Only: A Separatist Anthology*. London: Onlywomen Press.

Bulkin, Elly (1982) 'Heterosexism and Women's Studies', *Radical Teacher* 17.

Bunch, Charlotte (1975) 'Not for Lesbians Only', *Quest: A Feminist Quarterly* 2(2).

Burchill, Julie (1990) 'Sayings of the Week', *The Guardian*, 17 September.

Cameron, Deborah (1992) 'Review of Deborah Tannen's *You Just Don't Understand*', in C. Kitzinger, S. Wilkinson and R. Perkins (eds) *Heterosexuality*, Special Issue of *Feminism & Psychology* 2(3): 465–6.

Campbell, Beatrice (1980) 'A Feminist Sexual Politics: Now You See It, Now You Don't', *Feminist Review* 5: 1–18.

Campbell, J.C. and Alford, P. (1989) 'The Dark Consequences of Marital Rape', *American Journal of Nursing* 89(7): 946–9.

Caputi, Jane (1989) 'The Sexual Politics of Murder', *Gender and Society* 3(4): 437–56.

Carabine, Jean (1992) '"Constructing Women": Women's Sexuality and Social Policy', *Critical Social Policy* 12(1): 23–37.

Card, Claudia (1985) 'Virtues and Moral Luck', Institute for Legal Studies Working Paper No. 4. University of Wisconsin-Madison Law School.

Chaplin, Jocelyn (1988) *Feminist Counselling in Action*. London: Sage.

Chodorow, Nancy (1978) *The Reproduction of Mothering*. Berkeley, CA: University of California Press.

Clausen, Jan (1991) 'My Interesting Condition', *Out/Look: National Lesbian and Gay Quarterly* 7: 10–21.

Comely, Louise, Kitzinger, Celia, Perkins, Rachel and Wilkinson, Sue (1992) 'Lesbian Psychology in Britain: Back into the Closet?', *Feminism & Psychology* 2(2): 265–8.

Croghan, Rose (1991) 'First-time Mothers' Accounts of Inequality in the Division of Labour', *Feminism & Psychology* 1(2): 221–46.

DeHardt, Doris (1985) 'Can a Feminist Therapist Facilitate Clients' Heterosexual Relationships?', in L. Rosewater and L.E. Walker (eds) *Handbook of Feminist Therapy*. New York: Springer.

Dinnerstein, Dorothy (1976) *The Rocking of the Cradle and the Ruling of the World*. London: The Women's Press.

Doyle, James A. and Paludi, Michele A. (1991) *Sex and Gender: The Human Experience*. New York: William C. Brown.

Ehrenreich, Barbara and English, Deidre (1978) *For Her Own Good: 150 Years of the Experts' Advice to Women*. New York: Anchor/Doubleday.

Finch, Jane (1990) 'Can a Good Man be Sexy?', *The Guardian*, 21 June: 38.

French, Marilyn (1992) *The War Against Women*. London: Hamish Hamilton.

Friday, Nancy (1973) *My Secret Garden*. New York: Pocket Books.

Frye, Marilyn (1990a) 'Lesbian "Sex"', in Jeffner Allen (ed.) *Lesbian Philosophies and Cultures*. New York: State University of New York Press.

Frye, Marilyn (1990b) 'Do You Have to Be a Lesbian to be a Feminist?', *Off Our Backs* XX(8): 21–3.

Gagnon, John and Simon, William (1973) *Sexual Conduct*. New York: Aldine.

Gilman, Charlotte Perkins (1898) *Women and Economics*. New York: Harper and Row.

Gove, W.R. (1972) 'The Relationship between Sex Roles, Marital Status, and Mental Illness', *Social Forces* 51(1): 34–44.

Hamblin, Angela (1982) 'What Can One Do with a Son? Feminist Politics and Male Children', in Scarlet Friedman and Elizabeth Sarah (eds) *On the Problem of Men: Two Feminist Conferences*. London: The Women's Press.

Hamblin, Angela (1983) 'Is a Feminist Heterosexuality Possible?', in Sue Cartledge and Joanna Ryan (eds) *Sex and Love: New Thoughts on Old Contradictions*. London: The Women's Press.

Hanisch, Carol (1971) 'The Personal is Political', in J. Agel (ed.) *The Radical Therapist.* New York: Ballantine Books.

Hanscombe, Gillian E. (1987) 'Preface', in Gillian Hanscombe and Martin Humphries (eds) *Heterosexuality.* London: Gay Men's Press.

Hite, Shere (1989) 'Love on the Rocks', *Marxism Today*, 14–19 December.

Hoagland, Sarah Lucia and Penelope, Julia (1988) *For Lesbians Only: A Separatist Anthology.* London: Onlywomen Press.

Hollway, Wendy (1983) 'Heterosexual Sex: Power and Desire for the Other', in Sue Cartledge and Joanna Ryan (eds) *Sex and Love: New Thoughts on Old Contradictions.* London: The Women's Press.

Hollway, Wendy (1992) 'Review of Terry Pattinson's *Sexual Harassment*', in C. Kitzinger, S. Wilkinson and R. Perkins (eds) *Heterosexuality*, a Special Issue of *Feminism & Psychology* 2(3): 484–6.

hooks, bell (1984) *Feminist Theory: From Margin to Center.* Boston, MA: South End Press.

Hopkins, June (1969) 'The Lesbian Personality', *British Journal of Psychiatry* 115: 1433–6.

Irvine, Janice M. (1990) 'From Difference to Sameness: Gender Ideology in Sexual Science', *Journal of Sex Research* 27(1): 7–24.

Jeffreys, Sheila (1990) *Anticlimax: A Feminist Perspective on the Sexual Revolution.* London: The Women's Press.

Jennings, Paula (1986) 'Lesbian Liberation Later', *Gossip: A Journal of Lesbian Feminist Ethics* 3: 77–81.

Johnson, G. David, Palileo, Gloria J. and Gray, Norma B. (1992) '"Date Rape" on a Southern Campus', *Sociology and Social Research* 76(2): 37–44.

Johnston, Jill (1972) *Lesbian Nation: The Feminist Solution.* New York: Simon and Schuster.

Jones, Justine (1981) 'Why I Liked Screwing? Or, Is Heterosexual Enjoyment Based on Sexual Violence?', in Onlywomen Press (ed.) *Love Your Enemy: The Debate between Heterosexual Feminism and Political Lesbianism.* London: Onlywomen Press.

Kelly, Liz (1992) 'Review of Tilman Furniss' *The Multi-Professional Handbook of Child Sexual Abuse*', in C. Kitzinger, S. Wilkinson and R. Perkins (eds) *Heterosexuality*, a Special Issue of *Feminism & Psychology* 2(3): 473–6.

Kinsey, A.C., Pomeroy W.B. and Martin, C.E. (1948) *Sexual Behavior in the Human Male.* Philadelphia, PA: W.B. Saunders.

Kinsey, A.C., Pomeroy, W.B., Martin C.E. and Gebhard, P.H. (1953) *Sexual Behavior in the Human Female.* Philadelphia, PA: W.B. Saunders.

Kitzinger, Celia (1987) *The Social Construction of Lesbianism.* London: Sage.

Kitzinger, Celia (1992) 'Sandra Lipsitz Bem: Feminist Psychologist', *The Psychologist* 5(5): 222–4.

Kitzinger, Celia (1993a) 'Update on Homophobia', in Lilian Mohin (ed.) *An Intimacy of Equals: Essays in Lesbian Feminist Ethics.* London: Onlywomen Press, in press.

Kitzinger, Celia (1993b) 'Problematising Pleasure: Radical Lesbian Feminist Reconstructions of Sexuality and Power', in H.L. Radtke and H. Stam (eds) *Power and Gender.* London: Sage, forthcoming.

Kitzinger, Sheila and Kitzinger, Celia (1989) *Talking With Children About Things that Matter.* London: Unwin Hyman. (Published in North America as *Tough Questions*, Harvard Common Press.)

Koss, Mary P., Gidysz, Christine A. and Wisniewski, Nadine (1987) 'The Scope of Rape: Incidence and Prevalence of Sexual Aggression and Victimization in a National Sample of Higher Education Students', *Journal of Consulting and Clinical Psychology* 55(2): 162–70.

Leeds Revolutionary Feminist Group (1981) 'Political Lesbianism: The Case Against Heterosexuality', in Onlywomen Press (ed.) *Love Your Enemy: The Debate between Heterosexual Feminism and Political Lesbianism*. London: Onlywomen Press.

Lidstone, Margot (1992) 'Review of Sue Llewelyn and Kate Osborne's *Women's Lives*', in C. Kitzinger, S. Wilkinson and R. Perkins (eds) *Heterosexuality*, a Special Issue of *Feminism & Psychology* 2(3): 477–9.

MacKinnon, Catharine A. (1987) 'A Feminist/Political Approach: "Pleasure Under Patriarchy"', in James H. Geer and William T. O'Donohue (eds) *Theories of Human Sexuality*. New York: Plenum Press.

Mainardi, Pat (1970) 'The Politics of Housework', in Robin Morgan (ed.) *Sisterhood is Powerful*. New York: Vintage Books.

Matlin, Margaret W. (1987) *The Psychology of Women*. New York: Holt, Rinehart and Winston.

Mayne, Ann (1992) 'Review of Lee Ann Hoff's *Battered Women as Survivors*', in C. Kitzinger, S. Wilkinson and R. Perkins (eds) *Heterosexuality*, a Special Issue of *Feminism & Psychology* 2(3): 470–2.

Midgely, Mary and Hughes, Judith (1983) *Women's Choices: Philosophical Problems Facing Feminism*. London: Weidenfeld and Nicolson.

Miller, Jean Baker (1976) *Toward a New Psychology of Women*. London: Penguin.

Muehlenhard, Charlene L. and Linton, Melaney A. (1987) 'Date Rape and Sexual Aggression in Dating Situations: Incidence and Risk Factors', *Journal of Counseling Psychology* 34: 186–96.

Nichols, Margaret (1987) 'Lesbian Sexuality: Issues and Developing Theory', in The Boston Lesbian Psychologies Collective (ed.) *Lesbian Psychologies: Explorations and Challenges*. Urbana and Chicago: University of Illinois Press.

Oakley, Ann (1974) *The Sociology of Housework*. Oxford: Martin Robertson.

Oakley, Ann (1981) *Subject Women*. Oxford: Martin Robertson.

Ohlson, E. and Wilson, M. (1974) 'Differentiating Female Homosexuals from Female Heterosexuals by the Use of the MMPI', *Journal of Sex Research* 10(4): 308–15.

Olins, Renate (1989) *The Guardian*, 29 November.

Onlywomen Press, ed. (1981) *Love Your Enemy: The Debate between Heterosexual Feminism and Political Lesbianism*. London: Onlywomen Press.

Parker, Jan (1987) 'The Tables Need Turning', in Gillian Hanscombe and Martin Humphries (eds) *Heterosexuality*. London: Gay Men's Press.

Penelope, Julia (1986) 'The Mystery of Lesbians II', *Gossip: A Journal of Lesbian Feminist Ethics* 2: 16–68.

Penelope, Julia (1987) 'The Illusion of Control: Sado-Masochism and the Sexual Metaphors of Childhood', *Lesbian Ethics* 2(3): 84–94.

Phelan, Shane (1989) *Identity Politics: Lesbian Feminism and the Limits of Community*. Philadelphia, PA: Temple University Press.

Phillips, Anne (1987) *Divided Loyalties: Dilemmas of Sex and Class*. London: Virago Press.

Pogrebin, Letty (1980) 'The Secret Fear that Keeps Us from Raising Free Children', reprinted in Laurel Richardson and Verta Taylor (eds) *Feminist Frontiers II: Rethinking Sex, Gender and Society*, 2nd edn. New York: Random House.

Ramazanoglu, Caroline (1989) *Feminism and the Contradictions of Oppression*. London: Routledge.

Rich, Adrienne (1980) 'Compulsory Heterosexuality and Lesbian Existence', *Signs* 5(4): 631–60.

Rich, Adrienne (1981) Letter to Ann Snitow, Christine Stansell and Sharon Thompson, reprinted in Laurel Richardson and Verta Taylor (eds) *Feminist Frontiers II: Rethinking Sex, Gender and Society*, 2nd edn. New York: Random House.

Rich, Adrienne (1989) 'Foreword to "Compulsory Heterosexuality and Lesbian Existence"', in Laurel Richardson and Verta Taylor (eds) *Feminist Frontiers II: Rethinking Sex, Gender and Society*, 2nd edn. New York: Random House.

Russell, Diana E.H. (1990) *Rape in Marriage*. Bloomington and Indianapolis: Indiana University Press.

Scully, Diana (1990) *Understanding Sexual Violence: A Study of Convicted Rapists*. Boston, MA: Unwin Hyman.

Segal, Lynne (1983) 'Sensual Uncertainty, or Why the Clitoris is not Enough', in Sue Cartledge and Joanna Ryan (eds) *Sex and Love: New Thoughts on Old Contradictions*. London: The Women's Press.

Shameem, Shaista (1992) 'Review of Thanh-dam Truong's *Sex, Money and Morality*', in C. Kitzinger, S. Wilkinson and R. Perkins (eds) *Heterosexuality*, a Special Issue of *Feminism & Psychology* 2(3): 468–70.

Sherman, Julia A. and Denmark, Florence C. (1978) *The Psychology of Women*. New York: Psychological Dimensions.

Shulman, Sarah (1982) Letter, *Maenad: A Women's Literary Journal* 2(3): 7–8.

Shulman, Sheila (1982) 'Hard Words and Why Lesbians Have to Say Them', in Lilian Mohin (ed.) *Beautiful Barbarians*. London: Onlywomen Press.

Sichtermann, Barbara (1986) *Femininity: The Politics of the Personal*. London: Polity Press.

Siegelman, Marvin (1972) 'Adjustment of Homosexual and Heterosexual Women', *British Journal of Psychiatry* 120: 477–81.

Silber, Linda (1990) 'Negotiating Sexual Identity: Non-lesbians in a Lesbian Feminist Community', *Journal of Sex Research*: 131–40.

Smith, Dorothy (1992) 'Review of Cynthia Fuchs Epstein's *Deceptive Distinctions*', in C. Kitzinger, S. Wilkinson and R. Perkins (eds) *Heterosexuality*, a Special Issue of *Feminism & Psychology* 2(3): 479–82.

Spender, Dale (1984) Untitled contribution to R. Rowland (ed.) *Women Who Do and Women Who Don't Join the Women's Movement*. London: Routledge.

Stein, Sarah (1984) *Girls and Boys: The Limits of Non-Sexist Childrearing*. London: Chatto and Windus/The Hogarth Press.

Stoltenberg, John (1990) *Refusing to be a Man*. London: Fontana.

Tieger, Todd (1981) 'Self-rated Likelihood of Raping and Social Perception of Rape', *Journal of Research in Personality* 15: 147–58.

Tong, Rosemarie (1989) *Feminist Thought*. London: Unwin Hyman.

Ussher, Jane (1991) (Chair, BPS Psychology of Women Section) Letter to the Chair of the BPS Scientific Affairs Board, 21 May 1991, reprinted in *British Psychological Society Psychology of Women Section Newsletter* 8: 66.

Uszkurat, Carol Ann (1990) 'A Classic Mistake: Review of Betty Friedan's *The Feminine Mystique*', *Trouble and Strife* 18: 42–6.

Walsh, Mary Roth, ed. (1987) *The Psychology of Women: Ongoing Debates*. New Haven, CT: Yale University Press.

Wetherell, Margaret and Griffin, Christine, eds (1992) 'Feminist Psychology and the Study of Men and Masculinity: Part I: Assumptions and Perspectives', *Feminism & Psychology* 1(3): 361–92.

Whitelegg, E. et al., eds (1982) *The Changing Experience of Women*. Oxford: Basil Blackwell, in association with the Open University.

Williams, Juanita H. (1987) *Psychology of Women: Behavior in a Biosocial Context*, 3rd edn. New York: W.W. Norton.

Wilson, Anna (1981) 'Statements from Individual Members of the Collective', in Onlywomen Press (ed.) *Love Your Enemy: The Debate between Heterosexual Feminism and Political Lesbianism*. London: Onlywomen Press.

Wilson, M. and Green, R. (1971) 'Personality Characteristics of Female Homosexuals', *Psychological Reports* 28: 407–12.

Wittig, Monique (1992) *The Straight Mind*. Boston, MA: Beacon Press.

Heterosexual Feminist Identities:
The Personal and the Political

Celia KITZINGER and Sue WILKINSON

EDITORS' INTRODUCTION

The personal is political. Out of our lived experience we construct theory, drawing, in turn, upon that theory to understand the meanings of our lives. For this Special Feature we invited feminists, most of them psychologists, to reflect on the role of their heterosexuality in developing feminist theory, and to consider the implications of feminism for their heterosexual identities.

Contributions for the Special Feature were invited by mailing nearly 300 feminists, identified from a range of sources — including lists of conference attenders, membership lists of feminist and 'psychology of women' groups and editorial boards of feminist journals. We sent out two versions of the letter: known — or assumed — psychologists were asked 'How does your heterosexuality contribute to (a) your feminist politics? and (b) your feminist psychology?'; others were asked simply 'How does your heterosexuality contribute to your feminism?'

The following pages present autobiographical accounts from some of the women who responded to our invitation to reflect upon the complex, and sometimes contradictory, relationship between their feminism and their heterosexuality. We selected these pieces, from among the many fascinating contributions we received, in order to represent as wide and varied a set of views as possible. The pieces included are sometimes controversial, often vivid, always thought provoking. Taken together, they provide an intriguing glimpse into the ways in which the raw data of our lives may be translated into feminist theory, and the ways in which feminism informs our interpretations of the conditions of our lives.

1. How My Heterosexuality Affects My Feminist Politics

Carol Nagy JACKLIN

Being asked to contribute to this Special Feature as a 'heterosexual' was offensive. Why? Because of what it means to say 'I am heterosexual'. More specifically:

1. Saying 'I am heterosexual' implies that my sexual preference is an unchanging and essential personal attribute. It is, however, certainly not clear that one's sexual preference is either unchanging or an essential attribute. No one should be limited by this or any other label. Sexuality is complex. Our lives are complex, and growth (or at least change) is the only constant.
2. Because heterosexuality has been an established sexual preference, 'I am heterosexual' also says 'I am traditional'. At the very least it connotes that I do not have to struggle with society about my sexual preference. I feel I do have to struggle with society about limiting anyone's sexual preference. Moreover, I do not want to think of myself as a member of the establishment, even though I know I have many of the privileges and rewards of the establishment.

Heterosexual feminists live, work and may be in love relationships with the 'enemy'. That is, they will be in more close-up and entangled situations with members of the group — men — that have traditionally had power over women than are asexual feminists or lesbian feminists. Heterosexual women are at greater risk of having inequitable personal relations. The disadvantages are clear, the advantages somewhat less so.

I lived for 20 years in a non-equitable heterosexual relationship. During that time I moved from wanting a traditional relationship (and not being able to imagine an alternative!), through many stages, to wanting an intimate heterosexual relationship based on mutuality and equity. An example of my own traditionalism still haunts me. At one time (*c.* 1965), I thought I would not work when my first child was born. After being unemployed, outside the home, for six months, I realized I had to work or emotionally and intellectually die. I got a full-time job teaching psychology at a junior college. I always carefully described my partner as the 'breadwinner' and myself as the 'jam-winner'. I consciously did not want to be threatening to him (or the status quo) in any way. Yet the desire, the need and finally the demand for 'a little respect when you get home' (in Otis Redding via Aretha Franklin's words) became greater and greater.

Changes in the culture paralleled (and probably made possible) my own changes. The Aretha Franklin version of the song 'Respect' was important to many of us because it articulated and validated some of our deepest longings. It made it acceptable for a woman to ask directly for both respect and sex. Being able to ask for sex was an important example of being able to ask for what we wanted. (Sex and respect are still conjoined in ways I do not understand.) It was to that song that I and many other heterosexually partnered women I knew danced together, *not* with our partners.

The disadvantages of a non-equitable relationship are clear. Much of my energy was taken up by doing the traditional servicing for my partner. Even at the time I wondered what I would have been able to do if I had a 'wife'. There has recently been some measurement in monetary terms of what a 'wife' does contribute to a career. A study of Stanford graduates nine years after graduation found women *and* men whose spouses or partners do all or most of the household tasks made 13 per cent more money than their classmates. For both women and men, having a 'wife' at home is profitable even after accounting for the effects on earnings of occupation, hours of work and the presence of children (Strober et al., 1991).

Being the 'lesser' member of a pair (a belief I shared with my partner), took a toll on my self-esteem and on my career. I was unaware of how much of a toll until I was out of the relationship.

What could be the advantages of a non-egalitarian heterosexual relationship?

Firstly, my experience helps me to understand and help other women in similar situations. I know how difficult it was for me to see the inequity in that relationship and finally to leave it. It was difficult to see the inequity because of my own low self-esteem. In part, I felt that I didn't deserve, wasn't worthy of, more than what I had. In retrospect, I realize that a second difficulty I had in leaving the relationship was a fear of living alone. Yet the experience of living alone later felt like a gift. I learned that living alone was unrelated to being lonely. It was an experience that freed me from dependence on relationships.

Secondly, there were advantages of having been able to grow in spite of the relationship. I now know deeply that change and growth are possible in many areas of my own life and in others' lives. I do not suggest we groom girls for traditional relationships so they can grow out of them, but those of us who survived traditional relationships learned from them.

Thirdly, it was clearly pressure from the larger culture, and not pressure from my family of origin, that kept me from seeing the inequity in my relationship. This fact was one of the first clues I had in my professional work, in the area of socialization of gender roles, of the strength of the larger culture over the family.

Fourthly, I have always had women's friendship and support apart from my sexual relationship. These friendships have given me a perspective on that relationship. It may be that lesbians have the same perspective on their sexual relationship from friends or even from males. This is something that requires discussion, a dialogue between lesbian and heterosexual feminists.

Do heterosexual relationships have to be non-equitable? No. I am currently in an egalitarian heterosexual relationship. I know, moreover, of many equitable heterosexual relationships as well as inequitable lesbian relationships. But the asymmetry of power is more common in heterosexual relationships.

My 20-year unequal heterosexual relationship has been important to my feminist politics. For it made clear to me, emotionally and intellectually, how central issues of power are to intimate relationships and to other institutions. Power inequity continues to be the basis of many heterosexual relationships. The personal is the political. My experience of power inequity has helped me to understand how pervasive this inequity is in larger societal issues.

ACKNOWLEDGEMENTS
I would like to thank Barrie Thorne, Myra Strober, Richard Caputo, Beth Meyerowitz, Tollie Grimes, Catharine Stimpson and Mary Hayden for comments on earlier drafts of this paper.

REFERENCE
Strober, M., Jackson, D. and Chan, A. (1991) 'Determinants of Income among Stanford Graduates of the Class of 1981: A View after Nine Years', unpublished manuscript.

Carol Nagy JACKLIN is a Professor and Chair of the Department of Psychology and Professor in the Program for the Study of Women and Men at the University of Southern California, Los Angeles, CA 90089–1061, USA.

2. The Authority of the Name

Alison YOUNG

I have written previously in the name of heterosexuality. In a text on the press coverage of the Greenham Common protest (an encampment of women protesting against nuclear weapons outside a missile base in England, which began in 1981 and which continues, in residual form, today), in order to meditate on representations of femininity and criminality, I have written of myself as heterosexual (Young, 1990). Such a self-naming took place in a section of the text dealing with the press representation of the Greenham women as lesbian. I was discussing the evaluation of lesbian politics, while attempting to acknowledge my self-constitution as heterosexual: 'For me, practising a hetero- rather than a homo- sexuality, and therefore situated at present on that side of the boundary, I am trying to discover further meanings of the taboo [on lesbianism], its meanings for those, like me, on the authorised side, who have never yet crossed over' (Young, 1990: 78). And now, in addition to naming myself 'heterosexual', I have been so named by the invitation to contribute to this Special Feature.

That invitation produced in me the profound sense of being labelled. This had a salutary effect: through experiencing how the act of self-naming is radically different from the act of naming *the other*. To be invited to write *in the name of heterosexuality* by another is to experience the force of being positioned as Other. In this context, the name 'heterosexual' seems far more permanent and concrete than in my own use of it. Now my identity feels out of control. My sexual being is in the control of others: those who issued the invitation and those who may read this publication. No longer the subject of the text, I experience objectification and remember as illusory my previous sense of autonomy and self-control. This experience has been salutary since it is all too easy for an academic, feminist, legal theorist/criminologist, who researches, teaches and writes, to forget that the shape of subjectivity comes from the attributions of others, far more than from our own acts of self-naming.

From such a position, caught in the names of Others, what does it 'mean' to speak as a heterosexual feminist woman? The anagrammatical inverse of 'name', 'mean', has two senses here. First is that of understanding: how should we understand the position of the heterosexual feminist woman? The second is that of the average: heterosexuality is constituted as the average, the norm and the mean of contemporary society. Any understanding of the heterosexual feminist woman's position must take place in the context of her heterosexuality as privileged over alternative modes of sexual relation (lesbianism, bisexuality, homosexuality).

When I speak, think and write as a heterosexual feminist woman, what I am doing is primarily describing a relationship. This relationship exists in four ways: with the self; with men; with women; and with the social sphere. I will take each of these in turn. In terms of the relationship with the self, as Denise Riley (1988: 96) has written, on womanhood: 'It's not possible to live twenty-four hours a day soaked in the immediate awareness of one's sex. Gendered self-consciousness has, mercifully, a flickering nature.'

So it is with the self's relation to heterosexuality. There are moments at which one may feel intensely aware of a self-defined, self-chosen sexuality, which can be experienced both positively and negatively. With regard to men, the heterosexual woman has to negotiate several factors. For example, they are her chosen objects of desire; this may inflect the relationship she has with them. Further, she has positioned herself as potential object of desire for men; this can bring the possibility of pleasure, of unwanted attention or of victimization in intimate relationships.

With other women, the heterosexual woman experiences both community and alienation (sometimes simultaneously). This is most profoundly so in respect of lesbian women. As women together, there may be acknowledged similar values, fears, political perspectives, all or any of which can draw connections between separate individuals. However, as sexual beings, all too often the women may feel enormously apart, even on 'opposite' sides of a fence. Classic feminist texts, such as that by Adrienne Rich (1983), can serve to make the heterosexual woman feel guilt, annoyance, sympathy, but most of all, difference. In current feminist political practice, it is the heterosexual/lesbian division which appears to have the greatest (and most alienating?) effect.

This is not to claim that either 'side' (the notion of sides is an injurious myth; better perhaps to think of shades in a spectrum of colours) is 'right' in their suspicion of the other. Such an argument could never be won and should not be attempted: more fruitful would be an analysis of the terms of each position, with the aim of gaining a deeper mutual understanding.

Finally, the heterosexual feminist woman exists in relation to the social sphere. This is a position of paradox and contradiction: to be heterosexual is to be privileged over other forms of sexuality; however, to be a woman is to be always already derogated and denigrated, placed habitually below man (we could call this the 'missionary effect').

To end what has been an inevitably sketchy and superficial account of the contribution of my heterosexuality to my feminist politics, I can only sum up thus: since sexuality is relational, it can never be straightforwardly 'mine'. Heterosexuality is constituted in a matrix formed by the intersection of negotiated situations, desires, fears and attitudes. We all contribute to this: self, men, women, social structure, lesbians, homosexuals. Just as it was different to be named as heterosexual by others in the invitation to contribute to this publication, so my assertions of the 'meaning' of my heterosexuality will be subject to the rereadings of others, immediately.

REFERENCES

Rich, A. (1983) 'Compulsory Heterosexuality and Lesbian Existence', in E. Abel and E. Abel (eds) *The Signs Reader*. Chicago, IL: Chicago University Press.
Riley, D. (1988) *Am I That Name? Feminism and the Category of Women in History*. London: Macmillan.
Young, A. (1990) *Femininity in Dissent*. London: Routledge.

Alison YOUNG is Lecturer in Law at the University of Lancaster and author of *Femininity in Dissent* (Routledge, 1990). ADDRESS: Department of Law, Lancaster University, Lancaster LA1 4YF, UK.

3. On Being Ordinary

Halla BELOFF

Of the many influences I have tried to find for my ideas and my work, my heterosexuality has not come to mind before. As a social psychologist, the way in which one's formal academic studies are part of one's identity work must be a matter for nice analysis. And here are not only issues of priorities within one's group memberships, but the delicacies of how far one dare 'come out'. Which labels are too dangerous to expose? Although the status of 'heterosexual' is a safe one, Goffman was right when he wrote a whole book, *Stigma*, to argue that we all have something to hide. The status of heterosexual is a safe one and so has remained simply latent.

Being heterosexual has several benefits. The first is that it means being 'ordinary'. Having said 'heterosexual', there is nothing to hide on that front. One's experiences can be shared with many others. There is one less reason for the children to be ashamed of one. One can enter into most cultural narratives, that is novels, films, fine art, on the basis of simple and satisfying identification.

The second benefit, which I value as highly as the first, is that, with the required skill and energy, and a significant degree of luck, one can enter into and maintain the status of wife and of mother and have as a base for all of one's life, a family home. Others can have that, but the cement seems harder when a nexus has formal recognition all around. My good fortune has been that both my husband and I come from backgrounds in which loyalty was the only conceivable course. And my privilege was to be accepted by marriage into a family that I consider to belong to the Jewish intellectual aristocracy of Britain. The challenge within the family was for psychology to vie with history and biochemistry.

So a heterosexual position brings one 'inside'. But in critical other ways, I am an 'outsider'. I accept as a compliment, Stalin's insult and anathema, 'Rootless Cosmopolitan'. As a refugee, déclassé, atheist of Jewish background, highbrow woman with a career, perhaps it's my best claim. There is no doubt in my mind that this deviant position has shaped my work from school on. It seems that at every choice-point, a non-dominant alternative was taken. I stayed outside: science and not arts; psychology; personality study and a Freudian question; social psychology and the topic of non-conformity; and then gender and the social psychology of photography.

At South Hampstead High School, we were, in the 1940s, the last, fervent remnants of the Vera Brittain cohort of feminists. We read *Testament of Youth* at the same time as we tried to understand Marie Stopes (who was still being passed round in a brown paper cover which we labelled 'Heat & Light' — an allusion to the physics text), and were taught by the spinster bluestockings whose fiancés had been killed in the Great War. (Although there were the Miss Brodie kind of sets, I was, of course, kept outside of those too.) It was taken for granted that we would not accept the role of little women from our husbands, although husbands were thought to be a good thing. When, for reasons which could only have been its oddness, I nominated psychology rather than physics for university application, my teacher blithely wrote down child psychology. I did not bother to contradict her, but knew that was feminine and mentally opted instead for industrial, whatever that might be.

If Freud was right and all our life choices are meaningful then my early work on personality and conformity (or rather non-conformity) was a self-interested exploration of the meaning of nurture rather than nature and of the positive value of alienation. But, again, heterosexuality was a taken-for-granted quality. And it must be remembered that for my generation there was no political dimension involved, either for the straight or the lesbian position. An overarching *modernismus* did not necessarily include one's sexual orientation.

More recently my work on the social psychology of visual arts subjects is obviously without kudos within the current climate of academic research. And 'pictures' (or visual information, as I would call it were I wanting to be respectable) give direct pleasure. That itself is suspect. Just the kind of field that women would practise in. As a mature person I think I can bear that. I have always been a feminist, have stood up not only for myself but for women in a group and have tried not to practise psychology as a man in skirts.

In that being heterosexual is the common category, and the dominant one, I see members having an obligation not to abuse their position. Now it's going to be hard to continue without expressing arrogance or sounding patronizing. But also as an outsider I have seen an obligation to ally myself with other outsiders. That means I've tried to understand the lesbian and gay male experience. My first academic learning here came from Celia Kitzinger's teaching in her fine PhD thesis, of which I was external examiner. She advanced my simple liberal stance, adding the appreciation of active negation of heterosexuality to the plain tolerance of another orientation. This is a rearrangement of my mental furniture that I'm still arduously engaged in.

If commitment to psychology, and within it the particular stance of social psychology, is in the outsider domain, where the stranger can see what the native cannot, then perhaps heterosexuality was needed to provide a safe base. And is it because of an implicit feeling that male chauvinism, anti-Semitism and ageism exist somewhere, that we in Britain never speak about personal issues, and that this is the first time that even some of my colleagues will see me naked like this?

Halla BELOFF is Senior Lecturer in Psychology at the University of Edinburgh, Edinburgh EH8 9YL, and author of *Camera Culture*.

4. Hypatia Unbound: A Confession

Sandra Lee BARTKY

I have been heterosexual as some homosexuals say they have been homosexual: forever. Already, at the age of 5, I was attracted (in some diffuse sense of 'attract') to male movie stars in ways that were different from my fascination with female stars. Demands by lesbian separatists earlier in the Second Wave that heterosexual feminists vacate their relationships with men seemed to me then and seem to me still both cruel and impossible. The cruelty lies in the suffering we are asked to inflict on men to whom we may have made long-term commitments (with the enemy, presumably, all bets are off) and with whom we may have shared years of intimacy and trust. The impossibility, for women like me, is akin to the impossibility I would feel if, in obedience to political fiat, I were asked to change my fingerprints. The felt impossibility of changing one's sexual orientation is not an argument for the desirability of this orientation; indeed, I have often wished that I could love women erotically, but I can't. An appeal to the feminist psychologist readers: invent a therapeutic technique for releasing the heterosexual woman 'who always knew what she was' from the prisonhouse of necessity into the free space of choice.

Dr Freud has much to answer for, especially to women, but he did me a really good turn. The circle of aspiring young intellectuals to which I belonged in the 1950s had thoroughly assimilated a psychoanalytic perspective into its way of viewing the world, so much so that when I went after college graduation to study in Germany I found myself quite unable to share my inner life with German students who at that time didn't know the lingo. I had had some sexual and some non-sexual romantic experience here; there, released from the constraint that my behavior might be reported back to my parents, I was free as never before to continue my erotic explorations. At some point, I began to reflect on what it was I was up to, not just in Europe, but back home as well. I began to see that I was attracted only to certain kinds of men — men who were older than I, who were somewhat arrogant and occasionally tyrannical, men to whom I needed to ascribe, whether they really had them or not, qualities of talent and intelligence far superior to my own. It was important too that these lovers gave me no more than a grudging and sporadic approval of my own worth; I needed to be kept jumping, like a monkey on a string. Continuities began to suggest themselves between these men and the heroes of film and fiction that had most excited me in adolescence: the arrogant and sarcastic Rochester of *Jane Eyre*; the distant and melancholy Max de Winter of *Rebecca*; the cold and harsh combination guardian and piano-coach of *The Seventh Veil* and, of course, Rhett Butler. With me, nice guys clearly finished last.

The whole thing came to a head in Germany when I fell passionately in love with a count. Quite a nice guy, actually (unlike his predecessors), the count collaborated nonetheless with my fantasies. His title did much of the work; moreover he was ten years my senior, smart and worldly. His occasional good-natured jibes at the inadequacies of my American public education were sufficient to call forth not only the social inferiority I felt in his presence but my more familiar sense of intellectual inferiority as well.

I could live in denial no more: something fishy was going on here. Given the terms in which I saw the world, hypotheses began to form in my mind. Feeling woefully inadequate much of the time, perhaps I was hoping that one of these 'pricks' would endow me with a penis. More likely, though not incompatible with this hypothesis, was another: I had a father fixation: I was caught in an unresolved Oedipus complex. A permanent liaison with one of these fathers would make me perpetually a daughter. I was at risk of putting myself in bondage to a male Other whose praise would make me soar but whose coldness or criticism could just as easily send me crashing to earth. I knew, at first only intuitively, that I would suffocate in such a relationship; I could go nowhere; I would remain a nobody, defeated by an infantile need for a total approbation from some man selected by my unconscious precisely for his inability to provide it.

Laboriously, I began to change my 'sexual orientation' — a change neither recognized nor valorized in separatist theory. For fathers, I substituted brothers. I don't know exactly how I did this. Once or twice I consciously chose not to pursue men whose sadism excited me. As I began to succeed in graduate school, perhaps it came to me that I could raise my status in the eyes of the world and in my own eyes through my own efforts and that I needn't wait for some capricious male to bestow this great good upon me. The fathers cooperated too, as they were on the prowl not for peers but for daughters. Returning in time to my alma mater, I ran into an old flame, PB, the handsome, cultivated and arrogant son of Viennese refugees. In undergraduate days, PB had suffered me to adore him as he paraded before my dazzled eyes his familiarity with European *Kultur*. Two years later, I'd laid up a store of *Kultur* of my own and suddenly it came pouring out of me: stanzas from Heine (in German), quotes from Goethe (in German), familiarity with wines of the proper regions, talk of the intricacies of the *Daseinsanalytik* of Heidegger whom I was then studying. Understand that I laid all of this at the feet of PB as one would lay an offering at the feet of a god. But an odd look came over him; he was clearly disconcerted and he never dated me again. A year or so later I learned that PB had married a woman who was in no way his intellectual equal.

With several of these brothers I have had long-term and very loving relationships — relationships that provided me with companionship and acceptance and which did not require that I abase myself before a powerful masculine Other. But even though my erotic repertoire has widened, I have not found in the latter relationships the powerful erotic charge of the former. The approbation I need I found in a supportive feminist community. I have carved out a life for myself I would never have led as Daddy's girl. I have been, if not passionately sexual, then passionately political. My professional success, though modest, is something I never imagined I could achieve when I was consort to the count. I have flourished. My narrow escape has, of course, been purchased at a price, that price a certain fracturing of myself. Given things as they are and all things considered, not a bad bargain.

Sandra Lee BARTKY is Professor of Philosophy and Women's Studies at
      the University of Illinois at Chicago and author of *Femininity and
  Domination: Studies in the Phenomenology of Oppression* (Routledge, 1990).
  ADDRESS: Department of Philosophy (M/C 267), 1524 University Hall,
                                     Box 4348, Chicago, IL 60680, USA.

5. Identity, 'Passing' and Subversion

Mary CRAWFORD

I remember the first time I was accused of being a heterosexual (bourgeois heterosexual at that). It was 1971, and I had just joined my first CR group. My 'natural' sexual and emotional attachment to men was thoroughly attacked and disparaged by the Marxist lesbian feminists I had naively joined in the name of sisterhood. I began to wish I'd stayed in the closet.

The early 1970s were a pivotal time for my identity. Around me, friends were coming out as lesbians. Important feminist theorists were espousing separatism. Women were naming sexism, exploring the conditions of our lives, and making connections with each other. During those years I changed my thinking about women and gender relations in massive ways — yet, here I am, in 1992, still living with a man. Still living with the *same* man.

One thing that feminism has taught me is to question oppositional categories. 'Heterosexuals' can't exist without the corresponding category of 'homosexuals'. The opposition of the two categories allows either to be used as an instrument of social control. It also obscures the many dimensions along which an individual might choose to place herself as a sexual, sensual and social being.

It is clear that women do not always mean the same things when they say 'I am a heterosexual' (or bisexual or lesbian) (Golden, 1987; Shuster, 1987). Sexual identity is much too fluid, and behavior much too variable, to be so neatly categorized. (This is not to say that everyone *experiences* sexual identity in terms of fluidity and possibilities — cf. Kitzinger, 1987.) Although I was asked to write this comment as a 'heterosexual feminist', I certainly do not ascribe unitary meaning to the notion of being a heterosexual.

A quandary for me, as a feminist, is how to acknowledge the instability of the categories and the possibility of oppression through categorization, while also acknowledging the right of women to name themselves as they see fit. For the moment, I resolve this dilemma by respecting women who identify as lesbian, bisexual or heterosexual but resisting a sexual label for myself. Naming can be an affirmative act of self-definition; labeling and categorization are acts of those in power directed at those with less power.

Moreover, none of the labels seems adequate for who I am. There are many women whom I love for their bodies, their minds, their quirks, their brilliant individualities and their ways of being in the world. I recognize my sexual attraction to particular women, and to particular men other than my life partner, though I choose not to act on it. As a rule, I prefer the companionship of women, though I make exceptions for a few gentle men. I also experience rage at what some men have done to women. The label 'heterosexual' as usually applied doesn't really encompass these complexities of love, respect, anger and sensuality. Rather, I think of myself as a woman-identified person who, because of a decision to enter into a long-term affectional and sexual relationship with a man, is situated in a largely heterosexual social context.

On passing. What are the costs and benefits of living in ways that others recognize as heterosexual? Although I do not accept the situation as morally right, I inevitably enjoy what my lesbian friends call heterosexual privilege — braided, in my case, with class and color privilege. Mundane life is *easier* for me. No one discounts my feminist analysis of social problems by calling me a man-hater. (They use other arguments instead!) No one hassles me at my child's school, at the doctor's office or at work. No one tells me I'm an unfit mother. Because I am legally married, my job provides health care benefits for my partner and family (an urgent necessity in the USA where health care is a privilege of the wealthy). Wills and mortgages, taxes and auto insurance, retirement pensions and school enrollment for the children — all the ways that individuals ordinarily interface with social structures — are designed to fit people like me and my partner.

Although we reject the notion of ownership in relationships, my partner and I live in a context that views women as properly the property of men. It is easy and comfortable to travel or go out socially with my partner. Waiters see us, clerks wait on us, while street harassers ignore us to focus on the woman who is alone or with another woman. Well-dressed white men and the women who 'accompany' them get respect! Even when we are not together, his presence in my social network cushions me — for example from the miseries of trying to live on a single wage or two 'women's' wages. On the other hand, the heterosexual cushion can be an illusion. In the first draft of this paragraph I wrote that my partner's presence in my life 'cushions me from (some) sexual harassment at work'. (I had wanted to make the point that men who do not hesitate to violate a woman's personhood with sexual harassment sometimes balk at violating another *man's* 'property rights' and thus choose to harass single more than married women.) Both my partner and my friend wrote indignantly on the margins. She: 'You've been harassed!' He: 'No, it didn't did it?!' My parenthetical 'some' had been my covert acknowledgment that male protection had failed me; my assertion of invulnerability had glossed my wishful thinking that *he* who loves me could/should have protected me.

On subverting heterosexism. Being taken for a standard-issue heterosexual bestows a credibility that can be used to subvert heterosexism. I always begin my psychology of women course with dialogue (Unger and Crawford, 1992; Crawford et al., 1992). I interview students, and they interview me, about why we have chosen to teach/learn in this course, what skills and interests we bring to it, and what personal background we feel is relevant to working together. Invariably the students ask whether I am married. I know that this question is at least partly a code for the 'L word'. I never respond directly. Instead, I ask them, What do you believe you would know about me if you knew my marital status? What does this fact tell you about who I am, how I might teach, what I believe? Is it more relevant in this class than if I were teaching, say, Experimental Methods? Is marital status a relevant dimension for evaluating your male professors? After we follow this discussion along its (always fascinating) byways, I ask them what they would 'know' about me if I were to state that I am a lesbian. In refusing to label myself, and in helping my students articulate their stereotypes of lesbians, straight women and heterosexual marriage as the normative human condition, I speak from a position of heterosexual privilege that grants me safety in my classroom — yet I use that position to subvert their comfortable assumptions. Paradoxically, I use heterosexual privilege to subvert heterosexism.

As for my feminist politics, I cannot personally accept theories that treat men as an homogeneous class, espouse separatism or emphasize fundamental personality differences between males and females. Such theories look too simplistic and oppositional to me. Being situated in a heterosexual social network means that there are boys and men I spend a great deal of time with and know intimately. I continue to believe in their possibilities as lovers, life partners and friends. At the same time, as a feminist and a woman-identified woman, I work to eliminate patriarchal inequities of status and power.

ACKNOWLEDGMENTS

I am grateful to my dear friend Mary McCullough and my partner Roger Chaffin for their comments on an earlier draft.

REFERENCES

Crawford, M., Unger, R. and Stark, A. (1992) Instructor's Manual to accompany *Women and Gender: A Feminist Psychology*. New York: McGraw-Hill.

Golden, C. (1987) 'Diversity and Variability in Women's Sexual Identities', in Boston Lesbian Psychologies Collective (eds) *Lesbian Psychologies*, pp. 18–34. Urbana, IL: University of Illinois Press.

Kitzinger, C. (1987) *The Social Construction of Lesbianism*. London: Sage.

Shuster, R. (1987) 'Sexuality as a Continuum: The Bisexual Identity', in Boston Lesbian Psychologies Collective (eds) *Lesbian Psychologies* pp. 56–71. Urbana, IL: University of Illinois Press.

Unger, R. K. and Crawford, M. (1992) *Women and Gender: A Feminist Psychology*. New York: McGraw-Hill; Philadelphia, PA: Temple University Press.

Mary CRAWFORD is Professor of Psychology and Women's Studies at West Chester University of Pennsylvania, co-editor of *Gender and Thought: Psychological Perspectives*, and author (with Rhoda Unger) of *Women and Gender: A Feminist Psychology*.

6. Sisters Under the Skin: A Politics of Heterosexuality

Kadiatu G. KANNEH

The discussion which has been raging over sexuality and sexual difference in its many political manifestations has centred, in certain feminisms, on the politics of sexual preference. The encoding of sexuality as a political issue becomes strident in the case of strategies of identity, and I use 'strategies' in a deliberate sense. The significance of *placing* oneself within or against a social order can be a choice as well as a coercion. Or, rather, the narrative which inscribes the meaning of that position can be both chosen and necessary.

It seems curious, writing in the times in which I find myself, to discuss the location of a narrative of heterosexuality. How is it possible to inscribe a safe, uncontested identity as a purposeful political stance? I certainly do not wish to write against the painful and triumphant histories of lesbianism, the subversive and positive critiques of the dominant straight and oppressive societies in which we live. I do intend to suggest or intimate a possible reading of heterosexuality which would insist on the value and significance of racial or cultural loyalties within a feminist politics.

Loving women in a world where women are forced into a daily posture of opposition and struggle, is a mode of delight and recognition of the self which I would not dream of letting go. I choose also to listen to another voice of self-recognition which insists on an urgency which I would not wish to equate with an anti-feminist stance.

Having belonged to various feminist theory reading groups, I notice, painfully, that we always come up against the question of racial or cultural identity within or against the boundaries of feminism. How can we articulate a commitment to loving our brothers, our fathers, our vilified and celebratory cultural backgrounds? I find the imperative within my self-understanding as a feminist is to view the politics of anti-imperialism, black struggles, nationalism, within the terms and from the perspective of gender and the feminist movement. In contrast, and to my confusion, I find myself viewing women-identified theories unshakingly from the perspective of my own racial positioning, my own experience of racism, the histories of black people and my own family. These two strategies need not be mutually exclusive, experientially or theoretically, and I will not make the decision to abandon feminism in an either/or dynamic which would unacceptably limit and reduce my life.

Feminism's response to heterosexuality has repeatedly been to dismiss it, to criticize it as a neutral or normalizing area, as a threat to women, as akin to capitalism and male dominance. The other story which remains almost in the guise of feminism's guilty shadow, is that of solidarity with a community, loyalty to a history which still needs, cries out, to be honoured. I think of the black and white lesbians whose emotional suffering rests on their feeling of exile from fathers, brothers, mothers, the warmth of familial acceptance, the joy of staying with ease within the boundaries of home. I am also, necessarily reminded of those women, like myself, who feel caught between two contradictory heritages, coerced alternatively into the context of one or the other, disqualified from forming an identity in harmony with both. The politics of identity do, of course, involve a mass of contradictions, lived as shocks and moments of acute anxiety, invisibility, that sickness of standing at one remove from the body. A mixed-race identity reads as a contradiction in terms. Similarly, but not the same, heterosexuality as a feminist political choice invites an argument.

Can we dream of a feminist movement which could allow women to make different sexual choices within different social categories? Can we dare to suggest a changing pattern of thought where women concentrate the focus of their struggles in different ways? I feel rebellious of a feminist insistence that this movement come first or only, that patriarchy is the first and only key to imperialism, racial domination and capitalism. The feel, the size of the loss I suffer in the face of this call for all my attention, all my love, the anger I am taught to believe is negative, leads me to insist on claiming it all, to recognize, in my own feminist commitment, other locations, other desires which do not necessarily speak the same language.

Feminism can detach itself from the reminiscence of middle-class, white exclusivity, and the strength of anti-racist, socialist or black feminisms is evidence of the flexibility, the recognitions which the feminist movement negotiates. I want to suggest that loving men — as well as women — is not an accident, a problem for feminist identification, but a valid move towards cultural or racial self-determination; another or temporary choice for full self-expression. We need to move beyond locating contradiction as a barrier to political organization. Heterosexuality needs to be recognized as another instance of standing in more than one place at the same time, when race, class, culture, nationality go deeper than the skin.

Kadiatu KANNEH writes on questions of identity in post-colonial literatures and theory. She is a Lecturer in English at the School of English and American Studies, Sussex University, Falmer, Brighton BN1 9QN, UK.

7. Heterosexuality and Parenting

Susie ORBACH

Heterosexuality has been especially focused for me since becoming a parent. Until I became a parent, my main emotional ties apart from the one with my partner were with women. I worked in a woman-centred setting, my work concern focused mainly on women and much of my social life was spent with women. In a peculiar way, being heterosexual was not an issue I consciously confronted. To be sure I had, in common with many feminists, agonized in the early 1970s about my (hetero)sexuality in the context of a life predominantly spent with women. But for the decade and a bit before I gave birth to a son it was my relationships with women that were at the fore and not my heterosexuality. Since becoming a parent, the prejudices I have encountered — my own and other people's — coupled with my fantasies about raising children in a heterosexual family, have forced issues on me in a particularly poignant way.

First a word about my own situation. My partner and I committed ourselves to joint child-rearing with the addition of female child minders, au pairs and nursery workers. We both work from home and so have had an unusual amount of flexibility. The joint enterprise of parenting has worked well so far, with neither of us doing a larger share.

We have a son of seven-and-three-quarters (at present deeply enamoured of the World Wrestling Federation) and a daughter just three complete with pink ballet tutu and froufrou. We were both raised in left-wing households which restricted the range of reading material we could have access to, separating us somewhat from the culture of other school children, and this has led to a desire on both our parts to allow the children access to the wider culture. This proves problematic because of the deeply sexist nature of so much of children's activities. We have wanted the children to be able to manage in a sex-role stereotyped culture without being bound by heterosexism. It continues to be a difficult balance to achieve but our particular adaptation has been to focus our activities on creating *emotionally literate* children so that our daughter will not have to reiterate a situation in which girls and women provide for the emotional needs of others without receiving that attention themselves, and so that our son can be both articulate about what he is feeling and be responsive to the emotional expressions of others.

So participating in the constructing of new masculinities and femininities is for me predicated not on discouraging girls' interests in dolls or nail polish or boys' interests in swords and trains but in offering them substantial emotional attachments that are not gender restricted. The social circle of our friends includes several fathers who also engage in joint child-rearing so that masculinity and femininity for these children is not defined by who does or doesn't do the emotional labour and the household labour.

Outside our social circle this does cause considerable disjuncture for the children but I have been interested to observe my son's ability to be, as it were, bilingual. On first starting school he said, 'Well I'm extremely nervous but I suppose all the other children will be too.' A few days later he reported that they (the boys) might be nervous but they showed it by bashing one another up. The following week he said regretfully to his father, 'I'd like to be a gentle boy Dad, but I just don't think I can manage it.'

But while the children have a wider range of activities, fantasy personas and emotions than those who do not have gender-conscious parents, the overwhelming nature of the heterosexual world in which they are located, constructs future relationship scenarios in heterosexual terms. It takes a valiant effect to challenge that. When my son reported 18 months ago that he didn't want to kiss a girl and he was certainly never going to, my tease about how he might be changing his mind ten years from now was greeted with a resounding 'Yuk!' When I said he might want to kiss a boy the 'Yuk' was even louder and more determined. These interventions on my/our part where one tries to insert that there is a homosexual experience suffer, I believe, from their lack of exposure to homosexual couples or individual lesbians or homosexuals raising children. They don't see it represented on television or in the books they read and it just so happens that in their classes at school or nursery no one is (openly?) parenting in such a situation, so their access to homosexuality as an idea and a practice is curtailed by the limits of the world they encounter. And it is here that I am up against my own homophobia and forced to reckon with my heterosexuality. For although my work life involves work with lesbians, and lesbian mothers, nearly all the families we spend time with as a family ourself are heterosexual. This can't be an accident. It must reflect at some level the pressure of parenting as well as my own internalized prejudices.

I have not in parenting wished to valorize heterosexuality but raising a son after spending years working on the mother–daughter relationship has made me anxious to offer him a masculinity that is secure and not burdened by being responsible for patriarchy and being guilty for being a man. Since the only masculinity I have intimate knowledge of is his father's, I remain conscious of the fact that his is a heterosexually inclined masculinity and that my son will doubtless internalize something of that. Masculinity is represented to him more strongly in heterosexual terms than is femininity as our circle includes lesbians but not male homosexuals.

So parenting has forced me to identify myself as both emotionally and sexually heterosexual. Where gender politics from 1970 to 1984 located me almost exclusively within a woman's world, parenting has catapulted me back into the heterosexual mainstream engaging daily with the impact of patriarchy on the lives of my family. I can't say I like that aspect of parenting all that much. But I am also aware of the fact that as a parent I am accepted in this society as a woman in a way not legitimated before. I wonder how much of this legitimation would fall away if my parenting didn't take place in such an obvious heterosexual arrangement.

Susie ORBACH is a psychotherapist and writer. She co-founded The Women's Therapy Centre in London and The Women's Therapy Center Institute in New York and is the author of many books, including *Fat is a Feminist Issue*. ADDRESS: 2 Lancaster Drive, London NW3 4HA, UK.

8. On the Inadequacy of Our Sexual Categories: A Personal Perspective

Sandra Lipsitz BEM

How does my heterosexuality contribute to my feminist politics? That is an impossible question for me to answer because, although I have lived monogamously with a man I love for over 26 years, I am not now and never have been a 'heterosexual'. But neither have I ever been either a 'lesbian' or a 'bisexual'. What I am — and have been for as long as I can remember — is someone whose gender and sexuality have just never seemed to mesh very well with the available cultural categories, and *that* — rather than my presumed heterosexuality — is what has most profoundly informed my feminist politics.

When I say that my sexuality does not mesh with the available cultural categories, what I mean is that the sex-of-partner dimension being referred to by the three categories of heterosexual, homosexual and bisexual simply seems irrelevant to my own particular pattern of erotic attractions and sexual experiences. I have no desire to specify exactly what my pattern is in a public forum, but one thing I can say for certain. Although some of the (very few) individuals to whom I have been attracted during my 47 years have been men and some have been women, what those individuals have in common has nothing to do with either their biological sex or mine — from which I conclude not that I am attracted to both sexes, but that my sexuality is organized around dimensions other than sex.

Similarly, when I say that my gender does not mesh with the available cultural categories either, what I mean is that, since earliest childhood, my own particular blend of temperament and behavior has not only seemed to fall outside the categories of male and female, masculine and feminine, but also that being female has itself never seemed a salient feature of my self-concept. Like being human, in other words, it is a fact, but a taken-for-granted background fact rather than one of the nuclei around which I have constructed my identity. (Being a feminist, on the other hand, is one of those nuclei.)

None of this is to say, of course, that I live my life outside the culture's categories. No matter how marginal or alienated from the culture's categories I may feel subjectively, the outward pattern of my life is so completely in harmony with the culture's heterosexist institutions that I experience little or none of the flak that I would if I were living my life as anything other than a heterosexual.

Living in a heterosexual marriage and rearing two children have themselves contributed to my feminist politics, of course, because they have prompted me to theorize about, and also to experiment with, both egalitarian relationships and gender-liberated child-rearing. But it is still my subjective sense of being outside the culture's categories that has most profoundly contributed to my feminist politics because it has enabled me to see how the culture's categories *construct and constrain* social reality by providing the historically specific conceptual framework through which we perceive our social world.

My ability to understand and to articulate this insight in the domain of gender and sexuality has evolved dramatically over the past 20 years. In the early 1970s, I focused almost exclusively on the concept of androgyny because it seemed to challenge the traditional categories of masculine and feminine as nothing up to that time had ever done. By the late 1970s and early 1980s, however, I had begun to see that the concept of androgyny inevitably focuses so much more attention on the individual's being *both* masculine and feminine than on the culture's having created the concepts of masculinity and femininity in the first place, that it can legitimately be said to reproduce precisely the gender polarization that it seeks to undercut. Accordingly, I moved on to the concept of 'gender schematicity' because it enabled me to argue even more forcefully that masculinity and femininity are merely the constructions of a cultural schema — or lens — that is gender polarizing.

Finally, in a forthcoming book tentatively entitled *The Lenses of Gender: Transforming the Debate on Sexual Inequality* (Yale University Press, 1993), I am able to theorize the concept of the gender-polarizing lens more completely and also to expand the underlying insight into a comprehensive analysis of how a society's gender lenses systemically perpetuate not only the oppression of women, but the oppression of sexual minorities as well.

In particular, I now believe that there are actually *three* gender lenses embedded in the culture which, in addition to shaping how individuals perceive social reality, also shape how they construct the more palpable and material things — like unequal pay and inadequate daycare — that constitute social reality itself. The first lens is *gender polarization*, which superimposes a male/female distinction on virtually every aspect of human experience, including even how one is supposed to experience sexual desire. The second lens is *androcentrism*, which defines males and male experience as a neutral standard or norm and females and female experience as a sex-specific deviation from the norm. And finally, the third lens is *biological essentialism*, which rationalizes and legitimizes both of the other two lenses by treating them as the natural and inevitable consequences of the intrinsic biological natures of women and men.

It should now be clear that my unwillingness to squeeze my sexuality into any of the three sex-of-partner categories provided by the culture is not only a continuation of my 20-year-long challenge to the lens of gender polarization. It is also a challenge to the lens of biological essentialism because it suggests that — as biologically natural as the sex-of-partner category system may now appear to be — there may be nothing natural or inevitable about organizing one's erotic life around the dimension of biological sex.

Sandra BEM is Professor of Psychology and Women's Studies at Cornell University, Department of Psychology, Uris Hall, Ithaca, New York 14853–7601, USA.

9. The (Dis)Comfort of Being 'Hetero'

Nira YUVAL-DAVIS

The question being asked follows, I suppose, the new interest in hegemonic identities, such as that of men, whites, etc., and as such is very welcome. Only inquiry into hegemonic identities and collectivities can destroy the construction of 'naturalness' of hegemonic ways of being and behaving.

However, I am a bit worried that the assumption behind this question is that I define myself as a heterosexual in the same way that other women define themselves as lesbians; i.e. that my identity is my ideology and that I am committed to the binary universe which divides women into heterosexuals and lesbians.

Many lesbian women get upset when women, like me, who have had most, or even all, of their meaningful sexual relationships (and one-night stands) with men, refuse to call themselves heterosexuals in an essentialist way, rather than just in a descriptive way. Obviously we have not had to suffer the exclusions and discriminations that lesbian women who have 'come out' have had to suffer from the state, employers, general public prejudice and often family and former close friends. However, for me, and for many other women that I know from the same 'leftist' and feminist politics background, one of the exciting discoveries that feminism has brought to us has been the social construction of sexuality and the realization that we all have, to a lesser or greater extent, bisexual desires. Reducing sexuality to politics (which is a very different endeavour to including sexuality within the domain of the political) is very problematic for me.

Given this reservation, I shall now answer the question as a heterosexual feminist, to the extent that one can answer such a question in 1000 words.

One obvious response to the question is, of course, that, as a heterosexual (as well as a mother of a son) I could never have the luxury in my feminist politics of 'doing away with men' and attempting to build a separatist self-contained social and emotional world from which men would be excluded. Early on in my development as a feminist, in the early 1970s I had the occasion to interview (as part of my PhD fieldwork) heterosexual feminists who had chosen to become celibate. The trapped and hopeless way in which these women were talking about their lives has been a major warning for me not to choose this path (one of them, at least, ended up two years later marrying a rabbi and forsaking feminism altogether). The trap of celibacy is not the loss of sexual satisfaction (of which masturbation can take care splendidly): it is the loss of physical as well as emotional intimacy — which no close non-sexual friendship can replace.

Of course, this is where the problem lies for heterosexual feminists — how to develop intimacy with 'the oppressor'. Lesbians might be oppressed in the public domain, but heterosexual women — according to all feminist analyses and especially radical feminist separatist ones — enter unequal partnerships in which sexist norms and power relations prevail. The comforts of the ghetto experience which alternative lesbian communities can offer are not open to heterosexual feminists. In order to develop non-sexist (or, at least, more limited sexist) partnerships (or sexuality in general), many of the heterosexual women I know, including myself, have had to 'reinvent' the 'rules of the game' all the time — to lead a complex dance on a tightrope that often ended up with broken relationships and broken hearts, and, just as importantly, with a feeling of deep social isolation. (This is true especially for the immigrants/exiles among us who had no family or long-standing friendship networks to lean on and for whom the 1970s 'alternatives for families' have proved especially disappointing.) But we could not stay in the Marcusian stage of the 'Big Refusal' in our relationships with men, and personal — if not general social — life strategies had to be developed; and we had to learn to be strong, which is probably the most important precondition for any heterosexual feminist. . . .

Rejecting separatist feminism, however, has had for me to do with much more than just my sexuality and my motherhood. It has had also to do with my realization that the differences among women are as important and significant as the differences between women and men; that national, racial, class, place in the life cycle, and other social divisions are interrelated and enmeshed with gender divisions and therefore in no way could I have followed a feminist politics in which only the difference between men and women was the ultimate dividing line; and that on many fronts emotional and political bonds with men are as committing for me as are those with other women; that in some political struggles I have been engaged in, it was mostly men who were my partners at the time — the sexism of many of them notwithstanding. And on a more personal level — I have discovered enough men who were emotionally vulnerable and intellectually open to experience genuine friendship and intimacy on a roughly egalitarian basis in order to remain optimistic about gender relations. (To the extent that one can be optimistic about any progressive politics these days. . . .)

Moreover, I was always very weary of the politics of representation, especially of the 'inherent victim'. My political consciousness developed in Israel in the context of the struggle for civil and political rights of the Palestinians, and where I was constantly told that Jews could never be racists because they were the eternal victims of racism. I was weary of the 'tyranny of structurelessness' within the feminist movement from very early on, in which some women spoke in the name of all. And I was suspicious of the homogeneity of the 'raised consciousness' of women, this discovery of a shared 'objective truth' of 'The Condition of Woman' which was usually the direct result of the generally very narrow range of class, origin and age of the women who participated in the CR groups. So my heterosexuality has been just one of the factors which has shaped my socialist anti-racist feminism. And sexual politics have been just one of the elements which have shaped my politics.

Nira YUVAL-DAVIS is a Reader in Ethnic and Gender Studies at the University of Greenwich. She has written extensively on gender, racism and nationalism, and on the interrelationships between them. Her publications include her co-edited books, *Women–Nation–State* (Macmillan, 1989), *The Gulf War and the New World Order* (Zed Books, 1991), *Refusing Holy Orders: Women and Fundamentalism in Britain* (Virago, 1992) and a co-written book, *Racialized Boundaries: Race, Nation, Gender, Colour and Class Divisions and the Anti-Racist Struggle* (Routledge, 1992). ADDRESS: School of Social Sciences, Churchill House, Woolwich Campus, Wellington Street, Woolwich, London SE18 6PF, UK.

10. Heterosexuality: Challenge and Opportunity

Sheila KITZINGER

I never planned to be heterosexual, of course. If I had known my three radical lesbian feminist daughters back then, I would probably never have made that decision. I just *was*. A child of patriarchy, I was shaped by it. I expected to love a man, and did. I married, made a home, had a family, established deep loyalties.

My husband Uwe and I have always shared fundamental values — values which may, just possibly, have had something to do with the fact that three of our five daughters are lesbian feminists, and that we both admire their strength and idealism. He knew what it was to be a Jew as a child in Nazi Germany. We first encountered each other (briefly) at a meeting exploring the problems and challenges of building a better society. We were anti-racist, anti-sexist, anti-discrimination of any kind, yet after the last world war, the language we used at that time was different from, and in a way more positive than that used now. We called for world government, full employment, international understanding, world peace.

We sought to analyse society and to understand human behaviour. We married in the Quaker Meeting House at Oxford, and in doing so, we committed ourselves not only to each other, but to work for political and social change as equals, 'flying wing to wing'. We continue to share the same fundamental values. Where there are disagreements, my relationship with him, and the discussions we have, help me to define my feminism with more precision, in different ways, but just as powerfully, as my relationships with my daughters.

Of course, discussions with a man are different from those with women, and of course they involve compromise. I acknowledge that compromise with men can easily become treachery to women. I realize that I walk on a tightrope. Yet I look at who I am and where I am and try to determine how I can use this creatively. Most women are heterosexual and are under constant pressure to service the men in their lives. When they give birth they are controlled by a male-dominated, autocratic, hierarchical medical system. Many remember birth as a kind of rape. In challenging the male model of childbirth and in offering women the knowledge they need if they are to make informed choices between alternatives, to question medical authority and to develop self-confidence, I strive towards reclaiming our bodies in childbirth — to take birth back for women.

My politics spring from powerful personal experience. But it is vital to go beyond the purely personal and specific. My own birth experiences were very positive, and it would be simple for me to talk only about the joy of birth. Yet I spend much of my time listening to women who have been subjected to violence in childbirth, and my political understanding has been sharpened by awareness of the abuse that many women suffer.

My starting point was women's satisfaction and fulfilment in the experience of childbirth. What I have learnt in the last 35 years or so has opened my eyes to women's rights in childbirth, our rights to informed choice, to humane care, to control of our own reproductive health. How women give birth is part of a much wider challenge that concerns our lives as a whole, women's lives everywhere in the world. In the West we are among the most privileged nations. There are many countries in the developing world where women often die as a consequence of abortion or in childbirth. These account for nearly half of all deaths among women of childbearing age in the Third World.

The concept of 'freedom' in childbirth must mean more than freedom from pain, freedom from unnecessary intervention or freedom to do our own thing. It must mean a whole range of reproductive freedoms for women everywhere: freedom to choose whether or not to have a child in the first place, the right to free contraception, to safe abortion, freedom from compulsory sterilization, the right to adequate health care, freedom from grinding poverty that causes stillbirth and neonatal death, and freedom from exploitation by multinational companies who dump drugs in the Third World and offer 'free gifts' of dried milk to new mothers, with the result that lactation fails and their babies die from dehydration and diarrhoea. In the same way, the concept of 'freedom' as applied to heterosexuality and lesbianism is not simply a matter of personal choice, but of the social and political structures within which choices are made.

I didn't plan my life. Instead, I have taken opportunities. It may even be that, in challenging me, heterosexuality has somehow also energized me. I would not have it any other way.

Sheila KITZINGER is a social anthropologist and birth activist, author of 22 books including the classic *The Experience of Childbirth* (Penguin, 5th edn, 1986) and *Homebirth* (Dorling Kindersley, 1991). Her most recent book is *Ourselves as Mothers* published in the UK and Australia by Doubleday, September 1992. ADDRESS: The Manor, Standlake, nr Witney, Oxon OX8 7RH, UK.

11. Heterosexual Feminist Identities: Private Boundaries and Shifting Centers

Hilary LIPS and Susan Alexandra FREEDMAN

As we reflected on and discussed our identities as heterosexual feminists, several themes emerged: time, privacy/separateness and the sense of divided or shifting loyalties. These themes appeared as we pondered our relationships, our work, our feelings about the feminist movement.

Time is a major issue. We think it probable that, in women, heterosexuality is correlated with time spent in the company of men. Those men may be feminists or fellow travelers; they may be husbands or lovers or friends — yet being in their presence is not a neutral experience in a world that differentiates women and men according to roles and status. We think of the studies, including those by Alice Eagly and Wendy Wood (1991) and by Kay Deaux and Brenda Major (1987), that show gender-stereotypic behavior more likely to occur in the presence of an audience, or of those that suggest that reciprocal roles maintain each other, including the work of Michael Lamb et al. (1979), and we are forced to contemplate the idea that heterosexual women who are feminists are almost bound to experience a great deal of tension between the 'demand characteristics' of their social environment and the ideals of their feminism. We think of the consistent evidence that men dominate conversations, including the research done by Dale Spender (1989) and that of Don Zimmerman and Candace West (1975), and we wonder if, in concert with spending considerable time in the company of men, heterosexual women spend an inordinate amount of time keeping our feelings to ourselves, holding our opinions — especially our feminist opinions — privately.

The amount of time spent with men may expose heterosexual women to more masculine-oriented thinking and values. It may also make it more difficult for us to disengage from patriarchal standards. The resulting tension between feminist and mainstream perspectives can be challenging, encouraging the heterosexual woman continually to wrestle with and redefine her priorities. Sometimes, because of a sense of divided loyalty, that struggle is engaged privately, without the knowledge or collaboration of either a male partner or female feminist friends.

In a very real way, heterosexual women experience boundaries between our feminist activities and our sexual and intimate relationships. Time spent within roles of feminist and lover may not easily overlap. Any feminist woman can sometimes feel torn between the significant men her life — brothers, fathers, friends — and her loyalty to women. However, for the heterosexual feminist woman, such tension can sometimes be unrelenting, involving the long-term couple relationship in which she is most constantly and permanently involved.

A heterosexual woman who is part of a couple may experience conflict between her identity as a feminist and her identity as an intimate partner. She may sometimes have an inescapable sense of separateness, a feeling that her feminism is private, not shared completely with her partner. She may feel that her strong feelings about certain feminist issues are simply not totally explainable to even the most significant, supportive man in her life. The understanding provided by her partner is likely to be limited, intellectual rather than emotional, similar, perhaps, to heterosexual women's understanding of homosexuality.

Heterosexual feminists, then, may experience feminism as something that threatens our closest relationships. We are expecting husbands and lovers to support choices and behaviors that many men perceive as threatening. If a man is demonstrably supportive of his partner's feminism, he risks alienation from the masculine world. In this sense, heterosexual women can feel that we are implicitly requesting from our partners, not merely support, but an actual shift in loyalties.

There may also be tension in relationships with other feminist women. Even the anticipation of a feminist gathering is fraught with the unspoken possibility of divisions and barriers versus mutual affirmation. Will there be tension between women of different sexual choices or will there be mutual acceptance and an ability to transcend boundaries? Sexuality has the potential here, as elsewhere, to be used as a wall, creating an emphasis on group divisions rather than on individual diversity.

The experience of being different from a group of people with whom one shares ideals is in itself of value. Being a heterosexual woman in a movement that includes many lesbians gives one the opportunity and the push to try to confront and understand the perspectives of women who are different from oneself. Talking about differences in the abstract is one thing, but acknowledging or confronting those differences in the context of actual relationships raises more substantial possibilities for dialogue. Forming personal relationships with women who have different experiences invites us to think about differences in more than intellectual terms. These relationships can nurture a personal investment in understanding differences instead of a theoretical or ideological obligation to attempt do so.

Feminist gatherings can be, for heterosexual women, crucial times to escape the feeling of separateness, to be open with other women, to claim some listening space. This space is compacted in time, and the focus is on experiencing, even luxuriating in, that which we do not and cannot obtain elsewhere. For heterosexual women, feminist activities are places to be free of an often unrelenting cultural emphasis on female–male sexuality. With relief, we focus on feminism, work, friendship, not sexuality. When relationships here are inclusive of sexuality, it is not heterosexuality. On these occasions, there is for us as heterosexual women a sense of stepping back, of watching, rather than participating. We are richer for the opportunity to stand witness to the claiming of validation for something so personal and fundamental. The experiences of observing and participating are different, and both inform our lives in different ways. We may occasionally feel part of a marginal fringe as heterosexuals, just as elsewhere we may feel that way as feminists. Despite our sidestepping of our (hetero)sexuality on these occasions, it sometimes seems, paradoxically, that the tone of these gatherings, the sense that this is *our* time, is set by the lesbians who attend. This tone may be what gives these occasions their truly women-oriented focus and warmth.

Just as an emphasis on heterosexuality is not the focus of our feminist time, our sexuality is not our place of difference most salient to society. For heterosexual feminists what clashes with the mainstream is our feminism, not our sexual preference. We may believe that our sexuality is private, as we do not violate societal norms regarding object choice. However, depending upon the social circles in which we find ourselves, our sexuality may still be a source of confusion to those around us. Others may assume that, because we are feminists, we must be lesbians.

Heterosexual women may experience the mild marginalization of being different from those around us both in day-to-day life and in the feminist movement. We may feel ourselves a minority at some feminist gatherings, by virtue of our heterosexuality. We may find ourselves marginalized and even feared at other times by virtue of being feminists. This marginalization is not necessarily extreme. It may, however, imply great personal risk, take the form of threatening relationships (with heterosexual or feminist friends who do not fit into both of these categories) in which one has invested a great deal.

In the world outside feminist conferences, identifying oneself as a feminist is frequently marginalizing. Yet being a feminist has become respectable enough to get by with, particularly if the feminist woman in question stays within the bounds of tolerable feminine behavior. A heterosexual feminist can be considered 'safe' (although she may not *feel* safe), even though she is operating near the margins of a male-identified social world. She has more to lose than does her lesbian counterpart, who is already more completely marginalized, and so may take fewer risks in her behavior.

Here again, heterosexuality is associated with privacy. People may assume that a heterosexual woman thinks/feels/acts in certain ways considered appropriate for women. We may not conform to those assumptions, but we can hide behind them in ways that our lesbian counterparts cannot.

REFERENCES

Deaux, K. and Major, K. (1987) 'Putting Gender into Context: An Interactive Model of Gender-related Behavior', *Psychological Review* 94: 369–89.

Eagly, A. and Wood, W. (1991) 'Explaining Sex Differences in Social Behavior: A Meta-analytic perspective', *Personality and Social Psychology Bulletin* 17(3): 306–15.

Lamb, M., Tresch Owen, M. and Chase-Lansdale, L. (1979) 'The Father–Daughter Relationship: Past, Present and Future', in C. Kopp and M. Kirkpatrick (eds) *Becoming Female: Perspectives on Development*, pp. 89–112. New York: Plenum.

Spender, D. (1989) *The Writing or the Sex*. New York: Pergamon.

Zimmerman, D. and West, C. (1975) 'Sex Roles, Interruptions, and Silence in Conversation', in B. Thorne and N. Henley (eds) *Language and Sex: Difference and Dominance*, pp. 105–29. Rowley, MA: Newbury House.

Hilary LIPS, author of *Women, Men and Power* (Mayfield, 1991) is Director of, and Susan FREEDMAN is the Research Associate for, the Center for Gender Studies at Radford University, Radford, VA 24142, USA.

12. Love and the Politics of Heterosexuality

Caroline RAMAZANOGLU

Those of us who identify ourselves as both in some sense 'really' heterosexual and in some sense politically feminist, come up against a feminist consciousness which is both critical of our most intimate being and entails at least some resistance to close relationships with our nearest and dearest men.

Feminist heterosexuality in my experience is politically sensitive, personally painful and insufficiently studied. Both the sensitivity, and the extent to which heterosexuality has been taken for granted, mean that not nearly enough attention has been given within feminism to how women can have safe, pleasurable and unoppressive heterosexual relationships and sexual practices. We have not yet developed a critical but positive political heterosexuality which supports women. This has left individual feminists in a state of political isolation in tackling relationships with men.

Being asked to consider the political implications of heterosexuality focuses on contradictions and compromises which can be uncomfortable in the limelight. The unbalanced struggles and compromises that constitute my personal heterosexuality are painful and private. Whatever enlightenment and empowerment we can bring to our personal lives, our sexuality is still socially constituted in an unequal world, and no individual can successfully resolve the general problems of loving men and raising children within the patriarchal structures and cultures of the UK today. Since feminism has lacked positive collective strategies for sustaining satisfying relationships with men, there is no 'politically correct' feminist way of bringing the men out of our closets.

For many heterosexual women, sex is not particularly satisfying or pleasurable, but they may still value the social (and socially recognized) relationship with a man. Feminism has made little headway against the ways in which women learn to be feminine, and not nearly enough has been said about the fears of loneliness in industrial societies, the misery of failing to demonstrate womanhood by attracting a man, the fear of losing a man or the practical problems of constructing satisfying, close, balanced relationships. Political correctness is no comfort on a lonely Saturday night.

Heterosexuality, however, like any other relationship, does not have to be oppressive. Sex with men can be thoroughly pleasurable for women and feminism can promote rather than deny or limit this pleasure. The problem is how individual women can manage safe and unoppressive relationships within which pleasure is possible. Being a heterosexual feminist can require a relatively high level of knowledge, confidence and assertiveness. Since heterosexuality in the UK is socially constructed in men's interests for women to service men, it puts enormous social pressure on women to conform, but we are not passive victims of patriarchy. Our sexual orientation does not make us incapable of negotiating our sexuality with men if we have the support and confidence to do so, just as women can decide to be celibate or avoid any relationships with men.

Rather than seeing heterosexual and lesbian women as politically opposed, I see heterosexuality optimistically as an area of potential political action in working on men, but one in which women could do more to support each other practically and politically. Women who are in emotional and sexual relationships with men are at one of the battlefronts of sexual politics. As individuals they may have little power, be unable to change individual men or be unaware that their situation is anything other than natural. But with a critical feminist consciousness, belief in themselves, emotional stamina and the support of others, women can resist the particular ways in which heterosexuality has become institutionalized and empower themselves in practical ways to negotiate less oppressive relationships.

The struggle for unoppressive heterosexuality is complicated by women's relationships with each other, since social divisions such as class, race, ethnicity and ability privilege some women in relation to others, and give some men and women shared interests. Within feminism, critical debate is needed to ensure that struggles to transform heterosexual relationships do not lock some women into the pursuit of privilege within patriarchal structures. The problem of how to do this without attacking each other is always with us.

Feminism has an important role to play in educating and encouraging men to resist the construction of patriarchal relationships, and to negotiate other forms of heterosexuality. We do not need to see all men as personally oppressive, but what is urgently needed is a sense of how *difficult* it is for both men and women, day in day out, to counter social pressures in transforming heterosexuality. Mostly, I just feel tired. Men have much less reason to struggle and go on struggling than women. This can leave feminist heterosexuals fighting lonely battles in the kitchen, over childcare, in bed and about money. Separation from partners or divorce is one strategy, but while this may ease a personal situation, separation in a patriarchal society does not have any long-term transforming effect on heterosexual relationships. Unreconstructed men will hope to find new and usually younger partners who may be more accommodating in servicing their needs.

Everyone needs to love and be loved, but feminism cannot direct women into secure or happy relationships with reconstructed men. Such relationships require men to reflect critically on their masculinity, but very few men have really grasped the meaning of shared responsibilities (though we should acknowledge, and not be threatened by, those who have). Even when men do have such understanding, the greater social and economic value of their work outside the home can easily unbalance a hard won domestic equilibrium.

I cannot see how it is possible to raise sons as a heterosexual feminist without a working notion of contradiction, and without resisting guilt at continual failures to balance opposing pressures adequately. I decided some time ago that I could either succumb to terminal guilt, or do the best I could in the circumstances I had landed myself with. Support comes less from feminism, which I am largely failing, than from family and other mothers of sons who share my experiences.

Close relations with men can bring home the damage that heterosexuality can do to males, and the many ways in which men damage each other. There have been few practical strategies for how mothers can counteract the strength of social and peer pressures which value competition, aggression and potency, and leave men little space for fears, dependency, caring, womb envy or expressing emotional closeness. It is one thing to give your sons dolls to play with, it is another to let a seven-year-old boy take his baby doll to school when you know he will be jeered

at and assaulted by other children. Raising sons is an area which gives women potential power in transforming sexism, but the obstacles we are up against are strong and
intransigent. The balance between attacking oppressive masculinity and fighting
one's own children and their friends is an unstable one. One of my sons complained
bitterly that I had no idea what it was like trying to be anti-sexist and anti-racist in
the playground. More extensive and practical support is needed for ways of child-
rearing which pull against the weight of patriarchal culture and institutions.

Heterosexual women, like lesbian mothers, can make an impact on the complex
processes of sexual politics, which gives us some hope for the transformation of
patriarchal relationships. But while feminism gives women and daughters a basis for
political solidarity in empowering themselves, our partners and sons have no comparable political platform for their own disempowerment. Our strategies for change
must be clear and workable as this is a site of struggle in which we can all get hurt.
Feminists need all the optimism and tolerance we can manage if we are to enjoy relationships that neither subordinate heterosexual women nor oppress lesbians or those
who do not want close relationships with men.

Caroline RAMAZANOGLU lectures in sociology; has taught and
researched in Uganda and Turkey, and is currently a member of the
Women, Risk and AIDS project researching the sexual behaviour of young
people. ADDRESS: Department of Sociology, Goldsmiths' College,
University of London, New Cross, London SE14 6NW, UK.

13. Unbundling Our Binaries — Genders, Sexualities, Desires

Mary GERGEN

My (acculturated) experience of receiving the invitation to participate in this forum has been complicated.

My initial reactions were enthusiastic. I was pleased to be included in this project, and curious about its outcome — what my own synthesis and those of others will be.

I also became aware that no one had ever actually called me a heterosexual before. . . . Yet I don't deny it; I do not murmur, 'There must be some mistake.' No, I do affirm some basic self-identification tag. No vague memories of uncertainty plague me for this choice. (This is soon to become problematic.)

Then, my reaction shifted to a mingled puzzlement, resentment, a slight annoyance. Why address me so categorically as a heterosexual? Why was anyone so sure? Because I am married? Or because my husband seems 'straight'? Is it about my hairdo or my shoes or the things I have said, or not said? Or perhaps it is otherwise self-evident. A 'lesbian' once told me, 'If you count yourself gay you just know how to pick others out of a crowd.' Maybe it is that no one I've ever had a sexual liaison with or desire for is known to be gay by those who select?

Perhaps it is a political question. Do I not belong to some inner circle? Is there a conspiracy afoot? How did the heteros get picked out?

Why not, anyway, bisexual? Do they/we count in the pecking order?. . .

And then I felt fear — of pecking of another sort — of having the grain of writing flung before me, and then as I open my beak, whack . . . the axe falls. Death by self-proclamation. Or perhaps, to be less dramatic, I receive a few unpleasant pecks about the head and neck. All in the name of open, political exchange.

What is the underlying agenda here? We know the work of various editors. We are aware of Celia Kitzinger's writings, her public statements, and have some notions of her views on the oppressiveness of the heterosexual world. Is this a witch trial, or a trial by witches? Are we being rounded up for confessions in a public forum? For well-rounded feminist 'heterosexuals' this route may be open to us; confess our culpabilities; open our chapters of crime; commit ourselves to reform. The litany would be easy to recite. Yet, this path does not go very far. We all end up on opposite sides of the room. Only the judges and the prisoners have changed places. The oppressed become oppressors; the oppressors are oppressed.

But then, pondering, I catch a hint of hope. There is the slim possibility for something new to be gained by entering into this conversation. A way that springs beyond the dilemmas of binary oppositions: straight vs gay. This leap invites, makes me want to take a chance, to stick my neck out. To wing it.[1]

Let's try to talk together about identity, and gender, and desire.

A first question to pose within my part of the dialogue: Do we need to insist on being one, of being knowable, consistent, identifiable selves? Can we let go of our 'unity'? What if we were to slink into a multiplicity? or a temporary? or an oscillation among versions of identity? What could happen to our bifurcation then?

If we give up singular selves, then we call into question any consistent naming of any of the pieces that compose our selves. As Judith Butler argues, we might consider 'a thoroughgoing appropriation and redeployment of the categories of identity themselves, not merely to contest "sex," but to articulate the convergence of multiple sexual discourses at the site of "identity" in order to render that category . . . permanently problematic' (p. 128). Could we chance the giving up of any sort of self, thereby deconstructing the source of our distinction?

What about the part of our identities that is called woman? Does this word weight heavily upon us? Can we consider its constructed nature? Can we put a parenthesis around it? Is it possible for us to float away from that mooring? Where will we be carried? What anchors pull us back?

'Woman itself is a term in process, a becoming . . . Gender is the repeated stylization of the body, a set of repeated acts within a highly rigid regulatory frame that congeal over time to produce the appearance of substance' (Butler, 1990: 123). Woman is a name we might sometimes wish to use. Must it hold us in place? Not if we see it as a partial, incomplete filling in of ourselves. Or perhaps we wish to make a definition that can hold every word and deed. The whole of everything could become womanly.

And what about sexual orientation? Must we think in binary? What are the reasons to have such strong contrasts? To what extent do we invent and bring into being that which threatens us most? Is the function of heterosexuals to create the occasion for homosexuality to exist? Do homosexuals allow for heterosexuals as well? Each is required. This is a dangerous line of thinking.

> Lesbianism that defines itself in radical exclusion from heterosexuality deprives itself of the capacity to resignify the very heterosexual constructs by which it is partially and inevitably constituted. As a result, that lesbian strategy would consolidate compulsory heterosexuality in its oppressive forms (Butler, 1990: 128).

Do we want to keep ourselves tidied up in two bundles: straight and gay? How does 'gay' and 'straight' happen into being, but through the language of opposites? Can we imagine 're-signing' the two? Can we escape from the habit of making one the inverse of the other? Do the barriers hurt more than they help? There may be more than one answer. It may not be easy to tell. Answers may fluctuate and depend.

At the crux of our controversy is desire . . . or desires. That which we desire as sexual others, and the politics of these desires. Can we recode these signs, these sensibilities? Can we re-sign this itch from the binary codes now in contestation? Let us try by adding a bit of chaos theory in this realm.

Desire may depend on the very act of the unexpected that mingling categories can achieve. Desire's mystery may depend on violation, on unpredictability in special form. Perhaps, as Butler describes it, 'the object . . . of lesbian-femme desire is neither some decontextualized female body nor a . . . masculine identity, but the destabilization of both terms as they come into erotic interplay. Similarly, some heterosexual or bisexual women may well prefer that the relation of "figure" to "ground" work in the opposite direction — that is, they may prefer that their girls be boys' (p. 123).

Deconstructing gender, sexual orientation and desire imparts great possibilities for freedom, as well as 'trouble', in Butler's term. Playing at the edges of social conventions, withdrawing allegiance from the troublesome binaries of ordinary life, providing for multiple, partial and complex relationships can be revolutionary and satisfying practice. For psychology, putting this life form into play would create alliances from many quarters of feminism against those who live with the stuck assumptions that our social worlds are composed of a host of binary opposites, beginning with males and females. This alliance might erode the practice of drawing sexual/gendered antinomies without acknowledgment of the socially constructed nature of any distinction. Within new practices, the faceting of identity would be continually under question, destabilized as a matter of course. Notions of stable, internal, fixed qualities would be discouraged, in favor of temporary positioning. People would be formulated within the flux of sexual discourses.

In this world of my fantasy, more attention would be given to relational forms of activity, in which individuals would be seen as co-constructors of reality. Sexual relations would be one area of exploration, in which the terms of the relationships would be codependent on the actors, and the analysts. Further research activities would develop new forms of definition that would emphasize the partial, shifting and irrational flux of desire-actions, that would encompass many former, and antagonistic, names. A feminist psychology that could evolve into this form of research endeavor, one that could encompass the interests of 'gays' and 'straights' alike, could ultimately result in the decentering of current practices among more traditional groups who today take for granted that the everyday language is the everyday world.

NOTE

1. I would like to pay a special tribute to Judith Butler for her book, *Gender Trouble: Feminism and the Subversion of Identity* (1990), from which I borrow heavily in this text.

Mary GERGEN, an Associate Professor of Psychology and Women's Studies at Penn State University, is editor of *Feminist Thought and the Structure of Knowledge* (New York University Press, 1988) and is currently writing a book on the social construction of life stories. ADDRESS: Penn State University, 25 Yearsley Mill Road, Media, PA 19063, USA.

14. How My Heterosexuality Contributes to My Feminism and Vice Versa

Shulamit REINHARZ

Since I have neither read much nor thought much about this question, I assume it must be important and that some sort of silencing must be going on. That idea is essential to my notion of feminist research — pay attention to what you have not been paying attention to (see Reinharz, 1992). Another essential idea is that the process is part of the product and that consultation is part of the process. I began by asking a few feminist friends what they thought; then I posted a message on the women's studies e-mail bulletin. Some said they 'wouldn't touch it' because 'it brings you into a conflict with feminists who believe that only lesbians are feminists'. This response made it seem even more imperative that I try to write something, but also left me feeling wary.

The result of this consultation and reflection is a series of questions: to what extent is my heterosexuality a product of cultural messages that promote heterosexuality and to what extent is it something independent of those messages. If, as Adrienne Rich (1980) proposes, heterosexuality is compulsory, and I am heterosexual, then am I heterosexual only because it is compulsory? Would I be homosexual in a society where homosexuality was compulsory? Could a society exist in which homosexuality was compulsory? How about a society where homosexuality was 'as good as' heterosexuality? Where would I then fall on the 'lesbian continuum'? Actually, 'lesbian continuum' is losing its appeal to me as an idea because it suggests fixed positions. I prefer to think that we move around, perhaps on a continuum, in different stages of our lives.

Freud's idea about children being polymorphously perverse always appealed to me politically because of its inclusivity. But that idea did not challenge my heterosexuality the way 'compulsory heterosexuality' does. Adrienne Rich's (1980) concept of 'compulsory heterosexuality' emphasizes the idea that a repressive process takes hold of the polymorphous perverse child. She points out that heterosexuality has the 'power of a non-conscious ideology', to use a phrase of Sandra and Daryl Bem (1970). Adrienne Rich enables us to see the hegemony of heterosexualism. She reminds us that while Hitler's facism included genocidal homophobia, other more liberal societies are also homophobic[1] and thus dangerous. Heterosexuality may indeed be produced by the compulsory messages of cultural hegemony and what Herbert Marcuse called 'surplus repression'. How do lesbians and gays avoid 'surplus repression', how do people avoid cultural and social oppression? Is heterosexuality learned? Freud, Rich, Marcuse, the Bems and being a daughter of Holocaust survivors gave me a starting point for asking questions — they did not provide answers.

But then the puzzle arises: *Why am I both heterosexual and (apparently) lacking in homophobia*? If my heterosexuality is a product of learning unconsciously to hate lesbianism, then shouldn't I be homophobic? Why, instead, am I a heterosexual woman with lesbian friends? Why am I a member of a long-standing group most of whose members are not heterosexual? Why did I sponsor a course that undergraduates and graduates taught on gay and lesbian issues? Why do I try to educate my daughters in a way that will not make them feel compelled to be heterosexual but doesn't ridicule heterosexuality either?

I cannot answer most of the questions I ask myself. But I don't think being heterosexual means identifying with heterosexual culture. For example, I like the distinction Charlotte Perkins Gilman made in *Women and Economics* (1898) between heterosexuality and 'excessive sex differentiation'. Instead of being similar or complementary, men and women had differentiated themselves into the provider and the dependant. Gilman sarcastically called men 'the food supply of women'. Excessive heterosexuality is often the theme that drives a culture — supplying the energy for art, music, poetry, humor. I dissociate with that. I dissociate with the way heterosexuality overlaps with sexism and sexual oppression. It seems possible to me to envision a heterosexuality that does not originate in the male standpoint and that does not transform women into sexual objects. But female heterosexuals have not taken hold of their heterosexuality enough to make it a force in their own production of culture. I have no idea what that would look like. Women have been wonderful at expressing the pain, rage and shame they experience at the hands of men, but not the pleasure that is possible without succumbing to a male-identified view of themselves.

The only feminist literature about heterosexual pleasure I have located concerns women and eroticism and women being helped/protected/supported by husbands at crucial times. An example of the latter is Annette Kolodny's (1989) essay, 'I Dreamed Again that I Was Drowning', in which she recounts a recurring nightmare. In the dream she is drowning in a body of water close to the shore where a woman is walking who refuses to rescue her because it is inconvenient. Annette Kolodny wakes from her nightmare in her husband's arms and he comforts her. So too during the day, women abandoned her and her husband helped. This essay stands out in my memory because it is rare. Expressions of gratitude to husbands in the acknowledgments of many feminist books seem sincere. These are heterosexual women, helped by their husbands or male partners, so they can have time to write feminist books. Having a good husband seems to be many feminists' well-guarded secret.[2]

I assume the vast majority of the world's women live in heterosexual relationships and I think we feminists are abandoning them (as in Annette Kolodny's dream) if we do not study their (our) lives. We cannot dismiss heterosexual women as having 'false consciousness'. And yet it would be good for us also to empower women to understand their lesbian potential. It seems to me that most young and adolescent girls experience lesbian desire and then suppress it. In old age, women who have lived heterosexual adult lives and are widows could benefit from allowing themselves to live in lesbian relations (Reinharz, 1988). When I have talked about this with old women (I teach gerontology), they express very little interest.

Finally, I think being heterosexual makes it imperative to be vigilant against overlooking or silencing lesbians (Karon, forthcoming). The review of introductory psychology textbooks that found lesbians hardly mentioned at all, and pathologized when mentioned, is appalling to me (see Kitzinger, 1990). I once had a lesbian teaching assistant who would raise her hand in the middle of many lectures and say, 'What about lesbians?' I think she trained me well. But we who are heterosexuals must be more cognizant of omitting lesbians in our discourse — we should remember lesbians in discussions of sexual harassment, in children's literature, in advertising, in social texts — everywhere.

NOTES
1. The *New York Times* (22 January 1992:1) announced that the New York State Chapter of the Hibernian Society (Irish-Americans) had barred the Irish Lesbian and Gay Organization from marching in the annual St Patrick's Day Parade.
2. An exception is Letty Cottin Pogrebin (1991).

REFERENCES
Bem, Sandra and Bem, Daryl (1970) 'Case Study of a Nonconscious Ideology: Training the Woman to Know Her Place', in Daryl Bem (ed.) *Beliefs, Attitudes and Human Affairs*. Belmont, CA: Brooks/Cole.
Handa, Amita (1990) 'Heterosexuality and Contradiction: New Feminist Comments on Old Questions', *Resources for Feminist Research* 19: 5–6.
Karon, Sara (forthcoming) 'The Politics of Naming: Lesbian Erasure in a Feminist Context', in Shulamit Reinharz and Ellen Stone (eds) *Looking at Invisible Women: An Exercise in Feminist Pedagogy*. Washington, DC: University Press of America.
Kitzinger, Celia (1990) 'Heterosexism in Psychology', *The Psychologist* September: 391–2.
Kolodny, Annette (1989) 'I Dreamed Again that I Was Drowning', in Mary Lynn Broe and Angela Ingram (eds) *Women's Writing in Exile*, pp. 170–8. Chapel Hill, NC: University of North Carolina Press.
Phillips, Sara Rengel (1991) 'The Hegemony of Heterosexuality: A Study of Introductory Texts', *Teaching Sociology* 19: 454–463.
Pogrebin, Letty Cottin (1991) *Deborah, Golda, and Me*. New York: Crown.
Reinharz, Shulamit (1988) 'Feminism and Anti-ageism: Emergent Connections', in Regula Herzog, Karen Holden and Mildred Seltzer (eds) *Older Women: Research Issues and Data Sources*. Farmingdale, NY: Baywood Press.
Reinharz, Shulamit (1992) *Feminist Methods in Social Research*. New York: Oxford University Press. (With the assistance of Lynn Davidman.)
Rich, Adrienne (1980) 'Compulsory Heterosexuality and Lesbian Existence', *Signs: Journal of Women in Culture and Society* 5: 631–60.

Shulamit REINHARZ is the author of several books, including *Feminist Methods in Social Research* (Oxford University Press, 1992), directs the Women's Studies Program, and is based in the Department of Sociology, Brandeis University, PO Box 9110, Waltham, MA 02254–9110, USA.

15. Heterosexuality, Feminism, Contradiction: On Being Young, White, Heterosexual Feminists in the 1990s

Rosalind GILL and Rebecca WALKER

As friends, our many hours of conversations have always been fora for discussing the latest in women's struggles against sexism. In our conversations about topics as diverse as relationships with friends and lovers, the meaning of Madonna or our experience of sexual harassment, the subtext has always been — what does it mean to be a young (mid-20s), white, heterosexual feminist in the 1990s? Thus, when we actually had to sit down to discuss this in relation to an article about feminism and heterosexuality, the simplicity of the task was somewhat taken for granted. All that was needed was to put on paper the thoughts and ideas that formed the basis of our discussions.

Yet we discovered that thinking about heterosexuality and feminism was not quite so simple. It was precisely those taken-for-granted assumptions that caused us to really stop and question what it is about being heterosexual that offers a different dimension to feminism. In so doing we have found writing this to be an educative process in itself — forcing us to recognize the way in which 'heterosexual' is always a silent term (like 'man' or 'white') — assumed unless otherwise stated. We found it difficult to think about ourselves *as* straight feminists; it was much easier initially to think about ourselves *in relation to* lesbian women — except that this in turn opened up the whole uncomfortable issue of our power as heterosexual women. This is something which we touch upon in this article, but we also wanted to say something about our experience as heterosexual feminists more generally — to treat it as something worth discussing in its own right.

In beginning to address this, we have opened up a whole barrage of questions (many of which are not unique to heterosexual feminists) which we would, ideally, have loved to address: the desire to live outside the nuclear family, yet the constant pressures which push us towards reproducing some version of our parents' lives; our need to be taken seriously at work, yet our conviction that we do not want to imitate the competitive styles of male colleagues; our wish to be supportive to students and co-workers, yet not to be forever positioned only in a caring role; wanting to assert our feminist identities with our parents, without implying that the different choices which they (especially our mothers) made were worthless; our anxieties about becoming mothers, and our especial ambivalence about bringing up sons — to name but a few. The same themes recur — negotiation, compromise and, above all, contradiction. To be white, heterosexual feminists in the 1990s is to live inside contradictions — of which the contradiction between recognizing patriarchal oppression in all its subtle and pernicious forms and yet wanting to have profound friendships and sexual relationships with men is only the most obvious example.

What we want to deal with in the rest of this article is another — painful — contradiction which we constantly struggle with: the contradiction between what we think or know rationally and what we sometimes want or feel. We have no adequate language to theorize this. We know it sounds like we are talking about feelings as if they existed in some realm untouched by our feminist principles — and yet this is exactly how it feels. It is as if our deepest fears and desires remain solely constructed by patriarchal discourse: they are parts which feminism has failed to reach — yet. Because of this we spend our lives negotiating the contradiction — trying to find positions which feel comfortable, or, rather, less uncomfortable.

One such contradiction concerns the minefield that is the politics of appearance. For both of us *The Beauty Myth* by Naomi Wolf was an important book. Arguing that the policing of women's appearance constitutes a backlash against feminism and a new way of silencing women, it articulated a kind of oppression which we had both experienced from childhood. More than any book about economic inequality, unequal domestic labour or lack of political representation, this book spoke to an experience of oppression that attacks us in our most fragile, vulnerable and intimate area. As heterosexual feminists we want to be found attractive and desired by a man (or men), but we do not want to collude with the silencing and exploitation of women, and nor do we (as if it needed saying) want to be valued only in terms of our appearance. How are we to deal with this and to negotiate it in our relationships with men? One 'solution' which some anti-sexist men have adopted is to never mention their partner's appearance at all. But being feminists does not mean that we are immune from wanting to feel attractive, and needing to be told this by partners. To live with a man who believes that to say anything about our appearance would be sexist is to live feeling afraid and unconfident — and to hunger for someone to tell us that we are attractive to them. Paradoxically, it increases our anxieties about our appearance. It is not just that we fear that our partner will leave us for someone he finds more physically appealing, but that — however much we do not want it to — our very sense of identity is bound up with feeling attractive.

This contradiction between our anger at women's continued oppression by the beauty myth, and our desire to feel attractive is mirrored in so much of our lives. Feminism has given us a discourse to speak of our oppression, but it has not *displaced* the other discourses, it has not stopped us wanting (no, craving) things which we know are unsound.

We both want partnerships with men that are egalitarian, democratic and supportive. Yet we also have fantasies which owe far more to Mills and Boon than to feminism. In these deeply unsound fantasies men 'sweep us off our feet', wrap us in their 'strong, tanned arms' and, of course, adore us. Unlike many sexual fantasies these dreams are not limited to particular times nor are they fantasies which are not meant to be acted on. On the contrary, they accompany us through our daily lives as narratives, making us feel disappointed and cheated by the humdrum reality of our actual relationships with men. Unlike sexual fantasies, then, they do not *enhance* pleasure, but contribute to the destruction of our relationships with men — because these can never live up to our fantasies. We feel so hungry, so needy, we want so much *more*, but we live these desires through the discourse of patriarchal romances, not feminism. And the irony is that *we know it* — but that does not make the desires go away.

Against this backdrop it is perhaps not surprising that sexual relationships with men remain difficult and confusing. In common with those involved in HIV/AIDS and Safer Sex campaigns, we are constantly struggling to persuade partners to see sex as more than simply penetration. It is not just that penetration can feel like one more invasion, or simply that we find it less pleasurable than other forms of sexual contact, or only that it has always held particular dangers for women — and never more so than today. It is all of these things, but it is also that it feels such an impoverished view of sexual potential. What we come up against again and again in our sexual relationship is the need to *teach* men, always being the one who suggests something different, always being in the role of sexual educator. It is tiring, emotionally draining and often feels like work rather than pleasure. The fact that our culture has persuaded itself that it has had a sexual revolution makes this *more* difficult rather than easier — for women are now supposed to orgasm (multiply, of course) within moments of the man entering our vagina. Not to do so is to expose your unliberated self — you are not a real woman. The 'real woman' of the 1990s is the Madonna *and* the Whore, the superwoman of *She* and *Cosmo* — successful, attractive, intelligent, a supermum who is also sexually hungry for penetrative sex. She can 'have it all', but never dreams of having anything different. It seems to us that living in an age when we are told that sex can be openly discussed, paradoxically makes it even harder to point out the silences, the experiences that are not represented. In the thousands of books about sex, everything other than penetration remains treated as 'foreplay'. When with male sexual partners we raise the possibility of some other forms of sexual contact, we are made to feel that we have broken a taboo. The discourse says 'experiment, try different positions, anything goes', but try actually doing anything different and we know we've transgressed some unspoken rule.

And then there's the sexual encounter itself — so awkward and difficult. We know the rules of penetrative sex, but anything else . . . it becomes like giving bearings: 'up a bit, yes, that feels good, ow! can you touch me how you were before . . .'. We've both lain there feeling not pleasure but guilt that we're putting our 'nice' men through this, and anger that they have no idea what makes us feel good. We crave satisfying sexual experiences, but feel angry that such a transient pleasure is such an uphill struggle.

As young, heterosexual feminists we feel that we are on the frontline of the struggle to work out mutually satisfying and egalitarian sexual relationships. We wish we had better news!

We have spoken so far of negotiation, compromise and contradiction in our relationships with men, but this is also true of our relationships with women. The importance of women friends is paramount. To be able to express ideas, anxieties and fears in a supportive and understanding environment is a wonderful feeling which is difficult to match. We feel strongly that these relationships are as important as the 'partnerships' to which our culture accords status. Our own friendship and the writing of this article bears witness to how liberating it is to dare to say something which you know is deeply unsound and to have it understood, affirmed and even be told that it is shared. Would either of us have dared to write as individuals that we 'owned' such reactionary fantasies? No way — at least not without knowing that we were not alone. In this way friendships with women repeatedly bring alive the slogan that the personal is political.

But they are not without problems. Above all, we have each experienced many times the shattering of expectations, the feeling that we have been let down by other women. It is as if our idealized notion of the romantic hero is mirrored in our expectations of women friends. Why do they let us down? Why do they not find our friendship as important as we do? It would be too easy to say that this happens only when there is a man involved — we all know our culture's story of the woman who jettisons friends as soon as she meets a new lover. But this is not the whole story — women also let each other down in ways which have nothing to do with men. We feel that we are constantly battling against the low value which our society places on women's friendships.

Whilst men let us down too, what is different, we feel, about when women fail to live up to expectations of support and friendship is the difficulty we feel in expressing our anger towards them, as though a woman friend would not be able to cope with our anger, or as though we have 'no right' to be angry. For us, this difficulty in expressing anger to women is particularly acute in our relationships with lesbian women — tied up as it is with power. Both of us have had the experience of 'losing' our closest friend because she has 'fallen in love' with us and feels unable to remain friends knowing that her sexual feelings are not reciprocated. For both of us, in different situations, this has led to feelings of pain, loss and anger, but perhaps overwhelmingly, to feelings of guilt which have stopped us expressing our other emotions. There are several issues here: the difficulty of being angry with another woman, being 'eroticized' in unwelcome ways, the feeling of pain associated with the loss of an important relationship with a woman. Linking all these in the situation we describe are a whole set of issues concerning the accountability of heterosexual feminists to lesbians: we feel guilty about our heterosexuality which is not 'lived' as a political identity (although of course it *is* political) and we feel great discomfort about our position of power in relation to our lesbian friends (both the power to 'reject' and our more general power as heterosexual women in a heterosexist society). We are not saying that these experiences have made us somehow wary of forming friendships with lesbian women, we are merely trying to explicate some of the tangled webs of power which characterize such relationships.

We have each, at times, been accused of 'betraying women' for no other reason than our heterosexuality — of 'sleeping with the enemy'. To us, as straight feminists, struggling in our relationships, this is felt as an unjust attack. But again our response is not the anger that we feel at its injustice, but a kind of apologetic defensiveness. Because our heterosexuality is not *felt* as a political identity (who would want to mobilize around being straight?!), and because in many ways lesbianism appears to be the most appropriate political identity for feminists, we feel guilty. We even felt ambivalent about writing this — we did not want to be seen to be attacking our lesbian sisters, who already get attacked enough as it is. And yet not to respond is to collude with our own silencing. Isn't it? There must be a way of being able to speak our anger without it being taken as an attack on our sisters. We are still searching for it.

We have tried to be as honest as possible in this article. We have said things which are uncomfortable to admit, hoping that more 'right on' sisters will not judge us too harshly — and may even find echoes of their own feelings. We have also said things which, as we are all too aware, may be used against feminists or women generally. But we write out of the conviction that those who want to attack women will do so anyway, and that the importance of talking about our experience of heterosexuality transcends this. Overall, our own experience as young, white and privileged heterosexual feminists is one of continuous struggle and contradiction.

ACKNOWLEDGEMENT
We would like to thank Erica Burman for her helpful comments on an earlier version
of this piece.

Rosalind GILL is Lecturer in Communication Studies at Brunel University.
She is currently writing a book about gender, ideology and pop radio.
Rebecca WALKER is a Research Associate at the Health and Education
Research Unit at Goldsmiths' College. She has published in the area of the
doctor–patient relationship, and is currently working in the field of nursing
and HIV/AIDS. ADDRESS: Brunel University, Kingston Lane, Uxbridge,
Middx UB8 3PH, UK.

16. Retelling Myself

Janet SAYERS

Life stories have a notorious habit of changing in retrospect — as an effect of personal and political developments, not least those wrought by feminism. Little wonder, therefore, the uneven certainties of the following reconstruction of my own sexuality and feminism which I now attribute, perhaps paradoxically, to lack of men.

The facts seem to speak for themselves. My father left when I was 6, just as my grandfather quit my mother's childhood home. But was that because both men were victims, as one story has it, of being ousted by the family's matriarchs? How then explain my mother's and my own overweening awe of men? Was this, and our heterosexual desire — which, but for feminism and psychoanalysis, I took to be biologically given — triggered by men's absence? Was it their elusiveness that endowed men with such god-like status?

What is certain is that, long before many of my school friends, I became obsessed with securing a man — with what psychoanalyst Karen Horney, in similar circumstances, referred to as 'endless vagabonding'. Nor is there any question that my first lover was the double, at least in my eyes, of my father — the Aryan Adonis my barely adult Jewish mother had 15 years previously taken to be her spouse. Undoubtedly I also orgiastically enjoyed sex with one man after another, even though its pleasures might have been rooted in the illusion of thereby possessing a longed-for ideal — a figment of the imagination that always ran ahead of itself, so little could it ever be embodied in any one person.

No illusion, however, was its obverse: the all too real fact that sex, and its excesses, almost proved my undoing — at school, university and work. For this I unquestionably and unquestioningly blamed myself. Not that this did not coexist with fury at the sex to whom I felt so in thrall. How this became politicized is less certain. Undoubtedly sharing with other women experiences otherwise so readily attributed to the quirks of individual culpability and fate was crucial. So too was feminism's exposure of men's social dominance whereby I came to reconstrue the near disasters of my life as a result of paradoxically risking myself in sex with men in the hope of thereby gaining the affirmation their status seemingly conferred.

Certainly I continued to defer to men — and, in my work, to Freud. When, in the mid-1970s, psychology again turned its attention to psychological sex differences (as it also had in relation to an earlier women's rights movement) I translated feminist psychologist Sandra Bem's concept of androgyny into Freud's theory of infantile bisexuality. Not that I sought thereby to challenge heterosexuality. Quite the reverse. Rather I reiterated Freud's insistence on the erotic attraction of the penis. Indeed this formed the centrepiece of my first book, *Biological Politics*, and its critique of relativism, whereby women's social subordination has been attributed not so much to economic factors and their intersection with men's and women's biology, as to variations in the latter's social and psychological construction.

Nevertheless, my absolutism and seemingly settled heterosexuality were not to last. They were thrown into disarray by the increasing foregrounding of lesbianism within the women's movement. Undoubtedly this was a major factor causing me to rethink my life and sexuality. But the theory I used was still that of Freud. This time, however, in using his concept of bisexuality, I dwelt less on masculinity and femininity than on the indissoluble and conflict-ridden simultaneity of sexual wishes for both mother and father, of conjoint homosexual and heterosexual desire — a central theme in my book *Sexual Contradictions*, and in my introduction to Viola Klein's *The Feminine Character*.

But neither life history nor political movements stand still. Or else they are dead. No sooner had lesbianism become more visible than so too did its mother–daughter precursors and archetypes. Again I found myself retelling my own story, and with it that of psychoanalysis. No longer would the Freudian father–daughter saga do. It had to be supplemented, as I tried to do in *Mothering Psychoanalysis*, with the woman-to-woman life stories of his female colleagues and their patients. These included Helene Deutsch's challenge of Freud's attribution of lesbianism to rebellion against the father, in which she drew attention to the maternal components — both fraught and fulfilling — of homosexuality and heterosexuality alike. Then there was Anna Freud's close and lifelong partnership with Dorothy Burlingham; and Melanie Klein's observations on our attempts through sex to repair the damage done by hatred — in the first instance, hatred of the mother.

No sooner brought out of the closet, however, than the pluralities of sex and mothering have again suffered eclipse. The causes are unclear. Perhaps it reflects renewed ascendancy of patriarchy and heterosexuality. Certainly lesbianism and feminism are now less confident, more defensive. No longer does women's shared sex or sexual orientation seem so secure a basis for organizing politically. And this is given theoretical vent in the nihilistic deconstructionist dictum: woman does not exist, nor man neither. Whatever the reason, I again reconsider the past — once more through Freud — this time not, as long ago, in terms of the phallus, but in terms of its absence and the uncertainties and illusions to which it is heir. Maybe they will surface in another book called *Absent Men*. Perhaps not. What is certain is that my father, though alive, was not there. And that, as I have sought to explain, now seems to have been the beginning, though surely not the end, of my sexuality and work as a feminist psychologist.

Janet SAYERS is the author of several books on feminism and psychoanalysis, and is based at Keynes College, The University, Canterbury, Kent CT2 7NP, UK.

17. Radical Feminist Heterosexuality: The Personal and the Political

Robyn ROWLAND

I don't go about saying 'I am heterosexual' and do not feel I am particularly identified as heterosexual. In fact, in my political work against the new reproductive technologies in Australia, at least one journalist has believed for eight years that I am lesbian. In the women's liberation movement I think I have always been seen as a woman-identified, radical feminist, which is how I would name myself. It's important to note, too, that in Australia the delineations between heterosexual and lesbian feminists are not as fiercely contested as they have been in the USA and in the UK. There is a greater acceptance of feminist activists and their work, regardless of their personal sexuality.

I would not call myself heterosexual, but rather say that I am in a heterosexual relationship. This is because I feel women can and do exercise decisions about sexuality. Our radical feminist analysis, my friends' lives and my own desires have taught me that we can be wilful (in Sheila Jeffrey's [1990] term) in our sexual decisions. My current decision is to be heterosexual. I intend the relationship I am in to be permanent. This decision did not predate my feminism. I had had both positive and negative relationships with men; had experienced male violence and sexual violence; had been attracted to a number of women; and would have been reinforced by friends in a decision to begin a relationship with a woman rather than a man. I decided on the man I currently live with. This does not mean that I do not think I am as socialized as the next woman into heterosexuality. I know all of the pressures on us to conform. And it was not the risk of being lesbian which worried me, though sometimes I think the courage of lesbian women in patriarchy is too easily forgotten.

The wilful decision to be heterosexual did not have as much impact on my personal feminist politics as did the wilful decision to have a child. As a feminist mother, having a son brought me face to face with the kind of cruelties that are perpetrated on boys; it made me start to question how it was that traditional masculinity is generated. It raised those original questions again: Why do men hate women? How is patriarchy reinforced? In understanding these dilemmas, I came to believe that the men our sons are close to, whether they be born into heterosexual or lesbian relationships, are crucial in giving them appropriate role models; in creating an image of masculinity contrary to the destructive patriarchal conceptualization into which most men are conscripted.

I do recognize the reality of our analyses of the institution of heterosexuality as central to women's oppression. Through this institution women have been tied into a patriarchal family structure where they and their children are economically dependent and where domestic, sexual and emotional servicing are required in the contract between men and women called marriage. Sexual violence has also been used as part of the enforcement of women's submission and lower status, when the law, financial dependence and physical force are not enough to intimidate (Rowland, 1988; Rowland and Klein, 1990).

While critiquing heterosexuality, radical feminists have also given us concepts such as the 'lesbian continuum' (Rich, 1980) and 'Gyn/affection' (Raymond, 1986) which create an identity and place for women who may not be lesbian but who 'put women first' in 'some or all ways' — what I would call woman identified. To radical feminists such as myself living in heterosexual relationships, this has been crucially important.

Andrea Dworkin's damning *Intercourse* (1987), turns our stomachs with a gruesome exploration of masculine brutality. She argues that intercourse is often an expression of power by men over women and that it often expresses hostility or anger. Her analysis is solid and real and true. Dworkin also touches on other truths: the efforts to reform the context of intercourse and the act itself. Contextual reforms to what Raymond referred to as 'heteroreality', 'would then provide for the possibility that intercourse could be experienced in a world of social equality for the sexes' (Dworkin, 1987: 126). Feminist women working for social change also work for change at an individual level. Though patriarchal institutions are implicit in our intimate relationships, at that level there is sometimes more room for negotiation.

Sheila Jeffreys, in her thorough dissection of male-defined heterosexual desire, has located it within marriage. She sees heterosexuality as based upon difference, a difference that carries power differentials. Homosexual desire, however, is the eroticization of sameness, 'a sameness of power, equality and mutuality' (Jeffreys, 1990: 299–300).

How might a feminist heterosexual relationship differ from this patriarchal heterosexuality? It would include an equitable power distribution in terms of economic independence, where the woman does *not* engage in domestic, sexual and emotional servicing; a relationship in which sex or intercourse is not the primary way of relating, but merely a part of the relationship alongside other important dimensions, such as friendship and companionship. It is important to me that the man I live with has a similar politics. There are, of course, areas in which it is very difficult to have similar passion, particularly with respect to male violence. I think men carry with them a great deal of guilt and/or distaste about belonging to a social group whose main relationship to women is through rape. But men themselves have to work at coming to terms with that belonging and to distance themselves from such an experience of masculinity.

Love, as Carol Anne Douglas (1990) has pointed out, has been given a pretty bad press by feminists. This is understandable when love has always been defined for women as a self-abnegation, a self-sacrificing, self-disappearing act. Romantic love has been used to seduce women into domestic slavery. But this does not mean that love cannot be created and cannot exist. The love which involves a trust, reciprocity, knowing another and being known, a sustenance and vulnerability, a wisdom and friendship, is something that both heterosexual and lesbian women alike seek in their relationships. Heterosexual feminists do love their male partners. Male partners can also be friends. This is not to say that this friendship is the same as the friendship we have with women. The creation of that intimacy is different. Different does not necessarily mean better. Ironically, contrary to our feminist theory, often emotional relationships with a man are less demanding than they are with a woman. The intense intimacy involved in women-to-women relationships is not usually a part of a heterosexual partnership.

In reality no one relationship can supply all of a person's needs. To have such expectations is unfair and overdemanding and the loved one can never supply all of this emotional support, unless it be at risk of their own selfhood. One of the fears in lesbian relationships is the anxiety of merging; the anxiety of not knowing where you end and the other begins. For some I think this is reminiscent of relationships with mothers; for others it was not there but the closeness was desired. I think it is one of the reasons I remain heterosexual: the fear of merging is not part of a heterosexual relationship. Because of the obvious differences — physically and in our approach to the world — separateness is retained. For others too, it may be this space, this difference, this distance, this aloneness, this independence, which is part of the attraction to a man.

The power dimensions outlined by Jeffreys (1990) and Dworkin (1987) do not operate for me. I am not objectified in my relationship. I am not less powerful. Unlike many heterosexual couples, my partner and I live apart about 75 percent of our time in different cities and in different (but joint) households. I have my own job, my own bank accounts, my own friends and activities. I am not married. I earn an equivalent income. I run my own household. This makes, in my experience, a massive difference to the mutuality which can be gained with a man. We share a mutual commitment to each other and now to our son whose arrival has meant a renegotiation of our respective independence. I do not feel in any way trapped, frightened or abused. So the context of our heterosexual relationship for me as a feminist is different from the traditional relationships which many radical feminists critique.

If this is the context, then what about sexuality? This is one of the great taboos. Yet heterosexual feminists agree that one of the reasons for being with a man is that we like having sex with a man. Heterosexual sexuality is not always intercourse. And intercourse does take place which is *not* degrading. Penetration is *not* always rape. Having experienced penetration which was, I know the enormous difference between the feeling of fear, anxiety and disembodiment which comes with forced sex, and the feeling of intimacy, oneness and sensuality which comes with intercourse which is not. What is important in a sexual relationship is for each participant to feel integrity, self-respect and self-empowerment — and not at the cost of another. Hopefully feminists, and the men they decide to sleep with, bring these into a sexual relationship.

Dominance and submission are conceptualizations which male-defined heterosexuality has deified. Unfortunately, as Jeffreys points out, this sexuality can be practised between two women. What we have learned is that the violence and dominance involved in some sexual relationships spring basically from power and power difference, and not from the sex of the participants. I once felt that being with feminists anywhere in the world was being in a safe place. I no longer have that assurance.

If a woman has a partner who is independent, self-nurturing and not draining her through domestic servicing, I think we move away from Sheila Jeffreys' concept of eroticization of power difference and move towards the eroticization of the person. What I find erotic in my relationship is the particular male body that I am attracted to. But also the person himself: his goodness, his kindness, his gentleness, his strength, his values and his humour. He himself: a decent, non-oppressing man.

I think there are enormous difficulties for men in living with radical feminists: the learning curve must be heavy going. We set up a prototype of perfection. The rules are hard and the aloneness that these men feel must be as powerful as the companionship they experience with their feminist partners who set limits on how much emotional support they will give. Unwilling because of their political beliefs to demand the excessive nurture women partners are supposed to give, they often don't have, as we do, friends who will feed their need for intimacy. They need to like and respect themselves while acknowledging that men as a social group oppress women. Yet it is important for these men (as it is for women) not to feel disempowered personally.

The contradictions of living in a heterosexual relationship are less profound to me now than they were a few years ago. Now I am more concerned to use theory and analysis to help us to move always closer to an egalitarian relationship. I believe in the feminism we have articulated — that change is possible and has to be worked for. By living with a man in some senses I do support and perpetuate heterosexuality, but I hope it is a feminist-defined heterosexuality.

I am not saying that living with a man is not problematic. And I am not saying that my relationship has reached a feminist ideal. All relationships need constant work. But every woman has to live a life where she is and according to her own sense of political and personal belief. Sometimes our own critiques overpower us. Monolithic institutions like motherhood and heterosexuality are revealed as insidious, pervasive and obdurate. Often we solve the problem of their nature by absenting ourselves; if your relationship with a man is difficult, leave or find a woman; if motherhood is hard and ambiguous, don't do it. But many of us do not want to solve these problems by withdrawing. Dworkin encapsulates this struggling resistance well when she writes:

> Women have also wanted intercourse to work in this sense: women have wanted intercourse to be, for women, an experience of equality and passion, sensuality and intimacy. Women have a vision of love that includes men as human too: and women want the human in men including in the act of intercourse. . . . These visions of a humane sensuality based in equality are in the aspirations of women . . . they are deep humane dreams that repudiate the rapist as the final arbiter of reality. They are an underground resistance to both inferiority and brutality, visions that sustain life and further endurance (Dworkin, 1987: 128–9).

I live in a heterosexual relationship as a single person in partnership with what I have learned from feminism. This is not a defence, then, of male-dominated, male-defined heterosexuality. It is rather an exploration of one woman's attempt to live a feminist-defined relationship with a man. I do not call myself a heterosexual feminist. I call myself a woman-identified radical feminist whose partner is male.

NOTE
This personal experience is of course influenced by the opportunities available to me as a middle-class woman from a white Anglo-Irish Australian background.

REFERENCES

Douglas, Carol Anne (1990) *Love and Politics, Radical Feminist and Lesbian Theories*. San Francisco, CA: ism Press.

Dworkin, Andrea (1987) *Intercourse*. New York: The Free Press/Macmillan.

Jeffreys, Sheila (1990) *Anti-climax, A Feminist Perspective on the Sexual Revolution*. London: The Women's Press.

Raymond, Janice G. (1986) *A Passion for Friends, Toward a Philosophy of Female Affection*. Boston, MA: Beacon Press.

Rich, Adrienne (1980) 'Compulsory Heterosexuality and Lesbian Existence', *Signs, Journal of Women in Culture and Society* 5 (4): 631–60.

Rowland, Robyn (1988) *Woman Herself, a Transdisciplinary Perspective on Women's Identity*. Melbourne and New York: Oxford University Press.

Rowland, Robyn and Klein, Renate D. (1990) 'Radical Feminism: Critique and Construct', in Sneja Gunew (ed.) *Feminist Knowledge, Critique and Construct*. London: Routledge.

Robyn ROWLAND has established women's studies programmes at several universities in Australia and New Zealand. She has written extensively on feminist theory and on reproductive technologies, her most recent publication being *Living Laboratories: Women and Reproductive Technology* (Lime Tree, 1992). She is currently Associate Professor in women's studies at Deakin University, Geelong, Victoria 3217, Australia.

18. Heterosexuality: Beginnings and Connections

Victoria ROBINSON

It is only in the last two years that I have 'come out' as a heterosexual woman in my Women's Studies course (and more recently in other classes). The act, I feel, marked a transition from a theoretical recognition of the validity of the assumption that our sexuality is socially constructed, and not a biological given, to a personal and political acceptance of that acknowledgement. The fact that this was in the context of my work as a Women's Studies teacher was very relevant. This was because it was in the feminist classroom, with its emphasis on disclosure and personal experiences, that I felt able to do this, and recognized the necessity. Also, this was a conscious public utterance of my heterosexuality, as opposed to the private knowledge of that identity.

It could be argued that it is tactical not to reveal one's heterosexuality in an attempt to use uncertainty and ambiguity around sexuality to challenge students' expectations of how lesbians/heterosexuals act and look. This deliberate decision to conceal identity could be useful in specific situations such as an individual lecture or seminar; with my Women's Studies students, though, I would be engaged in a tutor–student relationship for at least 2 years. As these classes are charged with vulnerability, passionate emotions and sometimes personal revelations, I feel it is important for an honest dialogue to occur (say, when a lesbian student comes out in class), that I should respond with a similar level of openness, whilst recognizing power imbalances between us.

When heterosexuality was discussed in private, for me it was usually with friends, both lesbian and heterosexual, and with male partners. *How* I discussed it, though, was often different. With heterosexual friends and partners it tended to be implicit in conversation. I might discuss relationships, sexual desires and practices, as well as emotions, for example, but not always in an explicit context of problematizing heterosexuality. This more often happened with lesbian friends. One reason for these different discussions is that heterosexual women have different stakes in relationship to heterosexuality both as experience and as institution. Another aspect is that when I discussed heterosexuality it was in the context of sexual relationships — sometimes in terms of how they conflicted with or contradicted my feminism, but not in terms of how my heterosexuality was connected to my work situation or public roles, for instance.

The reasons for this are diverse, but certainly one of them is the lack of a coherent body of theory from heterosexuals, on heterosexuality either as experience or as institution, or indeed as political practice. One argument for this from heterosexual feminists has been that the powerful statement from some revolutionary feminists in the 1970s — to fuck men was to fuck the enemy — had created a correct political stance equating feminism with lesbianism. The conclusion from this was that heterosexuality was perceived as ideological suicide in terms of what a real feminist should be doing under the sheets. But given that we are in the 1990s, this view cannot adequately explain the silence (mainly) from heterosexual women on their sexuality, especially as many feminists from a diversity of positions have seen such a notion as simplistic, not taking into account women's economic need, or their choice to be in heterosexual relationships. Athena Tsoulis (1987) asserted:

> The women's movement has failed heterosexual feminists because it hasn't adequately explored alternatives for women. It has become a 'no no' to talk about heterosexual relationships. I mean you can't talk about problems in heterosexual relationships, the only things we can talk about are the disaster areas, violence and abortion. But the nitty gritty of working on relationships with men to try and forge a new sort of relationship has not been really acceptable.

There have been times when I felt that to talk about my heterosexuality in terms of the problems or pleasures has been seen as a luxury by lesbians or those not in relationships with men, at a time when women are faced with male power and violence. It has been difficult, for instance, to discuss publicly particular aspects of sexuality, like vaginal intercourse. This has tended to be discussed in symbolic terms — as a metaphor for men's colonization of women in economic, social or political terms — or, for example, in the very real context of rape and child abuse. It has also been an issue in the women's movement in the debates around lesbian sexuality and penetration, for example. But to acknowledge the diverse experience of women in relation to vaginal intercourse does not invalidate some women's enjoyment of it, sometimes. This acknowledgement, though, does not necessitate a rejection of the fact that other women do *not* enjoy it (as Shere Hite's research in the 1970s and since has revealed), nor does it mean that we don't need to re-evaluate the centrality of male pleasure in relation to this particular sex act, and the importance given to penetration at the expense of other forms of sexual/erotic expression.

Tsoulis (1987) also accepts that:

> There has been a reluctance on our part to discuss our relationships with men. Some of the responsibility for this situation must lie with heterosexual feminists and the initial reactions to lesbian demands to be made visible within the women's movement.

So, assertions by some heterosexual women that their heterosexuality is not seen as a political act or choice means the ensuing silence is partly a self-imposed one. The silence has meant that heterosexuality has remained largely uncharted and unexplored.

Part of this silence, too, comes from the fact that lesbians and gay men, because of their position in heterosexist societies, have had to theorize homosexuality and heterosexuality, whilst the heterosexual silence in both a public and theoretical sense has effectively positioned homosexuality as 'other' to heterosexuality — and has meant, by definition, not having to justify itself by discussion and debate. The argument put forward by Black women (e.g. (charles), 1992) for white feminists' need to deconstruct and problematize the category of 'whiteness' serves as a useful analogy for the necessity of critiquing heterosexuality as experience and institution.

The lack of theories on heterosexuality has meant that heterosexuality remains a monolithic term instead of one which reveals the diversity of women's experience in relation to it. The sense of contradiction between, for example, the oppressive aspects of heterosexuality, and issues of choice and pleasure has not been fully articulated. How, for example, can we talk about male violence *and* acknowledge the potential pleasure involved in heterosexual relations (sexual or otherwise) for some women — and indeed the connections? Part of the lack of theorizing heterosexuality stems from the failure to distinguish between ongoing struggles with individual men and the oppressive nature of heterosexism, so that any criticism of heterosexuality is perceived as a direct criticism of the relationships of, and engagement with, heterosexuality. This confusion means that any attempts to change heterosexual relations, for example by arguing for non-monogamous relationships, are sometimes viewed by heterosexual feminists as not being seen as constituting political action; or that heterosexuality is not seen as dynamic and open to change; or that this cannot be interpreted as feminism in practice — because of the failure to separate out the institution of heterosexuality, as opposed to the experience.

There has been some acknowledgement that it is important to look at heterosexuality in a wider context than (sexual) relationships, but we also need to see how heterosexuality interacts with 'race', class and age, for example. For instance, the workplace affords a realization of how such categories cut across and inform each other in specific contexts. I am a tutor employed on part-time contracts with no access to university resources, and lack of power in a personal and structural sense for myself and for the courses for which I am responsible — how does this relate to and compare with the institutional power of a lesbian and/or Black woman, who, in a full-time tenured position, may have more institutional power than myself, but who will face heterosexism and racism at work? Or in a teaching situation, how does my power in the dynamics of the classroom interact with a student who may be a lesbian and/or Black? Such a discussion of heterosexuality and other categories must be one which sees the power of heterosexuals in a personal and structural sense, but avoids creating those hierarchies of oppression which were so counterproductive to genuine and diverse discourse in the 1980s. What we need to do now is to discuss heterosexuality in terms of power and connections in a public way, without being either apologetic or defensive.

REFERENCES
(charles), Helen (1992) 'Whiteness — the Relevance of Politically Colouring the "Non"', in H. Hinds, A. Phoenix and J. Stacey (eds) *Working Out: New Directions for Women's Studies*. London: The Falmer Press.
Tsoulis, Athena (1987) *Spare Rib* no. 179 (June).

Victoria ROBINSON is a lecturer in women's studies in the Division of Adult Continuing Education at the University of Sheffield, UK, and is co-editor, with Diane Richardson, of *Introducing Women's Studies: Feminist Theory and Practice* (Macmillan, 1993).

19. The Heterosexual Feminist: A Paradoxical Identity?

Alison M. THOMAS

Writing this piece has been a fascinating (and at times puzzling) experience. Asked to explain myself, my psychology and my politics as a heterosexual feminist, I have had to reconstruct why I accept either or both of those labels, and in the process have realized that although in principle one might consider them mutually incompatible, for me they are, in fact, fundamentally (if paradoxically) interrelated. For, contrary to the logic which maintains that feminists should not in any way collude with those who oppress them (a logic which intellectually I can accept), I believe that I am actually a feminist *because* I am heterosexual.

For me, the two are linked both historically — in terms of how I first came to identify myself as a feminist — and in the present, in terms of why (as a happily married woman with two children) I remain committed to feminism. As I see it, my feminism arose initially out of my difficulties in understanding myself as a woman in relation to men and male-dominated society; today, as a feminist social scientist, my concern goes beyond those personal uncertainties to the wider socio-psychological issues underlying them, and the generally problematic nature of relations between men and women in contemporary society. These are, nevertheless, concerns which still very much reflect my own experience, as a heterosexual woman, of the routine frustrations and perplexities of everyday life.

I attempt here to separate out, firstly, why and how I came to be heterosexual and, secondly, how this relates to my seeing myself as a feminist.

Explaining why I am heterosexual is not an easy task: we are generally prompted to become aware of ourselves only when we realize that we are in some way different from the norm, and are required to account for that difference. Living in a predominantly heterosexual society means that one's sexuality is generally assumed to be 'straight' (by oneself as well as others) unless proven otherwise, and few of us therefore ever stop to question why we are heterosexual. For me, then, this is a story which is ill rehearsed: as far as becoming heterosexual is concerned, I can honestly say that it never occurred to me to be anything else, even if that does proclaim me the dupe of the heteropatriarchy and politically incorrect!

By contrast (and for the reasons already stated), I find it much easier to explain why I am a feminist. This story consists of a personal history and an intellectual (and ultimately political) reinterpretation of that autobiographical material. The personal history goes back as far as childhood, and early recollections of non-conformity to the norms laid down for my gender. I do not suppose that I could have had any conscious awareness at that stage that the female role was deemed inferior to that of the male in our society, but I certainly had no particular desire to identify with it myself (indeed, in common with many young girls, I went through a period in which my chief delight lay in being mistaken for a boy).

This alienation from my own gender was further compounded in adolescence by a realization that, in my eyes at least, I failed to match up to the expected standards of femininity: I was too tall, too plain and a 'late developer'. The physical evidence appeared to me to support my inner conviction that I was not a 'proper' woman, and by contrast with most of my peer group (eagerly embracing both boys and womanhood together), I continued to maintain a sense of self focused on being a 'person', an individual, rather than identifying with my gender.

It seems altogether too much of a cliché to state that it was, several years later, my first 'proper' sexual experience with a man (as opposed to hesitant fumblings with adolescent boys of my own age) which made me finally identify myself as a woman — yet that is basically how it seemed to happen. I experienced a highly charged, though necessarily brief, affair while working abroad in the summer before I went to university, with an older, married man: the whole episode seemed quite unreal to me — more like fiction or fantasy – as well as thoroughly confusing. I was totally intoxicated with the awesome realization that this grown man actually desired me, and it was this, I suppose — the slowly dawning awareness of what I represented to him — which allowed me to believe in myself as a woman for the first time. A large part of the intoxication I experienced stemmed from the power dynamics involved in this relationship: in just about every respect this man was more powerful than I was, and yet emotionally and sexually he appeared in thrall to me.

So, not only did this quintessential heterosexual seduction confirm my sense of womanhood, but at the same time it led to my first ponderings on what it meant to be a woman in relation to men, and the complex interplay of male and female desire. Indeed, it was the generally perplexing nature of this whole experience which led me to read my first book by a feminist — Simone de Beauvoir's *The Second Sex* — just weeks before I went up to university. I suppose it was this which whetted my appetite for feminism, for, 2 years later, I decided to take a women's studies option in my final year, and there began to make the intellectual connections between the 'personal' and the 'political', as my own experiences were fitted into a wider framework and began to make more sense to me.

Perhaps it seems strange that my original route into feminism thus owed more initially to my feelings of alienation from my gender (and to a rather confused questioning of the roles attributed to me as a woman) than to any clear identification with others of my sex. While I now identify with other women far more than in the past (when I was motivated simply to assert my own equality as an individual vis-a-vis men), it is still the case that I am a feminist primarily because at a personal level I cannot accept the roles allotted to me as a woman — though I now identify this as an aspect of the oppressiveness of women's position in society, not just as a problem peculiar to me.

In recent years my general discomfort with the female role has, in fact, increased since I became (in society's eyes) that prototypical woman, the all-purpose 'wife and mother'. It is in these twin roles that I have been most keenly aware of the disjunction between my own sense of myself and what society expects of me as a woman. If a woman pays the price for choosing lesbianism by being labelled 'deviant', then her heterosexual sister pays for her 'normality' by jeopardizing her autonomy and her right to a separate identity: I am fed up with having to explain why I do not wish to be identified as 'Mrs X', and with assumptions that, as a married woman, I am no longer capable of doing any physically or mentally demanding task without my husband's assistance.

I am of course aware that my lesbian friends can (and do!) simply remind me that these are all instances of the oppression to which I implicitly consented in choosing a heterosexual relationship, and that I should expect little sympathy for 'colluding with the enemy'. Although that is an argument whose basic logic I respect, its logical corollary — lesbian separatism — could never be an option for me. Since I neither believe in original sin nor inborn 'masculinity', I could not bring myself to reject the men about whom I care — husband, son, father, brother — simply on account of their gender. Those beliefs also commit me to the view that males are not genetically programmed to oppress women but, rather, that they learn to become members of a gender class which does so collectively. As far as I can see, my 2-year-old son is at present no more 'masculine' than his twin sister, and I am therefore determined to preserve him (as well as her) for as long as possible from the pernicious influences of our male-dominated, sexist society. It is thus my refusal, as a mother, to accept that he should become 'one of them' that once again strengthens my commitment to the feminist struggle.

This 'personal' commitment is of course also a 'political' one, for — as a self-confessed 'liberal' feminist — I firmly believe that educating the next generation is still the most productive way to achieve long-term change. In order to make progress *for* women, and to achieve a more egalitarian society in general, I therefore believe that we have to work *with* men — however unfashionably idealistic and hopelessly naive that may appear to some.

To conclude, then, it seems to me that, as feminists, we can choose various ways of tackling our oppression as women: in writing this, what I have attempted to do is to explain my own chosen strategy, which for me provides the necessary rationalization for an otherwise paradoxical identity as a heterosexual feminist.

Alison THOMAS is a lecturer in psychology in the Department of Sociology, University of East London, Longbridge Road, Dagenham, Essex RM8 2AS, UK.

20. Against Separatism

Elizabeth MAPSTONE

'How dare you assume I am hetero?' It is part of my own feminist politics to refuse to allow people to assume without question that I am hetero, which makes an interesting problem when asked to go public on that very topic. This appears to be the obverse of the radical lesbian choice to reject heterosexuality as a political act.

I am firmly against any political separatism which emphasizes differences between people. In spite of the popularity of feminist theories which claim that women have a 'different voice', there seems to me little evidence for this, and such theories merely serve to maintain the cultural status quo. And though political lesbianism does mount a convincing argument that women who choose to work within the patriarchal system have achieved too little, with temporary advances constantly eroded and undermined, realistically its long-term prospects for effective power are poor. I share the view of activist female politicians like Barbara Jordan, the black Texan congresswoman, who said recently: 'Separatism is not allowed. We should not permit ideas like political correctness to become some fad that could reverse our achievements. . . . We seek to unite people, not divide them' (Jordan, 1992).

The letter of invitation suggested that heterosexuality is the 'taken-for-granted identity for women', which is precisely the problem for me. My immediate response is that my sexual choices are nobody's business. I never use my married name, always used Ms until permitted the sexless Dr, at least in part to avoid such assumptions. Because any account of my own sexuality is likely to reinforce assumptions about me as a woman, I fear that interest in the sexual lives of feminist psychologists in general, even for political rather than prurient motives, risks returning us to the ignominy of sexual objects.

I found great difficulty in writing this paper, an enormous resistance in myself to the suggestion that my sexuality is anything but irrelevant to being a feminist. In the end I concluded it must be a matter of my age, my experience as a woman before modern feminism. For more than 25 years now, I have been fighting *against* the sexuality which so many people — men, the media, and now feminist psychologists — seem to think is a central factor in all human relations. I do not look on the men I meet as potential sex partners, and do not wish them to regard me that way either. That I am largely successful in this now is no doubt because I am 55 and a grandmother; these days there are lots of younger, more attractive women around.

By the time I went to Oxford as a very mature student 11 years ago, I had experienced almost every form of sexual harassment I have heard of (with the exception of violent rape), although of course it did not have a label then. On one occasion, I did go to the personnel manager of the large company for which I worked (this was in 1969): my immediate boss had taken my refusal to have sex with him badly, said 'You'll be sorry'. I was told that yes, it was deplorable, but it would be better if I found another job. I resolved then that no man would look on me as a sexual object ever again. Sexuality was a nuisance, at work it was a disaster. From then on, I would cultivate only those qualities which men and women had in common. Academic training reinforced this.

So I am now asked to explain how heterosexuality contributes to my work as a feminist psychologist, when I have tried to exclude it from my working life; and how it contributes to my feminist politics.

The political question is easier to answer, as implicit in the above. I rejected being seen as a sexual object, not heterosexuality as such. This conscious decision did carry with it the implication that sex without some kind of special relationship with the other was not acceptable. I suspect this may be a generational thing. Nevertheless, it does mean that I make a clear distinction between a man as an individual human being, whom I can love, and men as a social group against whom I must struggle.

Though real world power lies in the hands of men, and they continue reluctant to let go of even a tiny fraction, individuals are not responsible for the social structures from which we suffer. They are certainly to blame, of course, when they persist in repairing the chains that our sisters arduously try to break. But we must recognize that there are men who reject their traditional role, and who wish to live with a woman, and to have women friends, as equals rather than exploiter and victim.

The Bem Sex Role Inventory (Bem, 1974) illustrates to me the difficulties of prescribing how feminists should conduct their lives, public and private. I had always assumed that I would come out androgynous on the scale: theoretically I embrace both feminine and masculine values, androgyny seemed a good theoretical way forward. But when very recently I applied it to myself, I scored too low on 'feminine' measures: I suppose it might be better to be soft-spoken and not to use harsh language, but who in their right minds would want to be gullible, childlike, flatterable and yielding? And the 'masculine' measures include exactly those qualities I value most highly: self-reliant, independent, analytical, decisive, self-sufficient, defends beliefs, willing to take a stand. As Geis (1983) pointed out, these are not male or female attributes, they are attributes stereotypically assigned to high- and low-status groups. I was pleased to see that in a recent interview (Kitzinger, 1992), Sandra Bem no longer thinks of androgyny as a measure of psychological health. Her analysis of the three 'lenses of gender' as sources of 'the social reproduction of male power' (see Bem, this volume) appears much closer to my own interpretation of the relations between women and men, and I look forward to her new book with interest. She, too, wishes to do without the concepts of homosexuality and heterosexuality.

It should be clear that I most strenuously work against separatism and all notions of 'a different voice'. It is precisely that division of labour, whereby women are responsible for affiliative values and men claim rational search for the truth as their own, that is a source of the strongest barriers against equality in the workplace. Social historian John T. Williams (1991) has shown that men have traditionally expected some other group (usually women, sometimes clergymen) to take care of emotional and spiritual values for them. In my analysis, to emphasize the special qualities of being 'woman' because women have so widely, perhaps universally in our culture, internalized the ideology of affiliation, is to collude with men in perpetuating inequalities. To claim that traditional scientific methods of research 'do not suit women' is to reinforce men's claim that they alone are rational, while we women are irrational, emotional and incapable of logical thought (Seidler, 1989). It is to confine us once more to the doll's house, the gilded cage, the ghetto of women's work. We need to repudiate that division, encourage those men who would like to take on feeling values too (taking a crying baby for a car ride is not enough), but above all, we need to make sure we are heard, by men as well as women.

The implication is that, for a psychologist, it is imperative not to throw out those 'objective empirical research tools' that are most likely to have an impact on our male colleagues. As Rhoda Unger says:

> Feminist psychologists are caught in a double-bind. . . . If [positivist empiricist] tools may not be used by feminist psychologists there is little likelihood that their insights will be taken seriously by the rest of the discipline (in Kitzinger, 1989).

As a psychologist I am interested in the social construction of gender, and agree with Wendy Hollway (1989, 1991) that we should look at how men as well as women are constructed. I have found in my own research into the social construction of argument (Mapstone, 1992) that both women and men in the general population are aware of gender-role expectations, especially that men be logical and rational and women be supportive and nurturing. Under the division of labour assumption, the man who disagrees is exercising his rational faculties, while the woman who disagrees is failing in her primary function as carer and nurturer, is unfeeling, inconsiderate. In a word, she is 'disagreeable'.

Men's accounts of arguments with women show a variety of strategies which vary depending on relationships, but which all appear to have as their purpose warding off women's challenge to men to treat them as their intellectual equals. High levels of anger are reported with women in a formal relationship, and overt use of power where possible, while arguments at work with equal-status women are treated as unimportant. Women in all relationships are assumed to be irrational, unreasonable and emotional.

Women report expending a great deal of effort in trying to convince men that they are at least as capable of logical and rational argument as any man. Notwithstanding notions of 'a different voice', their accounts vary depending on relationships: while they do show conciliation with husbands and lovers, women demand the right to be heard and accepted as rational beings by non-intimate men, and in formal relationships, talk of being assertive, even intransigent. My research suggests that women in general are far more committed to feminist principles of equality than is widely supposed, and that they, like me, make a clear separation between private and public lives.

It may be objected that this is a form of separatism. My answer is that it does not separate *people*, it separates roles. I keep my sexuality private because it seems to me quite irrelevant to my roles as feminist, or psychologist, or writer or editor, that my closest friend right now is a man: tomorrow it could be a woman, or I might want to give up sex altogether. How can that be of interest to anyone else? My sexual choice in no way lessens my response to men's exercise of power, their prejudicial judgements, their cosy chauvinistic assumptions: indeed, having refused the role of sexual being in the public arena, I feel free to challenge men on their own terms. My own life and my research both convince me that we women owe ourselves a duty to *be* 'disagreeable'.

REFERENCES

Bem, S.L. (1974) 'The Measurement of Psychological Androgyny', *Journal of Consulting and Clinical Psychology* 42: 155–62.

Geis, F.L. (1983) 'Women, Sex-roles and Achievement: The Self-fulfilling Prophecy', paper presented at the annual meeting of the Eastern Psychological Association, Philadelphia, PA.

Hollway, W. (1989) *Subjectivity and Method in Psychology: Gender, Meaning and Science*. London: Sage.

Hollway, W. (1991) 'The Psychologization of Feminism or the Feminization of Psychology?', *Feminism & Psychology* 1: 29–37.

Jordan, B. (1991) *The Guardian*, 15 July.

Kitzinger, C. (1989) 'Deconstructing Sex Differences: Rhoda Unger's Social Constructionism', *Psychology of Women Section Newsletter* 4: 9–17 (British Psychological Society).

Kitzinger, C. (1992) 'Sandra Lipsitz Bem: Feminist Psychologist', *The Psychologist: Bulletin of the British Psychological Society* 5: 222–3.

Mapstone, E.R. (1992) 'Rational Men and Disagreeable Women: The Social Construction of Argument', unpublished thesis, University of Oxford.

Seidler, V. (1989) *Rediscovering Masculinity: Reason, Language and Sexuality*. London: Routledge.

Williams, J.T. (1991) 'Bearers of Spiritual Values', *The Psychologist: Bulletin of the British Psychological Society* 4: 3–7.

Elizabeth MAPSTONE is Managing Editor of *The Psychologist: Bulletin of the British Psychological Society*, and is affiliated to St John's College, University of Oxford, UK.

21. Heterosexual Celibacy

Loulou BROWN

I was born during the Second World War and didn't know my father until I was three-and-a-half, when I tried to kill him. My brother, my only sibling, was born when I was four-and-a-half and he, too, I tried to murder. I was considered socially unacceptable and sent to a boarding school aged five. There was massive bullying on the part of the children, many of whose parents were badly fucked up as a result of the war. I was one of the bullied, forced to be part of the 'Wuzzy Faced Gang'. I was told I would be burned at the stake, was shut in a cupboard in complete darkness, and had to watch others shit standing up: 'doing ploppage', we called it. Aged six I had had enough and 'excaped', a feat I regard as my major childhood achievement.

I subsequently became a day girl — at the same school. (My parents were unaware of my intense unhappiness and were told by the Head that I had run away because of 'my great sense of adventure'.) I got to know the children in the village I lived in. Unfortunately, one of the older boys wanted to fuck me, aged 10, and very nearly raped me — which almost undoubtedly retarded my sexual development.

Once more a boarder at the age of 11, we girls in the dorm used to fantasize about some of our male teachers having 'SI' (sexual intercourse) with female teachers or some of the older girls. But 'SI' was remote and abstract. What seemed much more concrete and important was whether you had 'it' (sexual attractiveness/sexual charisma). 'It' was almost tangible: without it you not only lacked status but were not going to get married — the be-all and end-all of our lives in those long-ago days of the 1950s.

Most of my energies, after leaving school, were directed towards finding my imaginary prince. I never once considered becoming a lesbian, even though almost all my friends were women rather than men.

In the mid-1960s I got pregnant. I had been living with a man in a small flat with very civilized arrangements. He did the ironing while I cooked. I paid a third of the rent as I earned a lot less than he did. Neither of us did the washing. Then we married — and I was immediately expected to do the washing, cleaning, ironing, cooking, look after the children, give up my precious and wonderful job and not go out. It seemed as though the whole of my previous life had suddenly finished. I was suddenly, and almost at the same time, a wife and mother with no friends or future. This was happily ever after, so it was not surprising that I joined the Women's Liberation Movement in the early 1970s.

Shortly after I embraced feminism (the word was never mentioned in those early, heady days) I fell head over heels in love, and for 10 years was obsessed with a man I saw rarely, perhaps once a month, and usually only briefly at railway stations or in carparks. We communicated over the phone. Over the years I came to realize that almost all the talk we had was about him and his life and problems; my roles were those of listener and counsellor, and I was supposed to accept what was said without questioning its validity. Eventually I had had enough and stopped the connection.

I never want to go through the pain and futility of such an unreal relationship again.

The man I was, and am, married to knew about the relationship but it was not that that made him violent. In 1974 I went for a weekend away with women on a co-counselling course. On my return home I found my clothes had been thrown out of the window and messages scribbled on mirrors, walls and books. I was physically battered quite badly and saved from serious injury only by the phone ringing. The scars in my mind induced by the battering remain today. Since that time I have never been able to fuck with this man without an initial shudder. It was my going away with women which had angered him more than anything else. It would seem that men's greatest fear is for women to get together. Because when women act collectively they are strong. Sisterhood is powerful, but women alone can be battered more easily.

In 1981 I read the Leeds Revolutionary Feminists' pamphlet *Love Your Enemy?*, which was uncompromising in its belief that all women should give up fucking men. If you didn't fuck them you were allowed to join the ranks of right- (or rather left-) thinking feminists. There was no question of innate desire. A woman's sexual orientation was deemed to be political only. To be a lesbian was the only way to achieve political correctness. But changing one's sexual orientation is not as easy as giving up Cape apples from South Africa and the prescriptiveness was, to say the least, very worrying. Adrienne Rich (1974, 1980) believed that all women were really lesbians, because they were 'naturally' so as a result of their all-embracing relationship with their mothers. She put forward the idea of lesbianism being on a continuum, with celibate women at one end of the spectrum and active lesbians at the other. While I think that in many respects Adrienne Rich's ideas are profound, and feel glad that celibate women have at least been identified, I wonder about my desires, my orientation, why it is that while I find men disgusting I also desire them.

I don't know whether my sexual orientation is the result of 'natural' tendencies or environmental factors. But it is men's bodies, not women's, which excite me. And when I dream sexy dreams they are invariably and explicitly about men. If I consciously fantasize (very rare these days) I think of men, not women. And this is so even though I identify with the central message of *Intercourse* (Dworkin, 1987), that, in our patriarchal society, if a male sexually penetrates a woman's body this constitutes a fundamental violation, with a subtext of rape, branding, possession, contamination and even sadism.

I have been celibate for over 3 years now, though I still live with the man I married long ago. This is my choice. I have studiously avoided all (very few) male sexual advances — and also all overtures made by women. Several people have suggested that I'm frigid, but I'm not. I have strong desires and burn a lot in my dreams — very occasionally I wake up having an orgasm. My frequent and sometimes lengthy depressions are, I am sure, because of no sexual activity. But I prefer the lack of sex to having to engage with each and every aspect of heterosexuality.

I live a lonely life, but I prefer this to the nonsense of a heterosexual existence and I have no desire to be a lesbian.

REFERENCES

Dworkin, Andrea (1987) *Intercourse*. London: Secker and Warburg.

Leeds Revolutionary Feminist Group (1981) 'Political Lesbianism: The Case Against Heterosexuality', in Onlywomen Press (ed.) *Love Your Enemy: The Debate between Heterosexual Feminism and Political Lesbianism*. London: Onlywomen Press.

Rich, Adrienne (1974) *Of Woman Born*. London: Virago.

Rich, Adrienne (1980) 'Compulsory Heterosexuality and Lesbian Existence', *Signs* 5(4): 631–60.

Loulou BROWN completed an MA in Women's Studies at the University of Kent in 1979. She is a freelance editor and writer, has recently edited books on Sylvia Plath and on the history of women healers, and is currently working on an international handbook of women's studies, to be published by Harvester-Wheatsheaf. She lives in London.

Nicola GAVEY

Technologies and Effects of Heterosexual Coercion

I am concerned here with explicating some of the ways in which sexual coercion, including 'unwanted sex', takes place within heterosexual relationships. It is suggested that dominant discourses on heterosexuality position women as relatively passive subjects who are encouraged to comply with sex with men, irrespective of their own sexual desire. Through the operation of disciplinary power, male dominance can be maintained in heterosexual practice often in the absence of direct force or violence. The discursive processes that maintain these sets of power relationships can be thought of as 'technologies of heterosexual coercion'. Extracts from women's accounts of their experiences of unwanted and coerced sex with men are presented to show the operations and effects of these technologies of heterosexual coercion.

To say that women often engage in unwanted sex with men is paradoxically both to state the obvious and to speak the unspeakable. While this assertion will not come as a surprise to many women, it embodies a subjugated knowledge which usually remains private and hidden. Unwanted and coerced sex are thus an aspect of some women's experiences of oppression which have remained to a large extent unrecognized, yet implicitly condoned, and even encouraged.

In this study I want to show how language and discourses on sexuality have the power to effect the material practice of heterosexuality in ways that subordinate women. Dominant discourses on sexuality provide subject positions for women which are relatively passive, and which prescribe compliance with or submission to male initiatives or demands. This compliance can be seen to be an effect of 'technologies of heterosexual coercion', which reproduce relations of power and dominance in the domain of heterosexual sex such that men's interests take precedence. My specific focus in this study is an exploration of women's experiences of unwanted and coerced sex within heterosexual relationships. It has been shown that rape and sexual aggression are relatively prevalent within heterosexual relationships (e.g. Gavey, 1991a, 1991b; Russell, 1982). Feminists have suggested, however, that recognized forms of sexual violence are only the extreme manifestation of a more pervasive coercive heterosexuality (see Gavey, 1990, for a fuller discussion). Women can be coerced into having sex with men in many more subtle ways than through physical force, or violence, or the threat of violence (e.g. Finkelhor and Yllo, 1983, 1985; Gavey, 1989, 1990; Muehlenhard and Schrag, 1991). In this study, I was particularly interested in how to account for those operations of power that do not involve direct force or violence, and/or which appear to involve the woman's consent or, at least, lack of obvious resistance. Later, I present excerpts from some women's accounts of their experiences of, and their feelings and beliefs about, coercive heterosexual sex. Some of the instances I discuss involved subtle coercion, while others involved quite obvious coercion or force but were somehow unable to be conceptualized as 'rape' or sometimes even as 'forced', by the woman at the time. The sorts of dynamics that I look at relate primarily to heterosexual women, but some of the less subtle mechanisms of male sexual coercion will apply more generally to all women. I do not address the possibility of how some forms of sexual coercion may also operate in similar ways within lesbian sexual relations.

DISCOURSE AND SUBJECT POSITIONS FOR WOMEN

At this point, I very briefly outline a general theory of discourse that provides a framework for the analyses in this study. From a poststructuralist perspective, language is always located in discourse. Discourse refers to an interrelated 'system of statements which cohere around common meanings and values . . . [that] are a product of social factors, of powers and practices, rather than an individual's set of ideas' (Hollway, 1983: 231). It is a broad concept referring to ways of constituting meaning which are specific to particular groups, cultures and historical periods. Discourse both constitutes, and is reproduced in, social institutions, modes of thought and individual subjectivities. Within any discourse subject positions are available to the individual, but these are not coterminous with the individual (Henriques et al., 1984). Subject positions offer us ways of being and behaving, and of understanding ourselves and events in our world. Because of the relationship between discourse, power and subjectivity, most women are likely to be positioned within dominant, prevailing discourses — although these positionings will always be to some extent partial, as they are contested and interrupted by other discursive possibilities. Indeed, subjectivity is fragmentary and any individual's subjectivity would never be entirely consistent with a unitary subject position from any one discourse. Rather, subjectivity is a process which is likely to be the transient, always changing, product of a discursive battle (Weedon, 1987) — hence the contradictions and ambiguities in women's experiences.

SEXUALITY AS SOCIALLY CONSTRUCTED

It is by now widely accepted that what we think of as 'sexuality' is not a natural and pre-existent entity, but rather a social construction. Thus, sex is not a seething mass of natural drives and urges that our society has repressed, but rather, sexual practices, desires, subjectivities, forms of identity and so on, have been produced and continue to be produced through the 'deployment of sexuality' (Foucault, 1981). According to Foucault (1980, 1981), sexuality has been 'deployed' in relatively recent times as a domain of regulation and social control. This theorization of sexuality allows an understanding of how the positions available to women (and men) in dominant discourses on sexuality are not natural and fixed, and nor are they neutral — sexuality is deployed in ways that are directly related to relations of power.

DISCIPLINARY POWER

The analyses presented in this study also rely on some of Michel Foucault's ideas about power. Central to a Foucauldian analysis of power is the recognition that power is not a unitary force that is independent of us and operates only from the top down, through repression and denial. Rather, Foucault has argued that over time traditional sovereign forms of power have been intersected with (but not replaced by) what he has called 'disciplinary power' (Diamond and Quinby, 1988). 'Discipline' regulates human life, imposing particular forms of behaviour and 'assuring the ordering of human multiplicities' (Foucault, 1979: 218). It 'produces subjected and practised bodies, "docile" bodies' (Foucault, 1979: 138). In this sense, power is 'positive'. That is, it is *productive and constitutive* — it produces meanings, desires, behaviours, practices and so on. Discipline is infused in multiple and diffuse ways throughout the whole 'social body', and disciplinary power is exercised through its invisibility (Foucault, 1979). Disciplinary power thus works through 'subtle coercion' (Foucault, 1979: 209), making the exercise of power more effective.

The concept of disciplinary power promises fruitful openings for exploring sexual coercion (particularly subtle forms) within heterosexual relationships. However, the differential, gendered, operations of power through the deployment of sex for men and women must be highlighted (e.g. de Lauretis, 1987; Bartky, 1988). Disciplinary power may produce 'docile bodies', but there are profound gender differences in the forms this takes with regard to heterosexuality.

Apparent Complicity in Heterosexual Coercion

The concept of disciplinary power allows an understanding of how women may be persuaded into apparent complicity in the process of our own subjugation, through the regulation and normalization of our subjectivities and behaviours. The panoptic schema, which Foucault (1979) referred to for illustrating how disciplinary power functions, provides an interesting model for understanding how subjects are enlisted into the service of regulating their own behaviour, thus becoming their own jailors (Bartky, 1988). The Panopticon is an architectural model (designed by Jeremy Bentham) for a prison, which consists of a central watchtower surrounded by a circular building divided into cells. Each cell extends the width of the building and has a window on both the outside and inside walls, thus creating an effect of backlighting which makes the cell occupant visible from the central tower. Furthermore, the central tower is designed so that the observer is not visible to the prisoners in their cells. This arrangement ensures 'that the surveillance is permanent in its effects' (Foucault, 1979: 201), without needing to be continuous in its action (that is, the supervisor need not always be present). In this model, power is both visible and unverifiable. That is, the inmates are constantly aware of the central tower from which they are observed, but they never know if they are being looked at at any one particular time. Thus, the Panopticon induces 'a state of conscious and permanent visibility that assures the automatic functioning of power' (Foucault, 1979: 201). This model illustrates how subjects can be regulated and normalized through the operation of disciplinary power.

Sandra Lee Bartky (1988: 81), in a feminist Foucauldian analysis of 'femininity', has argued the following:

> The woman who checks her makeup half a dozen times a day to see if her foundation has caked or her mascara has run, who worries that the wind or the rain may spoil her hairdo, who looks frequently to see if her stockings have bagged at the ankle or who, feeling fat, monitors everything she eats, has become, just as surely as the inmate of the Panopticon, a self-policing subject, a self committed to a relentless self-surveillance. This self-surveillance is a form of obedience to patriarchy. It is also the reflection in the woman's consciousness of the fact that *she* is under surveillance in ways that *he* is not, that whatever else she may become, she is importantly a body designed to please or excite. There has been induced in many women, then, in Foucault's words, a 'state of conscious and permanent visibility that assures the automatic functioning of power'.

'In contemporary patriarchal culture', Bartky suggested, 'a panoptical male connoisseur resides within the consciousness of most women' (Bartky, 1988: 72). Many parallels can be drawn between Bartky's incisive analysis of the vigilance of some women over their feminine appearance and the 'obedience' of some women in our sexual relations with men. Women involved in heterosexual encounters are also engaged in self-surveillance, and are encouraged to become self-policing subjects who comply with the normative heterosexual narrative scripts which demand our consent and participation irrespective of our sexual desire. Thus, while women may not engage in conscious and deliberate submission, disciplinary power nevertheless produces what can be seen as a form of obedience. While the individual male's behaviour in the interaction is not insignificant, the operations of power involved may transcend his particular actions.

TECHNOLOGIES OF HETEROSEXUAL COERCION

In Foucault's use of the metaphor 'technologies of power', it is suggested that just as we understand technology as a set of applied knowledges and practices that develop and construct material objects in our physical world, which structure that world and mediate our relationship to it and its meaning, so too do *social* 'technologies' construct and reproduce practices in, and experiences and meanings of, our personal and social worlds. Teresa de Lauretis (1987: 28) uses the technology metaphor to discuss 'the techniques and discursive strategies by which gender is constructed'. Thus, gender 'is the product of various social technologies, such as cinema, and of institutionalized discourses, epistemologies, and critical practices, as well as practices of daily life' (de Lauretis, 1987: 2). Similarly, this metaphor can be extended to understand the ways in which the gender-specific deployment of sexuality enables, if not actually encourages, heterosexual practice which contains much invisible coercion. That is, the normalizing social technologies of sex produce a material practice of heterosexuality in which women are produced as subjects who are encouraged to regulate our own behaviour in ways which comply with androcentric versions of sexuality (see Jackson, 1984, for a discussion of androcentric and heterosexist sexuality). In these versions of sexuality, heterosexuality is assumed as a given and is 'compulsory' (Rich, 1980), women's sexual desire is relatively neglected and, concomitantly, women often lack power to determine our involvement in heterosexual relations — both in general, and in specific forms of sex. The practices, knowledges and strategies that reproduce this state of affairs can be thought of as 'technologies of heterosexual coercion'.

The discursive fields in which these power relations are prescribed, enacted and reproduced as social technologies are many and varied. They would include women's and men's accounts and representations of their heterosexual sexuality and relationships; representations of sexuality and heterosexual relations in popular women's magazines, film, television, romance and other fiction, pornography and sex manuals; sexology and the practice of sex therapy; practices of contraception; sexual humour; church prescriptions on sexuality; sex education in schools; legislation on sexuality and sexual violence; sociobiological explanations for sexual violence, and so on. Exploration of the representations of sexuality and heterosexual relations and practice in any one of these areas would also lead to some understanding of the technologies and effects of heterosexual coercion. In this study, I focus on women's accounts of their sexual experiences with men as one discursive field through which technologies of heterosexual coercion operate. Women's personal accounts provide direct access to the discourses available to these women, the subject positions offered by these discourses and the ways in which power operates through these discourses, and in relation to specific discursive positionings.

To say that there exist technologies of heterosexual coercion is not to say that it is not possible for women to be positioned in ways in which we do have power and agency in sexual relations with men, and in which our desire is articulated and acted upon (e.g. Hollway, 1984; and see Gavey, 1991c, for a discussion of the missing discourse of desire as it relates to understandings of sexual violence). There are certainly discourses (e.g. feminisms) that impinge on heterosexuality which do allow such power and desire, although such discourses are not available as yet to all women. Furthermore, it would be naive to believe that an individual woman will achieve 'liberation' by positioning herself in a feminist discourse on sexuality in an otherwise misogynist material context. It is important to remember that the continued existence of more brutal forms of male (sexual and non-sexual) violence against women acts as an important signification and reminder of the lack of *ultimate* control and power that many women have in our sexual and/or other relations with men. To forget this material condition of women's lives is, perhaps, to move onto the slippery slope of victim-blaming. There are also other conditions of women's lives, such as economic and social disadvantages, which contribute to what may be seen as women's complicity in our sexual coercion. These conditions can frame or contextualize the prospect of engaging in unwanted sex in a way that makes it seem like the best of all possible options to the woman involved.

Next, I describe some of the experiences that women have recounted to me, and show, by reference to their discursive framing of the experience, some of the operations and effects of technologies of heterosexual coercion.

SOME WOMEN'S EXPERIENCES OF HETEROSEXUAL COERCION

The descriptions and analyses that follow are based primarily on interviews with six women, but are also informed by several earlier interviews and, to a certain extent, my own experiences and informal conversations with women over many years. All of the six women could be described as articulate, educated, middle class, heterosexual, Pakeha.[1] They included friends, acquaintances and friends of friends. The process through which they became involved in the research was initiated either at their suggestion, my suggestion or the suggestion of a third party in the context of discussions about my research topic. They were chosen because they were interested in participating in the research, and not because they had identified themselves as having had any particular sorts of experiences — in fact, several expressed the reservation that their experiences of sex with men had been very ordinary, and that they might not have anything to say that would be of interest to me.

Informed consent was obtained from all the women and utmost care has been taken to protect their anonymity and confidentiality. Four of the women were interviewed in their own homes, one in my home and one in her workplace office. I was interested in talking with the women about some of their experiences of unwanted and/or coerced sex within heterosexual relationships or at least potentially appropriate heterosexual encounters. The interviews were not formally structured by adherence to a schedule of questions. Most of the interviews began with me asking the woman to describe her ideas about what an ideal sexual relationship between a woman and a man would be like. I then asked her how typical she thought her description would be for most of her relationships, or for most women's heterosexual relationships. I then facilitated a discussion, using her answer as a starting point, which moved onto her experiences of unwanted or coerced sex with men. It was usually productive to trace in detail some particular experiences or relationships. The interviews were taped and then fully transcribed. All of the six women were consulted about the way I had written their accounts into my first draft, and they all agreed that what I had written was acceptable to them.

From such limited sampling of almost exclusively Pakeha women, I obviously do not intend to make statements which are universally applicable to 'Women'. I do assume, however, that these women, whose experiences I represent and whose accounts I reproduce in part, are not unusual or idiosyncratic in any notable way. I regard their accounts not so much as individual constructions, but rather as personalized versions of a limited number of available culturally and historically specific shared interpretive repertoires (Potter and Wetherell, 1987). Even so, I acknowledge that it is not possible adequately to represent the diversity of experiences, both within and between, women. Differences in women's experiences according to culture, race, age, class, religion and sexual orientation, for example, may occur in ways I cannot imagine (e.g. see Fine, 1988, for a discussion concerning black and Latina young women from predominantly low-income families in New York City). Thus, I offer these descriptions and analyses as a partial account which may or may not resonate for individual women readers and for particular groups of women.

I now go on to discuss a number of *overlapping* themes under which I have organized aspects of the data of women's accounts. These themes were chosen from my reading of the interview transcripts, although some of them have also arisen in looking at other data (e.g. Gavey, 1989, 1990), and have developed in conjunction with a broader background of reading, thinking and talking about these issues.

KNOWLEDGE ABOUT WHAT IS NORMAL

Through the normalizing discourses of heterosexuality a tyranny of inferred 'normality' appears to be one of the mechanisms that operate to regulate the heterosexual behaviour of women. In many instances women have recounted experiences in which their knowledge (and lack of knowledge) about what was 'normal' — in terms of what to expect and what to do — in relation to sex with men, determined their sexual practice. It seems that there exists a powerful cultural narrative that structures and constitutes actual heterosexual encounters. Sometimes the regulating and normalizing characteristics of this hegemonic narrative can be seen to work by precluding knowledge of acceptable alternatives, and sometimes it appears to be manifest in a subtly different form whereby participants have an active desire to be normal. The desire to be normal, and the concomitant fear of being abnormal (which I will discuss later as a somewhat different dynamic), seem to act as powerful determinants of sexual behaviour for women, in some instances.

One obvious area where dominant discourses on heterosexuality regulate practice is by governing the frequency of sexual interaction for heterosexual couples. This was explicitly articulated by one woman:

> MARILYN: But I do think to myself, 'How long ago was it, um, and, and so how long can we sort of acceptedly put it off for?'
> NICOLA: And what do you think is a- you know, what's your answer about that? What's acceptable?
> MARILYN: Well, well, my, my answer, is um, (*pause*) at the moment, I, I sort of think to myself that once a month is alright, I'm doing okay, . . . but I mean, that's like, really changed. Beforehand I would have — a, a year ago — would have been like, if I could- I couldn't have sex twice a week, you know, I felt guilty, I felt bad about it. I'd, I would make myself sort of want to do it, or, or no I wouldn't want to but, you know, I would feel *bad* if it didn't happen twice a week.

The standard heterosexual narrative seems to dictate the situations in which sex is required as well as the form it will take. For example, we are all familiar with the dominant assumption that heterosexual intercourse (coitus) is synonymous with 'real' sex. For instance:

> CHLOE: I'd say just about every time that we had any sort of sexual contact it was *culminated* in sexual intercourse.
> LEE: . . . sex, which was- which in our case meant coitus.

So, as Bland (1981: 67) has said, 'the displacement of the sex act as penetration from the centre of the sexual stage remains a task still facing us today'. Situations where there is the possibility for this standard narrative, including a 'coital imperative' (Jackson, 1984: 44), to be exaggerated include relationships where sexual interaction is not possible at the home of either partner (e.g. young women and men who are living at home with their parents) and situations when women are having 'affairs' with men. Elaborate steps may be required for the two to get to spend time together, or the time together may be so limited that the inevitability of sex (usually sexual intercourse) taking place becomes predictable, and consequently the option for the woman to not engage in sex if she doesn't feel like it may be curtailed. For example:

> LEE: . . . sometimes we'd, we'd prearrange. We'd say okay, we're going to meet at such and such a time in such and such a place, and, I mean sometimes that might be a motel room, sometimes that might be, um, on a beach, when nobody else was around. And I suppose the implicit understanding was that we would have sex, which was- which in our case meant coitus. (*pause*) Um, so there were those times, I mean- and having, having prearranged those (*pause*) those meetings, I mean, I, I suppose I had a sense of- I'd always hoped that it would- I'd be really turned on, it would be wonderful and all that sort of stuff, but if I wasn't, um, I'd feel really *silly* if I, if I then said 'sorry I've dragged you out here but-'
> NICOLA: Because it's such a um effort to make the time to see each other?
> LEE: Yeah. So there was that pressure given that we'd simply arrange to meet, in the understanding was that we would have sex. I mean, you'd hardly get in, book into a motel room, I mean (*laughter*) go to a *huge* amount of effort to get rid of my child, to get, for him to be able to um put his work on hold and all those sorts of things and, living in a small town to sort of creep around the back streets and make sure no one had seen you. Then to have done all that and then say, 'I'm sorry, actually, I just wanted a cuddle and a cup of tea' (*laughter*).

This woman had been in an ongoing relationship with that man, on and off, over a period of several years, and, with the exception of their first sexual encounter, it had never really been sexually exciting. Nevertheless, the discursive framing, which includes the material practice, of these encounters made the possibility of an ending without heterosexual intercourse seem 'silly' (Lee). Another woman, who had been having a relationship with a married man over a 14-year period, described a similar phenomenon:

> PAT: If we went away to the beach he would drink quite a bit and I'd, I *detest* being made love to when somebody's been drinking. I absolutely detest it, I think it's, it's *revolting* and they *stink* and I- they're not all there, and, um, that was when he was at his most insistent, and that was when he took ages to actually have an orgasm because he'd drunk too much and I used to detest it. And, um (*pause*) because we hardly- because we didn't have many weekends together I used to go along with it.

This dynamic rendered her a passive object of the sexual interaction:

> PAT: And I mean (*pause, sighs*), because we never had many weekends together I just used to sort of let him get on with it. But I (*laughing*) can't say that I was (*pause*), you know, a, a full participant.

The same narrative can be seen to govern the behaviour of young women who are relatively new to heterosexual relationships with men. One woman (Ann) described a series of 'one-night stands' when she was around 14 to 16 years of age:

ANN: Yeah, it wouldn't have occurred to me to have said no. (*long pause*) And also that feeling of, 'well, I've led them on', you know, 'I've led them on this far, I've, I've done these things, I've gotten a bit drunk, I've danced a certain way, I've got in the car, we've come to the park'. And there is still, remember, very much that feeling where, you know, I mean, if you led boys on then that's what you did. Whereas, when I think about it, I think, well, did I, when I was sort of leading them on, did I want to have it to end in penetrative sex? I don't think I did really. I think it was just more the enjoying of the flirting, I mean I was definitely quite flirtatious and enjoying of the attention that that got me, um- but then sort of the getting in the car, it was like, well, it was like, you just had to pay your dues really, for the other three hours of flirting, you know.

This narrative also seems to operate in situations which are not so obviously constrained by limited opportunities for time together:

CHLOE: Like he always, when I used to stay the night a couple of times a week, he'd always wanted to have sexual intercourse in the morning and that was just, that was just how it was. Like, you know, you had a fuck then you got up and you had a cup of tea then you had your breakfast. (*laughs*) And I never really enjoyed sex. And I mean I just thought, you know, like I didn't even question it. There was nothing- There was so much taking the cue from the guy. There was, I don't know how, I guess I just wasn't tuned into my own feelings or that, or I couldn't have gone through with it. Because, you know, that person wanted me, and I was in a *relationship*, we were going out together and, isn't this what everybody does? And, you know, all that sort of stuff. Most unpleasant.

WHY CAN'T I SAY NO?

Not only do women sometimes engage in unwanted sex with men because it does not occur to us to question it, but also, sometimes, we do not have the language to be able to say no. For example, one woman spoke of the pressure on girls when she was younger to be 'promiscuous':

NICOLA: Where was that pressure coming from?
ANN: (*Gap*) . . . it's partly having the language to say no. Like, this sort of amorphous feeling of, 'Ooh, I'm not sure about this', but having the language to say it, and, and, and also I guess, feeling that if you said it, it would have any effect. Because there is always that fear that you could say no and it would carry on anyway, and, and being physically less, and then you'd be raped sort of thing, and then it would be terrible.

This woman said that she had been recently talking to her friend about these experiences they'd had together as teenagers, and had reconceptualized them as sort-of-rape:

ANN: I was saying to my friend, Kelly, the other day, it was amazing how . . . we weren't raped as teenagers, you know, like the things we used to do. And then I thought, well we were sort of raped, really, when you think we were driven off in cars and we would end up in the park somewhere and we would have sort of boys having sexual experiences with us that we didn't- We often- like it was quite disgusting, like 'wasn't he revolting, his body was so awful', mmm and a sense of, um, being isolated too, like not knowing, you know, you are by yourself with this boy and there is always that physical difference in strength, you know . . .

Another woman described how, once intercourse had started, she had a feeling of total lack of control over the process:

CHLOE: I just realize the total lack of my belief in any right to say to somebody- Like if someone was standing on my foot I'd fucking tell her- Someone's got their penis in my vagina and they're grinding away and I don't feel able to ask them to stop. It's *just ridiculous*! Honestly, it's just the pits. I mean there's a hell of a lot of powerful stuff going on-

Another woman said:

PAT: There've been times in my life when I have really felt like . . . 'What the hell did I go to bed with that man for? Why am I doing this, I must be mad. Why can't I say no?', you know. It's it's (*pause*) it's very hard, I find it- I have in the past found it very difficult to say no to a guy who wants to go to bed with me. Very difficult. Practically impossible, in fact. Not to someone I've just met, but to someone that I'm, I've known a while, and been to bed with. If you've been to bed with them once, then there's no reason why, that you shouldn't go to bed with them again in their heads. And of course (*pause*), I mean, you can see that point of view (*laughing*).

This difficulty, or near impossibility, of saying no can render women almost 'unrapeable'. As Ann noted, in the extract quoted, part of her difficulty in having the language to say no was related to her fear that it may have no effect. So, instead of risking being raped, she did not say no, therefore not signalling her non-consent prevented whatever followed from being construed as rape. Similarly, Pat noted incidents – one with a relative stranger and one within the context of her ongoing relationship — in which she did not signal her non-consent, thus rendering herself unrapeable. In the incident with the relative stranger, she had gone to his home and he had used 'emotional blackmail' (Pat) to coerce her to have sex with him:

PAT: He actually said, you know, 'you've come over here and, if you didn't want to make love, why did you come?' and, a lot of stuff like that. That actually probably stunned me a bit because it was really the first time anyone's put it on to me in such a heavy way in words.

They ended up having sex (Pat: 'and he said all these things, and he, you know, started undressing me and I just, you know, gave up, I suppose'), in which he was physically rough (Pat: 'He bit my thighs and he bit my breasts and [*pause*] um [*pause*] I had fingermarks on me as well and, and my legs and, and breasts were terribly bruised for two or three weeks . . . I was terrified. I was really quite scared, because he was quite violent.') Nevertheless, she did not consider this event to be rape:

> NICOLA: So when you look back on that do you consider that to be sexual assault,
> PAT: Oh yeah,
> NICOLA: Yeah, or rape?
> PAT: Well I wasn't raped, raped, because I did- I- See, I've actually never been raped, but I mean really it's a fine line, isn't it, between saying yes, whether you want to or not, to somebody like that, that I didn't really want to go to bed with. Ah, I've, I mean I suppose I've been (*pause, sighing*) sort of pushed around (*pause*) but, but not hurt. Just (*pause*) manhandled (*long pause*) but not (*pause*) violently. (*Gap*)
> He, he didn't rape me, because I really more or less consented.
> NICOLA: And how did you consent?
> PAT: I (*pause*) acquiesced, in my actions, but not my words. I didn't say 'oh, okay', I just let him get on with it.
> NICOLA: So what would have been, what would have made that rape in your mind?
> PAT: Well, if I'd sort of- a- If I had tried to keep my clothes on (*pause*), and he'd taken them off, or if he'd simply forced his way into me without even bothering to take my clothes off. (*pause*) I, I can remember the odd occasion when, (*pause*) when, I've been forced into having intercourse, (*pause*) but (*pause, sighs*) I've never really felt as though I was raped. I mean I didn't even really feel I was- I didn't feel as though I was raped then. I'm- my (*pause*) um, my feelings on that occasion, were (*pause*) I'd had a very narrow squeak. Because I really- (*pause*) he (*pause*) I was, (*pause*), I, I do think, I remember feeling I had actually overreacted, because probably he wasn't going to do any more than he did.

This woman also described occasions of having been forced to have sexual intercourse by her lover (who was married to someone else, but was her primary sexual partner). These instances occurred during periods in their long relationship when they had decided either to 'just be friends' (Pat) or to not see each other any more. Her lover was never violent but, in fact, he did not need to be in order to exercise control over the situation.

> PAT: Anyway (*pause*) he'd come in and he'd kiss me. Well that's fine, but kiss-there are kisses and kisses and our kisses are always reasonably sexual kisses. So, you know, I would only let those go on for, sort of 30 seconds or so and then I'd back off, you see. Well, if he was feeling like being difficult about this he wouldn't let me back off and he would keep on kissing me, and he would keep on touching me and he would manoeuvre me into the bedroom.
> NICOLA: And so it- would you still be trying to back off during this time?
> PAT: Well, I probably wouldn't be trying that hard or, maybe I- but I mean, I, I, I mean I wouldn't- I mean if I really got absolutely angry and furious and got into a physical struggle with him, he would simply never have persisted.

So (*pause*) while I say, he'd, he'd (*pause*) he'd made love to me by force, if
I had really yelled and screamed or even raised my voice or, or, or hit him,
or — which I would never have done — he would have stopped. So, really,
it's probably, it's- they're just games we played.
(*Gap*)
. . . when I think about it, um, I know perfectly well (*pause*) because of the
sort of person he is that if I really said 'absolutely no, no, no, not on any cir-
under any circumstances', then he wouldn't have persisted, but then, you see,
the other thing to that is, that maybe I wouldn't actually say 'absolutely no, no,
no, not under any circumstances', in case he never came back again.

So, although this woman believed that her lover would have stopped forcing her
to have sex if she had clearly and unambiguously resisted him, this man would
never have had to entertain the possibility of using violence to exercise power
or control in this relationship, because of the high improbability of her ever
resisting him. These seem to be clear examples of the effects of disciplinary
power efficiently operating to regulate a woman's behaviour so that force and
violence are not necessary to maintain relations of power which favour a man's
sexual interests.

CONSENT OR NON-CONSENT: WHERE IS THE CHOICE?

In some instances, women do not perceive that consent or non-consent represent
distinct choices. For example, '[when I was younger] I don't think I was aware
of (*pause*) what it meant not to [have sex], or to say no' (Ann). This is not surprising when we notice that both *consent* and *non-consent* are different options
available to a woman in response to something that is *being done to her* (Garnier
Barshis, 1983). When dominant discourses on women's sexuality are structured
around consent, and they neglect more active notions such as desire, it is little
wonder that women often don't really understand the concept of consent in a way
that is meaningful to us. As Irene Diamond and Lee Quinby (1988: 200) have
noted, 'given the current mechanisms of power in our society, sexual consent
is often a function of disciplinary power'. One woman told me of her teenage
sexual experiences with her boyfriend, in which she performed the role of sexual
partner which she assumed was demanded by her chosen position as a girlfriend.
(As someone who did extremely well at schoolwork, in a school where academic
achievement was not positively valued among her peers, the status of being a
particular sort of boy's girlfriend was desired by her as a part of her quest for
social acceptability among female friends, rather than for any intrinsic rewards
of the relationship.) She was 14 when the relationship with her first boyfriend
began. It was a relationship in which she perceived that it was necessary for her
to have sex with him in order for her to have the relationship with him:

MARILYN: Oh yeah, yeah, definitely. It was the- you know, that was like what-
well that was all it was really. I mean, he would never- we'd never have talked
about anything. We would've gone out, but as part of a group, and um then
it was just accepted that whenever we went out we would end up having sex
in his car or something, afterwards.

The actual sexual experiences were undesired and totally unsatisfying for this
woman. Her boyfriend was 'not a skilled lover', and 'he made no attempt to,
um (*pause*) be affectionate' (Marilyn). Furthermore, the actual details of the
scene of sexual intercourse were far from ideal: 'we'd gone to a carpark, and
he had a, sort of horrible old, um car, and then- and he propped the, the um
front seats up with paint cans, and made me lie in the back with my legs out
the window' (Marilyn). Sexual intercourse itself was seemingly totally uncon-
nected to her sexual desire:

MARILYN: I didn't really like having it, but, I pushed that away and I could do
it without thinking about it. I never enjoyed it, I never had an orgasm or
anything like that, but I mean, and I never got any feeling from it at all, but-
NICOLA: Any feeling, um physical feeling?
MARILYN: Any physical feeling, any (*pause*), no I don't even think I got any
emotional feeling really. I didn't really feel that I needed to be loved by him
and this was how he showed me that he loved me or anything like that.

However, 'the worst thing about having sex really was the contraception thing'
(Marilyn). Her boyfriend refused to use condoms responsibly, and so she was
regularly having unprotected sexual intercourse:

MARILYN: It was a terrible stress you know, I mean I really, it dominated how
I thought about things all the time. I felt, I was worried about it all the time
. . . I, I worried. Probably, probably for about um two years I would have been
just hysterical with worry.

MARILYN: I was really frightened of getting pregnant all the time, every, every
month I would just lie in bed petrified with fear about what I was going to do.
I used to think if I got pregnant I would commit suicide, and I knew how to
do it. I used to write, I actually wrote a letter to the *New Zealand Women's
Weekly* pretending to be a young mother worried about my children eating
poison, around the house, and said 'which ones should be locked up?', so I
could find out what would kill you. And that was what I would do, that is what
I thought I would do.

Despite the sexual experiences with her boyfriend being, at best, what could
be described as only tolerable, and despite extreme anxiety about pregnancy, to
the extent of potentially fatal consequences, she said, 'I never would have ever,
ever thought of saying no or yes, you know, until I was, until a few years ago'
(Marilyn). It is difficult, therefore, to understand these experiences in neutral

terms, merely as a young woman having been persuaded (definitely not even 'seduced') to have sexual intercourse with a young man. Her own appraisal of the situation, based on her knowledge of supposedly 'normal' behaviour between men and women, meant that sex was required and compulsory. There was no room for her own sexual desire. Her behaviour (or her body, if you like) became inscribed through this technology of heterosexual coercion, so that she complied with and submitted to unwanted sexual intercourse. No direct male force was necessary to 'encourage' or make her enact this subservient sexual role, in which her body was subjugated to a man's sexual wants. She was, thus, under self-surveillance and acted as a self-policing subject, to use the language of disciplinary power. Furthermore, the 'architecture' of the situation — an old car parked in a carpark at night, would have probably mitigated against both her desire and her control.

'THERE'S SOMETHING WRONG WITH ME': THE PRICE TO PAY FOR NOT BEING 'NORMAL'

The fear of being 'abnormal' is not an unrealistic fear, as the women I spoke with recounted various ways in which they were unfavourably positioned by male partners or rapists, or by themselves or others, for being sexually unwilling or unresponsive. This ranged from the subtle to the extreme, and the price to pay can be high for women who resist, or whose experiences do not conform to, the implicit common-sense scripts for normal sexual behaviour for women. I think that this dynamic, in which women are aware of specific consequences for not behaving in a certain way, is different from the dynamic discussed earlier, in which a woman's behaviour is regulated by implicit and explicit norms, in the absence of particular insights into the effects of transgressing these norms.

One woman told me about having been raped when she was 19 (10 years previously) by her 30-year-old flatmate (with whom there had been no prior sexual contact, or even 'flirtatiousness' [Ann]).

> ANN: . . . he was in the bed with me, and I was being woken up with him sort of groping me, as it were, and I was quite disorientated, and thinking God, it's Ralph, you know, he's in bed with me . . . (*gap*) I mean it all happened quite quickly really, but I remember thinking quite clearly, 'Well if I don't- If I try and get out of bed, perhaps if I run away or something . . . he might rape me (*pause*) so I had better just. . .
> NICOLA: If you try and run away you mean?
> ANN: If I tried it, if I'd resisted, then he might rape me, you know. So he did anyway, sort of thing, really, when you think about it, when I look back.

Although she did not conceptualize the experience as rape at the time, he had been rough, and had left her bleeding and, later, frightened, 'confused', 'nervous within the house' (Ann) and hypervigilant about making sure she was never asleep before he'd gone to bed. However, it was not just the direct consequences of the rape that she had to contend with. Ralph asked her on subsequent nights if she wanted to 'come and sleep with me tonight?' (Ann), to which she refused. In the aftermath, she was constructed and positioned, by Ralph, the man who raped her, as well as her other male flatmate, as 'sexually uptight' (Ann):

> ANN: And then what happened after that was that I got this image of being this uptight (*pause*) bitch and this, uptight little pain. You know, I got the image of being quite- I got the reputation within the flat with him and David because it had- I think it had been a bit of a joke between them, that I was a sort of uptight, I was pretty uptight. And I did get quite uptight, I did get quite uptight. (*Gap*)
> NICOLA: Do you remember, um, you know, you said the next morning you felt like you- couldn't, it's not something you wanted to talk about. Do you have a sense of why that was, you know, what was about it?
> ANN: I remember thinking it was me. Like (*pause*), 'cause this guy, Ralph, used to have lots of women around and used to sleep with lots of women, and I always knew that, and so did David, the other flatmate, and I remember thinking 'it's me not understanding how things work in Melbourne or how things work with older people, or how I should be if I wasn't uptight'. (*Gap*)
> ANN: But our relationship, like I say, changed. I became quite, um (*pause*), he used to call me, they used to say 'Miss Prissy', 'Here's Miss Prissy', 'Here she comes in', and you know, 'Here's Miss Prissy', and it's like, 'Oh for God's sake, it was just a, just a bit of nothing'. And I didn't ever confront him about it.

This positioning may have had lasting effects for this woman:

> NICOLA: Do you think that that was significant in terms of like the way you saw yourself and the way you felt about yourself?
> ANN: Yeah I do. It's funny that, I've never thought about that before. But I still have that feeling sometimes that it's me, it's my fault if I don't want sex or I'm being uptight, or um (*pause*) If there's, ah maybe, another relationship since then if there has been things I haven't wanted to do I've often felt like (*pause*) I shouldn't be uptight, you know, I should be more- I think that thing of me being a bit uptight. That was the big thing, the big word that was labelled on me, that was exactly how I was seen after that. . .

One woman, who was violently sexually assaulted in her first marriage (approximately 30 years previously), at the time couldn't understand why she not only didn't enjoy sex with her husband, but found it physically painful. She wasn't aware that what was happening, behind closed doors, in her new marriage, was unusual: 'And I suppose I just really didn't know, I thought that was normal' (Rosemary). Her husband was having sex with her 'seven or eight or ten times a night, and through the day, and I was pregnant' (Rosemary). She went to her doctor, because of the severe pain she was suffering:

> ROSEMARY: And I went to the doctor about it and he just told me that I was, um, psychologically (*pause*) you know, undone, . . . I mean he virtually actually said to me that I was insane. And then my husband, just used to jump up and down on the bed every night, you know, telling me the same thing. And um, and I used to wake up in the morning and he'd be penetrating me before I was even awake, and when I was pregnant, I mean, it was just so *painful*, I just couldn't bear it.

Eventually, she came to believe that she might be schizophrenic:

> ROSEMARY: Well I thought there was, definitely thought there was something wrong with me and, more particularly, because I think at that same stage I found out that my father's father was schizophrenic. And so, and so I definitely made the link, and thought, well, you know, there's a chance that I am as well. And so I thought that I had these problems and, and, and couldn't, and just couldn't understand why I couldn't, um (*pause*), you, you know, couldn't get any pleasure out of being with him, and why it was so painful. You know, why people talked about it as being so wonderful, and why, for me, it was just absolute agony.

Other women report experiences which are perhaps more subtle than this, but nevertheless involve a form of violence. One woman spoke of arguments over sex in a long-term relationship of about four years:

> CHLOE: And, um, really getting, like getting into major arguments because I didn't want to have sex. Like, that- not actually being forced to have sex, but sometimes saying yes when I didn't really want to-
> NICOLA: To avoid the argument?
> CHLOE: Yeah. And the argument standing out as the most unpleasant thing. Things like actually being called a fucking bitch and having the door slammed. And trying always to explain that it didn't mean that I didn't care because I didn't want to have sex, but never ever succeeding.

One woman discussed her problem of having no sexual desire for her husband (whom she said she loved and, otherwise, had a good relationship with), and disliking having sex with him, yet feeling sexually attracted to a man she did not want a long-term relationship with. She told me about how she had gone to see a counsellor to seek some clarification about this 'ambivalence' and 'dilemma' (Marilyn). The counsellor seemed to avoid addressing this woman's problem, which left her frustrated and worried.

> MARILYN: And so I thought to myself, well God, maybe it's such a terrible problem that, you know, she just can't believe it, or she's really shocked by it, or never heard it before.

Another woman talked about her feelings of inadequacy about not feeling like having sex with her boyfriend who had taken her with him on an overseas trip he had won:

CHLOE: I remember sitting on the bed and him sort of making some suggestion that we made love or something and just not wanting to, just knowing that I didn't want to and just absolute- this feeling of absolute gloom sinking over and feeling really bad about myself too, because I didn't want to, and knowing that I wasn't actually prepared to, or able to, override it this time or any more, or whatever. And being there for ten days and going to this- oh, that made it really hard again because, this fantastic island, and fruit for breakfast, and sort of staying at the most expensive hotel. . .
(*Gap*)
Feeling like I'd come on this holiday with him and that somehow I wasn't doing my bit. . . . Um, that I was spoiling it for him. Yeah, just somehow that I wasn't doing what I should be doing. And just, yeah, just feeling like, even when I talk about it now, I sort of feel like I've got concrete in my legs. It's that sort of feeling of, um, (*pause*) it is, it- like it's a choice, sure, I'm saying I don't want to have sex, but it isn't a choice because I didn't have anywhere to go from there.

Another woman described her guilt around not feeling like having sex with her current partner, despite not feeling directly pressured by him:

ANN: I feel perfectly able to say no. I mean, I'm never pressured into it, but there is sometimes that feeling of guilt that, oh maybe I should, because, you know, it is, he is a lovely man, does these things, but you know, um. And I don't know why I have that, 'maybe I should'. It's me more than him, you know, but there is that slight feeling of guilt.

Other women have noted the restraints of such positionings, and how this has affected their behaviour in heterosexual encounters. For example: 'I'd still feel like I was being a bit prudish by saying "no"' (Lee), 'if we were still in contact now, I'd also feel, still feel um, prudish, and frigid and a bit unfair if I didn't, um, if I wasn't sexually responsible to him' (Lee). These sorts of negative positionings — which contribute to the constitution of a woman's identity, feelings and behaviour — are clear examples of some of the more obviously negative effects of technologies of heterosexual coercion.

NURTURANCE AND PRAGMATISM

In the face of a strong imperative for women to have sex with male partners irrespective of their sexual desire, some women act according to the dictates of nurturance or pragmatism, so that they are able to 'go along with sex' in the absence of sexual desire. This is a sense in which, as Diamond and Quinby (1988:201) noted, 'discourse within the technology of sexuality manufactures and conceals disciplinary power'. For, as Foucault (1981:86) noted, 'power is tolerable only on condition that it mask a substantial part of itself'. Such instances of women deciding to have sex with a man because he appears so 'needy' or 'pathetic', or she wants to give him something, or take care of him, or not hurt his feelings, can be seen to arise out of discourses on male sexual needs and female nurturance. Women discussed the operation of this dynamic in relation to their 'acquiescing' or 'consenting' to sexual intercourse with a male partner, but also in relation to not confronting or reporting a man who had committed acquaintance rape. The act of choosing to give sex may or may not be unpleasant and, indeed, it would be unnecessary to imagine that all nurturant 'giving of sex' reflects an act of submission in the face of relations of dominance. As one woman summed it up:

> ANN: Sometimes there is giving of, of your own accord and sometimes there is giving because you feel you have to.
> NICOLA: Yeah, so that's a distinction you'd make, too, between the giving thing.
> ANN: Mm, giving spontaneously and giving begrudgingly.

One woman talked about her long-term 'affair with a married man', in which she had been consistently sexually 'available', because 'sex is always frightfully, frightfully important to him', 'he can't live without it' (Pat):

> PAT: Now (*pause*) the sex was a, actually has been quite an important part of that. But, I have often gone to bed with him when I haven't really wanted to, when I haven't felt that I wanted to. And I've (*pause*) what you do is, you simply, um, suppress your own needs, because what he wants is to go to bed with you and you tell yourself it really doesn't matter much either way.

This woman was in somewhat of a bind, because her sexual 'availability' and responsiveness were probably perceived by her as central to her relationship. As she noted:

> PAT: Oh, I've said no to him occasionally, but hardly ever, hardly ever. And 'cause, you see, he- That was absolutely wonderful to him. The fact that I never ever turned him down. I mean, it was of *major importance in his life*, that I never said no.

Another woman described vividly how her partner's neediness, which was unappealing to her, nevertheless made it difficult for her not to have sex with him:

> LEE: . . . it wasn't that he was unkind, though. And I suppose that made it even worse. I mean if he had been, um, despicable, and power hungry and all those other sort of macho type things, then, I, I'd have no problems really in sort of metaphorically kicking him in the balls (*laughing*). But because he wasn't like that. He was actually quite cute, and, and pathetic- Ahh, that's what it is, and that's what used to turn me off as well. It was pathetic.
> NICOLA: The way that he-
> LEE: Pleaded. And wanted to have sex with me. And so I'd land up feeling sorry for him. I'd certainly land up feeling turned off.
> (*Gap*)

It was me feeling sorry for him. Him, he had these big sort of puppy dog eyes and (*laughs*). You just imagine little sort of tears running out of them, 'Oh, please, mummy'.

Women have often mentioned that it is easier to 'let sex happen', than to keep resisting when they don't want it. Thus, pragmatic ends, such as getting some sleep, can also enter into the decision. For example, one woman described a situation in which she'd allowed a lover to stay the night when he was in town on business. She'd said to him, "I don't want to make love, but come and stay", and he said, "Oh, okay, that'll be fine, I, I promise I won't touch" sort of thing' (Lee), but once he was there:

> LEE: . . . he kept saying, just, just, let me do this or just let me do that and that will be all. And, and, I mean this could go on for an hour, sort of thing, and, I, I mean I just wanted to go to sleep really (*amused*) when I had a busy day the next day (*both laughing*). So, in the end, in order to do that, in order to both go to sleep and for him to um, to finally relax, I mean he, he seems to be an amazingly sexual person, and I can just feel that sexual sort of energy there and he, he's no sooner going to go to sleep than fly to the moon. So, so after maybe an hour of, um, saying, me saying, 'no', and him saying 'Oh come on, come on' (*pause*) um I'd finally think 'Oh my, God, I mean, (*laugh*) for a few, for a few hours rest I may as- Peace and quiet, I may as well'. (*pause*) Um, I mean I'm not quite sure how I'd translated all those sorts of messages, but I suppose, I suppose he knew when I was saying okay (*laughing*), we may as well. So we made love, if you can call it that.

As may be expected, consenting to sex for nurturant or pragmatic reasons is not always neutral in its effect on the woman concerned. One woman who had discussed a relationship that was characterized by what she came to redefine as sexual coercion, commented on some of the emotional costs of her involvement in this.

> NICOLA: Do you think, um, there were emotional costs from that, sort of, direct-ly related to that, sort of sexual, what you're calling sexual coercion?
> LEE: Um, yeah, I think, I think there was. I think, I think there was for our friend-ship. (*Gap*) . . . I didn't respect myself I, I guess in, in my relationship with him . . . I, I gave, yeah, no, I gave away, I gave away some of my power I guess. I allowed him to exert some power over me.

When sex is engaged in for pragmatic reasons, it can take on specific meaning as something which is mundane, an ordinary physical activity (see also Gavey, 1989). One woman described some of the things she would be saying to herself under the pressure of a lover trying to get her to have sex with him:

> LEE: One was that, um, oh, why don't you just say 'yes', I mean it's, it's a nothing- it's like, having sex is like getting up and having breakfast. . .
> (*Gap*)
> I think in a way that, um, I was going to say, that was a way of making it,

making the *ordinariness* of it okay. I think it was just ordinary, it is just like having a cup of tea.

NICOLA: It's a way of making the ordinariness of it okay?

LEE: Mmm, so rather than it being really special and exciting. . .

Perhaps the ultimate pragmatic reason for apparently 'consenting' to (i.e. not resisting) sex, is to avoid being 'raped'. Examples of this are discussed in the section on women not having the language to say no to sex.

Not only may nurturance lead to women's compliance with unwanted sex, but it may also be implicated in actions which, following rape, protect a man from negative consequences. For example, Ann said in relation to her experience of being raped by her flatmate:

ANN: We just make it easier, it's like- and he doesn't have to think of it as rape. It's just what he does to women that he wants to sleep with, you know, he wants to fuck with, I mean, you know, but- He doesn't ever have to confront his behaviour, or the effects of it, um, and because, you sort of protect them from it. You know. And you internalize the distressing effects of it as well so that they don't — as the victim or whatever — have to see you as the victim or whatever, so they don't even have to see the distressing effects.

(*Gap*)

I remember thinking, oh well, maybe I wore my nightie around the house a bit too often, or maybe I encouraged him in some way or, you know, he was just being friendly, he was drunk and, you know. I really did think about it in such a way as to not blame him although I acted, my behaviour towards him and my attitudes certainly conveyed that, that I was pissed off. And I remember thinking I shouldn't be so uptight, I must be nicer to them, but it was like I just couldn't stop myself, I just couldn't, my body just couldn't bring itself to be-

She described how she would react differently now, in a way that would clarify it as rape, if the same thing happened:

ANN: If it happened now, if he got into my, if somebody got into my bed like that, a flatmate, and I said- I would be a lot stronger for a start. I wouldn't say 'What are you doing Ralph, you are in the wrong bed, I think maybe you should go back to your own bed', or whatever, I would say 'Fuck off'. And um, I, I think I'd really- it's funny, I don't know if, I, I mean I can imagine I could get raped now, but I would *really* fight it. I'd just fight it every, every- I mean I'd physically fight it much harder. I mean I really would. I wouldn't just go rigid and say nothing and- . . . if that happened I, I would have done anything, pinched him, bitten him, scratched him, scraped him, anything. And if it still had have happened, I would have pressed charges, you know, I would have, yeah. And I guess part of that in a way, by resisting so strongly it would have built it up to the point which I, then made it easier to conceptualize as rape.

RESISTANCE: AND TOWARDS REDEFINITION

The very fact that the women I spoke with related experiences which they recognized as undesired, unwanted and not enjoyed — despite often being within socially acceptable parameters — represents the necessary preconditions for resistance. That is, these women's positionings as subjugated heterosexual subjects was not complete and uncontested. Their experiences of dissatisfaction, and perceived coercion and abuse, highlight that the production of women as compliant subjects in the heterosexual script is not always completely successful. Some of the women I spoke with had come to a new point in their lives, whereby in positioning themselves within a feminist discourse on sexuality, they were able to access the power to resist those traditional injunctions to have sex irrespective of their desire. For example:

> ANN: I'm not prepared to have sex just for the sake of having sex as it were because I feel I should.

Some women were beginning to engage in the redefinition and redeployment of a new form of heterosexuality. One woman talked about how her current heterosexual relationship was special and positive in a way that previous ones had not been:

> NICOLA: How's it special now?
> LEE: (*laughs*) Um, I think, I think that that's really complex, um, and (*pause*) it's complex because of my relationship with Michael, and um (*pause*). But it's yeah, I mean there's lots of things there about (*pause*) being in love and, um thinking the person's wonderful in every respect. . . . but also there's a change in what it is that we do, um physically. Um (*pause*), and, and I guess, and that's really personal I suppose.
> (*Gap*)
> It's not ordinary now, because there's a feeling of being creative about what it is that we do. Um, (*pause*), yeah, there's a, there's a feeling that together we have, um, worked out our own (*pause*) wonderful and ever changing- I hope I'm not idealizing this, I don't think I am (*both laughing*). I'm pretty sure, oh, I'm not in fact. Um, we've worked out these wonderful and ever changing ways of sexually relating. So, so in that sense it's not ordinary because it's never, it's never the same. And I think I think it's like that because we've allowed, um (*pause*) we've allowed ourselves to do unordinary things. We've allowed ourselves to sort of move beyond, um, common-sense notions about what it is that people do in their bedrooms.

Suggestive, however, of the dominance of common-sense understandings of heterosexuality, movements of resistance and redefinition are not always easy or complete. For example, one woman who was attracted to celibacy within her marriage did not see this as a validated choice:

> MARILYN: I think there's a thing in, um, *Our Bodies Ourselves*, or something, you know, about celibacy. It's seen as being something that you do when you're single. You don't be in a relationship and be celibate. And I, and I sort of believe that, you know, I do. I kind of (*pause*) I mean maybe I shouldn't. I've never, I haven't actually thought that before, that maybe that's, that is viable. But, but (*pause*) but I'm not convinced or something (*laughs*).

Although she had read a newspaper article about a (married) woman who had written a book recommending celibacy, she was acutely aware of the negative positioning of this 'choice' within dominant discourses on heterosexuality:

> MARILYN: I felt that she was painted as quite a, um, sort of (*pause*) um, ball-breaking feminist, you know, like denying her husband sex. And he, he was sort of portrayed as quite a, um (*pause*) a, a sort of ineffectual, wimpish, little man to let this horrible woman do this to him. And when I read, when I saw it, it was at a time when, um, I really didn't want anybody to touch me or come near me and I thought, 'God, I could be just like that', um, um, and maybe, maybe I am.

Thus, the perceived negative value socially ascribed to the possibility of being celibate within a marriage made this option seem not viable for this woman. This can be seen as an example of how 'the power of all forms of subjectivity relies on the marginalization and repression of historically specific alternatives' (Weedon, 1987: 91). Another example of this sort of process is the guilt described by Ann when she didn't feel like having sex in her current relationship — despite believing that it is her right to not have sex when she doesn't want it, and not feeling directly pressured by her partner.

I think such resistance and ongoing redefinition is extremely important, both in its own right *and* as it relates to a continuum of sexual violence. A feminist political agenda which is concerned with both sexual violence and female desire is, in articulating women as active, desiring subjects who are interested in a range of practices and identities, more likely to deconstruct the phenomenon of compulsory heterosexuality and the highly prescriptive (and sometimes coercive) norms for heterosexual practice.

CONCLUSIONS

In this study I have discussed some of the ways in which the deployment of sex through technologies of heterosexual coercion constitutes possibilities for the domination of women through heterosexual practice, even in the absence of overt physical force or violence. By examining discourses on heterosexuality through women's accounts of their experiences (which, of course, do not exist in isolation from other discursive fields and material practices), we can see how 'language functions to create us as subjects' (Diamond and Quinby, 1988: 201), who are sometimes solicited into the processes of our own subjugation. In sampling from the data of six women's accounts of some of their experiences of coercive heterosexuality, including unwanted and forced sex with men, I have highlighted some of the ways in which this happens.

One way heterosexual coercion occurs is through the discursive framing of heterosexual encounters within a narrative in which (past a certain point in the encounter and/or relationship) certain forms of sex are prescribed, and sexual intercourse is required. Anything else is not easily accommodated. It may just seem 'silly', or it may lead to a woman being positioned as 'uptight', or it may, from her perspective, be regarded as an alternative to rape. Being positioned as 'uptight', as in Ann's case, may even occur when a woman is not gracious about having been raped by a man she knows. Or, as in Rosemary's case, a woman may be regarded as 'psychologically undone' because she cannot physically tolerate repeated violent sexual intercourse (rape), carried out on her by her husband.

Another important factor in this constitution of women as passive, compliant heterosexual subjects, seems to be the relative silence in articulating positions for women as active, desiring subjects (Gavey, 1991c). When, as Catharine MacKinnon (1983: 650) has observed, 'sex is normally something men do to women', consent can be a very passive action. Women are thus sometimes not aware of consent and non-consent as distinct choices (given certain, acceptable, parameters of the relationship). This is not surprising given the power of normative prescriptions for heterosexual practice — *and* given that women's sexual desire is often invisible, unspoken. When desire is absent in discourses on female sexuality, 'this constriction of what is called sexuality allows girls [and women] one primary decision — to say yes or no — to a question not necessarily their own' (Fine, 1988: 34). This silence allows the unwitting perpetuation of a form of (compulsory) heterosexuality in which women's agency and resistance exist only to the degree to which we can *limit* and *control* male sexual access (women's traditional imperative within heterosexuality). (We must remember, however, that sexual desire itself is not essential or unproblematic, but that it, too, is constructed and produced through the deployment of sexuality, and is itself inscribed by gender/power relations.)

I have also discussed actions arising from nurturance and pragmatism as examples of how the mechanisms of disciplinary power function in ways which conceal the operation of such power. By appealing to these nurturant or pragmatic reasons for having sex, women are 'disciplined' — our behaviour is regulated in ways in which the gender-specific operation of power is disguised. This invisible operation of power is extremely efficient because it obviates the need for overt force and violence.

The political implications of this analysis differ from some traditional analyses. Traditional feminist analyses have often relied on the notion of a simple top-down domination of women by patriarchal power, which is exercised by individual men and from which (all) men directly or indirectly benefit. This traditional understanding of domination, and its expression in the language of control, 'presumes a centering of power that may no longer exist in contemporary society: we are asked to seize power when power is no longer held by a clearly identifiable and coherent group' (Diamond and Quinby 1988: 195). An analysis which focuses on the regulating and normalizing functions of disciplinary power, however, does not rely on the presumption of unitary and centralized sources of power. It is, therefore, particularly useful for explaining women's compliance with unwanted sex and those forms of heterosexual coercion which do not involve overt force or violence.

One of the aims of this research was to interrogate, contest and disturb dominant conceptualizations of heterosexual sex. The deconstructive impulse of this research is not neutral, however. Women I have talked with about heterosexual coercion have sometimes told me that they have come to see their experiences in a different light as a result of talking or thinking about such experiences in the context of this research. To the extent that these new ways of making sense of their experiences create space for new discursive positionings which are more positive and open up possibilities for both resistance to coercion and the active pursuit of pleasure, then this is a positive, political implication of the research. We cannot avoid technologies of sex but, by understanding some of the ways in which they work, we can hopefully resist, challenge and contest technologies of heterosexual coercion.

ACKNOWLEDGEMENTS

I am very grateful to the six women who talked so openly with me about their experiences and allowed me to tape our conversations and quote them here. I am also grateful to the many other women I have talked with over the years about the sorts of questions posed in this research, both informally and more formally in the process of the research. I would like to thank Karen Newton for stimulating my interest in Michel Foucault's work on power, and Chris Atmore, Lise Bird, Sylvia Blood, Russell Gray, Tim McCreanor, Kathryn McPhillips, Karen Newton, Fred Seymour and Margaret Wetherell for careful and helpful comments and/or encouragement on an earlier draft. I would also like to thank Sue Wilkinson, Celia Kitzinger, Rachel Perkins, Susan Kippax and Corinne Squire who as editors and reviewers offered many helpful suggestions for revisions.

The research reported in this study was partially funded by a grant from the University of Auckland Research Fund and a University Grants Committee Postgraduate Scholarship to the author. An earlier version of these findings appeared in Gavey (1990).

NOTE

1. Pakeha refers to New Zealanders of European descent. The women's ages at the time they were interviewed were: Ann, 29 years; Chloe, 31 years; Lee, 33 years; Marilyn, 28 years; Pat, 52 years; Rosemary 50 years. (Names have been changed to protect anonymity.)

REFERENCES

Bartky, Sandra Lee (1988) 'Foucault, Femininity, and the Modernization of Patriarchal Power', in Irene Diamond and Lee Quinby (eds) *Feminism and Foucault: Reflections on Resistance*, pp. 61–86. Boston, MA: Northeastern University Press.

Bland, Lucy (1981) 'The Domain of the Sexual: A Response', *Screen Education* 39: 56–67.

de Lauretis, Teresa (1987) *Technologies of Gender: Essays on Theory, Film, and Fiction*. Bloomington, IL and Indianapolis, IN: Indiana University Press.

Diamond, Irene and Quinby, Lee (1988) 'American Feminism and the Language of Control', in Irene Diamond and Lee Quinby (eds) *Feminism and Foucault: Reflections on Resistance*, pp. 193–206. Boston, MA: Northeastern University Press.

Fine, Michelle (1988) 'Sexuality, Schooling, and Adolescent Females: The Missing Discourse of Desire', *Harvard Educational Review* 58: 29–53.

Finkelhor, David and Yllo, Kersti (1983) 'Rape in Marriage: A Sociological View', in David Finkelhor, Richard J. Gelles, Gerald T. Hotaling and Murray A. Straus (eds) *The Dark Side of Families: Current Family Violence Research*, pp. 119–30. Newbury Park, CA: Sage.

Finkelhor, David and Yllo, Kersti (1985) *License to Rape: Sexual Abuse of Wives*. New York: The Free Press.

Foucault, Michel (1979) *Discipline and Punish: The Birth of the Prison*. Trans by Alan Sheridan. London: Penguin (Original work published in 1975).

Foucault, Michel (1980) in Colin Gordon (ed.) *Power/Knowledge: Selected Interviews and Other Writings 1972–1977, by Michel Foucault*. Trans by Colin Gordon, Leo Marshall, John Mepham and Kate Soper. New York: Pantheon.

Foucault, Michel (1981) *The History of Sexuality (Volume 1: An Introduction)*. Trans by Robert Hurley. Harmondsworth, Middlesex: Penguin (Original work published in 1976).

Garnier Barshis, Victoria, R. (1983) 'The Question of Marital Rape', *Women's Studies International Forum* 6: 383–93.

Gavey, Nicola (1989) 'Feminist Poststructuralism and Discourse Analysis: Contributions to Feminist Psychology', *Psychology of Women Quarterly* 13: 459–75.

Gavey, Nicola (1990) 'Rape and Sexual Coercion within Heterosexual Relationships: An Intersection of Psychological, Feminist, and Postmodern Inquiries', unpublished doctoral thesis, University of Auckland.

Gavey, Nicola J. (1991a) 'Sexual Victimization Prevalence among Auckland University Students: How Much and Who Does It?', *New Zealand Journal of Psychology* 20: 63–70.

Gavey, Nicola (1991b) 'Sexual Victimization Prevalence among New Zealand University Students', *Journal of Consulting and Clinical Psychology* 59: 464–6.

Gavey, Nicola J. (1991c) 'Women's Desire in Sexual Violence Discourse', Paper presented at the Fourth International Conference on Language and Social Psychology, August, Santa Barbara, CA.

Henriques, Julian, Hollway, Wendy, Urwin, Cathy, Venn, Couze and Walkerdine, Valerie (1984) *Changing the Subject: Psychology, Social Regulation and Subjectivity*. London: Methuen.

Hollway, Wendy (1983) 'Heterosexual Sex: Power and Desire for the Other', in Sue Cartledge and Joanna Ryan (eds) *Sex and Love: New Thoughts on Old Contradictions*, pp. 124–40. London: The Women's Press.

Hollway, Wendy (1984) 'Women's Power in Heterosexual Sex', *Women's Studies International Forum* 7: 63–8.

Jackson, Margaret (1984) 'Sex Research and the Construction of Sexuality: A Tool of Male Supremacy?', *Women's Studies International Forum* 7: 43–51.

MacKinnon, Catharine (1983) 'Feminism, Marxism, Method, and the State: Toward Feminist Jurisprudence', *Signs: Journal of Women in Culture and Society* 8: 635–58.

Muehlenhard, Charlene, L. and Schrag, Jennifer, L. (1991) 'Nonviolent Sexual Coercion', in Andrea Parrot and Laurie Bechhofer (eds) *Acquaintance Rape: The Hidden Crime*, pp. 115–28. New York: Wiley.

Potter, Jonathan and Wetherell, Margaret (1987) *Discourse and Social Psychology*. London: Sage.

Rich, Adrienne (1980) 'Compulsory Heterosexuality and Lesbian Existence', *Signs: Journal of Women in Culture and Society* 5: 631–60.

Russell, Diana, E.H. (1982) *Rape in Marriage*. New York: Macmillan.

Weedon, Chris (1987) *Feminist Practice and Poststructuralist Theory*. Oxford: Basil Blackwell.

Nicola GAVEY is based in the Department of Psychology, University of Auckland, Private Bag 92019, Auckland, New Zealand.

S.P. SCHACHT and Patricia H. ATCHISON

Heterosexual Instrumentalism: Past and Future Directions

Two distinct strands of feminist thought have emerged in the past 20 years in explaining the behaviors of rape, sexual harassment, incest, prostitution and the presentation of these found in pornography. One group of theorists construes these behaviors and pornography as violent and terroristic outcomes of male dominance, while a second group views them simply as forms of heterosexuality. Utilizing, primarily, the theoretical insights of the latter group, this article offers a conceptual definition of heterosexuality — as an eroticized, hegemonic ideology of male dominance. The literature on the above behaviors and pornography is reviewed to determine if there is support for such a conceptualization. Finding support, suggestions are made for future research and the need for a unified feminist theory of sexuality.

Feminist literature on the behaviors of rape, sexual harassment, incest, prostitution and the presentations of these found in pornography[1] has become quintessential in explaining male dominance (Millett, 1970; Brownmiller, 1975; Herman and Hirschman, 1977; Daly, 1978; Barry, 1979; Dworkin, 1979, 1987; Rich, 1980; Shulman, 1980; Herman, 1981; Bart 1983a; MacKinnon, 1979, 1982, 1983; Russell, 1975, 1982, 1984; Jeffreys, 1985; Sheffield, 1987; Glass, 1988; Kelly, 1988; Smith, 1989). While there is general agreement among these feminists about the importance of understanding these behaviors in terms of explaining pre-existing gender inequalities, epistemologically speaking, there is also widespread disagreement about their origin. The disagreement over cause can be conceptualized into two dichotomous groups of theorists: one group views these behaviors as a product of male dominance, while a second group views these behaviors as part of the larger social practice called heterosexuality.

The first group of feminists conceptualize the behaviors of prostitution, sexual harassment, rape, incest and pornographic depictions in terms such as sexual terrorism (Sheffield, 1987) and sexual violence (Brownmiller, 1975;

Hanmer and Maynard, 1987; Kelly, 1988) and conclude that only when male dominance ends will these aberrant behaviors and pornography disappear (Herman and Hirschman, 1977: 756; Russell[2] and Lederer, 1980: 29). Assuredly, rape, sexual harassment, incest, prostitution and pornography are terroristic and violent; however, these are the most extreme and blatant forms of heterosexual behavior. Further, from this perspective one is often led to believe that these behaviors have nothing to do with sex, let alone hetero-sexuality. By primarily focusing on these five blatant forms as outcomes and mechanisms of male dominance these authors have perhaps limited themselves from gaining a full understanding of heterosexuality. Perhaps this explains why these and numerous other authors with this perspective treat other forms of heterosexuality as irrelevant or as residual categories.

In an attempt to deal with this conceptual problem, another group of feminists has extended its analysis to consider how heterosexuality in general is practiced as a form of male dominance (Millett, 1970; Dworkin, 1979; Rich, 1980; Russell, 1975, 1982, 1984; Bart, 1983a; MacKinnon, 1979, 1982, 1983). Catharine MacKinnon, perhaps the foremost spokeswoman of this group, in numerous sources (MacKinnon, 1979, 1982, 1983, 1987, 1989) has consistently posited that one must look at heterosexuality in total to understand its true meaning: a socially constructed form of power. Since sex is something men do to women, or as she more adamantly states (MacKin-non, 1982: 541), 'man fucks woman', through sexual relations — the inter-personal level — men dominate and control women. As such, sexual acts that involve coercion, violence and even consent are all viewed as falling under a dynamic of male dominance and female subordination (MacKinnon, 1983: 650). At the interpersonal level, 'sexuality does not have a gender; it creates gender' (Stoltenberg, 1990: 33); and the gender scripts found in hetero-sexuality prescribe male dominance and female subordination. In turn, heterosexuality provides the underpinnings of a system where women are controlled in all settings.

This broadened perspective also has important practical implications for the women's movement. Unlike the first group of feminist authors, which predicts that behaviors such as rape and sexual harassment will end only once male dominance disappears, this second perspective points to just the opposite: only once heterosexuality as an ideological practice ends will male dominance disappear. In other words, heterosexuality is the foundation of the social structure of male dominance, and successfully attacking it could bring down the whole house.

In short, the first group of authors fails to recognize that a high proportion of sexual relations occur in consenting situations that lead to the same out-come, male dominance (Brownmiller, 1975; Sheffield, 1987; Hanmer and Maynard, 1987; Kelly, 1988). Although the second group of feminist theorists (Millett, 1970; Russell, 1975, 1982, 1984; Dworkin, 1979; Rich, 1980; Bart, 1984; MacKinnon, 1979, 1982, 1983) has extended its analysis to include consenting acts, neither group has developed a unified, definitive conceptualization of heterosexuality, nor carried its discussions much beyond the already noted blatant forms.[3] In this article, we offer a straightforward, clear conceptual definition of what heterosexuality is — an eroticized, hegemonic ideology of male dominance.

HETEROSEXUAL INSTRUMENTALISM

In an attempt to clarify the dichotomy above, and to provide a useful conceptualization of heterosexuality as an instrumental ideology of male dominance, we offer the following conceptual definition.

Heterosexual instrumentalism refers to the behaviors which reflect and sustain the expectation that all heterosexuality is to be practiced with explicit requirements of dominance and subordination. The immediate goal is the exertion of power and control by the dominant actor over the subordinate actor: accomplished by force, coercion or consent (implied or otherwise). The ultimate goal of such behavior is the maintenance of pre-existing gender inequalities.

The expectation in this context is indicated not only by actual sexual behaviors, but also by depictions and suggestions of sexuality consistent with such a goal. The most obvious examples are pornography and other cultural depictions on television, in magazines and throughout society, which give explicit, eroticized societal support for the control of women through heterosexuality. Further, not only are coercive and violent acts of heterosexuality means to the continuing subordination of women, but *all* sexual acts that entail male dominance and female subordination fulfill this function.

We wish to add two provisos to this conceptual definition. First, some sexual relations between women and men are egalitarian in manner; thus, they would not be seen as forms of heterosexual instrumentalism. Second, some of the sexual behaviors found in lesbian and gay relationships are quite consistent with this definition; this is exceedingly evident in lesbian/gay sadomasochistic relationships and the supporting pornographic propaganda (Linden et al., 1982; Jeffreys, 1990). We would hold that these are indirectly supporting heterosexual instrumentalism. For as Robin Morgan has concluded:

> . . . through no fault of its own, the homosexual subculture often finds itself mirroring the dominant culture (patriarchally heterosexual), with the very standards which oppressed that homosexual subculture in the first place now being adopted by it (Morgan, 1982: 116).

Our definition of heterosexual instrumentalism is posited as quite consistent with *both* the first and, the inclusion of consent notwithstanding, the second mentioned groups of feminist writings on heterosexual dominance. This assertion is now tested.

A CATECHIZATION OF EXISTING LITERATURE

Rape

In the past 20 years the topic of rape has received a great deal of attention from both feminist and non-feminist researchers. Beginning, perhaps, with Susan Griffin's (1971) classic article, 'Rape: The All-American Crime', feminists began to question many of the myths that surround the 'crime' of rape. Some of the most vociferous of these myths are that rape is a relatively rare crime, committed by strangers who are typically psychologically sick individuals, and once a rape has occurred, societal response is swift — supportive of the raped women and punitive toward the assailant. Each of these myths is now addressed in turn.

Since the vast majority of all rapes go unreported, to date there are only two legitimated estimates of rape rates in the USA (Johnson, 1980; Russell and Howell, 1983). Using the limited Uniform Crime Reports data and the National Crime Survey (which both admit to underestimating true rates of rape), Johnson (1980) estimates that girls currently age 12 in the USA have a 20–30 percent chance of suffering from a violent sexual attack. Russell and Howell (1983) found this rate to be much higher. They found, using a representative sample in San Francisco, that a woman has a 46 percent chance of experiencing an attempted rape and a 26 percent chance of suffering a completed rape within her lifetime.

Regardless of whose estimates are used, a clear picture emerges: a very significant minority of women in the USA will experience an attempted rape, which has a better than 50 percent chance of being completed. Also noteworthy is the fact that neither of these estimates considers cases where a woman is raped by more than one man or more than once within her lifetime. In sum, rape is a relatively common experience for women in the USA.

Just the opposite is found when addressing the myth of rape as a crime committed by strangers. Overwhelmingly, the majority of rapes are committed by someone the woman knows and typically has been or is currently intimately involved with: i.e. date and marital rape (Kanin, 1957, 1967; Kirkpatrick and Kanin, 1957; Gelles, 1977; Makepeace, 1981; Russell, 1982, 1984; Frieze, 1983; Finkelhor and Yllo, 1985; Lane and Gwartney-Gibbs, 1985; Warsaw, 1988). Russell (1982) found that only 16 percent of the women's assailants were strangers in attempted or completed rapes. Of completed rapes, 6 percent were committed by strangers, when multiple rape experiences were considered.

Pauline Bart (1983a: 53) has asserted, 'to label rapists "sick" is inaccurate unless one is willing to say a substantial percentage [if not majority] of the male population is "sick"'. This is especially true considering the prevalence of rape, general attitudes that situationally support rape (Burt, 1980), and that a significant minority (35 percent) of males indicate some likelihood of raping — a rape proclivity (Malamuth, 1981). Also, convicted rapists consistently do not view forced sexual relations as a crime, and psychological studies fail to differentiate rapists from the rest of the male population (Scully and Marolla, 1985; Scully, 1988). A profile of the typical or potential rapist is not that of the psychopath or criminal but, rather, the 'normal' male.

Institutional reactions to rape generally reflect what has been presented thus far. Should a raped woman decide to report the offense — most do not — she will come in contact with the police. If she is persistent enough to convince the police that the rape is a criminal matter, she may also come in contact with hospital personnel and the courts. Typical treatment of all three is quite consistent: indifference, suspicion and indignation toward the raped woman (Griffin, 1971; Brownmiller, 1975; Bohmer, 1977; Clark and Lewis, 1977; Holmstrom and Burgess, 1978; Gordon and Riger, 1989). Although changes in rape laws, increasing numbers of female officers and doctors and rape crisis centers have made inroads in dealing with these problems, the majority of raped women still find little if any institutional support to pursue charges of rape against men (Rose, 1977; Dworkin, 1988; LeGrand, 1977; Gordon and Riger, 1989). On the contrary, implicit, and sometimes explicit, support is given to the rapist and his behavior.

In total, rape personifies heterosexual instrumentalism. Often practiced, this act of sexuality carries explicit requirements of dominance and subordination. Further, as Scully and Marolla (1985) have reported, rape allows the immediate exertion of power — often reported as a reward — over the submissive actor. Rape is obviously accomplished by force, coercion or implied consent (e.g. marital rape, still legal in some states in the USA or in date rape; or 'she said no, but her eyes said yes'). Finally, concerning the maintenance of pre-existing inequalities, rape definitely has this effect if one considers the constant fear with which most women live and the corresponding limits on the behaviors they exhibit (Griffin, 1971; Brownmiller, 1975; Riger and Gordon, 1981; Schepple and Bart, 1983; Herman, 1984; Warr, 1985).

Prostitution

If one uses the simplest definition of prostitution, the sale of sexual acts (Cooper, 1989) — which includes a great deal of sex found in dating and marriage — then an overwhelming majority of women experience prostituted sexuality. The contexts of dating and marriage notwithstanding, MacKinnon (1987: 52) estimates that 12 percent of all women in the United States are or have been prostitutes.

Cooper (1989), a liberal feminist, posits that the majority of women who are prostitutes sell sex out of economic choice. Such a position logically holds women accountable for their own plight — they freely chose to be prostitutes. Antithetical to this position is that put forth by Barry (1979), who holds that most women are procured, forced or manipulated into prostitution by males (Barry, 1979). Regardless of whether the woman is coerced by economic considerations (the general lack of employment opportunities for women, especially those without job skills, i.e. young women and divorced housewives) or by a man, prostitution is a form of forced sexuality. Although the violence and explicit coercion found in rape may also accompany prostitution, they need not — since money serves the same function of ensuring heterosexuality. In a sense, money creates a situation of implied consent. In exchange for money, a woman literally submits to the control of a man through sexuality.

Interestingly, the 'reward' women who adhere to heterosexual instrumentalism in the form of prostitution receive is explicit societal hatred (Millett, 1970; Barry, 1979). Perhaps this is due to the myth of women freely choosing to be prostitutes — a plight a 'good' woman would surely *never* choose. More likely, prostitution is indicative of general societal misogyny toward all women; by definition, expressed by heterosexuality.[4]

Prostitution is also representative of heterosexual instrumentalism. Money creates a situation where consenting actors willingly enter a sexual relationship. Of course, this is a male scenario, since female actors are often neither willing nor consenting but forced to profess such consent. Money allows the male customer to fulfill the immediate goal of heterosexuality: the exertion of power and control over a subordinate actor. Further, through the ideology of heterosexuality, prostitution not only allows males to control and dominate a given woman, but also to control other males' sexual access to her. In other words, the essential act of heterosexuality allows the scenario to be carried one step further, in allowing males economically to exploit women also. Through pimps, the monetary exchange and the act itself, prostitution provides another mechanism where pre-existing inequalities are maintained.

Sexual Harassment

Like rape, this form of heterosexuality has recently received increasing attention (Farley, 1978; MacKinnon, 1979; Gutek and Morasch, 1982; Maypole and Skaine, 1982; Martin, 1984; Benson and Thompson, 1982; Russell, 1984; Glass, 1988). Also like rape, sexual harassment has been found to be quite prevalent (estimates in the USA vary between 23 and 53 percent of working women), with institutional responses ranging from non-existent to tacitly supporting its occurrence (Weeks et al., 1986; Maypole and Skaine, 1983).

An early definition by Lyn Farley (1978: 14–15) is representative of most researchers' conceptualization of sexual harassment:

> [It] is best described as unsolicited nonreciprocal male behavior that asserts a woman's sex role over her function as a worker . . . an act of aggression at any stage of its expression, and in all its forms it contributes to the ultimate goal of keeping women subordinate at work.

This emphasis focuses on structural mechanisms — sexual harassment being one — and how they operate. Benson and Thompson (1982) have shown how sexual harassment operates similarly in the university. Sexual harassment at college or work is an instrument by which males erode and control females' career aspirations — especially in traditionally male-dominated areas — and ultimately ensure that women remain subordinate to men (and more easily exploited).

The importance of all of these studies is their explicit recognition of how sexuality is used to control and keep women subordinate. Unfortunately, the emphasis is narrowly restricted to economic settings. Sexual harassment assuredly does occur in these settings, but it also occurs in numerous other — and perhaps all — settings in which interaction between the sexes takes place. The explicit goal in all these settings is the same: the dominance of women through heterosexuality. As such, sexual harassment is much more prevalent than these studies of economic settings indicate.

Recognizing this, Becky Glass (1988) compared sexual harassment in the workplace and other settings, and found them very similar. She concludes (Glass, 1988: 55) that sexual harassment is indicative of 'normal' male–female relationships in society, not just economic, workplace relationships. This is very consistent with the broader definitions of sexual harassment proposed by Catharine MacKinnon (1979: 1): '[it] refers to the unwanted impositions of sexual requirements in the context of a relationship of unequal power'; and by Sue Wise and Liz Stanley (1987: 15): 'processes of social control enacted by men over women in which the totality of our lives are available to being policed by them'. Such 'requirements' and 'policing' both ensure, and are indicative of, unequal power.

Sexual harassment also exemplifies heterosexual instrumentalism. Whether at work, or in other non-economic settings, the purpose of the unwanted sexual advances is explicit: they serve as the means by which the roles of dominance and subordination are played out. If consummated, the initiator is able to exert control and dominance over an actor made submissive, through force; coercion ('want to keep your job?'); or implied consent ('I am your boss' or 'good girls do not belong in the bar alone'). Of course, this leads to the ultimate goal of the maintenance of pre-existing gender inequalities. Further, like attempted rape, the unconsummated act typically serves the same end: women often quit their jobs or refuse to enter any situations where they might expect sexual harassment (Schepple and Bart, 1983).

Incest

In an early article, Herman and Hirschman (1977: 740) argue that since the incest 'taboo is created and enforced by men, . . . it may also be more easily and frequently violated by men'. Supporting their assertion, numerous studies have found the perpetrators to be almost entirely male, typically fathers, step-fathers or brothers, while victims are overwhelmingly female (Herman and Hirschman, 1977; Herman, 1981; Russell, 1984; Parker and Parker, 1986). Sixteen percent of Russell's (1984) sample reported having experienced incestuous abuse and 38 percent had experienced at least one sexually abusive incident with an adult before reaching the age of 18. Considering the typically secretive and underreported nature of the act, combined with the general lack of an institutional response (when one *is* forthcoming it is generally punitive toward the victim), it is questionable if the taboo is but rarely enforced (Herman and Hirschman, 1977; Herman, 1981; Parker and Parker, 1986). As such, incest is very similar to the heterosexual behaviors discussed so far: fairly widespread; committed almost entirely by males against females; and with corresponding implicit societal tolerance.

As an obvious form of heterosexual instrumentalism, those forced into incestuous relations play out definite roles of dominance and subordination. Specifically, fathers or other adult male figures in the family are dominant actors to begin with, and through incest they are merely exercising and strengthening — or, in our view, blatantly abusing — their authority. In a sense, the girl/young woman who finds herself in an incestuous situation becomes a seemingly willing participant, because of the pre-existing family structure which gives implied consent that a male may exert his authority in such a manner (Herman and Hirschman, 1977). At this extreme, whether by means of rape, prostitution, sexual harassment or incest, if control through heterosexuality is regarded as a male birthright, then all of these acts involve implied consent. We would hold that most males, and the institutions they control, indeed view such behaviors in this way — unless it is a case of 'their women' being violated by other males (Scully, 1988).

The reason for this is also readily understood: incest, like all the previously discussed behaviors, serves the ultimate goal of maintaining pre-existing in-equalities. For many women it is the earliest and most powerful experience of behaviors to this end. As asserted by Herman and Hirschman (1977: 748), 'it is a betrayal [by someone] she is dependent on for protection and care'. Lover rape is often seen as very similar. Women report that the effects persist long after the incestuous acts have occurred. Young girls are taught to guard against sexual invitations from strangers. This also gives all girls a preliminary indication of what the meaning of heterosexuality is: a potential enemy that will control them for the rest of their lives. Conversely, while fathers and other trusted loved ones are supposed to protect them against such attacks, they are not supposed to partake in such behaviors lest they, too,

prove to be the enemy. The message all victims of incest receive is painstakingly clear: betrayed and rendered powerless, you can expect similar treatment by all males, for the rest of your life. Victims of incest just experience
the meaning and power of heterosexual instrumentalism a little earlier than
most.

Pornography

Robin Morgan's (1980) classic statement that 'pornography is the theory, and
rape the practice' perhaps best represents the powerful meaning of pornography. We would add to rape the practices of incest, sexual harassment,
prostitution and heterosexuality in general. Further, the production of
pornography prostitutes the bodies of countless women and children who
serve as the 'models' for this male propaganda (Lederer, 1980a; Rush,
1980).

Pornography, from the male perspective, is heterosexuality, and based on
the ideology of male dominance. Similarly, Andrea Dworkin (1979: 174)
posits that 'The major theme of pornography is male power, its nature, its
magnitude, its use, its meaning'. In numerous publications (whether soft or
hard porn) the image is the same: women are depicted literarily or pictorially
over and over in positions of submissiveness and subordination (Diamond,
1980; Griffin, 1981; Kittay, 1983; Pratt, 1986). Hard-core pornographic
themes shamelessly legitimate rape, other humiliating forms of degradation,
mutilation, child pornography and killing (snuff films) and the corresponding
extreme meanings — sadism and misogyny (Diamond, 1980; Dworkin, 1981;
Griffin, 1981; Bart, 1985). Barry (1979: 175) summarizes this focus by
stating that '[T]he most prevalent theme in pornography is one of utter contempt for women . . . women are raped, ejaculated on, urinated on, anally
penetrated, beaten, and, with the advent of snuff films, murdered in an orgy
of sexual pleasure'.

Without question, a great deal of pornography does assume the form of institutionalized women-hating (Dworkin, 1979, 1987). However, less blatant,
soft porn gives an equally powerful and disturbing message: women are to
be men's sexual subordinates and objects for their pleasure (Bat-Ada, 1980;
Lederer, 1980b; Steinem, 1980; Pratt, 1986). Although soft-porn images may
not overtly carry messages of sadism or degradation, these messages are still
implicitly present; and a message of eroticized dominance of women is still
clearly presented.

Pornography blurs all forms of heterosexuality into manuals of male
dominance. Pornography is the propaganda of male dominance (LaBelle,
1980), and not only 'widens the range of behavior considered acceptable
from men in heterosexual intercourse' (Rich, 1980: 641), but further
legitimates it as a mechanism of social control. The purview of pornography
is clear: images of what heterosexuality is and how it should continue —

male oppression and dominance carried out by force, coercion or consent where men are immediately and ultimately the most powerful. Correspondingly, women are portrayed as liking it, wanting it, pleading for it and ultimately satisfied by it (Bart, 1983b: 10). In the end, as Stoltenberg (1989: 121) states, 'Pornography tells lies about women. But pornography tells the truth about men'.

HETEROSEXUAL INSTRUMENTALISM: FUTURE DIRECTIONS

Strong support has been found for the proposed conceptualization of heterosexual instrumentalism. All four behaviors discussed do have expectations of dominance and subordination for those who willingly or unwillingly enter such relations. All of these behaviors have the immediate goal of exercising power and control, accomplished through force, coercion and consent. Pornography reflects and supports these ideological practices. All combine to fulfill the ultimate goal: the maintenance of pre-existing gender inequalities.

Our discussion of heterosexual instrumentalism has important implications for future feminist research and activism. Further, a range of other behaviors and cultural images must be explored in order to reach a full understanding of heterosexuality, and to counter and overcome it as an instrument of dominance. Such behaviors and images include: the obscene telephone call, obscene comments in public places, the peeping Tom, the flasher (all non-economic forms of sexual harassment), 'normal' heterosexual relations and pornographic presentations found in live entertainment. Examples of the latter include strip joints, topless/bottomless bars, wet T-shirt contests, jello and mud wrestling and peep shows. This list is far from exhaustive.

Although the obscene telephone call has received some research attention (Murray, 1967; Murray and Beran, 1968; Nadler, 1968; Russell, 1971; Sadoff, 1972), only a few feminist researchers have considered it as a secondary form of sexual harassment (Stanley and Wise, 1979; Warr, 1985; Glass, 1988; Kelly, 1988), and only two have investigated it as a primary form (Warner, 1988; Sheffield, 1990). Although both excellent starting points, the Warner study is almost entirely without a theoretical base, and Sheffield wrongly construes the obscene call entirely as a form of sexual violence. What is needed is an explicit investigation of how the obscene call — a form of heterosexuality — works as a mechanism of male dominance.

Another topic that has received little research attention is obscene comments in public places, although Bernard and Schlaffer (1989) consider why males sexually harass in public places; and Kelly (1988) explores the effects of sexual harassment in public places as part of a larger study on sexual violence. However, to date, we are unaware of any studies that specifically investigate the effects of such behavior on women and their daily activities. Possible appropriate settings for such an investigation could be bars, sporting events or jogging routes. In all of these settings, women are expected to have male escorts: what are the implications of not having a male escort, and how do women behave when entering these settings alone?

Feminist research is also lacking on both the peeping Tom (we found no studies) and the flasher (we found only two: Kelly, 1988; McNeill, 1987). Considering the sexual themes that underlie each of these behaviors, and the strong impact on those who experience these behaviors, this is quite surprising. In addition, we could find no feminist literature that investigates the pornographic presentations found in live entertainment.

Although a few feminist authors have discussed 'normal' heterosexuality (Millett, 1970; Russell, 1975; Dworkin, 1979, 1987; Rich, 1980; Bart, 1983a; MacKinnon, 1979, 1982, 1983), we are unaware of any studies that investigate the meaning of heterosexuality as it is widely accepted. That is, what is needed is a study of traditional heterosexual relations found in 'happily' married or dating couples, free of violent or coercive sex. The issue of how much sexuality is actually consensual vs 'altruistic' or 'compliant' (Bart, 1983a) could be explored. Similarly, the meaning of dominance and subordination could be addressed (i.e. is most consensual sexuality actually practiced in this manner?). The ultimate question is: Is consensual sexuality which entails male dominance and female subordination a form of social control? Obviously, we and others believe it to be so, and have presented evidence for this position.

TOWARD A UNIFIED FEMINIST THEORY OF SEXUALITY

The need for a unified feminist theory of sexuality is clear. If one concludes, as many feminists have, that heterosexuality is the primary and most powerful mechanism of social control, then understanding its meaning in all forms is imperative if male dominance is ever to be overcome. By focusing almost exclusively on the five most blatant, as most feminists have to date, neglects heterosexuality's power in numerous other contexts. This is especially true if one considers the overwhelming combined prevalence of these additional suggested areas in combination with the widespread societal acceptance that some of the forms receive (such as wet T-shirt contests or strip joints).

Heterosexual instrumentalism, like any ideology, must be flexible to survive. To attack one of its practices will mean it will deflect itself into others. In the 1960s when males' so-called birthright of sexual dominance in marriage came under scrutiny and was challenged, males countered by mass-producing pornographic magazines to reinforce what now was being questioned (Pratt, 1986). To make the images even more powerful, the act of heterosexuality was reinforced by presenting coercive and violent behavior as also acceptable (Lederer, 1980a). All of this is not to say pornography did not exist prior to the 1960s (de Sade is a frightening example), for it assuredly did. The point is that if one aspect comes under attack, heterosexuality compensates by expanding into other areas.

Heterosexual instrumentalism practiced at the interpersonal level allows men to dominate and control women, which, in turn, provides the underpinnings of a system where women are controlled in all settings. As previously noted, some feminists such as Herman and Hirschman (1977: 756) and Russell and Lederer (1980: 29) have posited that behaviors such as prostitution, rape and incest will only disappear when male dominance is ended. We have suggested just the opposite in this article; only when rape, prostitution, incest and all the other behaviors and images of heterosexual instrumentalism are eliminated will male dominance disappear.

ACKNOWLEDGEMENTS

We would like to thank Susan Schatzman, Sue Wilkinson and the three anonymous reviewers for *Feminism & Psychology* for the helpful comments and suggestions on earlier drafts of this article.

NOTES

1. We have purposely not included genital mutilation or women's access to birth control. These are not actual sexual acts, but rather are outcomes of heterosexuality — parts of women's physiology typically controlled by males. Also, we have not included sex murders or battering of women for similar reasons: i.e. they are behavioral outcomes of heterosexuality.
2. In all fairness, Diana Russell in other publications (i.e. Russell, 1975, 1982, 1984) takes a stance more aligned with the second set of theorists. As such, she has been cited here, but perhaps more accurately belongs to the second group.
3. All of this is not to say that either of these groups of feminists was wrong or misguided by first focusing upon these five blatant forms: most analysis starts with the obvious and then moves on to the more subtle.
4. Taking this conclusion to the extreme, this sort of logic is demonstrated in cases of serial murders, such as 'Jack the Ripper' and 'The Yorkshire Ripper', where the rationalization of these aberrant crimes is that the victims were prostitutes (Caputi, 1987; Cameron and Frazer, 1987). Then again, as Joan Smith (1989: 185) notes in her discussion of Peter Sutcliffe: 'he told the police he had wanted to kill prostitutes — not that he was seeking out women who sold sex for a living, but that he knew all his victims to be prostitutes simply because they were women' — thus explaining why several of his victims were not prostitutes.

REFERENCES

Barry, K. (1979) *Female Sexual Slavery*. Englewood Cliffs, NJ: Prentice Hall.
Bart, P.B. (1983a) 'Why Men Rape', *Western Sociological Review* 18: 46–57.
Bart, P.B. (1983b) 'Women of the Right: Trading for Safety, Rules & Love', *New Women's Times Feminist Review* 30: 1–11.

Bat-Ada, J. (1980) 'Playboy Isn't Playing', in L. Lederer (ed.) *Take Back the Night: Women and Pornography*, pp. 121–33. New York: William Morrow.

Benson, D.J. and Thomson, G.E. (1982) 'Sexual Harassment on a University Campus: The Confluence of Authority Relations, Sexual Interest and Gender Stratification', *Social Problems* 29: 236–51.

Bernard, C. and Schlaffer, E. (1989) ' "The Man in the Street": Why He Harasses', in L. Richardson and V. Taylor (eds) *Feminist Frontiers II: Rethinking Sex, Gender, and Society*, pp. 384–7. New York: Random House.

Bohmer, C. (1977) 'Judicial Attitudes Toward Rape Victims', in D. Chappell, R. Geis, and G. Geis (eds) *Forcible Rape: The Crime, the Victim, the Offender*, pp. 161–9. New York: Columbia University Press.

Brownmiller, S. (1975) *Against Our Will: Men, Women and Rape*. New York: Bantam Books.

Burt, M.R. (1980) 'Cultural Myths and Supports for Rape', *Journal of Personality and Social Psychology* 38: 217–30.

Cameron, D. and Frazer, E. (1987) *The Lust to Kill: A Feminist Investigation of Sexual Murder*. New York: New York University Press.

Caputi, J. (1987) *The Age of Sex Crime*. Bowling Green, OH: Bowling Green State Popular Press.

Clark, L.M.G. and Lewis, D.J. (1977) *Rape: the Price of Coercive Sexuality*. Toronto: The Women's Press.

Cooper, B. (1989) 'Prostitution: A Feminist Analysis', *Women's Rights Law Reporter* 11: 99–119.

Daly, M. (1978) *Gyn/Ecology: The Metaethics of Radical Feminism*. Boston, MA: Beacon Press.

Diamond, I. (1980) 'Pornography and Repression: A Reconsideration of "Who" and "What"', in L. Lederer (ed.) *Take Back the Night: Women on Pornography*, pp. 187–203. New York: William Morrow.

Dworkin, A. (1979) *Pornography: Men Possessing Women*. New York: Pedigree [E.P. Dutton, 1989].

Dworkin, A. (1987) *Intercourse*. New York: The Free Press.

Farley, L. (1978) *Sexual Shakedown: The Sexual Harassment of Women on the Job*. New York: McGraw-Hill.

Finkelhor, D. and Yllo, K. (1985) *License to Rape: Sexual Abuse of Wives*. New York: Holt, Rinehart and Winston.

Frieze, I.H. (1983) 'Investigating the Causes and Consequences of Marital Rape', *Signs: Journal of Women in Culture and Society* 8: 532–53.

Gelles, R. (1977) 'Power, Sex, and Violence: The Case of Marital Rape', *Family Coordinator* 26: 339–47.

Glass, B.L. (1988) 'Workplace Harassment and the Victimization of Women', *Women's Studies International Forum* 11: 55–67.

Gordon, M.T. and Riger, S. (1989) *The Female Fear*. New York: The Free Press.

Griffin, S. (1971) 'Rape: The All-American Crime', *Ramparts* 10: 26–35.

Griffin, S. (1981) *Pornography and Silence: Culture's Revenge Against Nature*. New York: Harper Colophon Books.

Gutek, B.A. and Morasch, B. (1982) 'Sex Ratios, Sex Role Spillover, and Sexual Harassment of Women at Work', *Journal of Social Issues* 38: 55–74.

Hanmer, J. and Maynard, M., eds (1987) *Women, Violence and Social Control*. Atlantic

Highlands, NJ: Humanities Press International.

Herman, D. (1984) 'The Rape Culture', in J. Freeman (ed.) *Women: A Feminist Perspective*, pp. 20–38. Palo Alto, CA: Mayfield.

Herman, J. (1981) *Father–Daughter Incest*. Cambridge, MA: Harvard University Press.

Herman, J. and Hirschman, L. (1977) 'Father–Daughter Incest', *Signs: Journal of Women in Culture and Society* 2: 735–56.

Holmstrom, L.L. and Burgess, A.W. (1978) *The Victim of Rape: Institutional Reactions*. New York: Wiley.

Jeffreys, S. (1985) *The Spinster and Her Enemies: Feminism and Sexuality 1880–1930*. London: Pandora Press.

Jeffreys, S. (1990) *Anticlimax*. London: The Women's Press.

Johnson, A.G. (1980) 'On the Prevalence of Rape in the United States', *Signs: Journal of Women in Culture and Society* 6: 136–46.

Kanin, E.J. (1957) 'Male Aggression in Dating–Courtship Relations', *American Journal of Sociology* 63: 197–204.

Kanin, E.J. (1967) 'An Examination of Sexual Aggression as a Response to Sexual Frustration', *Journal of Marriage and the Family* 29: 428–33.

Kelly, L. (1988) *Surviving Sexual Violence*. Minneapolis: University of Minnesota Press.

Kirkpatrick, C. and Kanin, E. (1957) 'Male Aggression on a University Campus', *American Sociological Review* 22: 52–8.

Kittay, E.F. (1983) 'Pornography and the Erotics of Domination', in C.C. Gould (ed.) *Beyond Domination: New Perspectives on Women and Philosophy*, pp. 145–74. NJ: Rowman and Allanheld.

LaBelle, B. (1980) 'The Propaganda of Misogyny', in L. Lederer (ed.) *Take Back the Night: Women on Pornography*, pp. 174–8. New York: William Morrow.

Lane, K.E. and Gwartney-Gibbs, P.A. (1985) 'Violence in the Context of Dating and Sex', *Journal of Family Issues* 6: 45–59.

Lederer, L. (1980a) 'An Interview with a Former Pornographic Model', in L. Lederer (ed.) *Take Back the Night: Women on Pornography*, pp. 57–70. New York: William Morrow.

Lederer, L. (1980b) *Take Back the Night: Women on Pornography*. New York: William Morrow.

LeGrand, C.E. (1977) 'Rape and Rape Laws: Sexism in Society and Law', in D. Chappell, R. Geis and G. Geis (eds) *Forcible Rape: The Crime, The Victim, the Offender*, pp. 67–86. New York: Columbia University Press.

Linden, R.L., Pagano, D.R., Russell, D.E.H. and Star, S. (1982) *Against Sadomasochism: A Radical Feminist Analysis*. East Palo Alto, CA: Frog in the Well.

MacKinnon, C.A. (1979) *Sexual Harassment of Working Women: A Case of Sex Discrimination*. London: Yale University Press.

MacKinnon, C.A. (1982) 'Feminism, Marxism, Method, and the State: An Agenda for Theory', *Signs: Journal of Women in Culture and Society* 7: 515–44.

MacKinnon, C.A. (1983) 'Feminism, Marxism, Method, and the State: Toward Feminist Jurisprudence', *Signs: Journal of Women in Culture and Society* 8: 635–58.

MacKinnon, C.A. (1987) *Feminism Unmodified: Discourses on Life and Law*. Cambridge, MA: Harvard University Press.

MacKinnon, C.A. (1989) *Toward a Feminist Theory of the State*. Cambridge, MA: Harvard University Press.

McNeill, S. (1987) 'Flashing: Its Effect on Women', in J. Hanmer and M. Maynard (eds) *Women, Violence and Social Control*, pp. 93–109. Atlantic Highlands, NJ: Humanities Press International.

Makepeace, J.M. (1981) 'Courtship Violence Among College Students', *Family Relations* 30: 97–102.

Malamuth, N.M. (1981) 'Rape Proclivity Among Males', *Journal of Social Issues* 37: 138–57.

Martin, S.E. (1984) 'Sexual Harassment: The Link between Gender Stratification, Sexuality, and Women's Economic Status', in J. Freeman (ed.) *Women: A Feminist Perspective*, pp. 54–69. Palo Alto, CA: Mayfield.

Maypole, D.E. and Skaine, R. (1982) 'Sexual Harassment of Blue Collar Workers', *Journal of Sociology and Social Welfare* 9: 682–95.

Maypole, D.E. and Skaine, R. (1983) 'Sexual Harassment in the Workplace', *Social Work* 28: 385–90.

Millett, K. (1970) *Sexual Politics*. New York: Doubleday.

Morgan, R. (1980) 'Theory and Practice: Pornography and Rape', in L. Lederer (ed.) *Take Back the Night: Women on Pornography*, pp. 134–40. New York: William Morrow.

Morgan, R. (1982) 'The Politics of Sado-Masochistic Fantasies', in R.L. Linden, D.R. Pagano, D.E.H. Russell and S. Star (eds) *Against Sadomasochism: A Radical Feminist Analysis*, pp. 109–23. East Palo Alto, CA: Frog in the Well.

Murray, F.S. (1967) 'A Preliminary Investigation of Anonymous Nuisance Telephone Calls to Females', *The Psychological Record* 17: 395–400.

Murray, F.S. and Beran, L.C. (1968) 'A Survey of Nuisance Calls Received by Males and Females', *The Psychological Record* 18: 107–9.

Nadler, R.P. (1968) 'Approach to Psychodynamics of Obscene Telephone Calls', *New York State Journal of Medicine* 68: 521–6.

Parker, H. and Parker, S. (1986) 'Father–Daughter Sexual Abuse: An Emerging Perspective', *American Journal of Orthopsychiatry* 56: 531–49.

Pratt, J. (1986) 'Pornography and Everyday Life', *Theory Culture & Society* 3: 65–78.

Rich, A. (1980) 'Compulsory Heterosexuality and Lesbian Existence', *Signs* 5(4): 631–60.

Riger, S. and Gordon, M.T. (1981) 'The Fear of Rape: A Study in Social Control', *Journal of Social Issues* 37: 71–92

Rose, V.M. (1977) 'Rape as a Social Movement: A Byproduct of the Feminist Movement', *Social Problems* 25: 75–89.

Rush, F. (1980) 'Child Pornography', in L. Lederer (ed.) *Take Back the Night: Women on Pornography*, pp. 71–81. New York: William Morrow.

Russell, D.E.H. (1975) *The Politics of Rape*. New York: Stein and Day.

Russell, D.E.H. (1982) *Rape in Marriage*. New York: MacMillan.

Russell, D.E.H. (1984) *Sexual Exploitation: Rape, Child Sexual Abuse, and Workplace Harassment*. Beverly Hills, CA: Sage.

Russell, D.E.H. and Howell, N. (1983) 'The Prevalence of Rape in the United States Revisited', *Signs: Journal of Women in Culture and Society* 8: 688–95.

Russell, D.E.H. and Lederer, L. (1980) 'Questions We Get Asked Most Often', in L. Lederer (ed.) *Take Back the Night: Women on Pornography*, pp. 23–9. New York: William Morrow.

Russell, D.H. (1971) 'Obscene Telephone Callers and Their Victims', *Sexual Behavior* 1: 80–6.

Sadoff, R.L. (1972) 'Anonymous Sexual Offenders', *Medical Aspects of Human Sexuality* 6: 118–23.

Schepple, K.L. and Bart, P.B. (1983) 'Through Women's Eyes: Defining Danger in the Wake of Sexual Assault', *Journal of Social Issues* 39: 63–81.

Scully, D. (1988) 'Convicted Rapists' Perceptions of Self and Victim: Role Taking and Emotions', *Gender & Society* 2: 200–13.

Scully, D. and Marolla, J. (1985) '"Riding the Bull at Gilley's": Convicted Rapists Describe Rewards of Rape', *Social Problems* 32: 251–63.

Sheffield, C.J. (1987) 'Sexual Terrorism: The Social Control of Women', in B.B. Hess and M.M. Ferree (eds) *Analyzing Gender: A Handbook of Social Science Research*, pp. 171–89. Newbury Park, CA: Sage.

Sheffield, C.J. (1990) 'The Invisible Intruder: Women's Experiences of Obscene Phone Calls', *Gender & Society* 3: 483–8.

Shulman, A.K. (1980) 'Sex and Power: Sexual Bases of Radical Feminism', *Signs: Journal of Women in Culture and Society* 5: 590–604.

Smith, J. (1989) *Misogynies: Reflections on Myths and Malice*. London: Faber and Faber.

Stanley, L. and Wise, S. (1979) 'Feminist Research, Feminist Consciousness and the Experience of Sexism', *Women's Studies International Quarterly* 2(3): 359–74.

Steinem, G. (1980) 'Erotica and Pornography: A Clear and Present Difference', in L. Lederer (ed.) *Take Back the Night: Women on Pornography*, pp. 35–9. New York: William Morrow.

Stoltenberg, J. (1989) *Refusing to Be a Man: Essays on Sex and Justice*. Portland, OR: Breitenbush Books.

Warner, P.K. (1988) 'Aural Assault: Obscene Telephone Calls', *Qualitative Sociology* 11: 302–18.

Warr, M. (1985) 'Fear of Rape Among Urban Women', *Social Problems* 32: 238–50.

Warsaw, R. (1988) *I Never Called It Rape*. New York: Harper and Row.

Weeks, E.L., Boles, J.M., Garbin, A.P. and Blount, J. (1986) 'The Transformation of Sexual Harassment from a Private Trouble into a Public Issue', *Sociological Inquiry* 56: 432–55.

Wise, S. and Stanley, L. (1987) *Georgie Porgie: Sexual Harassment in Everyday Life*. London: Pandora Press.

S.P. SCHACHT's recent areas of feminist research and publication include an ethnography of rugby players, an exploration of obscene telephone calls and an analysis of the anti-feminist emphasis of government funding of research on battered women. In the school year of 1992/93 Professor Schacht will be teaching a new course entitled 'Feminism and Sexuality', which will be grounded in many of the ideas presented in this article. ADDRESS: Department of Sociology and Anthropology, Southwest Missouri State University, Springfield, MO 65804, USA.

Patricia ATCHISON is Associate Professor in Sociology at Colorado State University. She specializes in the areas of gender roles, social problems, theory and social change. Her published work in gender roles includes comparison of Social Darwinism and anti-feminist social constructions, an analysis of the role complementarity of macho and his mate and work in heterosexual instrumentalism. She is also a published poet, emphasizing feminist themes and great plains pioneer culture. ADDRESS: Department of Sociology, Colorado State University, Fort Collins, CO 80523, USA.

Patricia DUNCKER

Heterosexuality: Fictional Agendas

This study considers the fictional construction of heterosexuality as social and sexual institution, drawing on selected novels of the 1980s by Margaret Atwood and Jenny Diski, with particular reference to The Edible Woman, Life Before Man *and* Nothing Natural. *I argue that the very ordinary daily oppression of women living traditional heterosexual lives, as well as the more extreme ritual humiliation of a woman involved in a heterosexual sadomasochistic relationship, are related products of sexual difference. I conclude with an argument, from a lesbian and radical feminist perspective, for the complete dismantling of the gender system which is the basis of heterosexuality.*

Yes, yes, of course there's a story behind this. Why am I talking about Margaret Atwood and Jenny Diski? Why these particular writers and why these particular fictions? Are they supposed to be quintessentially heterosexual? Well, I'll tell you. I got a new job. A relatively well-paid new job in a university department of English. My most immediate senior colleague suggested that I might feel moved to talk about Margaret Atwood's fiction on the first year lecture course as she was tired of doing so. I was anxious to please. I agreed at once.

Now, no one is lesbian unless she says she is. And everyone is who even mentions the word. Lesbian is no longer a word that cannot be spoken. But it still cannot be spoken with impunity. Or without consequences. I had let slip the fatal word — twice — in my curriculum vitae, by way of coming out. I then fully expected to keep quiet for a year or so, while I settled down and worked out who the opposition was. Unfortunately, there is always someone out there, at least one of them, maybe more, who already hates you, simply on account of who you are. You have to find out who he, or alas she, is.

And so there I stood, ready to deliver my inaugural lecture to a mass of expectant first years, all of whom I am to assume are heterosexual. My unspoken institutional agenda is to suggest to them that if they aren't they ought to be and to tell them what to expect of relationships between women and men by talking about fictional representations of heterosexuality. If you don't mention the alternative there isn't one. In fact, on our first-year course, we do mention the gay alternative. We teach William Golding's *Rites of Passage* (1980), a Booker Prize winning book by a Nobel Prize winning author. The homosexual man represented in that fiction is made drunk, sucks off a handsome sailor whom he's had his eye on, and subsequently dies of shame. So much for the gay alternative. The lesbian alternative, needless to say, is quite unthinkable.

Gender and all its attendant power structures is, crucially, one of the main concerns of the literature that we teach. Male homosexuality rises up from time to time and is either given a fair hearing or passed over in respectful silence. Shakespeare helps. But inevitably the Sonnets are used to prove that gay desire is ultimately no different from heterosexual desire. The torments of lust, anguish and jealousy are pretty much the same. And — so the more liberal version of the argument goes — as we're all in some way bisexual, insisting on homosexual difference is to make a loud noise about nothing.

Being a feminist in the academic literary world is now perfectly respectable so long as there are only one or two of you in the department. Many of the men are now equally concerned with 'gender theory' and are very interested in Elaine Showalter, Julia Kristeva, Luce Irigaray, Hélène Cixous and Toril Moi. Significantly, they aren't interested in Audre Lorde. We can talk about discourses of power, epistemological shifts and sexual difference. And, sur- prise, surprise, the men even want to give the lectures, so that the theory is cor- rectly presented. But I was handed Margaret Atwood, because she was seen to be in some sense irreducibly feminist: a woman writer who talks about women and heterosexual sex from the woman's point of view. Better give her to one of the women.

'Margaret Atwood', I began ponderously, 'is a writer who has always been intriguingly ahead of her times.' And what now follows is the lecture that I did not give. The things I did not say, which have choked me ever since.

By an accident of literary history Margaret Atwood's first and fourth novels were published together in Britain during 1979–80. *The Edible Woman*, written and set in the mid-1960s, when the women's liberation movement was no more than a tingle of desire, was first published in Canada in 1969. *Life Before Man* (*sic*), set in the years 1976–8, was first published in 1979. Both books are urban Canadian novels, set in Toronto. They have the same theme; they are novels of sexual manners which offer an analysis of the heterosexual contract. This is white, middle-class fiction. No one is black, disabled, homosexual or unemployed. In *The Edible Woman*, the cast are all in their early twenties. The young men are busy making it. They are either lawyers and soap men on the verge of being successful or they are intriguing alienated sensibilities writing their graduate theses in English studies. The women, so far as the action is con- cerned, sit on the rim of the book. They are either wives, or women waiting to be made wives, or underpaid, undervalued employees. The novel centres on women's perceptions and experiences, but makes it clear that we cannot significantly influence the conditions within which we live our lives. We will never get to be the boss. By the time we get to *Life Before Man* the lawyer has given up his job, and taken to making home crafts in the basement. The women have apparently progressed, been to university, attended the obligatory off-stage women's group, stopped going to it and got decent jobs. It is ten years on. They are all thirtysomething or pushing forty.

In *The Edible Woman* the decision is still up for grabs. Should our appallingly normal heroine (Maid) Marian opt for marriage to the lawyer and a life of dull, predictable respectability? Or not? What else is there? By *Life Before Man* we are caught, we have been married ten years, have two kids and are contemplating divorce. In *The Edible Woman* the heterosexual contract could still be negotiated, repudiated or recast in another form — but in *Life Before Man* marriage is a set of bars behind or around which the cast has to negotiate their various lovers and mistresses. In *The Edible Woman* the women still fight back indignantly. And in doing so it is clear that they have the writer's whole-hearted support. In *Life Before Man* Atwood's narrator takes up an ironic distance from the characters, male and female alike. The women are now either blood-curdling ball-breakers, who have certainly lost the narrator's approval, or vaguely suicidal, or both. The sparky rebelliousness of *The Edible Woman* has gone. Cynicism and despair are now the name of the game.

Margaret Atwood often writes a form of late twentieth-century Jane Austen: neat, smug prose, sex and marriage, class and manners. Except of course the dramatis personae writhe around in beds rather than simmer with repressed sex in drawing rooms. And, as in Jane Austen, atrocities never happen on the doorstep, but off-stage. In *Life Before Man*, the ex-lawyer, Nate, has a mother with a social conscience. She pins up the off-stage nightmares on a map of world horrors. The closest manifestation of social protest is a petition against the Mounties who have overstepped the mark in Québec. Nate's gloomy assessment of the public's attitude is probably accurate:

> . . . he knows that most people will allow six million Québeckers, Pakistanis, union leaders and transvestites to have their fingernails pulled out rather than admit that the paint is chipped on the bright red musical Mountie of their dreams (Atwood, 1982:305).

Lesbians and gays aren't explicitly included in the list, unless we are covered by transvestites. Heterosexuals are most people. We are part of the rest.

In Atwood's fictional world people have careers and enough to eat. Marian, our heroine in *The Edible Woman*, does her degree, then gets a job in advertising. Now advertising is always about selling you things that you don't need. And often about making the unacceptable desirable. The consumer and the thing consumed must correspond; therefore advertising produces images, images of ourselves and images of the product. Masculinity must be as carefully constructed as femininity if heterosexuality is to work. Take the example of the Moose Beer advertisement:

After a preliminary ringing, buzzing and clicking a deep bass voice, accompanied by what sounded like an electric guitar, sang:

Moose, Moose,
From the land of pine and spruce,
Tingly, heady, rough-and-ready. . .

Then a speaking voice, almost as deep as the singer's, intoned persuasively to background music,

Any real man, on a real man's holiday—hunting, fishing or
just plain old-fashioned relaxing—needs a beer with a
healthy, hearty taste, a deep-down manly flavour. The first
long cool swallow will tell you that Moose Beer is what
you've always wanted for true beer enjoyment. Put the tang
of the wilderness in YOUR life today with a big satisfying
glass of sturdy Moose beer.

The singer resumed:

Tingly, heady
Rough-and-ready,
Moose, Moose, Moose, Moose, BEER!!!

and after a climax of sound the record clicked off. It was in satisfactory working order (Atwood, 1980: 26).

Here we have heterosexual Canadian man, the huntin', shootin', fishin' type who has mastered the wilderness. The Moose Beer advertisement demonstrates the social construction of masculinity. Hunting, drinking, and consuming nature are the signs of sexually successful masculinity. The deep-down manly flavour is associated with casual killing.

Advertising constructs women too — as heterosexual, available to men, docile or wild according to male preference; as both desirable and domesticated. Marian's story, like many early feminist texts, is about the experience of being socially constructed as a heterosexual woman. This is a universal experience. All women are brainwashed from infancy to be heterosexual. Those of us who refuse to perform as required slide into the category labelled deviant. The interesting thing about being socially constructed as a heterosexual woman is that it is not just something other people do to you. You do it to yourself. For social expectations operate both within and without.

Marian spends a whole chapter brainwashing herself. The result is that she can no longer manage to tell the story. The narrative ceases to operate in the first person singular, confessional mode, the usual voice in which feminist escape stories are narrated, and lapses into the third person, the impersonal voice. Thus, the narrative moves from within to without — from I to she. Until we reach the end of the book and our heroine shakes herself free from the odious lawyer.

Life Before Man takes the three points of the conventional heterosexual triangle to tell the awful tale: wife, husband, other woman. Atwood uses first person narrative very rarely and sparingly because this would crack the ironic surface which holds her characters at a distance. In fact the material is too dangerously violent to risk narrating instantaneous feeling. Some of the violence happens off-stage: Elizabeth (the wife)'s lover Chris blows his brains out, the event which unleashes the novel. He reappears in flashback, a hairy Canadian Heathcliff, all penis and menace. In her heterosexual loneliness after his suicide, Elizabeth, who is given to slumming it sexually, tries a one-night stand with a naughty-knickers salesman. This is a disaster. Elizabeth is a monster, a vampire, a bitch: she is what happens to women who go for respectability at all costs, but she is still vulnerable to casual sexual assault:

> 'Hey, don't you want your turn?' the man says. His hand scampers like a spider up her thigh. 'I'm good, 'he says. 'Take a break and enjoy yourself.' His left hand holds the microphone as if he's expecting her to sing.
> 'Get your hand off my crotch,' Elizabeth says. She feels as if she's opened a serious looking-package and a wind-up snake has jumped out. She's never appreciated practical jokes (Atwood, 1980: 229).

The encounter is presented as funny. And we all laugh. But the undertow in the incident is nasty. She is alone with a man at night in his car. She wants to get out and walk home. She can't. Elizabeth is portrayed as a loathesome woman. Most of her readers, many of them women, have been set up to think that she's asked for it — and that she deserves all she gets.

Both *The Edible Woman* and *Life Before Man* are written within that extraordinary, peculiar moment of sexual history when contraceptives were fairly easily accessible for women and before the advent of AIDS. Both Ainsley, our heroine's best friend and confidante in *The Edible Woman*, — no, not her lover, that's unthinkable — and Lesje, the other woman in *Life Before Man*, decide to get pregnant of their own volition and in their own time. Ainsley actually picks, stalks and gets her man. Both women control their own reproductive force. This is (hetero)sex before AIDS in the style approved by heterosexual feminists. We can all entertain and act upon our desires, fairly fearless of the consequences. But in *Life Before Man* the sinister aspect of the heterosexual pact, and an aspect of male sexuality which was completely absent in *The Edible Woman*, is male violence. When Lesje's live-in lover William understands that Lesje is having an affair with Nate, his immediate response is to rape her:

> 'William, that hurts,' she says; then, 'William, cut it *out*!' He's got her jeans worked halfway down her thighs before it occurs to her that William is trying to rape her.
> She's always thought of rape as something the Russians did to the Ukrainians, something the Germans did, more furtively, to the Jews; something blacks did in Detroit, in dark alleys. But not something William Wasp, from a good family in London, Ontario, would ever do to her (Atwood, 1982: 185–6).

Here, respectability cracks. The veneer of civilized, sexual manoeuvring breaks down to reveal the ugliness of sexual force beneath. Despite Lesje's racism, Atwood is telling truth; most of us are raped by men we know well. And when it comes to heterosexual sex, women aren't ultimately in a negotiating position. It's not that easy to have sex on our terms — which is Atwood's point.

Behind every woman stands another woman, and behind every man stands his mother. This is Atwood's form of literary psychoanalysis, which has intriguing implications. In *Life Before Man* she elaborates her three points of consciousness, moving back into their childhoods and memories. Behind Elizabeth is Auntie Muriel, the evil stepmother, the witch she has to slaughter, the monster she is in the process of becoming. Behind Nate's awful, concerned understanding is his mother with her selflessness and noble causes: Save the Korean Poet. Behind Lesje are her passionate grandmothers, and her divided identity: Latvian/Ukrainian, Gentile/Jew. It is their voices which come back to her in her rage:

> She was too angry. If she tried to say anything at all, it would come out in the form of her grandmother's curses: *Jesus asshole poop! I hope your bum falls off! I hope you die!* (Atwood, 1982: 292).

In fact, this naked fury which erupts from time to time is the only thing which makes Atwood's analysis of the heterosexual contract feel clean. Her writing is a study in grey tones, fiction in ironic grey. The texture of her prose is dispassionate, unloving, cynical. What matters? What are the values being asserted? What is being argued for in this long grey stream of heterosexual misery? Should fiction argue for values? What indeed is the point of it all?

Adultery becomes a civilized arrangement if we can all sit on our feelings effectively. Religion becomes Auntie Muriel's torrent of hypocrisy, culminating in her black comic funeral. Sex is always disappointing. After ten years of making heterosexual love the earth has ceased to move. It all culminates in Lesje's reflection that:

> 'Man [*sic*] is a danger to the universe, a mischievous ape, spiteful, destructive, malevolent. But only theoretical.' Really she believed that if people could see how they were acting they would act some other way. Now she knows this isn't true (Atwood, 1982: 293).

Atwood uses a capital for Man. It's generic. The gloom, which has been deepening throughout the novel, is now complete.

So what *did* happen to feminism by 1978? Where have they gone, the women who caught the thinking disease? The women who said that post-feminism meant that you could wear your bra and burn your brains. Well, they have walk-on parts in Lesje's head:

> Lesje is doing something seedy. . . . Or even tacky. Very tacky, to be having an affair with a married man, a married man with two children. Married men with children are proverbially tacky, with their sad stories, their furtive lusts and petty evasions. Tackier still to be doing it in a hotel, of necessity a comparatively tacky hotel, since Nate is, as he says, a little broke. Lesje hasn't

offered to pay the hotel bill herself. Once, long ago, her women's group might
have sneered at this reluctance, but there is a limit (Atwood, 1982: 124).

Feminism belongs to 'once and long ago'. Whatever may have happened to
the women's group, she certainly doesn't frequent it any more. She opts for the
clichés instead. And the sadness of this book is in the irony of lines being
spoken, situations acted out, which are all predetermined elsewhere. The script
is already written; feelings are waiting to be felt, reproaches waiting to be
venomously delivered. And that's the subject of *Life Before Man* — Atwood is
examining the way in which heterosexuality doesn't evolve, doesn't change,
doesn't develop. The way in which women and men, in the hopeless attempt to
love one another, slink helplessly, miserably, into ruts.

What saves 320 pages of cynical, grey, ironic fiction from being a torrent of
sexual discouragement? Two things: naked rage and the wilderness. And this is
a pattern in Atwood's fiction. Do you remember the abysmal Moose Beer advert
in *The Edible Woman*? Well, there the wilderness was made safe for men who
drink the right beer. It's a billboard wilderness with no blood or fear. At the
climax of *The Edible Woman* our heroine and the awful lawyer give a party, the
first and last they ever give together. By this time our heroine can no longer eat.
Her mind has been brainwashed beautifully, but her body rebels. Refusing or
being unable to eat is always a form of self-punishment, but it is also a bid for
control. Marian is in a situation where she can no longer control what is happening to her. Her identity is about to be swallowed up in marriage, her body consumed. She does the sensible thing. She runs.

It's a good sign in Atwood's fiction when anyone does a bolt. It is always a
bid for freedom. Marian runs to the moody, loony English thesis-writing
graduate, who is another parasite, but at least an interesting one. And he opens
the door into the wilderness. He takes her across snow-covered Toronto to one
of the ravines. This is a startling scene. It is as if the urban text opens up, the
city cracks to reveal the wilderness beneath. The moment of danger is also the
moment of liberation.

> Marian gasped and took an involuntary step back: they were standing on the
> very edge of a cliff. The ground ended abruptly beyond their feet. Below them
> was a huge roughly circular pit, with a spiral path or roadway cut round and
> around the side, leading to the level snowcovered space at the bottom. . . . It
> seemed wrong to have this cavity in the city. . . . It made her suspect the white-
> pit bottom also; it didn't look solid, it looked possibly hollow, dangerous, a thin
> layer of ice, as though if you walked on it you might fall through (Atwood,
> 1980: 262).

The city breaks open and so does the sexual system between women and men.
The alternatives exist in the cracks. There is no question of marrying the lawyer
once she has seen the ravines.[1]

The same wilderness metaphor of ancient time exists in *Life Before Man*.

Underneath urban Canadian civilization lurk the dinosaurs, who exist as bones in the museum and as living beings in Lesje's imagination. Their presence suggests that there is a propositional element in human being. We have not always existed. In the chain of evolving life we are insignificant — a tiny recent addition — and we may not always exist. The heterosexual contract between women and men has become alarmingly tenuous, brutal and uncaring. Stripped of its property arrangements and economic rationale, the ideology of heterosexual love begins to look preposterous, negligible, bizarre. We may as well head for the wilderness.

Many women inhabit the wilderness. These are the women who ran, the women who invent themselves. During the 1970s there were women who decided to be lesbians, seeing the commitment to other women as the way out of the impasse of heterosexual feminism. As the economic climate of the 1980s darkened and they too became thirtysomething, like Atwood's characters, many decided to go back to the lives that they had left. They chose heterosexuality. The lesbians remained in the wilderness.

Do we, the wilderness women, care about the continuing, appalling state of relations between women and men? Should we be bothered with heterosexuality? Well, yes. We have to be concerned, for the following reasons. That most men prefer men seems to me to be an observable fact. Men prefer to work with men, to socialize with men, compete with men, write for men, read men. Sadly, it is also true that most women prefer men, even when they are not forced economically to do so, nor obviously brainwashed beyond repair. They work for them, wait upon them, take care of them, sleep with them, puff up their egos and bear their children. No one can deny that it is largely in our economic interests to do so. Heterosexuality is both a social and a sexual institution. We all live within it, in varying degrees, whether we want to or not. If you don't live with a man you will usually work for one or with one. You are probably related to one that you love.

Back in the 1970s feminists took upon themselves the terrifying task of changing the institution of heterosexuality from within. That project was the basis of the seven original demands of the women's liberation movement. We demanded equal pay with men, state-funded childcare facilities, security from men's violence, the right to determine our own sexuality, rather than being forced to be heterosexual in forms decided upon by our so-called masters, and an end to discrimination against lesbians. None of this was ever achieved. What we all failed to realize in the early 1970s was that these conditions of women's existence were the actual bricks of the heterosexual institution, the prison itself. They therefore cannot be changed. We can negotiate better conditions: no more slopping out, more frequent parole reviews, educational opportunities for long-term insiders, and we have done that for some. But the women's prison will always be there without a more radical rearrangement of all our lives.

So far as we, the lesbians, are concerned, I believe that ignoring the heterosexual world, however much we may loathe its customs, is madness. It is the world which bounds our own. Any fragile gains that we have made, our bars, our social spaces, the books we have published, the odd programme on TV, are all gains that can be clawed back at any time. Section 28[2] must have proved that to even the most sanguine among us. We have gained the few rights that we have by insisting that we too are as human as heterosexual women, and have the right to exist. We have only to be placed in another category to lose that right too; and, at best, to be forced back into economic dependence with our children on the ends of the umbilical cord, and violence as the threat if we put our noses outside the door.

Margaret Atwood — always ahead of her times — has already said this. In 1985 she published her eerie dystopia, *The Handmaid's Tale*. In the Republic of Gilead, religion rules. Identity becomes role, the women are wives, aunts, Marthas, handmaids. Heterosexuality is enforced. Women with viable ovaries become walking wombs. In a scenario resembling de Sade's fantasies, but without his sense of humour, the handmaid lies between the wife's legs, to be ritually fucked in the desperate attempt to breed. The only lesbian character in the novel fails to escape and is confined to a brothel, 'Butch paradise' as she ironically describes it, where the women can amuse themselves when the men have been sufficiently serviced. Lesbians are idealistic failures, with sentimental dreams of liberty. But Atwood is not going to abandon her heterosexual reader. In true Lawrentian style the chauffeur Nick turns up trumps. Free-range het sex is still interesting and erotic; and we are led to believe that he helps our pretty heroine escape.

Women and men, in an egalitarian society, would resemble each other. We would look alike, talk alike, move about in similar ways, dress in much the same clothes, and earn the same pay. In Atwood's dystopia women and men are sharply differentiated. They are not the same species. And it is this division, this brutal polarization, which is at the crux of the argument in another significantly successful heterosexual text.

In the same year that Margaret Atwood first published her terrifying vision of a theocracy in Britain — 1986 — Jenny Diski published a well-turned piece of realist fiction which was marketed as adult reading: an incisive analysis of a sadomasochistic heterosexual relationship. It was suggestively — indeed brilliantly — entitled *Nothing Natural*. It had wonderful reviews: hard sex, well written, the reviewers gloated. It is still in print, still selling well, there is a new paperback edition.

Nothing Natural is about being imprisoned in institutions and feeling well-off and secure inside them. Diski's novel takes up the same arguments about sexual difference and the ways in which it is oppressive to women that Atwood discusses in *The Handmaid's Tale*, but this time heterosexuality is discussed as a private sexual contract rather than as a state institution. But the idea that heterosexuality *is* an institution manipulated by the state is not absent from the text. The novel does a tour of various institutions: a home for abandoned, disturbed young people — in the subplot, our heroine befriends an alienated boy who shits himself — a prison, the mental ward of a hospital and a heterosexual relationship which is based on ritual patterns of violence, dominance and submission. The man gives orders, the woman bends over. Diski is absolutely explicit about what he does to her: spanking — ' "Christ", she thought, "this is new. What is this?" ' (Diski, 1990: 21); buggery over the kitchen table — 'She felt everything: violated, released, hugely and darkly excited' (Diski, 1990: 30); and, eventually, a rape scenario, her idea, in which she is tied up, beaten and then sodomized.

Nothing Natural is also about being programmed to respond in certain ways, playing along up to a point, then refusing to play the game any more. At the beginning of their relationship, Rachel, our heroine, feels that Joshua, her night visitor, not only has absolute control over what happens between them but that 'He had directed the evening as if he had had a script in his hand' (Diski, 1990: 33). At the end of the novel when she suspects that Joshua is being hunted for rape she sets him up by informing the police and writes the script for the rape scenario herself. The script is a web of pornographic clichés, and Joshua falls for them. The most astonishing thing about pornography is its repetitiveness: all the great classics, including de Sade, Bataille et al., propose the same scenarios.

Diski also suggests in the true Sadeian manner that the woman is really the mirror image of the man, with the same desires. It is essential that she should be like him, hard, cold, remote, for there is no pleasure in persecuting an entirely unwilling victim; and to explain this she gives them both brutal, unloving childhoods. Again and again Diski insists that 'it was precisely what Joshua revelled in that she wanted too' (Diski, 1990: 84). They both know the script. 'They were acting out a pantomime and they both knew it, although it wasn't to be said. As a pair of sophisticated post-Freudians they were giving each other therapy' (Diski, 1990: 85–6). What remained implicit in *Life Before Man* now becomes explicit: the fact of the heterosexual script.

Unfortunately, the post-Freudian therapy results in Rachel's severe and desperate suicidal depression. And just in case we were telling ourselves that mutual, loving, equal heterosexual sex was the answer, our heroine's confidante, Becky, discovers that her husband, who has lost interest in her, is having an affair. Round she comes for comfort — and here we have the lesbian sex scene. Pornography often presents lesbian sex as apéritif, the intriguing appetizer before the heterosexual main course. In most pornographic representations, lesbianism is portrayed as the fun-and-games end of heterosexuality. Male homosexuality (apart from its representation in the work of de Sade, who was genuinely gripped by the possibilities of buggery) is treated with caution, because it involves penetration, the 'real thing', and therefore introduces an unstable element into the drama of power and persecution.

This time, for her lesbian love-making, Diski uses the metaphor of the mirror and of Alice entering wonderland:

> And as she stroked and touched and felt her own body being caressed, she became enchanted by the confusion. She was Alice at the moment when the looking glass dissolved, kneeling on the mantlepiece, pressing her palms against the glass and feeling the reflection of her own flesh, touching another, touching herself, familiar but quite different, creating a third neither one nor the other, making love in a glass that became a liquid refracting pool, not you, not me, strange and strangely known (Diski, 1990: 152).

This is as finely written a passage as anything in the book, but what interested me was the fact that, apart from a little nipple-sucking, Diski became uncharacteristically vague about describing what it is that the two women actually *do*. Instead they are 'shockingly naked, shockingly women together, female form wrapped around itself' (Diski, 1990: 153), as if her lovers were a sculpture. They are not two women, but one flesh.

Heterosexuality, in this text at any rate, violently differentiates male from female, even while Diski insists that Rachel and Joshua are critically alike. Their natures are supposedly the same, but what they do to each other is different. So are their roles in the script: he commands, she obeys. I thought about this for a long time, because something critical about the construction of heterosexuality had emerged from the text of *Nothing Natural*. Let me explain.

One of the great nineteenth-century operas of heterosexual love is Wagner's *Tristan and Isolde*. I love it. So do many lesbians and gays who are in the habit of going to the opera. Why? At first glance it is not promising territory. I am not at all keen on the idea that the only way in which illicit passion can be consummated is in death — whether that passion is homosexual or heterosexual. So far as we, the lesbians, are concerned, our history is packed with far too many tales of noble self-sacrificing lesbians who either achieve greatness and respectability by dying off, or demonstrate that justice can and should be done by getting killed off. What is particularly extraordinary about *Tristan and Isolde* is the suggestion that what prevents their passion is the fact of sexual difference. And it is his idea, not hers. He demands to be 'Nicht mehr Tristan, sondern Isolde' (No longer Tristan, but Isolde). Homosexuals admire *Tristan and Isolde* because the opera argues that *difference* is unworkable, impossible, insoluble, to be resolved only in death. The lovers exchange names and identities. Passion is about being the other person. Not being different, but being the same. No longer being the Self, but the Other. Here, as far as I am concerned, is the answer.

The usual accusation levelled at lesbianism is that it is narcissism. I don't understand this objection, as — if it is a question of mutual passion — someone else is always involved. It is not narcissism to love the other who resembles you. To love the other as yourself, is to love yourself. The other has the same needs, the same desires, the same passion, and — were sexual difference dissolved — whether the other is man or woman would not matter. You are the other person. Sexual difference has ceased to exist.[3] The other is yourself.

But of course, in Jenny Diski's text, which conforms to the heterosexual fictional agenda, Rachel gives Becky the push. She turns chilly and cold. Becky is the loving other who must be shaken off:

> 'Rachel, what is it?' Becky insisted.
> I want you away, out of here, she thought; I want you to stop being so fucking pathetic, so fucking warm, so loving (Diski, 1990: 155).

When required to explain, Rachel argues that they are both 'hooked on men' (Diski, 1990: 157), as if heterosexuality was an unfortunate drug habit. As indeed, as far as the sadomasochistic relationship with Joshua is concerned, it is. Sameness cannot be perceived as, ultimately, erotically gratifying. If it were, Diski would have to rethink heterosexual sex — and the plot of the book.

'Nothing's a natural thing to do', snaps Diski's heroine. I think that's absolutely true — which is why any sexual act is as much about politics as it is about feelings. The urge to perform one particular sexual act rather than another doesn't rise up mysteriously from the gulf of our inward natures. There's a script. There is *always* a script. This is why we have to be precise about what it is that we do with one another, in bed and elsewhere, and even be prepared to argue it out.

There is no easy way of disentangling heterosexuality as sexual practice from the rest of the institution. But how could heterosex be transformed so that it did not turn women into willing victims and men into monsters? Unlike a substantial proportion of the human population, lesbian, gay and straight, I don't think that pleasure and pain are inseparable. I believe that gentleness is preferable to violence in all sexual circumstances, and that because sexual fantasies are dangerously linked to actual sexual acts, we must even be prepared to interrogate our fantasies.

There is nothing intrinsically horrible about fellatio or anal penetration — indeed, even vaginal penetration — if those practices have no political meanings which are oppressive, humiliating and destructive in the society at large. At the moment they do have such meanings. Should we then be prepared to obliterate heterosexuality as an institution? Well, this means getting rid of sexual difference. It also means abolishing most of the legal system, marriage, the family, most cultural and national traditions, the church, in all its forms, all sects, and most aspects of all other religions too, the tax system, work patterns, childcare arrangements, the distribution of wealth. It means rethinking the language, rebuilding our houses, remaking most of the sculptures, repainting the pictures and rewriting the books. We should have to argue for a radical restructuring of society. I for one will be glad to see it all go. I have been arguing that we should change it all for the last 20 years.

Can we imagine a world without sexual difference? A world in which gender was abolished? A world in which it had ceased to matter if your lover was a man or a woman? A world in which the polarization of heterosexuality in our dress codes, incomes and sexual practices was simply irrelevant? We would have to rethink the erotic. And that too would be no bad thing. This wonderful plan for complete demolition and rebuilding came from the extraordinary simple insight that the private, sexual space between two human beings is not free from external, public, political meanings. 'The personal is the political.' These two cartographers of heterosexuality's fictional agendas, Margaret Atwood and Jenny Diski, suggest that the sexual space is the political space. I agree.

NOTES

1. The Toronto ravines are also used in her later novel *Cat's Eye*. (Atwood, 1990)
2. The Section of the UK Local Government Act (1988), which banned the 'promotion' of homosexuality and 'pretended family relationships'.
3. Here I find myself in agreement with Sheila Jeffreys in her book about the sexual revolution, *Anticlimax*. See especially her Chapter 6, 'Creating the Sexual Future'.

REFERENCES

Atwood, Margaret (1980) *The Edible Woman*. London: Virago (First published Canada: O.W. Toad, 1969).

Atwood, Margaret (1982) *Life Before Man*. London: Virago (First published Canada: O.W. Toad, 1979).

Atwood, Margaret (1987) *The Handmaid's Tale*. London: Virago (First published Canada: O.W. Toad, 1985).

Atwood, Margaret (1990) *Cat's Eye*. London: Virago (First published Canada: O.W. Toad, 1988).

Diski, Jenny (1990) *Nothing Natural*. London: Minerva (First published London: Methuen, 1986).

Golding, William (1980) *Rites of Passage*. London: Faber and Faber.

Jeffreys, Sheila (1990) *Anticlimax: A Feminist Perspective on the Sexual Revolution*. London: The Women's Press.

Patricia DUNCKER is the author of *Sisters and Strangers: An Introduction to Contemporary Feminist Fiction* (Blackwell, 1992). She writes fiction, poetry and radical feminist criticism. Her most recent piece of fiction is 'Betrayal', published in *Sinister Wisdom* 46 (April 1992).
ADDRESS: Department of English, Hugh Owen Building, Penglais, University College of Wales, Aberystwyth, Dyfed SY23 3DY, Wales.

Allan HUNTER

Same Door, Different Closet:
A Heterosexual Sissy's Coming-out Party

One way to problematize heterosexuality is to acknowledge the tacitly assumed connection between heterosexual preference in males and their 'masculinity', i.e. their dissimilarity to women in personality and behaviour. The political implications of the 'masculinity' construct are central to what makes heterosexual participation by women a volatile subject for feminists. By analyzing and disentangling the ideological equivocation between men who are not sexually attracted to women and men who are considered to resemble women in personality and behaviour, it is possible to theorize a feminist heterosexuality that would involve women with males but which need not involve them with 'men'.

It is a universal fact of human existence that what we know best, that which forms part of our everyday mental landscape, is also that which we most take for granted, and question the least. And so some of the strongest jolts to our awareness, the deepest reorientations in our thought, often come from being confronted with the obvious (Miedzian, 1991).

There are two types of things that are very difficult for us to understand: the very deviant phenomenon, for which we have no name and no concept, and the very normal one, which we so often tend to take for granted because we have no concept of any possible contrast. Heterosexuality, for a long time in western culture, has been of the second category. Until recently, general awareness of non-heterosexual people and their lives was almost totally confined to off-color jokes and murky stereotypes, always looking at them from the outside. Only as gay rights and feminist social movements have drawn more attention to actual non-heterosexual people — their actual lives and their political and social concerns — have we started to acquire the beginnings of an understanding of heterosexuality in contrast. Even now, though, we tend to take heterosexuality for granted (and thus are not understanding it), except in the immediate context of gay, lesbian or bisexual people and their active communication of their perspective. *We* have not tended to look at the social forms particular to heterosexuality, or to consider the effects that heterosexuality has on a person, except for the limited times and occasions when *they* impinge enough on our consciousness to provide a momentary contrasting backdrop.

Consider the following question. My use of the referents 'we' and 'they' in the preceding paragraph show that I am consciously writing as a heterosexual person. Can I, a heterosexual person, write about heterosexuality itself if I have only limited second-hand access to the experiences and perspectives of gay, lesbian and bisexual people? What is the source of my authority to write? Is there any reason to assume that I understand this phenomenon from the inside if I have nothing in my direct experience or awareness to compare it to? The assumption behind that question is that heterosexuality exists only in contrast to differing *erotic* practices. Or, to turn an aphorism around, it is as if heterosexuals were interesting and worthy of understanding only for what we do in bed! At the insistence of theorists such as Adrienne Rich (1980), heterosexuals have been challenged to move beyond thinking only of the erotic practices of gay men and lesbians, to begin to understand the institutional aspects of sexuality. Insofar as heterosexuality is also more than a matter of what individuals with which body parts do to people with which other body parts, there are other possible contrasting positions from which it can be seen from the outside, so as to clarify the meaning of being on the inside. I would like to consider the matter of heterosexuality and what it means from a very deviant position, a phenomenon for which we have no simple name and only rarely even a blurry concept.

I assume that you are quite familiar with our culture's commonly shared notions of *masculinity*, in the sense of prescribed personality and behavioral characteristics associated with heterosexual men? This would seem to be a reasonable assumption. While there do exist multiple expressions of, and connotations for, the term 'masculine', I will be using the term throughout this paper to refer to these most commonly shared personality and behavioral manifestations of gender, as opposed to alternative 'masculinities', and as analytically separable from the biological sex to which they are culturally attached. Probably you are also aware of stereotyped notions of gay men as nonmasculine — more like women than they are like other (heterosexual) men, or at least less masculine and more feminine than heterosexual men are. What, then, is the proper name for a male who is *not masculine* in his general personality and behavior if he happens to be sexually oriented towards women? And what are the experiences of such males with heterosexuality — their own and the normative institutionalized variety which surrounds them? I explore these in this study.

This is not a research report. I do not have a nice collection of new, interesting, formal data to provide for the expansion of our understanding of heterosexuality. Instead, although I may make reference to various things as examples to illustrate a point I'm trying to make, I intend to work mainly with the large pool of everyday knowledge and shared meanings which we all know so well, and to look at it a bit differently. I tend to see theory as a verb, and to make reference to other people's work mainly when it serves the rhetorical purpose of example or clarification. Perhaps this explains the scarcity of references to psychoanalytic and poststructuralist theories within this study: I have never found them helpful in understanding myself, and, given my attitude towards theory-as-a-verb, I found it easy to ignore their hegemony within theory-as-a-noun. Feminist theory in general had its origins in analyzing everyday knowledge: it was not as if no one had ever noticed that men dominated women sexually, or got paid more to do the same work, until feminists did research to prove it, but rather that people had not looked at these things and questioned them and considered what it all meant.

I will supplement everyday knowledge with some impressions gained from my own life. You see, the unconventional male vantage point I have described is the only position from which I am directly able to consider heterosexuality, since this deviant position is the position of my own experience. Doing so as a male person is not without its theoretical implications. As Hearn (1987: 181) says, 'Men must not seek to appropriate feminism or feminist theory'. And yet, I don't pretend to know what we should call it when the male person seeks to theorize his own life honestly and from his own experience in relationships to the systemic context called patriarchy, with an attitude and politics geared towards agreement with what feminists have been saying, and with an adversarially critical intent focused on bringing patriarchy to an end. Also, I use the terms 'male' and 'female' here in places where you might expect 'man' and 'woman'. I use the term 'male' in order to distance biological maleness from the cultural construct of 'man', and I use the term 'man' specifically to invoke our shared understandings of what it means to 'be a man' in the patriarchal context. Similarly, I employ the term 'masculine' in its politically and socially embedded sense rather than its biologically essentialist sense. These choices are inherently political; I could have just as easily spoken of redefining what it means to be a man, or spoken of pluralistic, multifaceted 'masculinities' of which this was an alternative form. I chose not to do so. As John Stoltenberg (1989) has done, I have embraced the connotations offered by the observation that men who are not conventionally masculine are not men, and rejoiced in my refusal to be a man and in my location outside of masculinity.

BONDS: HOMOPHOBIA, MASCULINITY, HETEROSEXUALITY

For lack of any adequate pre-existent terminology, and since using long strings of words quickly becomes tiring, I will follow the lead of lesbians who call themselves 'dykes' and the militant gay rights group, 'Queer Nation', and I will seize a pejorative term that was hurled at me and other such males, and I will make it my own: 'sissy'. The word is etymologically derived from 'sister' and therefore directly connotes the sense of being like a girl or woman. Although this male-centered world tends to emphasize the worst of feminine characteristics, such as dependency and passivity, and the best of masculine ones, such as taking initiative and having courage, femininity is also associated with nurturing, caring and being sensitive, while masculinity is also associated with violence, vulgarity and an obsession with winning and dominating. A sissy is a male (regardless of sexual orientation) who is in some way *not* masculine, who is in some meaningful way more like women than men tend to be, or are 'supposed' to be. Maybe he is proud of it. Maybe he has reasons for not wanting to resemble other males in personality and behavior. In my case, I certainly am, and do.

To say 'regardless of sexual orientation' is to threaten an assumed connection, a bond which is so rarely challenged that it is rarely recognized as such. When I was being called 'sissy', I was also being called 'faggot' and 'queer' as I was being physically and verbally assaulted. To be a sissy is to be on the inside of homophobia, surrounded by it, experiencing it constantly. You don't even have to be physically attracted to males to get in.

Patriarchal heterosexuality — that is, heterosexuality in a context where male domination is normative and endorsed by the players — is tied to homophobia (Pharr, 1988). The most virulent and commonplace expressions of homophobia are directed towards homosexual males (Gagnon and Simon, 1973; Hart and Richardson, 1981). Since male gay behavior is first and foremost male behavior, it should seem provocatively odd that male domination would constrain male sexual behavior with such fervor. This is a qualitatively different kind of phenomenon from the functional constraints put on male sexual behavior in order to preserve various social institutions — for example, there are social sanctions against men raping women, molesting children, committing infidelities once married, and so on, and these sanctions appear to be geared towards the general maintenance of the institutions of marriage and family, but they exist in ambivalence, diluted in large part by men's tendency to permit themselves a wide latitude of sexual behavior as long as it doesn't immediately infringe upon other men. Given that, you would expect that the proscriptions against consensual male homosexual activity would be formal but not necessarily internalized or deeply enforced by strong and (almost) universally shared attitudes. You would expect, perhaps, winks and boasts of homosexual activities as something a man *got away with*, or intends to get away with. It should be an item of curiosity that an angry man in a bar or an angry boy in the schoolyard will shout 'You faggot', but not 'You rapist', as a term of abuse.

A closer look reveals that the primary image that heterosexual society has of the homosexual man is an image of a dominated man, one who is taking on the feminine sexual role or who has had that role forced upon him. The boys in the schoolyard don't just say 'You faggot'; they also say 'Fuck you'. In American prisons, it is widely whispered, there are males (especially young ones) who are utilized as receptacles, who are buggered, sodomized by force — they are considered to be homosexual, but those who rape them, or insert into them, are not.[1]

All sexual activity tends to require at least one deliberate actor, if not necessarily two; but the image that heterosexuals have of the active male who is volitionally *causing* gay sexual activity to take place focuses on the gay male who actively wants to sexually please *other* men: to arouse the erection, to provide the mouth or the anus, to be used as women are used. Homosexuality is somehow his doing. Effeminate men make it happen. In an interesting equivocation, even those males who can be *put* into a position of sexual subserviency through force and intimidation are assigned responsibility[2] and their identity is blurred with that of males who actively wish to give other males sexual pleasure. More deeply hidden in the shadows of the socially shared concept of gay male behavior is the image of the male who actively lusts after other males for his *own* sexual pleasure and seeks them out. Our conventional images have no easy word or image of the male who actively seeks his own pleasurable erotic sensations with other men. His existence is denied, ignored almost completely.

The gay liberation movement and the gay cultural motifs of the modern era seem to have addressed this, with gay men criticizing the stereotype of the gay male as effeminate and asserting their masculinity as well as their pride in their sexual preference. Fiction author John Rechy strongly implies that it has become almost 'politically incorrect' for men in at least some parts of the gay community in America to be effeminate (see, for example, *The Rushes*, Rechy, 1979). This threatens the association between images of masculinity and male heterosexuality and between those of effeminacy and male homosexuality.

The image of the male who *is* effeminate and whose sexual orientation is towards *women* threatens that same bond from the heterosexual side. The bond hasn't been threatened from that direction very much yet: people may be somewhat more likely to say or think that not all gay men are necessarily sissies, but they are not likely to assert or actively think that not all sissies are necessarily gay,[3] thus leaving heterosexuality the exclusive province of the masculine male. This is the foreground for an examination of heterosexuality: to recognize that heterosexuality is largely conceptualized, *unthinkingly*, as a relationship between women and *masculine* males. It is time to develop a more critical awareness of the effects of that bond and how the pieces fit together.

Gay men sometimes speak of having been 'born that way'. As a heterosexual sissy, I have a strong tendency to think that the attraction to females was something I was born with — I can recall an intense and erotic fascination with girls' bodies, such as the way that genital differences caused *that* part of their pants to be shaped differently, and it gave me strange naughty-sweet feelings to look at that or think about it. This was happening at an age where I was incredibly naive about sex (all I knew was how babies were made; no one had ever told me that sex was pleasant or that there was an appetite aspect to it), so I didn't know anyone else had ever had such feelings or that they were normal or anything like that. Therefore, when people tell me that sexual preference is all caused by socialization, I'm inclined to doubt them. While it may be true that all people have the capacity to have pleasant erotic experiences with either same-sex or opposite-sex partners (what Weinberger, 1972, called 'polymorphous' sexuality), I tend to think that some people may have strong preference tendencies to begin with.

I was not born a sissy, though. My sense of myself as more like the girls than the other boys developed over a period of time during early elementary school, and it had a lot to do with the social status of children. Children were all treated as immature, irresponsible people, not deserving of the respect that adults demanded for themselves. I wanted respect, dignity and equality with adults, and to my way of thinking at the time, if we demonstrated maturity and responsible control over our actions, we would earn the corresponding autonomy and proper treatment. Furthermore, it was obvious that the girls were doing a very good job of being good citizens and were appreciated for it: teachers and other people's parents had a strong tendency to trust girls and to praise them for being good, whereas the boys were all treated as discipline problems looking for a place to happen (Hartley, 1974). Therefore, there were many times when I was accused of being like a girl and I reacted by agreeing and being proud of it.

Meanwhile, although I had strong girl-oriented sexual *feelings* during these early years, the fact that I didn't know what they were or what the world expected from male sexuality meant that I didn't have a perspective on *heterosexuality* until later, when being a sissy ran me up against the scripted roles for sexual behavior.

The meaningful processes of heterosexual interaction can be divided into meeting and courtship, which is the first bundle of scripted sexual behaviors, and the structure and dynamics of ongoing sexual relationships, which is a related but separate bundle of roles and scripts.

FLIRTING: THE POLITICS OF GETTING HETEROSEXUALITY STARTED

When Kinsey laid to rest the part of the double standard that maintained women got no pleasure at all from sex, everyone cried out that there was a sexual revolution afoot. But such talk, as usual, was deceptive. Morality, outside the marriage bed, remained the same, and children were socialized as though Kinsey had never described what they would be like when they grew up. Boys were taught that they should get their sex where they could find it, 'go as far' as they could. On the old assumption that women were asexual creatures, girls were taught that since they needed sex less than boys did, it was up to them to impose sexual restraints. . . .

Adolescent boys growing up begging for sexual crumbs from girls frightened for their 'reputations' — a situation that remains unchanged to this day — hardly constitutes the vanguard of a sexual revolution (Susan Lydon, 1970).

These traditional images of heterosexual behavior are well known, widely shared and *expected* to be shared, enough so that virtually all the adolescents and young adults know that this is still more or less the way things are (e.g. Nonkin, 1985). Sometimes the flirtation stage actually occurs twice, with essentially the same rules but on two different levels. In a context where there is an implied sexual meaning to any male–female encounter, such as a singles bar or a dance, the first level is the occasion of meeting for the first time. Females often do a great deal to initiate this, but traditionally not in an overt, direct way. They make eye contact and draw attention to themselves, but it is up to the male to make the approach and say the first word. The second level is more universal, and revolves more specifically around the question of whether or not to engage in erotic behavior. Some variation on the following stereotyped assumptions tends to operate:

1. The females want to 'fall in love' and be loved in return by a cute guy who will be the boyfriend, and, within that context, they want good sex (in earlier times, marriage was necessarily first). The males don't really like most females that much, unless they are in love, and they aren't necessarily trying to fall in love at all, and, so, in or outside of that context, they want good sex. Therefore. . .
2. Males come on to females, usually because they are physically attracted to them, since their main interest is physical and appearance is a physical phenomenon. Sometimes they come on to a female because she has a reputation for being sexually available to males whether they love her or not. Either way, the females can reject the guys they don't have any interest in at all, but the other males have to be kept interested but slowed down so that proximity and time creates the possibility that he will really start to like her, perhaps fall in love. Females do not overtly come on to males.
3. Males who are rejected are allowed to keep on trying, since males who think they are not really being rejected, just slowed down a bit, are *supposed* to keep on trying, and sometimes you can't tell which is which anyway. But if a male thinks a female is being too hard to get, so that it isn't fun for him any more, he can quit paying attention to her — he doesn't have to keep on trying. Females are not supposed to pursue the matter. It is up to him to press the issue.

Feminists have made it apparent that the scripted roles for heterosexual behavior are oppressive and humiliating to women — keeping women passive, mutating their own sexual appetite so that it becomes the man's ally and the opposite of their self-determination, making sex a conquering of women by men and eroticizing male domination itself (Greer, 1970; Dworkin, 1981; MacKinnon, 1987). They have also indicted *masculinity itself*, as an identity construct that seems to depend for its existence on being extremely different from females and very glad of it, and contemptuous of all things female and feminine (Dinnerstein, 1976; Chodorow, 1978). Since the advent of the feminist movement, courting behavior has lost some of its gender-specific rigidity, but for the most part only to a degree. Some individual clauses of the silent 'contract' described here may not apply to certain age groups, certain ethnic or cultural subgroups and so on, but single heterosexual people seldom operate with a blank slate rather than a set of expectations, and those expectations are usually gendered, more or less according to the scripted roles given above.

Interestingly, a concept of women's oppression is actually embedded in the basic sexist courting roles. The assumption woven into the script is that casual sex (as opposed to sex in the context of an ongoing, loving relationship) is oppressive to women, and that men who seek it are preying upon them. Heterosexuality, then, is a competitive struggle between the male and the female. That men would want to prey upon women is assumed to be part of male nature.

A male person with little or no interest in trying to dominate and oppress females might find the male role script distasteful, and consider relating sexually to women differently; indeed, from overhearing female conversations, it might seem that women are perpetually on the lookout for such fellows. Unfortunately, women may demand a more sensitive man, but aren't sure of what to do with one when they find one.

The problem actually lies not with the inconsistency of women, nor even directly with an insufficiency of sensitive men, but rather in the structure of the scripted roles themselves. It is a much more serious problem for male sex-role nonconformists than for our female equivalents. There is not as strong a conceptual bond between femininity and heterosexuality for females as there is between masculinity and heterosexuality for males. Sex between males and females *can and often does* result when females do not obey the script — for example, they may take a far more active and overt role in causing sex to happen or they may act on an interest in casual sex by accepting male overtures without any attempt to play 'hard to get' or to slow the man down — and this is an important point, even though females who behave in this fashion are subjected to labeling and contempt from both males and females. Non-feminine females, or masculine females, have a range of images and stereotypes that include heterosexual activity: the slut, the bitch, the castrating dominating strong woman, and so on. These are negative, of course, but they could be (and sometimes have been) proudly adopted by nonconforming, assertive women, and in theory, at least, such women could eventually meet men who like them that way through the operation of the heterosexuality script. When males do not obey their scripted role, there is no provision within the script which calls for heterosexual behavior to take place. If it is to take place at all, it must do so *outside*, beyond the script and its assumptions about what various behaviors mean.

There is no happy medium. The sissy must behave against a patriarchal backdrop, not in a vacuum. Sexually assertive behaviors which would not be considered oppressive otherwise are open to being interpreted that way precisely because other men, in general, have behaved as they have. Nowhere does this have greater impact than in the matter of the simple, honest, declaration of sexual attraction. Surrounded by females complaining of the exploitative, insensitive nature of men's raw sexuality and often confronted head-on with the generic, automatic female response to all male expressions of immediate sexual interest, the sensitive young male who identifies with and respects women is likely to be rapidly polarized. He ends up being driven towards a masculinizing track of ceasing to feel hurt by such interpretations of his sexuality, or else towards complete (or nearly complete) cessation of expressing appetite for women in order to avoid being accused of, to put it tritely, 'being only after one thing'.

The sissy whose sexual orientation is towards women brings the possibility of very different concepts of heterosexuality, perhaps so much so that a new term may be needed for this as well. But the heterosexual sissy is conceptually homeless. And so was I, until I conceived of myself. Which I did. But that makes it sound easy, and getting to that point was an agonizing, stressful experience, and I had to do *that* alone.

I am a person who has been angrily or sneeringly accused of being gay all my life (usually in uglier terms), and therefore, because I always had a strong sexual interest and orientation towards girls (and later, women), I had all the seeds for homophobia planted in my head, too. You see, I was made to be afraid of the idea that homosexuality might be what 'happens' to boys like me *whether it's what we want or not*. Since I didn't particularly *like* other males, generally speaking, that just made it all the more scary. Constantly being confronted with it, having it shoved in my face as an accusation, I finally reached a point (while still virginally inexperienced with women) when I had to ask myself whether or not they were right — was I gay? Answer: well, I have the *capacity* to be, if I want to be. After a lifetime of being accused of it, I give myself *permission* to enjoy gay sex if I ever want to, and I'll be damned if I'm going to spend the rest of my life worrying about it, but that's not really what I *want* right now.

The real fear that was revealed by considering it as a possibility was the fear of never having the sexual experiences and close relationships that I had always wanted with *women*. I saw that I'd have to deliberately search beyond the norm. My sexuality was different.

And in that moment, I came out of *my own* closet, at least to myself (since I was *still* an invisible identity with no word for it, there was no easy way to express what I understood about myself to anyone else). I stood 'acquitted' of having to be anything I didn't want to be. I rejoiced in being a sissy and celebrated the fact that my sexuality is oriented towards women, *but isn't dependent on or defined by a committed effort to avoid sexual feelings and experiences with men*. And suddenly it all seemed really simple. The rest of it was just a matter of coming out to the rest of the world. . . .

EXCITEMENT: A TRANSITION PARAGRAPH

> Journalist Stephanie Gutmann is an ardent foe of what she calls the date-rape dogmatists. 'How can you make sex completely safe?' she asks. 'What a horribly bland, unerotic thing that would be! Sex is, by nature, a risky endeavor, emotionally. And Desire is a violent emotion. These people in the date-rape movement have erected so many rules and regulations that I don't know how people can have erotic or desire-driven sex' (Gibbs, 1991).

Stephanie Gutmann is not the only person I've heard say or come close to saying that sex would lose its sexiness if it no longer included the element of the 'hunt', the attempt to seduce and the thrill of the chase, any of which blur into coercion and domination if it is not just a game. In the times when I've overheard rare discussions about the heterosexual attractiveness and possibilities of sissy men, it has often been asserted that such men have too much in common with the women for either of them to feel much excitement. There is no gap for the spark to jump. You get two sweet, nice people together, and nobody's going to do anything except with the permission of the other, assuming that anyone has the 'balls' to bring the subject up. Nobody getting turned on, chased down and *had* by someone who knows how to arouse the traitor body. Nobody feeling the triumph of coming in for the 'kill', gleefully and sardonically taking and *having* the teasing sexy someone they'd been wanting so long. This is the only available image for getting together outside the scripted sex roles: bringing up the subject verbally and discussing the matter rationally and politely, so that all the cards are face-up on the table. The fun and spontaneity is dead on the cold, dry dissecting table of intellectual analysis, and there's no danger, tension or suspense.

This, they say to me, explains why opposites attract. It explains why heterosexual men *must* be masculine. Women want real men, and that's all there is to it.

I think they still might find it upsetting to be reminded that some of the women want real women instead. Until the middle of my own feminist-era lifetime, the idea of even one woman actively seeking sexual pleasure on her own initiative was censored from people's imagery, perhaps because it is so threatening to another one of those bonds, the bond between maleness and the 'masculinity' of active sexual lust. As I said before, all sexual activity tends to require at least one deliberate actor if not necessarily two. Lesbians are certainly oppressed, as women and as gay people, but, interestingly, a great deal of their oppression has taken the form of denying their existence or of rendering it 'safe' (Pharr, 1988; Rich, 1980), some kind of cuddly, unimportant, not-really-lusty female activity that some women engage in when they can't catch a man. In contrast, the idea of gay men seems so important for the institution of heterosexuality that I think that if there were no gay men they would have been invented as mythical creatures. There needs to be something that boys are afraid of becoming if they don't embrace the actively dominant, anti-woman attitudes of masculinity (Hartley, 1974; Hart and Richardson, 1981; Herek, 1987). At sexual maturity, the connection between sissyhood and homosexuality and the negative way of defining desired male behavior as not-a-sissy come together in a homophobic-sissyphobic-misogynistic pattern: the patriarchal trinity of masculinity as we know it. At any rate, the very existence of lesbians and of women's own lusty sexual appetite and tendency to act upon it directly does bring to mind one possible answer to the 'opposites attract' argument outlined above for why sissy males would be boring to women because no one would take the initiative — let dynamic, assertive women who are accused of being unfeminine seduce the sweet sissy guys! It would keep the old gendered scripts active, albeit running in reverse order, but at least the women wouldn't have to worry about oppressing the men by expressing and acting upon any sexual desire they felt for them.

But, really, it isn't that simple. For one thing, little boys do not grow up being warned about predatory girls, and for the most part males do not in any other way internalize stuff that would give them the complex of reluctances and ambivalences about sex that makes up that part of classical femininity. There is no danger and suspense because, to paraphrase Mae West, you cannot seduce the willing. To whatever extent we do need a sense of danger and suspense and tension in order to make flirtation sexy, putting the responsibility for sexual initiative on women will not provide it for sissy men, however many other things it might solve. In our society, which eroticizes domination and power conflicts, the most likely location of such an eroticized situation for a sissy male *would* be with other men — because it is forbidden, because it has been warned against, because it has been so effectively painted as a sexual phenomenon which stalks males and must be feared and fought against. This, really, is the crux of the argument about 'opposites attract'.

If it is true that all people have the capacity to experience pleasurable erotic sensations in sex with people of the same sex in some situations, and it is also true (at least in the world as we know it) that issues of power, conflict and vulnerability tend to add the fuel of excitement and suspense to potential erotic situations, then *all* men in western society have been set up to respond under the right circumstances with erotic passion to being seduced in some way by other men simply because it is possible and yet forbidden. In a short, tight loop, it becomes possible partly because it *is* scary, which is *why* it is so scary! Here, indeed, is the bottom of the valley of homophobia, and from here the links between homophobia, heterosexuality and masculinity in men start to make sense.

COUPLING: THE POLITICS OF KEEPING HETEROSEXUALITY GOING

If there is any widely shared image of a non-masculine man functioning in an actively heterosexual situation — a 'sissy archetype' — then it's Caspar Milquetoast, a mild-mannered ineffectual married man dominated by his wife.[4] He does what she wants him to do. Presumably, she married him in order to use him as a source of money or social status. We still can't visualize him flirting or participating in those brief hedonistic sexual encounters called 'one-night stands'. If the conventional male's sexual interests are constructed first around the fear of being gay and the need to prove otherwise, they are further shaped by a desire to avoid the fate of Caspar Milquetoast, who probably married *her* because that was the only way he was ever going to have any access to heterosexual erotic experiences. The applicable epithet is 'pussy-whipped'.

In patriarchal male-dominant society, the logical norm to which one might expect men to aspire would be the opposite of this: a man in an ongoing relationship with a woman in which she does what he wants her to do. And there are such images, head-of-the-family patriarch images, but they aren't the central masculine motif at all. In fact, *all* images of the male engaged in an ongoing relationship with a female are at least faintly tainted by the Caspar Milquetoast image, and the most masculine images are those in which male–female relationships are the most temporary and superficial, tightly constrained to an impersonal and oppositional erotic contact. These are the forms of male–female contact that are traditionally assumed to be exploitative of women, as discussed previously. In short, it would appear from the imagery that all heterosexual possibilities must involve the domination of someone, either men or women, and that the possibilities for men's domination lie mostly in short-lived superficial encounters. Since research seems to indicate that marriage is emotionally and psychologically good for *men* and bad for *women*, this is another assumption that should seem odd to us without further explanation.

Some forms of exploitation do seem to work best during occasions of short-term contact, such as robbery, whereas other work better over a protracted period of time, such as slavery. Interestingly, the forms involving short-term contact are usually exploitations of people who are not truly weaker in the context where exploitation is taking place: if the thief does not escape quickly, the person whose property has been stolen may gain useful access to systems of law enforcement and the exploitation will not work.

In the case of male domination in a close erotic context, the male is cloaked in shared images of male authority as well as far less ambivalence about the permissibility of his sexual behaviors, and furthermore he is in a much better position to use physical force — these all contribute to male domination, and sometimes suffice to do so over long periods of time.

But not always. Sexual sensations have emotional content in and of themselves, and have a tendency to create or strengthen empathic connections and shared identity.[5] Intimacy, in other words, has a tendency to spread. Domination that depends on an ideology of difference and superiority, as male supremacy tends to, is incompatible with a sense of connectedness and shared identification. If this is revolution, though, it is confined to the level of individuals. Shulamith Firestone (1970), writing in *The Dialectic of Sex* about how love is the pivot of women's oppression, said that the only thing that makes a man's feeling of connectedness and identification with a woman stand out and look so special is the backdrop of his attitudes towards women in general, within which women are not perceived as equal, interesting or even as people. And yet, this experience, the 'holy grail' of women's sexual existence within patriarchy, merely causes each woman to hope that one man will be led by sexual and related emotional experiences to identify with her and therefore see her as a person while continuing to view other women as subhuman, tangential, unworthy of consideration.

But intimacy has a capacity far more fearful than the mere capacity for undermining ideologies of superiority. When a sense of shared identity and connectedness has been created, and exists strongly, the individual's identity becomes enmeshed in the relationship itself, and with the other person or persons. Like a center of gravity, this shifted sense of identity affects personal orbits. To be in love is to be vulnerable to the opinions, needs and wants of the other who is now no longer strictly other at all. To be in love is to risk being more deeply in love than the other, to become subsumed in another's life and interests and immediate emotional condition and concerns more deeply than one's own — or, rather, they *become* one's own.

This is not to say that love is only about power and domination. The person who has the dubious distinction of having someone fall more or less unilaterally in love with her or him must often deal with an emotionally fragile, dependent person who follows about, puppy-eyed and pathetic. For most people, this is not preferable to a more balanced relationship with the richness of needing and feeling needed, enjoying the emotional intoxication of identifying while experiencing the joys of having another become intoxicated with them in turn. But love is not *separable* from power and the possibility of becoming thoroughly decentered and probably hurt in the process. Love is not safe and cannot be made safe.

Patriarchal custom makes a valiant try, however. When one considers how little the masculine personality construct and the overall male experience prepares males for the emotional interplay of interconnection and caring and need, it becomes readily apparent why it has to try so hard. Consider the masculinized male, for whom the vulnerability is that of desiring connection with She who is of the same gender as the (m)Other of original and primary connection (Hollway, 1983), because that is the connection denied and dreaded, the denial of which defines masculinity itself (Chodorow, 1978). This is a dreadful fear that makes even the elimination of freedom palatable in comparison. The marriage contract and the less formal structures by which ongoing heterosexual relationships are commonly assembled are generally geared towards promises of forever, promises of exclusivity, promises of ever continuing deep feelings on a mutual basis. In the current era of legal, obtainable divorce and greater individual freedoms in such personal matters, they don't tend to work very well. But to the extent that they do work, creating 'safe' situations where leaving the relationship or getting involved with someone else is out of the question for those involved, they result in boring, stagnant unerotic relationships dragging themselves off into the sunset. Because without the excitement and the fears and the vulnerability that would come from risking love with another *free* person, there is no gap for the spark to jump.

RESOLUTION

Erotic excitement, according to patriarchal ideology, depends on the tension created by setting men against women in a power struggle, setting them at cross-purposes with conflicting interests that create the possibilities of vulnerability and domination. The scene of this conflict is the period of negotiation for sexual experience: if he 'scores', he wins and moves on; if he falls in love and sticks around for an ongoing relationship, she wins; if he gives up and moves on without 'scoring', it's a draw (Hollway, 1983).

Heterosexuality with sissies involved doesn't include erotic excitement as constructed by *that* particular system, but if the false patriarchal division between courtship and ongoing relationship is recognized for what it is and discarded, there are other sources of eroticized vulnerability, and I've not found matters boring.

The sissy quite possibly has prided himself all his life for his development of 'feminine' strengths. Although contemptuously conceptualized as a dominated Caspar Milquetoast, he has no necessary reason to fear the ongoing relationship that would ordinarily characterize a female win. With no fragile rigid sense of identity dependent on how *different* he is from women, the possibility of falling in love and identifying deeply with a woman has a less frightening face, and so he is probably more ready to share and care. The hard part, other than figuring out who (or 'how') he is in the first place, is finding women who have recognized that there is nothing for them within the boundaries of the heterosexual game script of how boy meets girl and stays with girl, and are therefore looking outside beyond it. Most likely, these are women who are not committed to a sense of themselves as heterosexual feminine women. Fortunately, female identity is less constructed around proving that one is not a lesbian than is male identity around proving one is not gay, and feminism has certainly helped. Feminists understand best about discarding the role scripts and starting off from scratch with no sexist assumptions.

It is unclear who has the advantage at close range. The woman fascinated by and attracted to the sissy is probably more experienced with the specific dynamics of erotic and other intimate emotional connectedness, and could probably get involved with another man much easier than he could get involved with another woman. On the other hand, there are fewer men like him than there are women like her, and they both know it. Furthermore, most strong women are not *used* to playing with men who are their emotional equals in intimate relationships.

All in all, it tends to be rather risky and frightening for both, with lots of vulnerability and tenderness and sparks jumping around all over the place.

All this has a number of theoretical implications. First, for someone who has drawn so extensively upon feminist theory as I have here, is the 'men in feminism' question.

I have built my model from feminist tenets because, although as Doyle (1983), Herek (1987) and others have noted, sissyphobia is derived via projection from both misogyny and from homophobia, the question of primacy seems to me to answer itself almost the moment it is asked: I cannot believe for a moment that the masculine man's hatred and fear and contempt of women is due to the ways in which women remind them of gay men or sissies! Sissyphobia, therefore, is utterly patriarchal. I am going so far as to claim that patriarchy cannot survive without sissyphobia, but that is because the elimination of sissyphobia already necessitates the cessation of misogyny in (and as the definition of) men. The implication of ending sissyphobia for male homophobia is that 'heterosexual' and 'homosexual' become converted back to adjective descriptions of behavior rather than noun descriptions of people (as discussed by Herek, 1987), if sissyhood, a 'way' a given male person 'is', ceases to be attached to what he *does* (i.e. with whom) as the sexual expression of himself.

Some people will look upon this as further demonstration that males (if not men) have a stake in the success of feminist transformation; others, no doubt, will state that they are not at all surprised to see that another man (and what is a male, if not a man?) is trying to insert his stake into a feminism that wants nothing to do with it. Jeff Hearn writes,

> Can there be men's anti-patriarchal theory, that would parallel but not compete with women's theory? Some would say 'no'; it is ridiculous for an oppressor class to propound theory, contradictorily in an anti-patriarchal form. For example one could argue that it would be meaningless for bourgeois to construct bourgeois anti-capitalist theory, apart from as an extended and convoluted exercise in ideology and smoke-screening. Yet the comparison is not exact — for members of the bourgeoisie can change classes, both individually and collectively; men cannot. It is men's fix in biology that paradoxically creates the possibility of critical, anti-patriarchal theory and practice. If bourgeois are convinced that they want to oppose capitalism they can renounce their social class and change sides; men cannot do that in the same way. It is this contradiction of consciousness and biology that creates the possibility of anti-patriarchal theory — of theory against patriarchy whilst remaining a man (Hearn, 1987: 14).

Or while remaining male, at any rate.

The question 'Is a feminist heterosexuality possible?' (Hamblin, 1983) is inseparable from the question of whether men can really ever be anything to feminism other than either a 'masculinist reaction or a "gentlemen's auxiliary"' (Kimmel, 1987) of men who support women's causes for women's reasons. Until and unless the specifically sexual questions of feminism are addressed by what men do (or cease to do, or both), men cannot claim to have responded to feminism at all. Male sexuality and the heterosexual relationship, both metaphorically and as literal concrete reality, has often been cited as the core of patriarchy, and Hamblin's question has been answered more than once in the essentialist negative (Dworkin, 1987; discussed in Horowitz and Kaufman, 1987). Answers have also been posed from a qualified essentialism, as when one early reader of this work asked me if sissyhood in action implied refraining from penetration in order to eliminate male domination beneath the sheets.[6] The sissy theoretical perspective I've outlined here is thoroughly outside biological claims, and assumes that the essential relationship of gender to systemic oppression is a 'fluid-essentialism', in which dynamics can change; and that biology does not contain political meaning all by itself, even if it is true, as Horowitz and Kaufman (1987: 84) assert, that 'Male sexuality . . . isn't constructed out of nothing. . . . Culture does not write on a blank paper', and that this is similarly true for women as well. If there is an inclination among some females to esthetically prefer sexual expression with the male of the species, we cannot know it until it ceases to be compulsory (Rich, 1980), but we also cannot know of its absence until that same situation prevails. If some portion of the world's females are indeed inclined to desire males sexually for reasons not entirely attributable to the ideologies of social construction, this would explain part of the difficulty women have had in rising up against their own oppression.

I am saying, in essence, that males will benefit from a successful transformation of our world from patriarchy to the feminism-inspired world of voluntary co-operation that is most often visioned to replace it (Morgan, 1982; French, 1985). I am saying that sissies are those males most likely to understand this on an immediately personal ground, and that as they understand this, they will see themselves as having a personal stake in the success of feminism.

I should assert that it is not an equal stake: even as a sissy, as I get older, the rigid specifications of heterosexual behavior apply less and less to the people of my own age cohort, because individual experience brings its own deconstructive processes even as the same sexist script dynamics encode the sexualities of the generations behind us — meanwhile, I am not of the sex that must face systematic discriminations, and I'm not going to get raped in the parking lot on my way home tonight. But I think understanding the sissy as category clarifies the need to move beyond binary oppositional understandings of what patriarchy really is. Social structure and the social constructs of which it is formed can be re-understood from the position of the individual particles whose interactive dynamics are doing the constructing, but this only takes on revolutionary consequences when it is possible to see our way towards change on both sides, for reasons that both parties can appreciate. Perhaps the radical feminists were right all along when they said that no systematic form of oppression, whether you call it capitalism, state power or patriarchy, can survive collectively generalized, but individually personalized, political changes in what the sexes mean in interactive relationships.

There are many more theoretical implications and insights of which I *could* speak and write, which stem from the concept of the sissy. It is distinctively

thrilling to consider the ramifications of this being in print (a seductively powerful position, this business of being a published person!), and of being able to
refer back to it in order to go on to say other things. One corollary to the personal being political is that the theoretical is tactical, and the very fact of having
said what has been said here, if it has merit and makes sense against the
backdrop of people's understanding of the world, is that I have spoken sissyhood
into being, at least in a small way; and the more that this concept draws attention, the more it becomes a socially shared concept and a category of experience
from which definitions of self and society can and will respond. By the very act
of saying truthfully that the heterosexual sissy is inconceivable, I may well have
made it untrue.

NOTES

1. An old observation. A good analysis and discussion can be found in Kate Millett's
   Sexual Politics (1970).
2. Which is, of course, also true of the rape of females: the victim is blamed. A good
   and vivid fictional example of this attitude is developed in James Kirkwood's *Good
   Times, Bad Times* (New York: Crowell, 1975).
3. In a course I once took on sexism and gender roles, my teacher drew a continuum
   from 'all masculine' to 'all feminine'. It was asserted that a person could be in
   the middle (androgynous) and still be heterosexual, and *therefore* men should give
   up their homophobic concern with being 'all masculine'. When asked about the
   fate of a male who was much closer to the 'all feminine' pole of the continuum,
   the teacher shrugged and said, 'I think they'd probably all rather be gay over
   there'. In Richard Greene's research (*The Sissy Boy Syndrome and the Development of Homosexuality*. New Haven, CT: Yale University Press, 1987), the author
   provides case histories that are presumably representative of his total sample —
   boys who were sissies who grew up to be gay, boys who were masculine who
   grew up to be straight, boys who were sissies who became masculinized later and
   grew up straight, and so on. None of the case studies was of boys who were
   sissies, remained sissies and grew up to be heterosexual sissies. If *not one* of the
   sissies in his sample of boys had grown up to be heterosexual without becoming
   masculinized beforehand, that would have been a major finding, central to his
   research interest, but it wasn't even commented upon. On the other hand, neither
   was it stated that some sissies remain sissies and grow up to be heterosexual. It
   is seldom said that some sissies are heterosexual, and it is difficult to notice the
   pattern formed by an absence.
4. A cartoon character of H. T. Webster, Caspar Milquetoast was a caricature of the
   mild-mannered, overly proper ineffectual man thoroughly dominated by his wife,
   other men and essentially everyone else.
5. Audre Lorde writes:
   > The erotic functions for me in several ways, and the first is in the power
   > which comes from sharing deeply any pursuit with another person. The
   > sharing of joy, whether physical, emotional, psychic, or intellectual, forms
   > a bridge between the sharers which can be the basis for understanding much

of what is not shared between them, and lessens the threat of their difference (Lorde, 1980: 298).

(Or, I might add, it can threaten through its capacity to lessen difference.)

6. Which is perhaps worthy of an answer. My non-essentialist answer would be that not having penetration in mind as the goal of erotic expression — or for that matter any goal other than intimacy and sharing and pleasure — best characterizes the difference.

REFERENCES

Chodorow, N. (1978) *The Reproduction of Mothering: Psychoanalysis and the Sociology of Gender*. Berkeley, CA: University of California Press.

Dinnerstein, D. (1976) *The Mermaid and the Minotaur: Sexual Arrangements and Human Malaise*. New York: Harper and Row.

Doyle, J. A. (1983) *The Male Experience*. Dubuque, IA: William C. Brown.

Dworkin, A. (1981) *Pornography: Men Possessing Women*. New York: Putnam.

Dworkin, A. (1987) *Intercourse*. New York: The Free Press.

Firestone, S. (1970) *The Dialectic of Sex*. New York: Morrow.

French, M. (1985) *Beyond Power: On Women, Men and Morals*. New York: Ballantine.

Gagnon, J. and Simon, W. (1973) *Sexual Conduct*. Chicago, IL: Aldine.

Gibbs, N. (1991) 'When is it Rape?' *Time* 3 June: 63.

Greer, G. (1970) *The Female Eunuch*. London: MacGibbon and Kee.

Hamblin, A. (1983) 'Is a Feminist Heterosexuality Possible?', in S. Cartledge and J. Ryan (eds) *Sex and Love: New Thoughts on Old Contradictions*. London: The Women's Press.

Hart, J. and Richardson, D. (1981) *The Theory and Practice of Homosexuality*. London: Routledge and Kegan Paul.

Hartley, R. (1974) 'Sex-role Pressures and the Socialization of the Male Child', in J. H. Pleck and J. Sawyer (eds) *Men and Masculinity*, pp. 7–13. Englewood Cliffs, NJ: Prentice Hall.

Hearn, J. (1987) *The Gender of Oppression: Men, Masculinity, and the Critique of Marxism*. Brighton: Wheatsheaf.

Herek, G. M. (1987) 'On Heterosexual Masculinity: Some Psychical Consequences of the Social Construction of Gender and Sexuality', in M. S. Kimmel, (ed.) *Changing Men: New Directions in Research on Men and Masculinity*. Newbury Park, CA: Sage.

Hollway, W. (1983) 'Heterosexual Sex: Power and Desire for the Other', in S. Cartledge and J. Ryan (eds) *Sex and Love: New Thoughts on Old Contradictions*. London: The Women's Press.

Horowitz, G. and Kaufman, M. (1987) 'Male Sexuality: Toward a Theory of Liberation', in M. Kaufman (ed.) *Beyond Patriarchy: Essays by Men on Pleasure, Power and Change*. London: Oxford University Press.

Kimmel, M. (1987) 'Teaching A Course on Men: Masculinist Reaction or "Gentlemen's Auxiliary"?', in M. S. Kimmel (ed.) *Changing Men: New Directions in Research on Men and Masculinity*. Newbury Park, CA: Sage.

Lorde, A. (1980) 'Uses of the Erotic: The Erotic as Power', in L. Lederer (ed.) *Take Back the Night: Woman on Pornography*. New York: Morrow.

Lydon, S. (1970) 'The Politics of Orgasm', in R. Morgan (ed.) *Sisterhood is Powerful*, pp. 197–205. New York: Vintage Press.

MacKinnon, C. (1987) *Feminism Unmodified: Discourses on Life and Law*. Cambridge, MA: Harvard University Press.

Miedzian, M. (1991) *Boys Will Be Boys: Breaking the Link Between Masculinity and Violence*. Garden City, NY: Doubleday.

Millett, K. (1970) *Sexual Politics*. Garden City, NY: Doubleday.

Morgan, R. (1982) *The Anatomy of Freedom: Feminism, Physics, and Global Politics*. Garden City, NY: Anchor/Doubleday.

Nonkin, L. J. (1985) *I Wish My Parents Understood: A Report on the Teenage Female*. New York: Freundlich Books.

Pharr, S. (1988) *Homophobia: A Weapon of Sexism*. Inverness, CA: Chardon Press.

Rechy, J. (1979) *The Rushes*. New York: Grove Press.

Rich, A. (1980) 'Compulsory Heterosexuality and Lesbian Existence', *Signs* 5(4): 631–60.

Stoltenberg, J. (1989) *Refusing To Be a Man: Essays on Sex and Justice*. Portland, OR: Breitenbush Books.

Weinberger, G. (1972) *Society and the Healthy Homosexual*. New York: St Martin's Press.

Allan HUNTER first attempted to put the experiences and understandings outlined in this article into words in his freshman year in college in 1980 and was locked in a psychiatric hospital for doing so. He is now a graduate student of sociology, a participant in the psychiatric inmates' liberation movement and a conceptually problematic participant in the movement against patriarchy. This is his first professionally published work. ADDRESS: c/o Department of Sociology, State University of New York at Stony Brook, Stony Brook, NY 11794, USA.

Denise THOMPSON

Against the Dividing of Women: Lesbian Feminism and Heterosexuality

I am arguing for a continuity of interests between lesbians and heterosexual women, and that lesbians and heterosexual women have common experiences which enable them to understand and empathize with each other. I document the history of the feminist critique of heterosexuality from early radical feminism to the contemporary arguments of Rich (1980), Raymond (1986) and Penelope (1985a, 1985b, 1985c). From a lesbian feminist standpoint, I suggest that setting up an oppositional dichotomy between 'lesbian' and 'heterosexual' divides women from each other and perpetuates the heterosexual hegemony. The continuing revaluation and redefinition of lesbianism is essential in order to achieve the political priority of feminism: an end to male domination.

I write about heterosexuality from the standpoint of lesbian feminism because the change in perspective which came with lesbian feminism has irrevocably changed the way I view heterosexuality. From the standpoint of lesbian feminism, I can no longer approach heterosexuality as the only 'real' form of sexuality — having stepped out of heterosexual activity, I no longer find it real. Neither can I approach it even as a valid alternative — the feminist critique is too convincing and unanswerable. So this article, although structured around 'heterosexuality', refers constantly to lesbianism, because the lesbian commitment is central to the feminist critique of heterosexuality.

The chief burden of my argument is that there is a continuity of interests and experience between 'lesbian' and 'heterosexual' women, that lesbians are not a 'different' category of women, but part of a continuum of being female. Lesbianism, as it has been redefined by feminism, is not just the 'sexual preference' of a 'minority', but central to the redefining and recreating of what it is to be a woman.

What I mean by this continuity is that all women share a common interest in opposing male supremacy, wherever they are situated in relation to men. The existence of political lesbianism demonstrates that women *can* withdraw from the heterosexual system which maintains the male as the 'human' norm and the female as his ancillary. It demonstrates, too, that women can love other women, and can recognize other women and ourselves as fully human individuals lacking nothing.

Within the liberal pluralist framework, lesbians are perceived to be like heterosexual women in everything but the sex of the 'person' they 'choose' to have sex with (see Kitzinger, 1987). However, as a lesbian feminist, I am not arguing that there are no differences between lesbians and heterosexual women. To be heterosexual, all a woman needs to do is to fall unthinkingly in with what everyone does. She does not have to make a choice between equally valid alternatives — hegemonically, there are no alternatives to heterosexuality — she merely has to follow the dominant mores. To be a lesbian, however, requires some measure of self-reflection, or at least self-consciousness.[1]

Moreover, women identified as lesbians are subjected to the full force of the mechanisms designed to keep women in their 'place', sustaining men and fostering male interests, and as the 'appropriate' receptacles for male desire. At the same time, by refusing sexual intimacy with men, lesbians are less tied into the more immediate problems of relations with men. So there *are* differences between lesbians and heterosexual women, but those differences spring from a common root — the dividing of women from each other in order to keep the attention and energy of the 'normal majority' of the female population focused on men.

I *am* in disagreement, however, with the assertion of Monique Wittig and the radical lesbians that 'Lesbians are not women' (Wittig, 1980; Hoagland and Penelope, 1988: 439–500). Because all women have a common interest in liberating ourselves from male supremacy, lesbians included, I am worried about the consequences for female solidarity of the refusal to call ourselves 'women' — not out of a concern about 'alienating' heterosexual women — to the extent that they are alienated from us, it is not our doing.[2] What I am concerned about is that we could forget, ignore or deny the oppression we share because we *are* women, not just lesbians. I can understand only too well the impatience many lesbians feel with a feminism which remains tied into heterosexual concerns, at the expense of lesbian interests. But the solution is not to abandon feminism, but to continue making it relevant to lesbians.

The position I am arguing has been criticized on the grounds that it 'desexualizes' lesbianism. For example, the authors of the Introduction to *Desire: The Politics of Sexuality* asserted that the Radicalesbian manifesto, 'The Woman-Identified Woman' (Radicalesbians, 1970) 'opened the way for the desexualization of lesbian identity'. This manifesto managed, according to Snitow et al. (1984: 24–6), to 'completely unsex an identity that had been all sex just a short time before'. It did this by 'pointing to anger rather than eros as the wellspring of lesbianism' — the manifesto opened with: 'What is a lesbian? A lesbian is the rage of all women condensed to the point of explosion' — and by 'identify[ing] lesbians with all women by redefining lesbianism as the quintessential feminism'. Snitow et al. (1984: 24–6) comment: 'The sources of lesbianism, then, [according to 'The Woman-Identified Woman' paper] were political not erotic'.

But this criticism (deliberately?) misses the point. The opposition between 'political' and 'erotic' — *either* political *or* erotic — is untenable in feminist terms. From the beginning, feminism has pointed to the political nature *of* the erotic, not least within the institution of heterosexuality. More recently, it has become clearer that this mutually exclusive dichotomy between 'the political' and 'the erotic' is a hallmark of sexual libertarianism, which must insist that sexuality is outside political critique if it is to maintain its defence of lesbian sadomasochism and pornography. (For examples of this libertarian standpoint, see Vance, 1984, 1989; Rubin, 1984; Webster, 1981, 1984; Echols, 1984. For critiques of sexual libertarianism, see Jeffreys, 1990; Leidholdt and Raymond, 1990; Cole, 1989; Thompson, 1991.)

The Radicalesbian authors of 'The Woman-Identified Woman' paper were more in touch with what was actually happening in feminism than the editors of the *Desire* volume. By refusing to characterize the lesbian relationship 'simply by sex' (Radicalesbians, 1970: 20), they were broadening the definition of lesbianism to encompass:

> . . . the primacy of women relating to women, of women creating a new consciousness of and with each other which is at the heart of women's liberation (Radicalesbians, 1970: 21).

The insistence that lesbianism is not only genital sexual desire and/or activity, but also a redefining of women by women for women and outside male control, is not to 'desexualize' it. To say that lesbianism is not only genital sex is not to say that lesbianism is not sex at all. The slide from 'not only' to 'not at all' is so absurd that I can only explain it as a form of bad faith. Those who are now identified as sexual libertarians have a vested interest in not understanding or questioning current forms of sexual desire because those forms constitute their own feelings and emotions. They constitute, or have constituted, the feelings and emotions of all of us in one way or another. The difference lies in the willingness to question and the refusal to be implicated. Arguments like that of Snitow et al. are unconvincing in their attempts to dismiss and trivialize the central importance of lesbianism to feminism.

Early radical feminism was highly critical of heterosexuality. (The examples of early radical feminist writings I will be using are all from the USA. This is not an example of US cultural imperialism. As I remember the period in question — the early 1970s — these writings were the only ones available in Australia which were saying what we were saying and thinking anyway.) Whether it was called 'the sex-role system', 'sex class' or 'the institution of sexual intercourse', heterosexuality was the enemy to be struggled against. Its destruction was a prerequisite for the feminist revolution. Heterosexuality had to go. None of it was retrievable for feminist purposes.

The New York group of radical feminists, formed in October 1968, and calling themselves simply THE FEMINISTS, had a membership quota. Women
who were in sexual relationships with men could not comprise more than one-
third of their membership at any one time. (Given the heterosexual orientation
of THE FEMINISTS, the other two-thirds were unlikely to have been lesbians,
although this is conjecture on my part. They were more likely to have been
celibate.) 'We must destroy the institution of heterosexual sex', they said:

> . . . the institution of marriage [is] inherently inequitable . . . this institution
> [is] a primary formalization of the persecution of women . . . at present [the]
> psychology [of heterosexuality] is dominance-passivity . . . the female is
> coerced into sexual relations with the male . . . sexual relations [are] . . . pro-
> grammed to support political ends — that is, male oppression of the female
> (Koedt et al., 1973: 374, 376).

Ti-Grace Atkinson insisted that 'our society has never known a time when sex
in all its aspects was not exploitative and relations based on sex, e.g. the male–
female relationship, were not extremely hostile' (Atkinson, 1974: 19). Although
this statement could be read to mean that sex was bad for men too, her concern
was clearly with the oppressive consequences for women. The chief target of
her attack was 'the institution of sexual intercourse', which was, she said, 'in
the interests of the male and against the interests of the female', and which
'limit[ed] a woman's human possibilities'.

Along with the critique of heterosexuality went a scathing denunciation of
'love'. Ti-Grace Atkinson said with a fine rhetorical flourish:

> And love. As long as we're on sacred cows, let's finish them. What is love but
> the payoff for the consent to oppression? What is love but a need? What is love
> but fear? In a just society, would we need love? . . . Scratch *his* love, and you'll
> find *your* fear (Atkinson, 1974: 7, original emphasis).

Bonnie Kreps said: 'we must fight the corrupt notion we now call "love", which
is based on the control of another rather than on love for the growth of another'
(Koedt et al., 1973: 239). And THE FEMINISTS said:

> Love promotes vulnerability, dependence, possessiveness, susceptibility to
> pain, and prevents the full development of women's human potential by direc-
> ting all her energies outward in the interests of others (Koedt et al., 1973: 375).

According to Shulamith Firestone, 'love' (for men) placed women in an impossible situation because it was a relationship of inequality. 'Love', she said,
'requires a mutual vulnerability that is impossible to achieve in an unequal
power situation' (Firestone, 1971: 132). Although she could conceive of the
possibility of a love that led to mutual enrichment and growth, as things stood
at the moment, love became 'complicated, corrupted, or obstructed by an *unequal balance of power*' (Firestone, 1971: 130, original emphasis). Under

present conditions, it was dangerous for women to love men, she argued, because men could not love in return. Men were protected against the vulnerability of love by their membership of the superior class. Either the man idealized the woman he was 'in love' with, in order to raise her above the common female herd and to justify his interest in her: 'A man must idealize one woman over the rest in order to justify his descent to a lower caste' (p. 131). Or he degraded her in order to distinguish her from his original forbidden love object, his mother. Either way, the woman was faced with unrealistic expectations to live up to or struggle against.

Many of the early radical feminist critics of heterosexuality were themselves heterosexual. Their critique was a radical one, i.e. they were concerned not merely to reform heterosexuality, but do demolish it altogether. Nevertheless, by remaining focused on the problems of heterosexuality, they reinforced the idea that heterosexuality was the only 'real' sexuality, and they excluded consideration of lesbianism as a possible radical alternative. Sometimes this exclusion was inadvertent — 'sexuality' was entirely heterosexual and lesbianism was never mentioned.

Sometimes the exclusion was deliberate. Ti-Grace Atkinson, for example, argued explicitly against the revolutionary implications of lesbianism. In her view, lesbianism was no improvement on heterosexuality because, she said, it was 'based ideologically on the very premise of male oppression: the dynamic of sexual intercourse' (Atkinson, 1974: 85). But she herself defined 'sexual intercourse' as 'the interrelation between these two classes' (i.e. between the two sexes). Moreover, lesbianism has at least one crucial difference from heterosexuality, i.e. the absence of the penis, the organ which defines what counts as 'sexual' in male supremacist terms. Hence, the question of lesbianism's difference from heterosexuality does need to be raised. By failing to do so, Atkinson failed to demonstrate that lesbianism was as oppressive to women as heterosexuality.

The heterosexual feminist critique of heterosexuality was short lived. It had petered out by the mid-1970s (for two recent exceptions, see Sichtermann, 1986; Johnson, 1988), except, of course, for continuing feminist struggles for reproductive rights and women's autonomy and independence, and against rape, marital violence, child sexual abuse, sexual harassment, etc., none of which was labelled 'heterosexual' any longer (although it was sometimes attributed to 'the family'). If I were to speculate about the reason for this on the basis of my own experience of feminism, I would suggest that many of the 'heterosexual' feminists who mounted the initial critiques became lesbians (see below), and the source of the challenge to heterosexuality shifted to lesbian feminism. At the same time, the challenge developed and broadened and became even more unequivocal than the original critique.

There was some chronological overlap between the heterosexual feminist critique of heterosexuality and the lesbian feminist one. 'The Woman-Identified Woman' paper already mentioned was presented as early as 1970 (at the Second

Congress to Unite Women, as a challenge to the National Organization of Women and its refusal to acknowledge lesbians). The authors, who called themselves Radicalesbians and 'The Lavender Menace' (a phrase coined by Betty Friedan to dismiss the lesbian demands), argued that lesbians were ideally placed to question the conventional feminine role because they had never felt comfortable with it. The Radicalesbians also pointed out that any woman could be labelled a 'lesbian', and that the term was used to keep women in their place, subservient to and serving men. They argued that lesbians were a vital part of women's liberation, both because of the challenge lesbians posed to femininity, and because of the love and solidarity lesbians had for women. They said:

> As long as women's liberation tries to free women without facing the basic heterosexual structure that binds us in a one-to-one relationship with a man . . . this obviously splits our energies and commitments, leaving us unable to be committed to the construction of the new patterns which will liberate us (Radicalesbians, 1970: 21).

The lesbian feminist journal, *The Furies*, dates from 1972. In the collection of articles from the journal, called *Lesbianism and the Women's Movement*, the authors of the Introduction said:

> Lesbian-feminist politics is a political critique of the institution and ideology of heterosexuality as a primary cornerstone of male supremacy. It is an extension of the analysis of sexual politics into an analysis of sex itself as an institution. It is a commitment to women as a political group which is the basis of a political/economic strategy leading to power for women (Myron and Bunch, 1975: 10; see also Abbott and Love, 1973).

The later lesbian feminist accounts took the critique further. In 1978, the Leeds Revolutionary Feminists asserted baldly and unequivocally what many lesbian feminists were still saying and thinking, but either had been too frightened to say in public or had been intimidated into silence when they did say it (or were perceived to be saying it, whether or not they actually had):

> . . . any woman who takes part in a heterosexual couple helps to shore up male supremacy by making its foundations stronger . . . . Every act of penetration for the woman is an invasion which undermines her confidence and saps her strength. For a man it is an act of power and mastery which makes him stronger, not just over one woman but over all women. So every woman who engages in penetration bolsters the oppressor and reinforces the class power of men (Leeds Revolutionary Feminist Group, 1981: 6).

I find this something of an overstatement of the feminist critique of heterosexuality. While there is no feminist account which validates heterosexuality as a feminist activity, there are feminists who maintain their radical feminist politics — in the sense of recognizing male domination as the main enemy, and women loving women as their primary feminist commitment — despite their heterosexual desire and activity. Nonetheless, this public statement by the Leeds

Revolutionary Feminists needed to be made because it was exactly what so many women were saying among themselves.

My preference is for the accounts given by Adrienne Rich and Janice Raymond (Rich, 1980; Raymond, 1986), because both of them argue for a continuity of female experience between 'lesbian' and 'heterosexual'. Both argue that heterosexuality is imposed on women. They give numerous examples of the ways in which women are sometimes brutally coerced into 'heterorelations' (Raymond's term), sometimes subjected to more subtle violence by being deprived of any possible alternatives. The one criticism I would make of their accounts is that they give too little attention to the ways in which heterosexual desire is inculcated in women, the ways in which women are brought to embrace their own oppression. Both Rich and Raymond uncover a continuum of relationships between women, relationships which have always existed but whose historical continuity has been suppressed by the male supremacist requirement that women love and nurture only men. Rich's term for these relationships is 'lesbian continuum', Raymond's variously 'gynaffection', 'female friendship' and 'female affection'. Both situate the lesbianism of 'second-wave' feminism within this continuum of women loving women. It is this approach which most accurately describes what actually happened during this 'second wave' of feminist political consciousness and activity. We ourselves experienced the continuity in our own lives.

The phenomenon of women becoming lesbians with the advent of 'second-wave' feminism has received very little acknowledgement in feminist writings. One of the few writers who does acknowledge it, Julia Penelope, writes:

> In a sense, recruiting heterosexual women into the movement has served to recruit Lesbians, because so many wimmin shed the facade of heterosexuality once they're given permission to love themselves and other wimmin (Penelope, 1985a: 32).

The evidence for its happening, and continuing to happen, is largely confined to the experience, memories and current perceptions of those of us who are prepared to acknowledge it. It has been silenced, along with so much of radical lesbian feminist politics, by the continuing hegemony of the malestream and its continuing co-option of feminism. Nonetheless, it happened and is still happening, and is the strongest empirical evidence against the idea that lesbians are different from 'other' women. It demonstrates that lesbianism is neither something foreign to 'most' women as the conventional (malestream) wisdom would have us believe, nor a mark of automatic revolutionary consciousness setting lesbians apart from women in general as a certain sort of absolutist separatism asserts. (For my concept of 'absolutist separatism', together with my defence of separatism in Marilyn Frye's and Julia Penelope's sense of withdrawing recognition and energy from men and male institutions, see Thompson, 1991: 93–4.) If women can move from heterosexual to lesbian desire, permanently or temporarily, reluctantly or with relief and recognition, then to be a lesbian is not to be separate and distinct from 'other' women — it is part of a continuum of female existence. While the shift to a lesbian feminist consciousness is a radical rupture with the unthinking heterosexual norm, not only for women who were 'actively' heterosexual, but also for lesbians prior to the arrival of second-wave feminism, it does not constitute a complete forgetting. How could we forget, when it is still all around us, proselytizing daily, hourly?

'Lesbian' and 'heterosexual' are not two distinct and incommensurable categories of women. There are many lesbians who used to be heterosexual in the sense that they had sexual relations with men, were married, had children, etc., and who either changed their sexual orientation completely, or actively and consciously embraced a lesbian desire and passion which had always existed but which had not been identified until the arrival of 'second-wave' feminism. Even lesbians who have never been heterosexual in desire and activity cannot avoid the influence of a heterosexual hegemony which flaunts itself as the only 'love', and promotes its values endlessly as the only 'reality'. Lesbians are thoroughly familiar with heterosexuality, both through actual personal experience and through the all-pervasive ideology which saturates the whole culture.

Moreover, heterosexual women can recognize the familiarity of lesbianism. Although heterosexuality functions to divide women from each other in the interests of maintaining the female servicing of men, heterosexual women, too, know what it is to love women, through female friendship and support networks, through sisterhood and solidarity and through their own experiences of the maternal relation. While the latter is distorted and dehumanized under conditions of male supremacy, since its purpose is to service males and to train females to service males, daughters and the mothers of daughters can recognize each other despite the odds stacked against them. Although heterosexual desire functions to keep women from each other, even to turn us against each other, women can love women in spite of it.

To set up an oppositional dichotomy between 'lesbian' and 'heterosexual' is to falsify female existence. The malestream cannot avoid setting up the opposition. By defining women only in relation to men, the male hegemony cannot incorporate women who have no need for men, particularly women who have no need for men sexually. As women outside male definition, lesbians are not 'real' women. At best, they are a 'deviant minority', tolerated as an oddity as long as they do not impinge on the lives of men and 'their' women. The attitude that lesbians are not 'real' women was succinctly expressed by one stalwart citizen (male, of course, since women still hardly qualify as 'people', much less as citizens), caught on the outskirts of an abortion demonstration some years ago in Sydney. Fuming with rage, he burst out: 'She's not a woman, she's a lesbian. She couldn't have a baby if she tried!' His wife nodded beside him in tight-lipped agreement. (He couldn't have known, of course, but within range of his wildly thrusting finger, there were at least two lesbians who had four children apiece, not to mention me who had two.) 'The lesbian' must be made to be different from 'other' women in terms of malestream thought — how else can the male mind incorporate females who do not 'love' men?

Another example of the false opposition is the so-called 'heterosexual/lesbian split' within feminism, which supposedly happened in the 1970s. As I experienced this split here in Sydney, it was one within the ranks of lesbian feminism itself. While some lesbian feminists were insisting that lesbianism was central to feminism, other lesbian feminists were objecting that this stance excluded heterosexual women, either from the vanguard of feminism or from feminism altogether, because to acknowledge the importance of lesbianism to feminism would be too threatening to 'ordinary' women, or because lesbianism was 'irrelevant' to 'most' women. It was a lesbian/lesbian split, with radical feminist lesbians on one side insisting that lesbianism was necessary for the feminist revolution, and socialist feminist lesbians on the other worrying about being too threatening to heterosexual women, often referred to as 'most women' or 'the women out there' in 'the western suburbs' (in the case of Sydney).

But if large numbers of lesbian feminists had once been heterosexual in the most literal sense, and all lesbian feminists have a more than passing acquaintance with heterosexuality, then lesbian feminists ourselves had once been 'out there', and were, moreover, still struggling with 'out there' 'in here'. If we could recognize the political priorities of feminism from 'out there', so could other women. To assume that feminist politics needs to be sanitized and made palatable in order to attract more recruits is patronizing and dishonest. To quote Julia Penelope again:

> . . . *no* woman with a shred of self-respect is going to ally herself with a movement that has systematically and purposely set out to LIE to her in order to recruit her into its ranks. Diluting one's politics, denying one's principles, gutting one's ideology to seem more 'appealing' are all ways of LYING. . . . Any woman who really wants a different life for herself doesn't want essentially the same life with a few superficial frills here and there. She wants something other than what she has, or she isn't going to bother (Penelope, 1985b: 26–7).

Penelope attributes these attempts to 'euphemize' feminism to 'movement leaders', while I attribute them to socialist feminists. The difference is, I think, a national one. The USA is more likely to have 'leaders' than Australia — any 'leaders' we ever had, e.g. Germaine Greer, Anne Summers, tended to leave Australia's small pond to find bigger fish to fry elsewhere. And Australia has a more continuous, consistent and overt history of socialist politics than the USA.

Penelope also sees this drive to sanitize feminist politics as a fairly recent phenomenon, whereas I see it as one which has been around since the beginning of this 'second wave'. But Penelope herself locates its beginnings at an early date. She mentions International Women's Year as a starting point for the realization on the part of 'the organizations and "leaders" of the US WLM' that this was 'an opportunity to build a large political constituency, a movement of

NUMBERS of women' (Penelope, 1985a: 32, original emphasis). (The date of International Women's Year is given in this paper of Penelope's as '1977', whereas it was actually 1975.)

The antagonism towards lesbians and lesbianism within feminism seemed to be based on the assumption that lesbians were not only different from 'other' women, but *so* different that they (we) would scare 'other' women off. Bizarrely, this assumption was frequently made by lesbians about other lesbians, and about themselves. The absurdity of this can only be explained by locating it in the continuing influence of the heterosexual hegemony, the 'out there' alive and flourishing 'in here'. But to the extent that lesbian feminists *are* different from 'other' women, that difference in not an experiential (or ontological) one, but a political and ethical one. It springs from a recognition of the existence of male domination, a perception of its various subtle and overt manifestations and a refusal any longer to be subjected to its values and coercions. Although acknowledged and identifiable lesbians are subjected to a special form of harassment, any strong-minded, independent women can be labelled a lesbian and punished for it. As the Radicalesbians put it:

> Lesbian is a label invented by the man to throw at any woman who dares to be his equal, who dares to challenge his prerogatives . . . who dares to assert the primacy of her own needs. To have the label applied to people in women's liberation is just the most recent instance of a long history. . . . For in this sexist society, for a woman to be independent means she can't be a woman — she must be a dyke (Radicalesbians, 1970: 18).

It is not so much the lesbian's 'difference' which is so threatening, but her similarity. What the feminist redefining of lesbianism says to women still caught up in compulsory heterosexuality is: 'Here we are, not so very different from you in socialization, training and life experience, women like yourselves, and yet we have stepped out of the need for men and what they offer. If we can do it, so can you.' For women who can't, and who cannot live with the contradiction, it is the recognition of similarity and continuity which is so threatening. Why it should also have been other *lesbians* who found it threatening, I do not know. Perhaps it had something to do with their continuing commitment to the political priorities of the male left, with its vanguardism, its insistence on converting 'the masses'. However that may be, the heterosexual cause was certainly hotly defended by some lesbians within feminism almost from the beginning.

But why lesbianism? Why is it not possible to challenge and demolish the heterosexual hegemony through celibacy, or through a radical reassessment and rearrangement of heterosexual relationships? The short answer to that question is that that is not the way it happened. Although there are many women who happily chose celibacy rather than continue battling with men and in order to free themselves to be with women, celibacy in itself lacks the drive and passion of lesbian desire. And although there are women who carved out space and energy for themselves and other women while continuing in sexual relationships with men, the brick wall of the heterosexual hegemony is still too solidly entrenched, and its undermining too dependent on the goodwill of men. To give the last word to the Radicalesbians:

> Only women can give each other a new sense of self. That identity we have to develop with reference to ourselves, and not in relation to men. . . . For this we must be available and supportive to one another, give our commitment and our love, give the emotional support necessary to sustain this movement. . . . It is the primacy of women relating to women, of women creating a new consciousness of and with each other which is at the heart of women's liberation (Radicalesbians, 1970: 21).

NOTES

1. That does not mean that lesbians are invariably more aware than heterosexual women. Sometimes, the self-awareness around sexual desire can be combined with a greater conformity. Individual lesbians may not take advantage of the opportunity for self-awareness and resistance to social control. But because heterosexuality is the norm, the woman who 'chooses' it does not really have to make a choice.
2. The assertion that lesbians are not women works better in French than in English. It is no accident that it appeared first among Francophone lesbians. The French, 'Les lesbiennes ne sont pas de femmes', can mean both 'Lesbians are not women' and 'Lesbians are not wives'. Although Wittig's original French text makes it clear that 'les femmes' should be translated as 'women' rather than 'wives', French has no separate word to distinguish 'women' from 'wives'. Although such an argument has no political relevance — Francophone women have as much need for female solidarity as Anglophone women — it does suggest that the English word 'women' is more retrievable than the French 'femmes'.

REFERENCES

Abbott, S. and Love, B. (1973) *Sappho Was a Right-On Woman: A Liberated View of Lesbianism*. New York: Stein and Day.

Atkinson, T.-G. (1974) *Amazon Odyssey*. New York: Links Books.

Cole, S. G. (1989) *Pornography and the Sex Crisis*. Toronto: Arminita.

Echols, A. (1984) 'The Taming of the Id: Feminist Sexual Politics, 1968–83', in C. Vance, (ed.) *Pleasure and Danger: Exploring Female Sexuality*. London: Routledge and Kegan Paul.

Firestone, S. (1971) *The Dialectic of Sex*. New York: Bantam Books.

Hoagland, S. and Penelope, J., eds (1988) *For Lesbians Only: A Separatist Anthology*. London: Onlywomen Press.

Jeffreys, S. (1990) *Anticlimax*. London: The Women's Press.

Johnson, M. M. (1988) *Strong Mothers, Weak Wives: The Search for Gender Equality*. Berkeley, Los Angeles and London: University of California Press.

Kitzinger, C. (1987) *The Social Construction of Lesbianism*. London: Sage.

Koedt, A., Levine, E. and Rapone, A., eds (1973) *Radical Feminism*. New York: Quadrangle Books/The New York Times Book Co.

Leeds Revolutionary Feminist Group (1981) *Love Your Enemy? The Debate Between Heterosexual Feminism and Political Lesbianism*. London: Onlywomen Press.

Leidholdt, D. and Raymond, J. G., eds (1990) *The Sexual Liberals and the Attack on Feminism*. New York: Pergamon Press, The Athene Series.

Myron, N. and Bunch, C., eds (1975) *Lesbianism and the Women's Movement*. Baltimore, MD: Diana Press.

Penelope, J. (1985a) 'The Mystery of Lesbians: I', *Gossip* 1: 9–45.

Penelope, J. (1985b) 'The Mystery of Lesbians: II', *Gossip* 2: 16–68.

Penelope, J. (1985c) 'The Mystery of Lesbians: III', *Gossip* 3: 23–39.

Radicalesbians (1970) 'The Woman-Identified Woman', in S. Hoagland and J. Penelope (eds) *For Lesbians Only: A Separatist Anthology*. London: Onlywomen Press.

Raymond, J. (1986) *A Passion for Friends: Toward a Philosophy of Female Affection*. London: The Women's Press.

Rich, A. (1980) 'Compulsory Heterosexuality and Lesbian Existence', *Signs* 5(4): 631–60.

Rubin, G. (1984) 'Thinking Sex: Notes for a Radical Theory of the Politics of Sexuality', in C. Vance, (ed.) *Pleasure and Danger: Exploring Female Sexuality*. London: Routledge and Kegan Paul.

Sichtermann, B. (1986) *Femininity: The Politics of the Personal*. London: Polity Press.

Snitow, A., Stansell, C. and Thompson, S., eds (1984) *Desire: The Politics of Sexuality*. London: Virago.

Thompson, D. (1991) *Reading Between the Lines: A Lesbian Feminist Critique of Feminist Accounts of Sexuality*. Sydney: The Gorgon's Head Press.

Vance, C. (1984) 'Pleasure and Danger: Toward a Politics of Sexuality', in C. Vance, (ed.) *Pleasure and Danger: Exploring Female Sexuality*. London: Routledge and Kegan Paul.

Vance, C. (1989) 'Keynote Address: "Social Construction Theory: Problems in the History of Sexuality"', in *Homosexuality, Which Homosexuality? Essays from the International Scientific Conference on Lesbian and Gay Studies*. London: Gay Men's Press.

Webster, P. (1981) 'Pornography and Pleasure', *Heresies* 12: 48–51.

Webster, P. (1984) 'The Forbidden: Eroticism and Taboo', in C. Vance (ed.) *Pleasure and Danger: Exploring Female Sexuality*. London: Routledge and Kegan Paul.

Wittig, M. (1980) 'The Straight Mind', in S. Hoagland and J. Penelope (eds) *For Lesbians Only: A Separatist Anthology*, pp. 431–9. London: Onlywomen Press.

Denise THOMPSON was born in Mt Isa, Queensland, Australia, in 1940, but has lived in Sydney ever since. She is an independent scholar (a euphemism for 'unemployed academic'), with an Honours degree in Sociology from the University of New South Wales. She has been a lesbian feminist since the early 1970s, and is the author of *Reading Between the Lines: A Lesbian Feminist Critique of Feminist Accounts of Sexuality* (Sydney: The Gorgon's Head Press, 1991). ADDRESS: PO Box 132, Leichhardt-2040, Sydney, Australia.

Jackie GILFOYLE, Jonathan WILSON and BROWN

Sex, Organs and Audiotape: A Discourse Analytic Approach to Talking About Heterosexual Sex and Relationships

This article examines talk about sex and heterosexual relationships, based on a study of 12 women and 13 men who participated in semi-structured interviews, in order to identify the 'discourses' of sexuality which inform talk about heterosexual sex. One theme in talk about heterosexuality can be understood through the 'pseudo-reciprocal gift discourse': women are described as 'giving' themselves to men, whereas men 'give' women orgasms, reproducing dominant norms of male activity and female passivity — and thereby reinforcing the oppression of women. Men talk more graphically about sex than women — we suggest the resources of meaning concerning sex suit men's interests rather than women's, and reflect men's dominance in a (hetero)sexist society.

INTRODUCTION AND RATIONALE

This article explores how people talk about heterosexual relationships and sexuality. It concentrates on this topic for several reasons. First, the largely North American literature concerned with interpersonal attraction and 'dating behaviour' is unsatisfactory. For example, the currently influential 'equity theory' (Hatfield and Traupmann, 1981; Walster et al., 1978) treats relationships as sites where people consider costs and rewards for themselves and costs and rewards for the other person. Such theorizing does not address the possibility that the dominant ways of making sense of relationships are embedded in the heterosexual culture. Participating in such relationships, therefore, involves lived experience of this heterosexual culture rather than simply balancing costs and benefits. The best way to investigate this possibility, it seems, is to examine talk about relationships.

Second, the literature of the women's movement is concerned about heterosexual relations being a site of inequality, with women being disempowered in heterosexual sex (Hite, 1977). Heterosexuality, and in particular intercourse, is explicitly identified as a primary part of women's oppression (Dworkin, 1987). Indeed, it is often argued that heterosexual relationships are incompatible with women's interests and are imposed by a world which acts in men's interests, such that heterosexuality becomes 'mandatory' or 'compulsory' for women (Dworkin, 1987; Rich, 1980). The aim of this article, then, is to see how these inequalities might emerge in people's talk about heterosexual sex and relationships. Rich (1980) argues that women's sexual identity is not freely chosen but superimposed upon them. Institutionalized heterosexuality helps to maintain male dominance and ensures that women cannot easily define their own sexuality, not least because in many cases women are dependent on men economically.

Third, if women can address the power imbalances in sexuality, make explicit and analyse the male-serving assumptions about sex and women's role in it, then this is a positive step towards overcoming male dominance in this and other aspects of society.

A fourth inspiration for this study is a belief that sex is not simply a natural fact. Sex is a social construction, bound up with the economic, social and political structures of the world in which we live. The things people find attractive, or erotic or revolting vary from time to time and culture to culture. Even if we take a specific act like heterosexual intercourse, it seems that the social and personal meanings attached to this act in terms of sexual identity and sexual community have varied historically (Vance, 1983). The body and its actions are understood according to prevailing codes of meaning.

Finally, the study seeks to extend Hollway's (1984, 1989) analysis of talk about heterosexual relationships. Hollway proposes that there are 'discourses' within which people position themselves to make sense of and to talk about their sexuality. The use of the term 'discourse' in this article follows the usage established by Henriques et al., (1984: 105) where a discourse is a 'regulated system of statements'. However, a discourse is not necessarily written down in any one place; its level of articulation is social, rather in the way that ideologies or social representations are supposed not to be coextensive with any one person's mental contents or contained in their entirety in any single text. A discourse in this sense is shared by a social group of speakers and actors. It involves more than language, indeed it also organizes meaning and action. Our concern was to expand Hollway's analysis to include more of the texture and talk of participants' experiences of relationships and sexuality, and to show how this is embedded in larger sexist and heterosexist social representations or ideologies.

HOLLWAY'S APPROACH

Hollway (1984, 1989) provides one of the most comprehensive and influential attempts to analyse talk about relationships and heterosexuality. She argues that our roles arise as a result of the broader, socially articulated discourses in which we are embedded. These discourses provide us with subject positions from which to speak. From her analysis of men and women talking about sex, she identified three 'discourses' which inform people's talk and which provide gender-differentiated subject positions. The discourses are: the 'male sex drive discourse'; the 'have/hold discourse'; and the 'permissive discourse'. Hollway's (1984: 230) use of the term 'discourse' shifts the emphasis away from Foucault's (e.g. Foucault, 1979) explicitly historical use of the concept towards an approach which is located around the meaning derived from language (written or spoken) which makes available different positions and powers for men and women.

The Male Sex-drive Discourse.   This proposes that men are driven by biological necessity to seek out heterosexual sex. It relies on the claim that sex (for men at least) is a natural need and is not mediated socially. It positions men as pursuers of women, or as observers who critically evaluate women's bodies. In this discourse women's sexuality is sometimes seen as a lack, or is seen to be governed more by the need to reproduce than by the need for sex. Women are seen as the object of the male sex drive discourse, whereas men maintain the dominant position of being the subject.

The Have/Hold Discourse.   Although not centrally concerned with sex, this discourse is closely linked with ideas of monogamy, partnership and family life. It proposes that sex should take place within the context of a lasting relationship where the man is the head of the family and is responsible for his wife and children. These principles are embedded in the Anglican Church's vows, hence the term 'have/hold' discourse. In principle this discourse applies to both men and women, but in practice it applies more stringently to women, to the extent that it confers different positions for men and women in society. For example, during the 1950s it was commonly invoked to produce the required norms of conduct in women, encouraging them away from their jobs and back into the home so that demobilized servicemen could return to both a 'traditional wife' and a job.

According to the have/hold discourse, women's sexuality is a lack, somehow compensated for by the emphasis on her relationship with husband and children. Women are thus designated as the subject of this discourse, in that they must be married or at least conducting a relationship in order to enter a sexual relationship. Men, on the other hand, are the object of the discourse, since it is their acquisition as husbands and lovers which is required before a sexual relationship is allowed to exist for a woman.

The Permissive Discourse.   In this discourse the principle of monogamy is challenged — it is considered the right of both men and women to express their sexuality in any way they choose. In assuming that sexuality is natural and should not be repressed, the permissive discourse is closely allied to the male sex drive discourse; however, it differs from the male sex drive discourse in that it applies the same assumptions to both men and women. Despite this, the permissive discourse has limitations for the position of women, as Campbell (1980: 1–2) indicates:

> the permissive era permitted sex for women too. What it did not do was defend women against the differential aspects of permissiveness on men and women. . . . It was about the affirmation of young men's sexuality and promiscuity; it was indiscriminate and its object was indeterminate (so long as she was a woman). The very affirmation of sexuality was a celebration of masculine sexuality.

As Jeffreys (1990b: 22) points out, being included in sexuality, even having orgasms, is not necessarily pleasurable for women, nor does it mean that the ancient taboos or restrictions on women have been subverted or eroded.

It is this framework of discourses we draw upon and extend in the latter part of the article. Here, we simply make a number of points about Hollway's approach. First, she proposes that discourses make available positions for subjects to take up in relation to other people. Women and men are placed in relation to each other through the meanings which a particular discourse makes available. Second, because the traditional discourses surrounding sexuality are gender differentiated, the taking up of subject and object positions is not equally available to men and women. For example, the power of men over women is an important part of heterosexual eroticism (Jeffreys, 1990a: 2; Kitzinger, 1991: 307). However, once we imagine the man who yields and submits to the woman's aggressive pursuit we move outside the realm of everyday heterosexuality and into the more restricted realm of male fantasies of dominant women. Third, practices and meanings have histories developed through their role in human social life. People's lives are not the product of a single discourse but of many, which may be adopted almost simultaneously, in the same conversation, or over a longer time span.

The aims of this article in the following sections are (1) to discuss the role of the researcher in interviews of the kind we have conducted; (2) to elaborate on a fourth discourse for talking about heterosexual sex, i.e. in the manner of the 'pseudo-reciprocal gift discourse'; and (3) to consider some of the differences between women and men which are apparent in our data.

METHOD

This article is based on discussions with 25 people, of whom 15 were undergraduate students, conducted as part of undergraduate projects at Aston University. There were 12 female interviewees and 13 males. The male interviewer

TABLE 1

Participants

Participant number	Sex	Age	Occupation	Location of interview	Interviewer's sex
1	F	21	PhD student	Study/bedroom	F
2	F	22	Graduate employment	Study/bedroom	F
3	M	28	PhD student	Study/bedroom	F
4	M	20	Unemployed	Study/bedroom	M
5	M	21	Graduate law student	Study/bedroom	M
6	F	20	Student	Department	M
7	F	30	Student	Department	M
8	M	20	Student	Study/bedroom	M
9	F	20	Student	Study/bedroom	F
10	F	22	Student	Study/bedroom	F
11	F	24	Student	Study/bedroom	F
12	F	21	Student	Study/bedroom	M
13	M	22	Student	Study/bedroom	M
14	M	21	Unemployed	Study/bedroom	M
15	M	23	Researcher	Department	M
16	M	21	Student	Department	M
17	F	21	Student	Study/bedroom	F
18	M	26	PhD student	Study/bedroom	F
19	M	27	Unemployed	Study/bedroom	F
20	F	20	Student	Study/bedroom	M
21	M	23	Student	Study/bedroom	F
22	M	23	Student	Study/bedroom	M
23	M	30	Civil servant	Study/bedroom	M
24	F	25	Student	Study/bedroom	F
25	F	22	Student	Study/bedroom	F

(Wilson) interviewed 9 men and 4 women, whereas the female interviewer (Gilfoyle) interviewed 4 men and 8 women. It was felt that in dealing with a subject like heterosexual sex and relationships there is some difficulty in talking freely. Therefore, like Hollway (1984, 1989), the subjects were people presumed likely to talk freely about the subject material and to be relaxed and self-disclosing. A list of the participants is provided in Table 1. All but two were white. Most had middle-class cultural experience, either at home or at college, even though they might not be enjoying middle-class incomes. All participants were heterosexual.

Although the sample is small and does not represent a range of social divisions, the study was interested in language use rather than the people generating the language; in how language might correspond to broader structures of power in society, rather than in demographic relationships between the present sample and the population as a whole.

A set of 18 questions was used to initiate conversation, based on the interviewers' own experience of heterosexuality and relationships, and their

TABLE 2

Questions used as discussion prompts

1. Are you or have you ever been involved in a long-term relationship with the opposite sex?
2. What characteristics initially attract you to the opposite sex?
3. Why do you feel you initially got involved with members of the opposite sex?
4. What do you expect to get from a relationship with the opposite sex?
5. Are your expectations usually fulfilled?
6. What do you think your partner's expectations are?
7. Do you think that power struggles exist in a relationship? If so, what is your experience of them?
8. What can sexual relationships with the opposite sex give you which other kinds of relationships can't?
9. How important do you feel sex is in a relationship?
10. Do you think that sex can be a substitute for anything else in a relationship?
11. Who do you find usually initiates the sex act?
12. Who do you think usually enjoys sex the most?
13. How important is orgasm to you?
14. How important do you think it is to the opposite sex?
15. How important is the act of penetration in a sexual encounter?
16. Do you find that a good sexual relationship increases overall enjoyment of the relationship?
17. The penis is to the man as the _____ is to the woman. Fill in the blank in your own words.
18. What do you think would be a good question to ask?

conversations with friends as the project developed. The questions are presented in Table 2. The questions were not always strictly adhered to but gave a structure to the discussion. The interviewers attempted to create an informal, relaxed setting for the interviews, which lasted between 20 and 50 minutes. Participants were interviewed singly and were aware that the discussion was being tape-recorded. They were guaranteed anonymity.

Clearly, factors such as the researchers' sex, manner, questions and non-verbal reinforcers could be crucial in constructing the responses which people made. Griffin (1990) describes three stances which the researcher might take in informal interviews of this type. The first, researcher as 'Kewpie doll', involves keeping one's eyes and ears open and one's mouth shut (Polsky, 1969). The second, researcher as 'nodding dog', involves encouraging respondents with smiles and nods but keeping verbal interventions to a minimum. However, silence and nods and smiles are not neutral interventions, as respondents may read positive and negative connotations into this behaviour and it might itself put respondents on their guard. Third, Griffin describes the researcher who 'talks back'. This can involve challenging what the participant says or encouraging mutual self-disclosure in the form of a friendly discussion. In our interviews, a mixture of these three approaches was used in an attempt to achieve a participative rather than a voyeuristic approach to the subject-matter (Currie and

Kazi, 1987). This results in dropping the formal procedures which restrict variation in traditional interviews (Potter and Mulkay, 1985).

The analysis of the data reflected a number of concerns. First, we were particularly interested in patterns or themes which would indicate that the two sexes were positioned differently. Second, we tried to examine the function which different aspects of the participants' discourse might have in terms of sustaining a particular pattern of gender inequalities. Third, we were also interested in methodological issues — particularly reflexivity.

RESULTS 1: REFLECTING ON REFLEXIVITY

In considering how the interaction between participant and interviewer may be constructing the data, we were particularly interested in the way participants seemed to make sense of the interview situation. We sifted the material to discern any which satisfied Brown's (1988: 126) definition of reflexivity that 'an expression is reflexive if it indicates some awareness of the conduct or content of the discussion'. Part of this process can be conceptualized in terms of 'demand characteristics' (Orne, 1962) or the clues which give away the experimental hypothesis. In our case, some participants indicated that they perceived the interviewer to have some judgemental capacity over them, and had some sort of criteria whereby the answers were judged right or wrong. For example Participant 5, male (MP5):

> MP5: . . . apparently when men have an orgasm there is a chemical which is released in their brains which makes them drowsy and go to sleep. Am I answering properly? Am I giving you a full account?

Here, there is also an emphasis on technical information, almost as if the interview were a knowledge test. Perhaps we can also draw parallels with Foucault (1979) and suggest that the relationship between interviewer and participant recalls that between doctor and patient, or priest and sinner, in its power dynamics. Further, sometimes participants obviously felt their answers were inadequate. For example:

> MP8: I think you'd say that love was more important, if you see what I mean. I know it's not very good.

The disclaimer (Hewitt and Stokes, 1975) in this answer may serve two purposes. First, the participant may assume his answer is not up to scratch in terms of the criteria which might be operating in the situation. Second, the utterance may involve a display of self-worth (Goffman, 1959) in that he's presenting himself as someone who usually performs to high standards and this is a regrettable lapse.

A further example comes when the male interviewer (Wilson) is interviewing Participant 7, female (FP7):

> W: What is the most important aspect of sex to you?
> FP7: Well, you'll have to direct me if I'm going off the track . . .

There are two possible interpretations here. The first assumes that the interviewer had already decided what the proper answer was, and that it was his job to direct the interviewee to give this correct answer. The second interpretation invokes the grander roles which mainstream society proposes for women. The participant might have asked for direction because the way we talk about and conceptualize heterosexual sex may be more in line with male interests than female ones, as we shall argue below. Perhaps our language and culture provide only shaky and uncertain positions from which women's sexual experience can be described. Perhaps, then, FP7 was trying to adhere to a male account of sexuality. Another respondent, in the post-interview chat, seemed to doubt her ability to contribute anything novel:

> G: . . . we're wondering, you know, if men and women say anything different about it.
> FP11: I don't know, I don't know whether I've said anything other than the really totally blindingly obvious.

Here, it is almost as if the investigation was being conceptualized as a search for the bizarre and esoteric.

Several participants indicated that they were making assumptions about the orientation of the researcher to the subject matter. This was particularly clear with a male interviewer and male participants. Some seemed to assume that he was 'liberal' and would disapprove of overt sexism; others supposed he maintained 'traditional' sexist ideologies.

The first group, those who presented a liberal 'non-sexist' approach, sometimes showed interstices in their liberalism which hinted at a more conventional sexist orientation. For example MP15 distanced himself from what he presented as the common male position:

> W: How important is penetration in the overall sex act?
> MP15: Ah, it's not that important, although I would say the majority of men would actually define sex as a penetration, I consider it in a broader sphere.
> W: It's not the be-all-and-end-all then?
> MP15: No, certainly not, it's just my thing, but most people see penetration as sex.

While this quote presents a more sensitive and liberal version of masculinity, explicitly distinguished from the attitude of 'most men', there were overtones of a more conventional sexism. Elsewhere in the discussion, this participant described how certain types of female behaviour could be seen as 'tarty', suggesting complicity with conventional sexist assumptions about women's sexuality. In this way perhaps we have an example of the 'unequal egalitarianism' identified by Wetherell et al. (1987). To explain this it could be suggested that

MP15 had constructed a version of the aims and orientation of the research and was tailoring his remarks to the recipient.

The second kind of response made by participants operated in a rather different way. Here we found an easily distinguishable sexism; no effort was made to hide a sexist orientation; and these participants attributed similar views to the male interviewer. For example, consider the following exchange with MP5:

> W: What do you expect to get from a relationship with a woman?
> MP5: Well, it's somebody you need in the morning and somebody to shout at when you're in a bad mood. Somebody to make me something to eat when I'm hungry, or go out for a drink, when I want to go out. Just somebody to be there.
> W: A source of convenience?
> MP5: Yes, *it's terrible isn't it?, we all do it.* (emphasis added)

This participant is universalizing the statements he makes, saying that we all do it. He may even be extending his own (male) fragment of experience to all men, or to the human race as a whole. Perhaps he is also trying to disarm any criticism the interviewer might make of the statement by inducting him into a frame of reference which they might hold in common.

Further, as we discuss later, the format of the investigation might be better suited to men than to women. Methods tend to reproduce dominant ideologies. For example, the statement 'The penis is to the man as the ＿＿＿＿＿ is to the woman . . .' reproduces the assumption of men as 'hail fellow well met', with the goods in the front window, and women as being characterized by mystery — or even a blank!

We now move on to elaborate a variety of discourse which we believe usefully supplements Hollway's tripartite division: the pseudo-reciprocal gift discourse; and to show how this discourse underscores the inequality between men and women in heterosexual sex and relationships.

RESULTS 2: DEFINING A NEW DISCOURSE: INTERCOURSE AS A
PSEUDO-RECIPROCAL GIFT

In addition to Hollway's three kinds of discourse, another identifiable pattern appeared in our interview discussions. This led us to develop the idea of what we initially called the 'reciprocal gift discourse'. Later we changed this to the 'pseudo-reciprocal gift discourse' (on the advice that the original title connoted too much equality and mutuality). Indeed, we argue, this discourse is part of the fundamental inequalities which result in the oppression of women in heterosexual relationships and sex.

The central proposition of the 'pseudo-reciprocal gift discourse' is that men require heterosexual sex to satisfy their sexual urges (corresponding to the male sex-drive discourse). However, in order to do so, *this* discourse relies on men viewing women as passive receptacles who must relinquish all control over their bodies, in 'giving' themselves, or in 'giving' sex to their male partners. In return, the man must try to please the woman, which entails, in most cases, trying to 'give' the woman an orgasm.

Positioned in this discourse, women are seen as the object who is both 'given away' and 'given to'; while men, on the other hand, are seen as the subject, maintaining their dominance by both being the recipient of the woman and conferring on the object (woman) the gift of pleasure or orgasm. By implication, this discourse rules out the possibility of women having sensual pleasure or orgasms on their own. Moreover, it positions these 'pleasures' as necessarily good, natural and proper.

There are clear links between the formulation of this discourse and the analysis of sexology and sexual 'liberalism' provided by Jeffreys (1990a, 1990b), who notes that many (male) writers on heterosexual sex, from Stekel (1936; 'to be roused by a man means acknowledging oneself as conquered') through to Chesser (1946; 'complete surrender is the only way she can bring the highest pleasure to herself and her husband') have seen the woman's role in sex in these terms. Indeed, present-day sexual libertarians have eroticized the power difference between men and women (Jeffreys, 1990b: 25). Stoltenberg (1990) argues that (male) sexual desire, venerated and valorized by 'sexual liberationists' (see, among others, Comfort, 1979; Crichton, 1986; Weeks, 1985) is not necessarily benign, but can arise from men's needs to put women down (Jeffreys, 1991). Thus, we would argue that the 'pseudo-reciprocal gift discourse' is similar to the position offered in modern manuals of sexology. The mutuality in this discourse is illusory, in the same way as the mutuality offered in *The Joy of Sex* (Comfort, 1979) or in the pages of *Forum* magazine. Perhaps, then, our characterization of the pseudo-reciprocal gift discourse represents a modernization and particularization of the male sex-drive discourse.

Like Hollway's discourses, the pseudo-reciprocal gift discourse is a product of a number of components which enable subject and object positions to be adopted in relation to other people. As becomes clear from the data presented below, the most conspicuous manifestation of this position came from male participants. We might speculate, then, that the pseudo-reciprocal gift discourse not only confers more power on men, but gives them linguistic resources to develop more flattering descriptions of what it is that heterosexuality, and its associated sexual practices, involves.

We have divided our identification of the components of the pseudo-reciprocal gift discourse into three categories: passive woman; active man; and the role of sex as another kind of reinforcer.

Passive Woman

A general theme, which ran through several of the men's discussions, suggested that women were best fulfilled in their roles as inactive 'quarry' during the process of starting liaisons. For example:

> MP4: It always has been the role of the male to make the first move in any part of the relationship at all. It's always the man who is supposed to ask the girl to dance or is supposed to go over and give the girl the first chat-up line.

There were a myriad of suggested reasons why women should be so inactive during the formative stage of relationships. These were perhaps best summed up by MP23:

> MP23: I think historically, traditionally, it's the man who makes the play, who's chasing the woman. Historically that is his role. You see it presented to you in the media as well. I mean all the films you see it is the bloke chasing the woman.

This is curiously similar to Metcalfe and Humphries (1985) who include a discussion of male power and female passivity in media representations of sexuality.

As mentioned earlier, the pseudo-reciprocal gift discourse relates primarily to people positioning themselves in discussion about sexual activities, however the foregoing suggests that the passivity of women is an idea which pervades all aspects of relationships. Women's perspectives on this issue were not so readily offered. An example, however, was provided by FP17:

> FP17: I don't think, come to think of it, that I've ever really been looking for it [heterosexual relationship] but it just sort of happens, you know, there's always someone about, so I've never needed . . .
> G: To make the first move?
> FP17: Yeah, I suppose.

In this case there is no specific reference to making the first move — this terminology was supplied by the interviewer — but there is no particular passivity either. In the interviews themselves there was no critique offered of men's activity, but informal conversations with friends (and the experience of the first author) suggest that being 'pestered by wankers in pubs' is a common if regrettable experience.

With such a backdrop it is hardly surprising that men describe the role of women during sexual intercourse also as that of a passive object. This was most explicit in MP14's account:

> MP14: It's more important that the woman is giving herself to me. She is laying herself on the line.

MP14 appears to view intercourse not as a mutual interaction, but as his partner offering herself to him. The sacrifice he perceives her as making by giving herself to him is reinforced by his inference that his partner does not have any strong inclinations for intercourse. For example, he states that sex is not as important for him now as it was when he was younger, and that now sometimes he prefers 'to talk rather than jump into bed', because he likes to 'think of the other person as well'. He states that he is taking his partner's wants into consideration and he interprets these as not being interested in sex; this implies that when he does have intercourse, it is for his own gratification. Moreover, he seems to conceptualize his partner as a passive entity to meet his sexual needs. However, he does attempt to reciprocate her giving herself to him by giving something in return; he 'makes an effort' to 'give' her an orgasm because he thinks a lot of her.

The 'giving' on the part of women corresponds to the 'He asks; she gives' detected by Rubin (1976: 139). It is exemplified in our study by FP9, speaking in response to the question about who initiates the sex act:

> FP9: . . . it makes him happy so I always reckon I might as well give it to him.
> G: Even when you don't . . .
> FP9: Even when I don't want to, no I suppose if I really don't want to I don't want to, but sometimes I give it to him.

Giving oneself and giving sex to one's partner are not quite the same: the latter implies merely an activity, whereas the former is more likely to involve the whole person. Nevertheless, this discourse involves a relentless giving on the part of the women.

The perceived passivity seems to be the result of two factors. First, women are assumed, particularly by men, to have a much smaller 'sex drive' than men (if they have one at all!). This corresponds to the major tenet of Hollway's 'male sex-drive discourse'. It was mentioned equally by men and women in our discussions; however the position is best described my MP4:

> MP4: Women are much more affectionate than men. What I've always found, they're always much more ready to hold onto you and kiss you and things but when it comes down to sex they're not as vigorous I suppose. They don't have the same sort of sex drive.
> W: So what do you think it is about men? Do men have a sort of inbuilt . . .?
> MP4: Yeah, I suppose so, I suppose it's from the power syndrome thing. It's like men have always been more powerful at sex. They have more sexual urges, much more sexual vigour.

Notice the exclusion here of 'hold onto you and kiss you' from MP4's definition of sex. Apart from not having the biological urges of men, women are also assumed to have less interest in sexual intercourse from a recreational point of view:

> MP23: I find with women, they can't be bothered making the first move but once you've started it's great. I think it takes a bit to get them warmed up.

Women's responses to the issue of who initiates the sex act seemed to embody two themes. One was summed up by FP24: 'Oh god he's always wanting it!' Another respondent, who was living with a partner and slept with him every night, appeared to meet resistance sometimes in her quest for physical intimacy:

FP25: I mean sometimes I was feeling you know passionate and he would say like he had to get up in the morning or what was it, he would say I was making him itchy, that's it.

So her own efforts were not interpreted as sexual advances, but rather as keeping her partner awake, or as the source of unwelcome bodily sensations.

The second factor which contributes to women being placed in a passive role is the assumption that women's orgasms are a product of men's intervention, and that in order for a woman to achieve orgasm she must lie back and relax:

W: Do you think it has anything to do with a man whether a woman has an orgasm?
MP5: Yeah, definitely.
W: To what extent?
MP5: Well, firstly a woman . . . I think she has to be mentally relaxed then I think it's down to the bloke to experiment.

The presumption that women should be passive throughout heterosexual intercourse seems to result in women losing any self-determination of their bodies, or their orgasms. Once a woman enters a sexual encounter, she is no longer seen as in control of that particular facet of her physiology, and it seems as if an invisible contract is drawn up, whereby the man is responsible for both partners' 'pleasure'. Pleasure, it should be noted, is in this discourse constructed in much the same way as it is for the 'sexual liberals' discussed by Jeffreys (1990a, 1990b), in that sexual feelings, practices and orgasms are unproblematically good things. The notion of pleasure is often collapsed into the concept of orgasm. Particularly when experienced by women, moreover, it is supposed to represent some form of liberation. However, as Jeffreys argues, this is not necessarily so; and, as we hope will become clear from this article, it can reinforce inequality in relationships.

Active Man

Men are conceptualized as active in the pseudo-reciprocal gift discourse, as we have implied in dealing with the passive role assigned to women. However, there are additional components to the idea of the active man which merit further attention. First, the man, as the subject of the discourse, is the active agent — in that he is responsible for any activity that might take place during intercourse. This activity is not limited solely to the sexual side of the relationship — as some of the earlier quotes indicate, he is responsible for any initiative that might take place at the start of the dating procedure.

The concept of active man during intercourse was almost universally accepted by both our men and women participants, and many of the discussions were characterized by the assumption that it was the man's responsibility both to initiate any sexual advance, and to create any feelings of pleasure or enjoyment therein. FP12 sums up a position common to many of our women participants:

W: Who do you think enjoys sex the most?
FP12: It depends on the bloke because it's harder to have an orgasm or whatever so the bloke has to put a bit more effort in.

Again we can see how the woman has resigned responsibility for the enjoyment of sex, and is relying on the man to get any pleasure out of the encounter. This type of attitude is exemplified by many 'enlightened' men, who see it as their responsibility to give the woman as much pleasure as they themselves experience. We have used the term 'enlightened' because this position was contrasted with a more primordial and less mutualistic approach by MP23:

W: Who do you think enjoys sex the most?
MP23: Mmm. Depends on the individual. Personally I try to make the woman enjoy it as much as I can, and sometimes I haven't enjoyed it because the person I'm with hasn't enjoyed it either. I think it is an individual thing, it just depends on how good you are, how interested the bloke is. I mean it's easy for any bloke just to go in, belt away and finish and not even care about the woman.

It is clear, then, that if the woman does enjoy sex, it is not because of her activity or feelings, but instead because the man is 'good', or rather that his technique is 'good'.

This way of talking about sex is another salient feature of the pseudo-reciprocal gift discourse, and it exemplifies the active/passive dichotomy even further. For example, many men's talk about intercourse and sexuality was infused with mechanistic and technical metaphors:

MP5: Yeah, touching certain buttons does play a very big part of it, certain positions play a really big part of it.

Men's use of this type of language may signify that the act of sex is a male domain, and that there is no place for an equally active female partner. Throughout the discussions continual reference was made to women as passive objects to be controlled. Indeed, there seemed to be a repertoire of references to sex as work:

W: How important is orgasm to you?
MP14: Pretty important. I don't like to leave a job half finished.

Some women seemed to use this way of talking about their partner's attitudes to their orgasms:

FP17: When I was going out with Mark and I didn't come he was upset on my behalf because he didn't feel he had done a good enough job.

Or again with FP24:

FP24: Steve used to, he might have read it somewhere, but he used to think that he had to keep going. I used to feel sorry for him sometimes, the effort he put in, for ages and ages.

Thus, we have a bifurcation between the men's accounts mentioned earlier, and the women's accounts immediately above, wherein it is not quite the case of women giving themselves to the men and the men giving them orgasms ('pleasure'). Getting their partners to reach orgasm is a reinforcer for the men. It is not a no-strings-attached gift for the women. As some of Rubin's (1976: 151) respondents seemed to suggest, for women, perhaps, men's 'wish for their orgasm is experienced as oppressive and alienating'.

While it has been noted for some time that men's language is task oriented while women's is more socially oriented (Spender, 1980), it seems that the language men adopt when referring to sexual intercourse has special connotations for power in relationships. For example, how can you consider somebody as an equal partner when you describe them consistently as a passive object or when you describe their sexual pleasure using mechanistic and technical phrases?

While the man has adopted the active role, he is not only dominating the woman through his activity in conferring on her any pleasure she might experience, he is further defining, demeaning and relegating her position through his positioning of her as a passive object. His own activity is defined like that of the videogame expert — in terms of performance and competence. By implication, then, men become the source of all sexual pleasure. Thus, if men are absent then so is sex, and the possibilities of lesbian sex or women's autoeroticism are ruled out.

Sex as Another Kind of Reinforcer

While both men and women seemed sometimes to be inscribed within the pseudo-reciprocal gift discourse, it seems that the men's subject positions within it are more dominant than those available to women. This discourse may also seek to define an appropriate subjectivity for women, rather like the 'submission' advocated by Chesser (1946), or indeed the 'ecstatic submission' suggested as a title for this discourse by an external referee. Perhaps we can develop some insight into the role sex plays for our participants if we examine some of the functions of the positions available within the pseudo-reciprocal gift discourse.

For many participants, the positionings of the pseudo-reciprocal gift discourse, namely those of passive woman and active man, is seen to reinforce each person's gender role:

W: Do you think the male is responsible for the female's orgasm?
MP5: I would put it down to the man and his technique. Yes I think pressing the right buttons is important, but you also have to have the right mental attitude, because I think if a woman has an orgasm you probably feel more of a man. You know the other person has enjoyed it and it was because of you and your penis, you gave her that, you gave her one.

Also:

> W: How important do you think orgasm is for women?
> MP5: I think it's pretty important. I don't think a woman will feel quite as feminine
> if she couldn't experience one.

As MP5 describes the active role he adopts there is no doubt as to where his partner's pleasure comes from — himself and his penis. He attributes her pleasure to his technique. Thus, he perceives her sexuality as moulded to fit in with, and react to, his own; he regards her sexuality as passive and dependent upon his actions.

In effect, then, intercourse is seen as clearly distinguishing between the sexes, as building masculinity and femininity. A possible speculative implication of this is that it is passivity which to some extent, at least, confers upon women their femininity, and hence may delineate their role in wider social contexts.

Therefore, it can be concluded that the man positioned as subject of the pseudo-reciprocal gift discourse, and the woman as object, involves him perceiving her as a passive entity who will react to his sexual advances and respond to his technique. It is ironic, then, that the 'enlightened' male discourse, in which men take some responsibility for their partner's pleasure, is yet another example of men abrogating power to themselves, as they take away women's ability to be an independent sexual agent. The discourse denies the possibility of such agency, as men become not only the dominant sexual partner but also the experts on sexual pleasure for themselves and for women. The use of mechanical metaphors by men when talking about sex constitutes more evidence for men regarding women as passive sexual objects. Therefore, when men adopt this subject position in the discourse, intercourse acts as a reinforcer of the passive and active roles which are conferred on women and men respectively. It appears that men's positioning of women as passive in sexual activity is consonant with the passive roles conferred on women in other spheres of society.

THE LANGUAGE OF MEN?: REFLECTIONS ON GENDER AND TALK ABOUT SEX

In presenting this account of the pseudo-reciprocal gift discourse we have drawn extensively on four men's and five women's accounts of the process of finding partners and conducting heterosexual life. In this final section we voice some of our misgivings about the fact that the men in our study were much more forthcoming than women. Women's version of sexuality was much more difficult to determine from this study. From a Foucauldian perspective one might argue that the 'discourses' available in the contemporary western language community within which we speak about sex are geared to articulating men's interests and accounts of sexuality. We suggest there is much less space in western twentieth-century culture for women than men to build accounts of their sexuality. As

Spender (1980: 172) says, 'Only male sexual characteristics have been named as real within the patriarchal framework'.

Of course, we are not saying that there is a total absence of discourse about sex which foregrounds women's interests. Clearly, heterosexual feminism has produced alternative discourses concerning women's sexuality in heterosexual sex. Equally, we must acknowledge the productivity of lesbian feminist theorists (see, for example, Frye, 1990; Hoagland, 1988) in producing alternatives to the dominant (malestream) sexual discourse. Moreover, there is a tradition of psychological work on the topic of gender differences in self-disclosure. Early work, such as that by Jourard (1964), suggested that women were more self-disclosing than men (although, more recently, Rosenfeld et al. [1979] suggest that age differences, situational and personal factors may override any general masculine or feminine patterns). Miell (1984) notes that women are often expected to disclose more and may be pressed to do so. Overall, there are *a priori* grounds for expecting women to self-disclose more than men. However, we found greater difficulty in generating and analysing accounts from women than men. Why should this be the case?

We are given clues in some parts of the interview discussions as to what women's version of sexuality might be like. For example, comments in response to the question 'What characteristics initially attract you to the opposite sex?' suggest much less of an orientation to attractiveness on the part of women than men:

> W: What about physically, does that. . .?
> FP7: Well, I don't think physically is high on my list, I would tend to sort of steer away from someone who is hugely fat or tall, but other than that average sort of looks.

Also:

> G: What initially attracts you about them when you start?
> FP2: It's personality, but I wouldn't go out with them if they were a hunchback . . . cos I'm small I couldn't go out with someone who's about six foot seven and I couldn't go out with someone who was 20 stone.

We are given further clues as to the nature of women's talk about sex by means of responses to the question: 'The penis is to the man as _____ is to the woman. Fill in the blank in your own words.'

Eight men said 'clitoris', four said 'vagina' and one didn't know. Apart from one woman who said 'clitoris', women in general said there was no equivalent. The men interpreted this question from a physical standpoint and defined women's sexuality in the same way as they defined their own: as being centrally concerned with one zone or organ. Those who replied 'vagina' are perhaps seeing women as a receptacle for their sexual gratification. Ann Koedt (1970), in her article 'The Myth of the Vaginal Orgasm', states that the myth persists not because of ignorance on the subject, but because it is not in men's interests to acknowledge that women's orgasms are not dependent on penetrative inter-course. Johnston (1973) warns against the danger of the equally problematic myth that the vagina is insensitive. Of course, men viewing women's sexuality as vaginally based helps them more easily continue with a phallocentric sexual-ity. However, the extent to which men replied 'clitoris' to our question suggests that sexual knowledge has been popularized over the last 20 years.

Women's responses to our 'penis analogue' question expressed uncertainty, and doubts as to whether the issue could be summed up so simply:

> G: So how would you describe it in your own words?
> FP1: I think it's an overall sexuality about a woman rather than a particular object.

Or FP9, interviewed by Gilfoyle, in response to the same question:

> FP9: I don't think it's all concentrated in one little tiny zone.

In the few accounts we have of women describing what they find erotic it seems that female desire is described as being capable of attachment to many different things. For example, Galloway (1990: 28) describes her delight at being fed fish by a partner in a restaurant (possibly not so delightful for the fish). If we find such descriptions quaint and unusual, this indicates the extent to which our culture is informed by phallocentric notions of sexuality. This diffuse eroticism is rather different from the fascination with, say, high heels and stock-ings which might be found in stereotypically male accounts of fetishism, because it is not specifically and obsessively located in one subject or situation, but rather is capricious, flexible and surprising.

Also our female respondents' talk about sex contained some analogies bet-ween sex and communicative activity. FP1 refers to intercourse as having ex-pressive qualities:

> FP1: Sex is something special and I basically think is an expression of intensity of feeling between two people, which can't be expressed in any other way.

And:

> FP6: . . . sex in a relationship builds the intimacy up.

On being asked what roles or functions sex played in a relationship, another female respondent said:

> FP7: Sex is probably an expression of intensity of feeling which isn't matched in any other way.

At the same time there was some attempt by the women to represent male sex-uality. There was, for example, an account of the alleged ubiquity and in-evitability of men's orgasms:

W: How important is it [orgasm] for males?
FP7: It's a foregone conclusion, it just exists, it is very important.

One further possible reason why the men were more forthcoming than the women is that our investigation might have suited them better. The exercise — and the particular questions asked — may have been geared to men's interests.

If an investigation is constructed in such a way that it makes it difficult for women to talk about sex then we are much less likely to get a full and candid account from them. If the nature of the investigation is different from the sorts of topics and issues around which women's everyday talk centres, we can be much less sure of the generality or representativeness of what they may say. There may be realms of untapped feminine discourse.

For example, it was suggested to us that a group of older feminist heterosexuals would have no difficulty in articulating their account of sex and sexuality. Certainly, our results are profoundly local to the age, ethnic, class, sexual and educational characteristics, and the able-bodiedness of our participants, to name but a few of the salient characteristics. Were we to repeat the exercise we would be looking for ways of eliciting more from women and trying to make the investigation correspond more closely to women's interests. We would also want to represent the concerns of a more diverse group of women.

CONCLUSION

Despite the energy with which the topic of heterosexual sex and relationships is theorized and debated, there is an enormous amount of work to do to open up the field. In particular, the possibilities of articulating women's experience of sexuality are only beginning to be tackled. We have briefly mentioned Frye (1990) and Hoagland (1988). Hite (1977: 363–97) provides some insights, but despite the large number of women on which her book is based, it is in itself a very small step towards reforming heterosexuality.

We hope to have made two points strongly in this article. First, we have supplemented Hollway's account of the discourses of heterosexuality by the addition of the 'pseudo-reciprocal gift discourse', whereby women are conceived of as giving themselves or giving sex to men, while men give women orgasms. This, we have suggested, reinforces the oppression of women by encouraging their passivity in the face of the activity, and crass notions of technical expertise, it encourages in men. It seems to colonize the terrain of women's pleasure in a way which is profoundly confirming for and reinforcing to men, much as is argued by Jeffreys (1990b).

Second, we have noted some of the differences in men's and women's talk about sex. Specifically, women seemed to apply what could be described as a 'critique of silence' (Morley, 1980) to talk about sex. Apart from inviting us to question our data-gathering procedure, this relative silence on the part of women also invites us to speculate that dominant ways of talking about sex correspond more closely to men's interests than to women's.

Taken together, these findings suggest the resilience of prevailing notions about sex. In particular, we would highlight the way in which the pseudo-reciprocal gift discourse has condensed women's desire for pleasure into an entity called 'orgasm', which is called into existence by men's skill and technique. The recent development of so-called 'women's erotica' (Barbach, 1988; Chester, 1989; Reynolds, 1990; see also Galloway, 1990; Campbell, 1990 for discussion) invites us to ask whether these publications reflect autonomous, woman-oriented discourse about sex, or whether they are publishable, readable and comprehensible precisely because they reflect the dominant way in which stories about sex are told in a (hetero)sexist society. Even if women can produce alternative languages and concepts which they are able to control (e.g. Daly, 1987), this is very different from actually attaining equality between the sexes in heterosexual relations — or in any other aspect of society.

ACKNOWLEDGEMENTS

We would like to thank all the people who took part in this study and gave us something to think about. Particular thanks are also due to Dr Chris Griffin of Birmingham University whose encouragement and helpful suggestions were much appreciated, and the referees, Wendy Hollway, Rachel Perkins and Celia Kitzinger whose comments served to extend our own thinking as well as providing a basis for revising the manuscript.

REFERENCES

Barbach, L. (1988) *Erotic Interludes*. London: Futura.

Brown (1988) 'Watching the News: Towards an Understanding of the News Reception Process', unpublished doctoral dissertation, Leicester University.

Campbell, B. (1980) 'A Feminist Sexual Politics: Now You See It Now You Don't', *Feminist Review* 5: 1–18.

Campbell, K. (1990) 'Whatever Turns You On', *The Guardian*, 6 November, p. 36.

Chesser, E. (1946) *Love and Marriage*. London: Pan, 1957.

Chester, L. (1989) *Deep Down: New Sensual Writing*. London: Faber.

Comfort, A. (1979) *The Joy of Sex*. London: Quartet.

Crichton, S. (1986) 'Going for the Big "O"', *Ms*, May.

Currie, D. and Kazi, H. (1987) 'Academic Feminism and the Process of Deradicalisation: Reexamining the Issues', *Feminist Review* 25: 77-98.

Daly, M. (1987) *Webster's New International Wickedary of the English Language*. New York: Beacon Press.

Dworkin, A. (1987) *Intercourse*. London: Arrow Books.

Foucault, M. (1979) *The History of Sexuality: Vol 1*. Trans. J. Hurley. London: Allen Lane (Original work published Paris: Gallimard, 1976).

Frye, M. (1990) 'Lesbian "Sex"', in J. Allen (ed.) *Lesbian Philosophies and Cultures*. New York: State University of New York Press.

Galloway, J. (1990) 'The Phoney Search for Women's Erotica', *New Statesman/Society* 3(132): 26–8.

Goffman, E. (1959). *The Presentation of Self in Everyday Life*. New York: Doubleday.

Griffin, C. (1990) 'The Researcher Talks Back: Dealing with Power Relations in Studies of Young People's Entry in to the Job Market', in W. Shaffir and R. Stebbins (eds) *Experiencing Fieldwork*. Newbury Park, CA: Sage.

Hatfield, E. and Traupmann, J. (1981) 'Intimate Relationships: A Perspective from Equity Theory', in S. Duck and R. Gilmour (eds) *Personal Relationships 1: Studying Personal Relationships*. New York: Academic Press.

Henriques, J., Hollway, W., Urwin, C., Venn, C. and Walkerdine, V. (1984) *Changing the Subject: Psychology, Social Regulation and Subjectivity*. London: Methuen.

Hewitt, J.P. and Stokes, R. (1975) 'Disclaimers', *American Sociologial Review* 92: 110–57.

Hite, S. (1977) *The Hite Report*. London: Talmy-Franklin.

Hoagland, S.L. (1988) *Lesbian Ethics: Towards New Value*. Palo Alto, CA: Institute of Lesbian Studies.

Hollway, W. (1984) 'Gender Difference and the Production of Subjectivity', in J. Henriques, W. Hollway, C. Urwin, C. Venn and V. Walkerdine (eds) *Changing the Subject: Psychology, Social Regulation and Subjectivity*. London: Methuen.

Hollway, W. (1989) *Subjectivity and Method in Psychology: Gender Meaning and Science*. London: Sage.

Jeffreys, S. (1990a) *Anticlimax: A Feminist Perspective on the Sexual Revolution*. London: The Women's Press.

Jeffreys, S. (1990b) 'Sexology and Antifeminism', in D. Leidholt and J.G. Raymond (eds) *The Sexual Liberals and the Attack on Feminism*. Oxford: Pergamon.

Jeffreys, S. (1991) Review of J. Stoltenberg (1990) *Refusing to be a Man, Feminism & Psychology*. 1: 301–4.

Johnston, J. (1973) *Lesbian Nation*. New York: Simon and Schuster.

Jourard, S.M. (1964) *The Transparent Self*. New York: D. Van Nostrand.

Kitzinger, C. (1991) Review of S. Jeffreys (1990) *Anticlimax, Feminism & Psychology* 1: 306–8.

Koedt, A. (1970) 'The Myth of the Vaginal Orgasm', in S. Firestone and A. Koedt (eds) *Notes from the Second Year of Women's Liberation*. New York: Knopf.

Metcalfe, A. and Humphries, M. (1985) *The Sexuality of Men*. London: Pluto Press.

Miell, D.E. (1984) 'Cognitive and Communication Strategies in Developing Relationships', unpublished PhD thesis, University of Lancaster, UK.

Morley, D. (1980) *The 'Nationwide' Audience: Structure and Decoding*, British Film Institute Monograph No. 11. London: BFI Publications.

Orne, M. (1962) 'On the Social Psychology of the Psychological Experiment, with Particular Reference to Demand Characteristics and their Implications', *American Psychologist* 17: 776–83.

Polsky, M. (1969) *Hustlers, Beats and Others*. Harmondsworth: Penguin.

Potter, J. and Mulkay, M. (1985) 'Scientists' Interview Talk: Interviews as a Technique for Revealing Participants' Interpretive Practices', in M. Brenner, J. Brown and D. Canter (eds) *The Research Interview: Uses and Approaches*. New York: Academic Press.

Reynolds, M. (1990) *Erotica: An Anthology of Women's Writing*. London: Pandora.

Rich, A. (1980) 'Compulsory Heterosexuality and Lesbian Existence', *Signs* 5(4): 631–60.

Rosenfeld, L.B., Civikly, J.M. and Herron, J.R. (1979) 'Anatomical and Psychological Sex Differences', in G.J. Chelune (ed.) *Self-Disclosure*. San Francisco, CA: Jossey Bass.

Rubin, L.B. (1976) *Worlds of Pain: Life in the Working Class Family*. New York: Basic Books.

Spender, D. (1980) *Man Made Language*. London: Routledge and Kegan Paul.

Stekel, W. (1936) *Frigidity in Woman in Relation to Her Love Life*. New York: Livewright. (Originally published 1926.)

Stoltenberg, J. (1990) *Refusing To Be a Man*. London: Fontana.

Vance, C.S. (1983) 'Pleasure and Danger: Towards a Politics of Sexuality', in C.S. Vance (ed.) *Pleasure and Danger: Exploring Female Sexuality*. London: Routledge and Kegan Paul.

Walster, E., Walster, G.W. and Berscheid, E. (1978) *Equity: Theory and Research*. Boston, MA: Allyn and Bacon.

Weeks, J. (1985) *Sexuality and its Discontents*. London: Routledge and Kegan Paul.

Wetherell, M., Stiven, H. and Potter, J. (1987) 'Unequal Egalitarians: A Preliminary Study of Discourses Concerning Gender and Employment Possibilities', *British Journal of Social Psychology* 26: 59–71.

Jackie GILFOYLE. Jonathan WILSON and BROWN are at the Aston Business School, Aston University, Birmingham B4 7ET, UK.

Mary BOYLE

Sexual Dysfunction or Heterosexual Dysfunction?

The psychological literature on sexual dysfunction has been mainly concerned with the sexual problems of people in heterosexual relationships. This article takes as its starting point recent attempts to extend this literature to the sexual problems of homosexual women and men. It is argued that such attempts may not have taken sufficient account of the extent to which existing classification systems, nomenclature and theory of sexual problems are based on heterosexist and sexist assumptions about the nature of male and female sexuality, about sexual activity and about what is seen as sexually problematic.

It is well known that homosexual women and men have not been well represented in the mainstream literature on sexual problems. Masters and Johnson, for example, conducted their 1970 treatment programme only with heterosexuals, while the words 'homosexual' or 'lesbian' do not appear in the index of Kaplan's (1974) 'New Sex Therapy'. Similarly, most articles on sexual dysfunction in major journals do not discuss homosexual clients or suggest that theories of sexual dysfunction developed with heterosexuals might not be universal. Jeffreys (1990) has noted, too, the invisibility of homosexual relationships in popular sex manuals. It is not simply that homosexuality has been overlooked. Masters and Johnson (1970) saw a homosexual orientation as one of many blocks to 'natural' sexual functioning which could be removed by their treatment. Their use of terms such as 'indoctrination' (of men), 'seduction' (of women) and 'handicapped' to refer to becoming or being homosexual attests to their negative views. Similarly, Comfort (1987) listed bisexuality amongst 'sexual problems'.

More recently, however, attempts have been made to apply the ideas and practices of traditional sex therapy to the sexual problems of homosexual women and men. Lieblum and Pervin (1980: 321) for example, claim that 'Sex therapy with homosexual couples and individual clients is not significantly different from sex therapy with heterosexuals. The same dysfunctions exist and the same techniques are employed in treatment.' McWhirter and Mattison (1980: 322, 325) endorse this view: 'Homosexual couples experience the same range of sexual dysfunction as do heterosexual couples. . . . The new phenomenologically oriented categories of *DSM-III* provide a more precise descriptive diagnosis for sexual dysfunctions that apply to both heterosexual and homosexual persons.' Nichols (1989: 278, 287) appears to disagree and claims that 'Sex therapy with gay clients differs from that with heterosexuals in many respects' and that 'sex therapists must remember that the types of sexual dysfunction will be different among gay and lesbian clients'. Although Nichols discusses the influence of lesbian and gay culture on sexual practices, and has provided extremely thoughtful discussions of sex therapy with lesbians (Nichols, 1987a, 1987b), a good deal of the difference to which she refers seems to involve differences in prevalence of particular presenting 'disorders', expressed in the language of the American Psychiatric Association's *Diagnostic and Statistical Manual of Mental Disorders* (the *DSM*), and differences in the content of inhibiting factors. Thus, these differences may not involve a fundamental reassessment of the ways in which we construe sexual problems and the meanings we attach to them.

The idea that sexual problems in homosexual relationships can be described and conceptualized using existing nomenclature and classification systems, is based on at least two major assumptions which have rarely been subjected to critical scrutiny in the standard literature. The first is that modern nomenclature and classification systems rest on objective, scientific descriptions of sexual functioning and dysfunctioning. In other words, it is assumed that there exist 'out there' clearly definable *human* sexual problems; the task of the researcher or clinician is simply to 'find' and describe these in a value-free way. The second assumption is that it is reasonable to construe sexual complaints as a series of individual disorders. The *DSM-III* (APA, 1980: 6), for example, refers to its contents as '[mental] disorders that individuals have'. It can be argued that this individualistic or dispositional approach, which is apparent in spite of the attention paid to couple interaction, has contributed to the perception of sex therapy as a process of removing 'blocks' to 'natural' sexual functioning. Masters and Johnson saw therapy in this way and the idea appears to have been transferred by others to homosexuals. In this case, however, a major 'block' is 'homophobia'. Lieblum and Pervin (1980: 321) claimed that what is 'critical' in treatment is that the therapist be free of homophobia and '[assist] the homosexual individual or couple in overcoming his or her own homophobia'. Similarly, Hamadock (1988) and Nichols (1989) have emphasized the role of 'internalized homophobia' in interfering with, as Nichols (1989: 283) puts it, 'joyful sexual expression'. This presentation of people's hatred and fear of homosexuals as a personal disposition, or even disorder, internalized by homosexuals themselves and interfering with their sex lives, may perpetuate an essentialist view of sexual functioning as a natural attribute awaiting release; it also fails to take account of serious criticisms which have been made of the concept of homophobia and its roots in psychiatric theory (see, for example, Kitzinger, 1989).

Before we assume that these and other ideas in the existing literature can constructively accommodate homosexuality, or, as the title of one of Nichols's (1987b) papers suggests, be 'bent to fit a gay life-style', we need to examine the assumptions on which this literature is based. I argue that they are problematic and that the nomenclature of sexual 'dysfunction', and theories surrounding it, cannot be seen as generic, objective descriptions of sexual problems. Rather, both nomenclature and theories appear to have been derived at least in part from heterosexist and sexist views of male–female relationships and may have served to perpetuate power differences within them.

At least four closely related themes relevant to these assumptions can be identified in 20th-century sexological literature and these will be examined in turn, together with ways in which they seem to have been transferred to homosexual, particularly lesbian, sex therapy. The first is that of male–female sexual relationships as reflecting and enabling male dominance and female submission; the second is that of the centrality of heterosexual intercourse; the third that of female arousal being less important than male; and, finally, the theme of females being more sexually problematic.

'SEX' AS MALE DOMINANCE AND FEMALE SUBMISSION

The early sexological writers of this century were quite explicit about the fact that, in heterosexual sex, men dominated and females submitted. Stekel (1926), for example, claimed that 'To be roused by a man means acknowledging oneself as conquered' (he was, presumably, talking only of women). Lest women should be unsure of their script in this drama, he added that 'A woman should say "Do what you want with me!" and then: "Enough! I am at the end of my powers. I have had enough!" Then only she acknowledges herself defeated, subdued, in the game of love' (Stekel, 1926: 3). Long (1919: 142) described the perfect husband: 'He must be virile, bold, strong, aggressive, positive, compelling'. For Havelock Ellis (1936), the dominance–submission relationship was played out in courtship rituals:

> . . . the primary part of the female in courtship is in the playful yet serious assumption of the role of a hunted animal who lures on the pursuer, not with the object of escaping, but with the object of being finally caught. . . . The primary part of the male is by the display of his energy and skill to capture the female or to arouse in her an emotional condition which leads her to surrender herself to him.

Such explicit references to dominance and submission were common in sexological writings even well after the Second World War. Jeffreys (1985) has argued strongly that this depiction of heterosexual sex as male conquering female must be seen as part of more complex developments in sexology in relation to the social context of the early 20th century. One of the most important of these developments was the 'discovery' of female capacity for sexual pleasure and its corollary, female frigidity. As Jeffreys has shown, such 'discoveries' and attempts to remedy frigidity did not reflect sexologists' altruistic desire to increase women's sexual satisfaction; rather, they can be seen as a response to women's increasing social and economic independence, as well as to the increasingly visible preference of some women for sexual relationships with their own sex. The message was clear: if, as appeared to be the case, many women were sexually dissatisfied with men and now had opportunities to leave unsatisfactory relationships, or, indeed, never to enter them in the first place, then male dominance was seriously threatened. Sexologists thus had to convince women that they had a right to sexual pleasure and persuade men to provide it. Such ideas, however, might lead to mutuality and reciprocal exchanges of pleasure among heterosexuals. It was therefore not only necessary that women's pleasure be contained within a framework of male dominance, but also that women be persuaded of the rightness of this state of affairs. Sexologists thus claimed that women enjoyed male dominance, that it increased both male and female pleasure — indeed that it was necessary for male performance — and that it was natural. The final sanction for women who still did not enjoy intercourse was that they were said to be masculine and/or lesbian, with the attendant physiological, psychological and social horrors of these appellations (see, for example, Ellis, 1936; Stekel, 1926; Gallichan, 1927; Chesser, 1941; Van de Velde, 1961). Although expressed within the sexological literature, these ideas can be seen as part of a much larger movement which, as Rich (1980) has put it, imposes, manages and organizes heterosexuality.

Clear, if less explicit references to heterosexual sex as involving male dominance can be found in more modern and putatively scientific sexology writings. Masters and Johnson, for example, claimed that, 'Full penile erection is, for the male, obvious physiological evidence of a psychological *demand* for intromission. In exact parallel, full vaginal lubrication for the female is obvious physiological evidence of a psychological *invitation* for penetration' (Masters and Johnson, 1970: 195; emphasis added). Comfort (1987: 63), in a section where women supposedly told men about female sexuality, claimed that, 'obviously [male] strength is a turn-on'. It is notable that in these quotes, the term 'obvious' has replaced the earlier term 'natural', but arguably to similar effect.

This depiction of sex as a relationship of dominance and submission clearly creates problems for homosexuals. For lesbians, there is no partner who will 'obviously' turn them on by his strength, who will naturally be excited by their coquettish alternation between resistance and submission or who, if Kinsey et al.'s (1953) and Jeffreys' (1990) claims as to the uncommonness of penile substitutes in lesbian sex are accurate, will routinely accept an 'obvious' invitation to penetrate her partner. For gay men, there is no partner whom they are programmed to conquer or to excite by their aggression. This is not to suggest that issues of dominance and submission are irrelevant between homosexual partners. Differences in age, race or class may create disparities in power. And sadomasochistic sex, which can be seen as the most extreme and ritualized enactment of dominant and submissive roles, has been the subject of intense debate (Samois, 1982; Linden et al., 1982; Rubin, 1984; Jeffreys, 1990). Of particular relevance here is Nichols' (1987a, 1987b) discussion of the use of some sadomasochistic practices as a form of sex therapy for, among other problems, 'inhibited desire' in lesbians. Nichols notes Samois' (1982) emphasis on the consensual nature of sadomasochistic sex and argues that such practices are justified by the fact that sexual desire is enhanced by the maintenance of difference, of barriers in relationships.

These justifications of sadomasochistic sex as a goal of sex therapy — that it is consensual and that it enhances pleasure by maintaining differences — are closely related. As Linden (1982) has pointed out, a central issue is not whether people should be prevented from engaging in sadomasochistic sex, but whether 'consensual' can carry any of its usual meanings in this context. Both male and female heterosexual desire and, to a large extent, male homosexual desire, are constructed around ideas and images of dominance and submission, of activity and passivity, of the eroticization of difference (Rian, 1982; Coward, 1984; Jeffreys, 1990). For heterosexual women, the enactment of their assigned role in sex has been a replication of their social subordination. Rather than seeing sadomasochism as consensual or as a 'sexual enhancement tool' for therapeutic use (Nichols, 1987b: 250), we need to ask whether both consent and enhancement are not functions of our intense indoctrination into the eroticization of dominance and submission.

Nichols extends her argument by distinguishing between sadomasochistic sex which is desire enhancing and that which is addictive and destructive, but she reverts to the individualistic and pathologizing language of psychiatry to justify this: those who are psychologically or physically damaged by sadomasochistic sex are depicted as 'unstable' or as having 'borderline personalities'. Such an argument compounds the neglect of the cultural context in which sadomasochism has been constructed as erotic with a neglect of the social demands which may control its practice (see, for example, Linden, 1982).

The inclusion of even milder forms of sadomasochism as a goal in sex therapy with lesbians may not only perpetuate the dominance and submission so pervasive in images of heterosexual and male homosexual sex, it may also hinder the analysis — both personal and social — of *why* dominance and submission play such a central role in our erotic lives. Against this, Nichols (1987a: 111) argues that, 'it is more important at this stage in history to support women being sexual, however they are sexual, than to judge which aspects of their sexuality are non-patriarchal and which male-identified'. This is true only if we assume that being sexual is more important than any other goal and it is difficult to see how women can be encouraged to develop new models of sexuality while those most explicitly based on dominance and submission are being prescribed as therapeutic.

The debate over sadomasochism has not reached mainstream heterosexual sex therapy literature and may never do so; indeed it might be argued that modern approaches to sex therapy described in this literature concentrate on reciprocal pleasure. Direct references to male dominance and female submission are certainly rare. But they remain common in popular literature where consensual heterosexual sex is still often described in terms of women's 'surrendering' or 'yielding' and men's 'taking'.

THE CENTRALITY OF HETEROSEXUAL INTERCOURSE

For Masters and Johnson and for Kaplan, penis–vagina intercourse was the unquestioned goal of their therapy programmes. It was not simply in their choice of goal that Masters and Johnson made intercourse 'compulsory'; they frequently used the term 'natural' to refer to what they were trying to achieve. Similarly, their granting of volition to male and female genitals (erections which demanded intromission; vaginas which invited penetration) creates the impression that the only biologically correct way to deal with sexual excitement is to have heterosexual intercourse. Indeed, Masters and Johnson came close to resurrecting the idea that women need males to ejaculate in their vaginas for their psychosexual health. Describing the 'cure' of men who have never ejaculated during intercourse they claimed that:

> This is a moment of rare reward for the wife of any man suffering from ejaculatory incompetence. Some wives referred to the foundation have waited more than ten years to consummate their marriages. Their levels of psychosexual frustration during these barren years are beyond comprehension, despite their relative facility at multiorgasmic release of sexual tensions during their coital patterning (Masters and Johnson, 1970: 132).

(There was, incidentally, no suggestion that this frustration was caused by the woman's desire to become pregnant.)

While not making such grandiose claims for male-oriented intercourse, the third edition of the *Diagnostic and Statistical Manual, DSM-III* (APA, 1980) still defined some psychosexual problems which have no obvious connection with intercourse, in relation to it. 'Inhibited sexual excitement', for example, referred to 'Partial or complete failure to maintain [excitement] until the completion of the sexual act', with no suggestion that this latter term carried other than its usual meaning. Rather than seeing intercourse as simply a sexual act, Dworkin (1987) has provided an analysis of the relationship of intercourse, of penetration, to women's sexual and social inferiority. Similarly, Jeffreys (1985) has noted that the emphasis placed by early sexologists on heterosexual intercourse played an important role in maintaining male dominance, by making intercourse the means of women's 'surrender' and fulfilment, and by making men indispensable to this fulfilment. And, as Hite's (1982) and Hollerorth's (1986) data make clear, many men acknowledge intercourse as a means of dominating women.

The 1987 revision of the *DSM* substituted 'the sexual activity' for 'the sexual act' but there is no clear evidence that either this, or the decline in direct references to male dominance and female submission in heterosexual relationships, has been accompanied by a decline in the popularity of heterosexual intercourse as a central goal of sex therapy, even if it is no longer expected that women will usually achieve orgasm in this way. Perhaps this is not surprising, given the almost complete conflation of 'sex' with 'intercourse' in our culture (Hite, 1981, 1982). There is no reason why intercourse should not be one goal of heterosexual therapy or should not be one of many equally valued sexual activities. But what is strikingly lacking in mainstream literature is discussion of why this activity should form such a central part of heterosexual activities or of the different meanings it might have for males and females. This silence, as effectively as earlier pronouncements on the sacred quality of intercourse, creates an atmosphere of 'rightness' and 'naturalness' around heterosexual intercourse which masks the problems this creates for heterosexual women and for the ways in which homosexual activities are perceived.

It can be argued that the emphasis which has been placed on intercourse as a means of both male and female sexual satisfaction has also led to a concern with the length of time intercourse lasts, and thus with 'premature ejaculation'. Indeed, Jeffreys (1990: 23) has called this a 'wonderful example of an invented disorder'. Masters and Johnson clearly saw premature ejaculation as ejaculation which occurred too soon for the woman to reach orgasm during intercourse. In this they can be said to be the only modern sexologists who could provide a coherent answer to the question, 'premature for what?' Kaplan rejected their definition and stressed instead a man's lack of control over ejaculation. It is clear from her writings, however, that this control is thought necessary to provide the woman with sexual satisfaction. The *DSM-III-R* (APA, 1987) has maintained the idea of premature ejaculation as a problem of voluntary control, but has combined this with a focus on intercourse by defining the problem as 'Persistent or recurrent ejaculation with minimal sexual stimulation or before, upon, or shortly after penetration and before the person wishes it' (APA, 1987: 295). It is not necessarily unreasonable that people should want to prolong sexual excitement prior to orgasm but we need to ask why this should be seen primarily as a male problem, particularly when references to women climaxing rapidly, and before they would prefer, can be found in both modern and ancient texts (Hite, 1981; Jacquart and Thomasset, 1988). We need to consider also the different meanings which rapid orgasm, or orgasm before a certain point, might have in heterosexual and homosexual relationships rather than simply transferring the 'disorder' to homosexual men as McWhirter and Mattison (1980) appear to have done.

A much more indirect way of making intercourse central to heterosexual theory and therapy has been to emphasize the 'sexual response cycle'. Both Masters and Johnson and Kaplan have developed this idea and it is central to the *DSM*'s classification of sexual problems. Of course, modern versions of the cycle do not explicitly include intercourse but use general terms such as 'desire', 'excitement' and 'orgasm'. Older versions of the response cycle did, however, make intercourse and male orgasm central, with the female playing the role of passive receptacle (Darmon, 1985). It is also clear from Hite's (1981, 1982) data that modern heterosexual couples tend to define their sex cycles as including intercourse and as being completed by male orgasm.

The idea of a 'sexual response cycle' not only has connotations of male-oriented intercourse; it is part of an essentialist view of sex. A 'response cycle' conveys an impression of progression and completeness, of a natural and inevitable way of responding to sexual stimuli. Loulan (1988) has used the 'sexual response cycle' in therapy with lesbians but stresses the lack of inevitability, suggesting that 'Women skip some or all of the remaining stages [after "willingness"] or skip around between them' (Loulan, 1988: 226). It is important to emphasize the variability of sexual responses, but by discussing this in the context of a response cycle, women can be made to seem deviant, and Loulan places herself in the position of having to 'give permission' to lesbians to 'opt-out' at any stage of the cycle, of having to justify their doing so. Given this, and that the original formulation of the sexual response cycle both reflected and replicated male sexual dominance through intercourse, then we might ask whether the idea of a response *cycle* — as distinct from descriptions of a variety of sexual responses — is ever likely to work to women's benefit.

THE RELATIVE UNIMPORTANCE OF FEMALE AROUSAL

Both Masters and Johnson and Kaplan emphasized the similarities in female and male responses to sexual stimuli. Masters and Johnson (1970: 99), for example, remarked that, 'In a comparison of male and female sexual function, it should always be emphasised that in sexual response, it is the similarities of, not the differences between, the sexes, that therapists find remarkable.' In spite of these 'remarkable similarities', both Masters and Johnson and Kaplan described the sexual problems which men and women were said to experience in very different ways. The most notable difference is in the lack of attention paid to female pre-orgasmic responses, and in particular to female vasocongestion, in spite of the fact that this is recognized as the major sign of female arousal (Geer et al., 1974). Masters and Johnson's classification system, for example, has no female category analogous to that of male impotence, which is, of course, defined by a lack of vasocongestion in sexual situations. (Their tentatively suggested category of female low sexual tension is clearly not analogous to impotence.) Indeed, Masters and Johnson did not, apparently, even ask women about their pre-orgasmic responses during the initial history taking, in contrast to their detailed interest in men's. Kaplan's (1974) classification system does include a female category possibly analogous to her 'male erectile dysfunction', but which is given the non-specific title of 'general sexual dysfunction'. Comfort (1987:

63) does not even mention female vasocongestion and, indeed, appears to deny its existence: 'The fact that, unlike [men] [women] can't be visibly turned off and lose erection . . .'. The *DSM-III* did use the same category label (inhibited sexual excitement) to encompass both female and male pre-orgasmic physiological responses, or, at least, their absence. The 1987 revision, however, reverted to a language of difference, and of greater specificity for men, by its use of the category labels of 'Female Sexual Arousal Disorder' and 'Male Erectile Disorder'.

This de-emphasis of female pre-orgasmic changes, and the use of vague labels to encompass them, have at least two important implications. The first is that the attainment of male genital swelling is made to seem more important than the equivalent response in females. This disparity is reflected not only in the invisibility of female pre-orgasmic responses in some classification systems, but in the apparently greater efforts made to restore vasocongestion in males than in females (Stock, 1988). It is more important that men experience genital swelling during sexual encounters only if we believe that the act of penetration is the most important outcome. Women can, after all, participate in, or be subjected to, intercourse without experiencing genital swelling, particularly if an artificial lubricant is used. To pay more attention to male vasocongestion not only makes intercourse central, but reflects the cultural stereotype of women as the recipients of male action and desire, but whose own desire is secondary.

A second implication of de-emphasizing female pre-orgasmic responses is that women are restricted in the language available to them for thinking about and communicating their sexual responses. The importance of this lack can hardly be overemphasized. As Spender (1985) has pointed out — talking more generally about the lack of action words for female sexual responses — the highly restricted language available to females can make their sexuality seem unreal. Van de Velde (1961), in his classic *Ideal Marriage*, may well have been aware of this when he aimed his book at the medical profession and men, claiming that women could not provide much useful information on their sexual responses: 'Only few women are at present capable of observing and recording their own sensations, and then subsequently of analysing them' (Van de Velde, 1961: 7). Women's restricted access to a language for understanding and communicating their physiological sexual responses means that they may use a non-specific language of feelings (arousal, enjoyment) which could more easily be misunderstood or invalidated. This is not to suggest that describing bodily changes is a more accurate way to talk about sexual responses than to describe feelings. It is, however, difficult to see how women's understanding of their sexual responses can be helped by obscuring or overlooking an important aspect of them. Frye (1990) has eloquently argued this point in relation to lesbians. Talking about the extensive literature on gay male sex, she comments that she 'realized . . . that [gay male sex] is articulate to a degree that, in my world, lesbian ''sex'' does not remotely approach. Lesbian ''sex'' as I have known it . . . is utterly inarticulate' (Frye, 1990: 311). What is notable here is the extent to which the traditional literature has participated in reducing women to inarticulateness.

It is not only that this de-emphasis of women's pre-orgasmic responses has helped to deprive women of a sexual language; it has also impeded research into their sexual problems. It is well known that certain drugs and medical conditions can interfere with vasocongestion. Yet in spite of Masters and Johnson's observation of similarity in male and female bodily responses to sexual stimuli, research on the effects of drugs and disease on male vasocongestion far exceeds research on their effects on women. Although this disparity must be partly attributed to the relative lack of importance attributed to female vasocongestion, it seems also to reflect an unsupported belief that, painful intercourse apart, women are less vulnerable than men to the effects of medical conditions (see, for example, Kaplan, 1974). Nichols (1987b: 254) has extended this belief to lesbians and claims that, 'medical conditions are perhaps even more rare as the causes of lesbian sexual problems than is true for heterosexual women, because with heterosexual women these medical causes are usually tied to dyspareunia, a complaint rare among gay women'. In fact, we know very little about the relationship between medical conditions and women's sexual responses but we cannot assume that it is as unimportant as Kaplan and Nichols seem to imply.

But if the literature has emphasized the importance of male sexual responses at the expense of female, it may also have contributed to sexual problems in gay men, who may find themselves subject to the assumptions, apparently held by many heterosexuals, that male genital swelling implies action, that its disappearance marks the end of a sexual encounter and that its prolonged absence implies the end of all sexual encounters (Masters and Johnson, 1970; Hite, 1981; Stock, 1988).

WOMEN ARE MORE PROBLEMATIC

The idea of women being more sexually troublesome than men is one of the most persistent themes in the sexological literature. It is not, of course, always expressed in this apparently derogatory way. Havelock Ellis, for example, depicted women as more sensitive and more complex than men, with the implication that they were therefore more subject to difficulties. There was clear agreement among sexologists early this century as to why women should be more problematic. They were, first, slower to arouse than men (although whether this was a natural or socially acquired characteristic was never fully agreed) and, second, had to transfer the locus of their sexual pleasure from the clitoris to the vagina. Put simply, women had to learn mature sexual responsiveness; men possessed it naturally.

It is difficult to believe that it was entirely coincidental that these female attributes left women without an autonomous sexuality and created a dependence on men, and sexual intercourse, for fulfilment. Such ideas had the added advantage of reinforcing the dominance–submission relationship between men and women, as so much emphasis was placed on the husband's role of initiator of sexual encounters and teacher of the wife's sexual responsiveness. Although Kaplan (1974: 291, 348) did claim that women were usually slower to arouse than men, such direct claims have become less frequent in mainstream literature. It is also now uncommon to find the assertion that vaginal orgasm is associated with psychological maturity, although such a claim is made in a major psychiatric dictionary (Campbell, 1989). As with the idea of heterosexual sex implying male dominance, however, the theme of women being more sexually problematic is now expressed indirectly, in three main ideas.

The first is that women are more sensitive than men to psychological and situational aspects of all sexual encounters and relationships. Kaplan (1974), for example, claimed that it is easier to 'turn women off' during sexual encounters and that:

> . . . as compared with the female response, the sexual response of many males . . . is relatively insensitive to psychological influences. The male response is often impervious to the quality of the relationship . . . it is difficult to conceive of a normal woman who would consider tipping a masseur 45 cents for the favour of masturbating her to orgasm (Kaplan, 1974: 345).

Similarly, Comfort (1987: 34, 45) claims that the male sexual response is 'far brisker, more automatic' than the female and that many female 'turn-ons' are 'situational and atmospheric'. Masters and Johnson used a similar argument — that 'real identification with the male partner, and warmth and expression of mutual emotional responsivity' are of 'vital concern' only to women — to justify providing surrogate partners for males but not females. Ehrenreich et al. (1986) have suggested that when women noticeably behave in ways which suggest that these claims are false, the strength of the claims intensifies.

These assertions about the nature of female sexuality are very similar to those of early sexologists and have the same consequence: women are denied an autonomous sexuality and are presented as being dependent on particular men and relationships for their sexual fulfilment. They also receive the message that their concern for emotional and psychological factors is not reciprocated; their male partners would, it is implied, respond to almost any woman in the same way.

The second theme which suggests that women are more sexually problematic is that of women's sexual problems being located in the mind and men's in the body. Kaplan (1974) has expressed this clearly:

> . . . the essential pathology [of impotence] is the impairment of the erectile reflex (p. 256).

By contrast,

[Female] general sexual dysfunction (and frigidity) refer to conditions which are characterised by an inhibition of the general arousal aspect of the sexual response . . . these women manifest a universal sexual inhibition which varies in intensity (p. 342).

Comfort (1987) appears to share this view. His description of 'impotence' centres on vasocongestion and scarcely mentions feelings; the description of 'frigidity' centres on emotional responses and mentions neither vasocongestion nor lubrication. Comfort also asserts that, '[Frigidity], unlike male impotence which can often be removed by simple reassurance (though not always), isn't easily helped by books. Female sexuality is much less arranged in a straight line than male — where a woman has difficulties of this sort they *have* to be dealt with on an individual basis' (Comfort, 1987: 198; emphasis in original).

Such presentations of 'impotence' and 'frigidity' depict female sexual problems as attributes of the person rather than the body, and therefore arguably as more serious than the male mechanical dysfunction. They also doubly deny women their sexual autonomy. Not only are they more dependent on particular men for sexual fulfilment than are men on particular women; when problems arise, they cannot, unlike men, resolve them through their own efforts, but must become dependent on professionals. It is easy to see how the lack of an easily available physiological and action-oriented language to describe female sexuality may contribute to the impression that female sexual problems are psychological while male problems are physical, and the *DSM-III-R*'s categories of 'Female Arousal Disorder' and 'Male Erectile Disorder' are likely to exacerbate this problem.

The idea of women being more sexually problematic is suggested, thirdly, by recent discussions of women's need for clitoral stimulation to reach orgasm. The widespread recognition that women do not reliably attain orgasm through intercourse might at first glance appear to make them seem less problematic than before. Closer examination of the literature suggests that this is not the case. The *DSM-III-R*, for example, retains a category for women who do not climax during intercourse, while the language used to describe women's need for clitoral stimulation suggests that they need something extra, something that men do not need, in order to reach orgasm: 'additional stimulation', 'simultaneous clitoral stimulation', failure to climax 'in the absence of manual clitoral stimulation', and so on (Kaplan, 1974; Jehu, 1979; APA, 1987; Comfort, 1987). Such language obscures the fact that women and men climax most reliably when they receive direct stimulation of the clitoris or the glans penis but that intercourse provides this direct stimulation much more easily to men than to women. Instead, intercourse is subtly portrayed as a 'natural' means to orgasm for the sexually straightforward male, while the more complex and problematic female needs something more. The potentially damaging effects of this portrayal, in terms of women's perception of themselves and men's perception of them, is made clear by the comments of some of Hite's respondents:

> It's our fault if we can't be as natural as men are [and climax during intercourse] (Hite, 1981: 252).

> I feel perverted that I can't have orgasms during intercourse and need cunnilingus to make me come (Hite, 1981: 373).

> I didn't feel good for [women] [when I heard of their need for clitoral stimulation separate from coitus]. Like a car with a defect that the dealer wouldn't fix (Hite, 1982: 659).

If we were to say of a lesbian that she was unable to climax without additional clitoral stimulation or simultaneous clitoral stimulation, the inappropriateness of such language would be obvious. That it does not, apparently, seem inappropriate when said of women in general attests to the strength of belief in sexual intercourse as the central, natural most fulfilling sexual activity and our willingness to pathologize women who do not respond as if this were so.

Finally, the *DSM-III-R* provides a direct claim that women are sexually more problematic. Each class of 'disorder' is accompanied by information on prevalence, prognosis, sex ratio, and so on. For 'sexual dysfunctions', the sex ratio is given only for those 'disorders' which could be diagnosed in women or men. In each case, for hypoactive sexual disorder, inhibited orgasm and dyspareunia, the 'disorder' is said to be more common in females. Because these problems are presented as attributes of individuals, this suggests that, for example, difficulty in reaching orgasm is more a female than a male characteristic, rather than a consequence for women of the cultural organization of heterosexual relationships. As Hite (1981) has pointed out, it is not that women have difficulty having orgasms, but that society has difficulty coming to terms with the way they have orgasms. This point is emphasized by Hite's and Kinsey et al.'s (1953) observation of the greater frequency with which women appear to reach orgasm in homosexual relationships.

CONCLUSION

Hamadock (1988) has suggested that the present lack of sex education and sex therapy services for lesbians is a reflection of the pervasive heterosexual bias in the field of sexology. It is unlikely to be to the advantage of lesbians or gay men if this bias is seen merely as one of exclusion which can be rectified by extending current theory and services to them. As this analysis of sexual dysfunction nomenclature and theory has shown, the bias is more complex and pervasive than this. It involves the construction of an autonomous, performance-oriented male sexuality which can be used as a means of dominating women. Female sexuality, of necessity, is the reverse of this: receptive, dependent, feeling-oriented and presented as problematic when it does not conform to a male ideal of sexual practice. Heterosexual intercourse is at the centre of this system and sexual 'dysfunctions' have been largely defined in terms of the extent to which they impede it or its completion in orgasm. Neither homosexual women nor men are likely to gain if current theory and practice are applied to homosexual problems without these issues being addressed. It is certainly true that the literature on sexual problems written by and for lesbians shows more awareness of the issues than does the traditional literature; but the extent to which ideas which may not be in women's interests have been transferred to this new writing attests to their tenacity and pervasiveness. Both men and women have been disadvantaged by traditional theory. Women, however, have arguably suffered more, because, as Jackson (1989) has pointed out, it is male sexuality which has come to serve as a model for human sexuality and, within this framework, women have been rendered deviant, less powerful and less articulate. It is likely that, rather than participating in the integration of homosexuality into the heterosexual literature, women would derive greater benefit from the development of autonomous theories of female sexuality, both homo- and heterosexual, encompassing physiology and feeling and expressed in a female-centred language.

REFERENCES

APA (American Psychiatric Association) (1980) *Diagnostic and Statistical Manual of Mental Disorders*, 3rd edn. Washington, DC: APA.

APA (1987) *Diagnostic and Statistical Manual of Mental Disorders*, 3rd edn, revised. Washington, DC: APA.

Campbell, R.J. (1989) *Psychiatric Dictionary*, 6th edn. New York: Oxford University Press.

Chesser, E. (1941) *Love without Fear*. London: Rich and Cowan Medical Publications.

Comfort, A., ed. (1987) *The Joy of Sex*, rev. edn. London: Quartet Books.

Coward, R. (1984) *Female Desire: Women's Sexuality Today*. London: Paladin.

Darmon, P. (1985) *Trial by Impotence*. London: Chatto and Windus.

Dworkin, A. (1987) *Intercourse*. London: Secker and Warburg.

Ehrenreich, B., Hess, E. and Jacobs, G. (1986) *Re-making Love: The Feminization of Sex*. New York: Doubleday.

Ellis, H. (1936) 'Analysis of the Sexual Impulse, Love and Pain, The Sexual Impulse in Women', *Studies in the Psychology of Sex*, Vol. 1, Part 2. New York: Random House. (Originally published 1903.)

Frye, M. (1990) 'Lesbian "Sex"', in J. Allen (ed.) *Lesbian Philosophies and Cultures*. New York: SUNY Press.

Gallichan, W.M. (1927) *Sexual Apathy and Coldness in Women*. London: T. Werner Laurie.

Geer, J.H., Morokoff, P. and Greenwood, P. (1974) 'Sexual Arousal in Women. The Development of a Measuring Device for Vaginal Blood Volume', *Archives of Sexual Behaviour* 3: 559–66.

Hamadock, S. (1988) 'Lesbian Sexuality in the Framework of Psychotherapy: A Practical Model for the Lesbian Therapist', in E. Cole and E.D. Rothblum (eds) *Women and Sex Therapy. Closing the Circle of Sexual Knowledge*. New York: The Haworth Press.

Hite, S. (1981) *The Hite Report: A Nationwide Study of Female Sexuality*. New York: Dell.

Hite, S. (1982) *The Hite Report on Male Sexuality*. New York: Ballantine Books.

Hollerorth, H.J. (1986) 'The Uses Men Make of Sexual Intercourse with Women'. Roundtable presentation, the Annual Meeting of the Society for the Scientific Study of Sex, St Louis. Cited in W. Stock (1988) 'Propping Up the Phallocracy', in E. Cole and E.D. Rothblum (eds) *Women and Sex Therapy: Closing the Circle of Knowledge*. New York: The Haworth Press.

Jackson, M. (1989) ' "Facts of Life" or the Eroticization of Women's Oppression? Sexology and the Social Construction of Sexuality', in P. Caplan (ed.) *The Cultural Construction of Sexuality*. London: Routledge.

Jacquart, D. and Thomasset, C. (1988) *Sexuality and Medicine in the Middle Ages*. Cambridge: Polity Press.

Jeffreys, S. (1985) *The Spinster and her Enemies: Feminism and Sexuality 1880–1930*. London: Pandora Press.

Jeffreys, S. (1990) *Anticlimax. A Feminist Perspective on the Sexual Revolution*. London: The Women's Press.

Jehu, D. (1979) *Sexual Dysfunction: A Behavioural Approach to Causation, Assessment and Treatment*. Chichester: Wiley.

Kaplan, H.S. (1974) *The New Sex Therapy: Active Treatment of Sexual Dysfunctions*. London: Baillière Tindall.

Kinsey, A.C., Pomeroy, W.B., Martin, C.E and Gebhard, P.H. (1953) *Sexual Behavior in the Human Female*. Philadelphia, PA: W.B. Saunders.

Kitzinger, C. (1989) 'Heteropatriarchal Language: The Case against Homophobia', *Gossip: A Journal of Lesbian Feminist Ethics* 5: 15–20.

Lieblum, S.R. and Pervin, L.A. (1980) *Principles and Practice of Sex Therapy*. New York: The Guilford Press.

Linden, R.R. (1982) 'Introduction: Against Sadomasochism', in R.R. Linden, D.R. Pagano, D.E.H. Russell and S.L. Star (eds) *Against Sadomasochism*. Palo Alto, CA: Frog in the Well.

Linden, R.R., Pagano, D.R., Russell, D.E.H. and Star, S.L. (eds) (1982) *Against Sadomasochism*. Palo Alto, CA: Frog in the Well.

Long. H.W. (1919) *Sane Sex Life and Sane Sex Living*. New York: Eugenics Publishing.

Loulan, J. (1988) 'Research on the Sex Practices of 1556 Lesbians and the Clinical Applications', in E. Cole and E. Rothblum (eds) *Women and Sex Therapy: Closing the Circle of Knowledge*. New York: The Haworth Press.

McWhirter, D.P. and Mattison, A.M. (1980) 'Treatment of Sexual Dysfunction in Homosexual Male Couples', in S.R. Lieblum and L.A. Pervin (eds) *Principles and Practice of Sex Therapy*. New York: The Guilford Press.

Masters, W.H. and Johnson, V.E. (1970) *Human Sexual Inadequacy*. London: J. and A. Churchill.

Nichols, M. (1987a) 'Lesbian Sexuality: Issues and Developing Theory', in Boston Lesbian Psychologies Collective (eds), *Lesbian Psychologies*. Chicago: University of Illinois Press.

Nichols, M. (1987b) 'Doing Sex Therapy with Lesbians: Bending a Heterosexual Paradigm to Fit a Gay Life-style', in Boston Lesbian Psychologies Collective (ed.) *Lesbian Psychologies*. Chicago: University of Illinois Press.

Nichols, M. (1989) 'Sex Therapy with Lesbians, Gay Men, and Bisexuals', in

S.R. Lieblum and J. Rosen (eds) *Principles and Practice of Sex Therapy. An Update for the Nineties*. New York: The Guilford Press.

Rian, K. (1982) 'Sadomasochism and the Social Construction of Desire', in R.R. Linden, D.R. Pagano, D.E.H. Russell and S.L. Star (eds) *Against Sadomasochism*. Palo Alto, CA: Frog in the Well.

Rich, A. (1980) 'Compulsory Heterosexuality and Lesbian Existence', *Signs* 5(4): 631–60.

Rubin, G. (1984) 'Thinking Sex: Notes for a Radical Theory of the Politics of Sexuality', in C.S. Vance (ed.) *Pleasure and Danger. Exploring Female Sexuality*. London: Routledge and Kegan Paul.

Samois (1982) *Coming to Power*. Boston, MA: Alyson Press.

Spender, D. (1985) *Man Made Language*, 2nd edn. London: Routledge and Kegan Paul.

Stekel, W. (1926) *Frigidity in Woman in Relation to her Love Life*. New York: Liveright.

Stock, W. (1988) 'Propping up the Phallocracy: A Feminist Critique of Sex Therapy and Research', in E. Cole and E.D. Rothblum (eds) *Women and Sex Therapy. Closing the Circle of Sexual Knowledge*. New York: The Haworth Press.

Van de Velde, T.H. (1961) *Ideal Marriage: Its Physiology and Technique*. New York: Random House.

Mary BOYLE is Head of Clinical Psychology Training at the University of East London and has worked as a therapist with people with sexual problems. She has a particular interest in processes of theory construction in clinical psychology and psychiatry and in the development of alternatives to traditional theories. ADDRESS: Department of Psychology, University of East London, Romford Road, London E15 4LZ, UK.

Jenny KITZINGER

Sexual Violence and Compulsory Heterosexuality

This study examines psychological theorizing about the impact of childhood sexual abuse on women's sexuality. I argue that the psychological definitions of, and treatments for, 'sexual dysfunction' are instruments of oppression designed to enforce heterosexuality and obscure feminist questions about the links between sexual violence and 'normal' sexual relationships. We urgently need to reclaim a radical feminist way of understanding experience that rejects compulsory heterosexuality and demands social revolution, instead of simply promoting individual adaptation.

INTRODUCTION

There is a story about the role of psychology in combating sexual violence against girls. It is a story about progress. It goes something like this. Once upon a time, in the dim and distant past, psychologists, psychiatrists and psychoanalysts dismissed women's accounts of childhood sexual exploitation — they said it was just fantasy, or that it didn't do any harm, or they told women to forget what had happened and get on with their lives, or they locked them away in mental hospitals. But things are different now, *now* psychologists, psychiatrists and psychoanalysts recognize the widespread reality of abuse and they are at the forefront of acknowledging and documenting the full impact of such violence. *Now* they are really listening to women, taking their experiences seriously and responding to their needs.

This is an 'up the mountain' account of psychology's role (see Kitzinger, 1987: 7–10). It is a powerful rhetorical structure that perpetuates psychology's role as definer of reality. However, this 'up the mountain' account of psychology's progress has been challenged by many feminists and survivors of abuse who tell the story in a different way (e.g. Armstrong, 1987; Kelly, 1988). In this version, psychology is not part of the 'solution' to male violence. Rather, it is part of the problem. Psychology has not changed — it has merely dressed up old approaches in the new fashions of the time. Psychology has consistently operated as an instrument to police women's reactions to sexual assault — limiting and individualizing what we can learn from such experiences, and obscuring the political implications. I'm not just talking about the bad old days of the 1940s or 1950s. The thriving 'incest industry' of the 1980s and 1990s, which evolved partly in response to feminism, is riddled with psychological explanations which appropriate feminist rhetoric but which dismiss feminist ways of understanding our lives. Psychology has devised a framework for processing our 'personal experiences' which erases feminist questions about the implications of sexual violence for relations between men and women, and which enforces conformity to heterosexual norms.

MALESTREAM PSYCHOLOGY

A Brief History of Diagnosis and Treatment

Throughout this century psychologists have demonstrated great concern about the impact of sexual violence upon women's willingness to comply with heterosexuality. Psychiatric case studies from the 1940s, 1950s and 1960s identify 'penis envy', 'castrating impulses' and a 'morbid fear of heterosexuality' as among the possible consequences of sexual assault (Lustig et al., 1966; Medlicott, 1967). One author, for example, bemoans the fate of an incest survivor who was afflicted with such severe penis envy that 'when faced with the opportunity for intercourse . . . [she] had not known what to do with the erect penis offered her by a rather passive partner, but held it against her clitoris' (Butler Tompkins, 1940).

However, the consensus among many psychologists around this time, and, indeed, right up until the 1970s, was that there was probably nothing to worry about: most women who were sexually assaulted during childhood were left 'none the worse for the experience': the majority were married and 'were very devoted to their husbands and children' (Rasmussen, quoted in Armstrong, 1987: 18). Psychologists reassured the public that abuse could be a perfectly normal part of growing up (Lukianowitz, 1972) and that there was nothing inherent in the experience to alienate girls from relationships with men. On this principle, the experts applauded the sensible, accepting attitude of those women who were able to put their experiences 'in perspective' and they noted that incest seemed harmless within an accepting subcultural context. We are introduced to women such as 'Mrs V'. Her father repeatedly raped her between the ages of 8 and 15. However, she is 'happily married' and 'sexually well adjusted' and has no bad feelings towards her abuser: 'Oh, I don't mind it. I think it was quite natural for him to do so after his wife had left him' (Lukianowitz, 1972: 303).

The liberated child, portrayed in this early psychological literature, was free to submit to the sexual demands of her father (or any other man) without fear or guilt. She did, however, face one source of danger — her mother. These researchers emphasized that the girl could grow up without anxiety *only* so long as the mother was 'permissive and allows the incestuous behaviour to be expressed in an open and nonsurreptitious manner' (Raphling et al., 1967: 505). If mothers reacted with anger, 'outrage' or 'moralizing', then, they were warned, this could cause more damage to their daughters than the assault itself. Documenting the attempted rape of a 12-year-old, one author concludes that the only real harm was caused by the child's mother whose reactions 'ruined her daughter for sex with men'. The girl grew up to be a lesbian (Gundlach, 1977: 371–81).

By the end of the 1970s and during the 1980s the rise of feminism caused these psychologists' arguments to become increasingly untenable. In personal testimony, autobiography, anthologies and political theory, women named the 'seduction' of children as father–daughter rape and spoke out about the violence of sexual assault and men's use of power within the family (Angelou, 1983; Armstrong, 1977; Brady, 1979; Walker, 1983; Ward, 1984). Psychology was forced to adopt different strategies and the consensus among professionals shifted accordingly. Suddenly psychology became alert to the severe damage caused by abuse and experts agreed that sexual abuse often 'ruined' women for sex with men because the experience itself was so damaging.

Scanning the more recent mainstream psychological literature on sexual violence reveals a proliferation of case studies, research findings and diagnoses which demonstrate women's failure to survive sexual assault unscathed. Now, instead of reassuring the public that most abused girls grow up to get married, research starts to reveal the worrying fact that around 40 percent of survivors remain without husbands (Search, 1988: 47). Now, instead of telling us that raped girls will grow up to be sexually 'normal', experts seem to vie with each other to diagnose 'poor sexual adjustment', 'disrupted sexual functioning' and various 'symptoms of feminine sexual incapacity' (Bagley and Macdonald, 1984; Becker et al., 1984: 11; Giaretto, 1976).

Women who have been sexually assaulted are diagnosed as suffering from 'desire disorders', 'impaired sexual arousal' and 'sexual avoidance syndrome' (i.e. they may not want sex with men; they may not get excited by it; and sometimes they may even try to avoid it).

We are warned that a woman who has been raped (whether during childhood or adulthood) may reject feminine clothing and display 'homosexual tendencies' (Woodbury and Schwartz, 1971: 21). She may score poorly on the 'Female Sexual Arousability Scale' — for instance by expressing a distaste for pornography (Hoon et al., 1976). She may only be capable of clitoral orgasms — not the mature, vaginal variety (Steele and Alexander, 1981: 229). She may be disgusted by the masculine body and perceive the penis as a weapon. She may be incapable of having sex with her husband after an argument (Steele and Alexander, 1981: 230), and her 'clinical profile' may reveal a tendency to avoid virile, aggressive partners (McGuire and Wagner, 1978: 13).

Most troubling of all, according to these experts, is that many women display a profound distrust of men. This is clear evidence of a 'maladjusted reaction' which the psychologists variously explain as 'transference', 'projection' or 'displacement' (Katz and Mazur, 1979: 278; McGuire and Wagner, 1978: 14; Meiselman, 1978: 278–9). We are told that sexual assault can lead to a 'disturbance of the aggressive drive' resulting in 'an inability to get close to men because of suspiciousness and anger; frigidity, sexual unresponsiveness, or an intense competitiveness and need to be in control' (Geiser, 1979: 29). We are informed that sexual assault victims often 'confuse' sex and power (or powerlessness) and may exhibit symptoms of 'post-traumatic stress', such as an alarming tendency to refuse 'to take the inferior position during intercourse' (Goodwin et al., 1987). To the additional consternation of these experts, some women are even incapable of accepting a penis into their vagina at all. They suffer from what the experts call 'vaginismus' — a 'syndrome' characterized by 'disabling spastic contractions of the vaginal musculature' (Cole, 1988: 44).

The professionals who diagnose women's sexual maladjustments never question the politics of these 'problems'. They rarely address fundamental issues such as: Why *should* women get married? Why should we enjoy 'feminine' clothing? What is wrong with 'homosexual tendencies'? Why should we be turned on by pornography? Why shouldn't we fear and distrust men or feel anger about male sexual violence? What is wrong with choosing gentle, unaggressive partners, or preferring to be 'on top' during intercourse, or wanting to be in control? Why shouldn't a woman reject having sex with a man while she feels angry or upset? What makes a 'vaginal orgasm' superior to a clitoral one, and what is so important about a woman not wanting a penis inside her anyway? Indeed, why should women want sex with men at all?

Definitions of normality and sexual health are taken for granted and instead of addressing any of these questions, the experts set about ensuring a wide choice of treatments to meet what they have defined as women's needs. Some of the treatment described in the earliest literature are particularly brutal. If a woman's vagina was too tight to accept a penis, doctors cut through the muscles or surgically enlarged the entrance so that she became physically incapable of resisting penetration. Alternatively, she might be given sedatives to dull sensations of fear and pain. Other options included the use of electric shocks. 'Miss X', for example, who found male bodies repulsive, was treated with 'aversion relief therapy'. This meant being repeatedly subjected to electric shocks which she could only escape by turning to look at photographs of naked men. She soon reported a substantial improvement in her condition (Crown, 1976: 102).

These treatments, using knives, drugs and electric currents, common in the 1960s and 1970s, seem to be less popular today. Instead, many experts prefer to help women reduce their resistance to sex with men through more subtle forms of behavioural therapy.

It is not necessary to restructure a woman's body surgically if she can be educated to understand the marvellous elastic capacities of the vagina or be taught to accept penetration by inserting progressively larger objects into her vagina. A graded series of glass rods or plastic vaginal 'training instruments' are manufactured for this purpose.

It is not necessary to drug a woman into compliance if she can be taught to overcome her resistance through patience, gentle persuasion and extensive foreplay. Ever since the pioneering work of Masters and Johnson, sex therapists have advised couples temporarily to avoid penetration. Only once they have learnt such restraint can they slowly build up 'increasingly intense forms of sensual touching' leading, ultimately, to a restoration of full sexual activity. The therapists note that this treatment 'may provoke intense rage' in survivors of child sexual abuse, but are confident that women's anger can be 'redirected' so as not to interfere with the 'healing' process (Haugard and Reppucci, 1988: 257).

Nor need a woman be subjected to electric shock treatment if she can learn to behave 'normally' through repeated exposure to films showing women enjoying heterosexual intercourse. According to proponents of such methods, viewing sexually explicit films help to 'desensitize' women to feelings of disgust and has the added advantage that the actress in the film serves as a useful role model to demonstrate 'appropriate female reactions' to sex.

Many modern therapists are not content simply to work on women's physical reactions to sex, they seek to restructure the way that they think. They aim to alter women's basic understandings about themselves and their relations to men. Indeed, some women will require help to 'rebuild their entire world view' (Hancock and Burton, 1987).

Techniques for achieving such goals are rich and varied. Some practitioners advocate prompt family therapy. A girl will only be able to root out her distrust of 'the world', they argue, by restoring her faith in her family. They therefore advocate reconciling girls with their abusers, helping the victim 'to learn to trust the victimizer' and trying to increase 'mutual empathy' between them (Lutz and Medway, 1984: 324).

A more common approach to dealing with victim's disillusion is to encourage them to find some appropriate stand-in to represent a 'good male'. A sensitive male therapist is often recommended. The therapeutic relationship is apparently supposed to act as a model for equality and trust, although the fact that male therapists often abuse their patients is occasionally noted. (For discussion of the routine abuse of patients by doctors see Burgess and Hartman, 1986.)

Another approach is to enable a woman to learn the appropriate way to relate to men through her relationship with 'The Divine Therapist'. Christian-oriented therapy spells out the implications:

> When you have been through child sexual abuse, you have no respect for males. You don't trust them. So it's important to your healing to come to trust this masculine God; to honor [sic] him, to submit to him. The last thing a woman who's been defiled by a man wants is to be submissive to a man. Everything in you wants to fight men . . . [But] As you learn to trust God, you are healed

in your ability to love and trust your own husband. You stop being hostile to men in their maleness (quoted in Hancock and Burton, 1987: 86).

'Cognitive restructuring' is another popular technique. One practitioner, Derek Jehu, has developed a comprehensive programme specifically designed to correct the sexual attitudes of women abused as children. The treatment programme, described in his book *Beyond Sexual Abuse* (Jehu, 1988) involves categorizing and correcting every aspect of what he calls women's 'misunderstandings' about sex. Because cognitive restructuring depends on pinning down, dissecting and systematically replacing women's 'distorted' views, Jehu has to make *explicit* sexual values that are implicit in many other programmes but never openly acknowledged. As a treatise on the dominant sexual ideology his book makes fascinating reading.

Jehu instructs a wife who would rather not have sex at all that celibacy is 'inappropriate in marriage'. He persuades the woman who feels sexually harassed by her partner to realize that 'I need to accept the realities of our relationship — that it is to include a sexual relationship. That's O.K. because I want it too' (Jehu, 1988: 275–85). He convinces the woman who believes that men see her as 'a sexual object' that 'It is me who has the "screwy" ideas, not the man' (Jehu, 1988: 129). He teaches the woman who feels violated by penetration to experience it instead as 'vaginal containment' (Jehu, 1988: 259). Women's fear, distress and resistance are systematically dismissed as they are persuaded to come to terms with 'the realities' of relationships with men and assured that they really can, and what is more *really want*, to enjoy sex.

Any questions a woman raises about the connections between male violence and male sexuality are systematically silenced. Her negative experiences of sex are rendered irrelevant. Rape itself is defined out of existence because, according to Jehu's philosophy: '. . . a woman invariably controls her environment, and if she finds that a particular man can't be trusted she can deal with it at that point. . . . it's no big deal . . . she need not be coerced into a situation in which she does not feel comfortable' (Jehu, 1988: 129).

When a woman feels used and abused by men it is her own fault. As one woman was forced to acknowledge during the course of her treatment:

> . . . as long as I continue with my thinking that sexual sensations are frightening and hurt and that someone is only using me for his own kicks . . . then I'm just continuing the abuse. Only this time I'm responsible for it. . . . I'm turning the experience of having sex . . . into something that it's not through my own mental engineering (Jehu, 1988: 281).

Not only is rape written out of existence because, as Jehu would argue, 'a woman invariably controls her environment', but when sex nonetheless feels frightening and violating it is only because of the woman's faulty mental constructions and, therefore, she is responsible for abusing *herself*.

The Therapist and the Rapist: The Common Factors

These therapists never seem to doubt their own divine right to define the meaning of sex, the nature of relationships and the ultimate goal for 'true health'. They also appear to miss the irony of their various therapeutic interventions: the irony that identical techniques are employed by rapists who are preparing their victims to submit to abuse.

Just as the early treatments for 'sexual dysfunction' included the use of knives, drugs and electric shocks to 'cure' women who resisted sex with men, so abusers have always used outright coercion against their victims (including physical mutilation, drugging girls with alcohol or beating them into submission). But it is not only the brutal 'old-style' therapeutic interventions which parallel the tactics used by rapists. The new-style 'behavioural' and 'cognitive' therapies bear striking similarities to the treatment meted out to children by their abusers. Father-rapists have never been averse to a little 'behavioural therapy' or 'cognitive restructuring' alongside, or instead of, brute physical force.

Just as therapists persuade women to use 'vaginal training instruments' to encourage them to accommodate larger and larger objects into their vaginas, so the men who sexually assault children often prepare their victim for intercourse over several months by inserting things into their bodies (fingers, the stem of a pipe, candles, bottles and spoons).

Just as therapists encourage survivors to understand the marvellous expanding capacity of the vagina, so rapists are also concerned to educate their victims: 'he'd start up these conversations about how well it was all designed: how the vagina was so perfect for the penis to go into, and the penis was such a perfect shape for the vagina, and who could have designed it better, and the fact that it had evolved this way seemed miraculous' (Jude, quoted in Ward, 1984: 20).

Just as therapists encourage women and their partners to engage in prolonged foreplay, so abusers often painstakingly and patiently erode their victims' resistance by progressing from hugs and stroking to more intrusive acts, and by using children's own erotic responses against them.

Just as therapists encourage survivors to view pornography or 'instructional videos' to learn that other women take pleasure in sex, so rapists frequently use 'kiddie porn' — showing children apparently enjoying sex with adults — in order to convince their victims that they, too, should willingly participate in such acts.

Just as therapists teach women that if they experience sex with men as frightening it is due to their own 'mental engineering', so rapists teach their victims that their fear and distress is unwarranted: 'It's OK, there is nothing wrong in what we're doing together — it's perfectly natural.'

Just as therapists argue that sex is a special way of showing love and sharing intimacy, so rapists tell their child victims that the abuse is a symbol of the special relationship they share with their 'little princess': 'He mentally forced it, confusing me, and saying that it was because he loved me and if I loved him it didn't matter . . . he worked on my heart-strings.'[1]

The psychologists have a label for the process employed by abusers to prepare children for increasing levels of victimization: they call it 'grooming'. If this is 'grooming', then sex therapy centres are 'finishing schools'. The rapists 'groom' girls to submit to them as children; the therapists complete the job to ensure that women can continue to comply with the coercive etiquette of heterosexuality as adults.

RECLAIMING OUR LIVES: THE HEALING WAY

So far I have focused on mainstream psychology, the kind of work written up in academic textbooks and journals. However, since the mid-1980s, a new type of psychology literature about child sexual abuse has appeared: pop-psychology and self-help manuals. These are the books which cram the shelves of 'alternative' book shops bearing titles such as *Reclaiming Our Lives: Adult Survivors of Incest* (Poston and Lison, 1989); *The Healing Way: Adult Recovery from Childhood Sexual Abuse* (Kunzman, 1990); and *Reach for the Rainbow: Advanced Healing for Survivors of Sexual Abuse* (Finney, 1990). The authors proclaim their professional and personal qualifications, (e.g. 'Lynne D. Finney, JD, MSW, Survivor and Therapist) and the blurbs pronounce that the contents will 'empower' you to 'take charge of your life' and help you to 'claim a healthy sexuality as your right' (Kunzman, 1990).

Advertised as 'accessible' and 'free from jargon', such books address the reader in 'everyday language' drawing on 'good common sense'. They avoid insulting terms such as 'frigidity' or 'castrating impulses' and reject the pathologizing of lesbian relationships. Instead of labelling survivors 'sick and abnormal', these authors are committed to 'recognizing', 'legitimating' and 'validating' women's experiences and to 'giving women permission to feel'. They acknowledge the existence of inequality between the sexes; pay tribute to the role of feminists and survivors in highlighting sexual exploitation; and talk about 'power', 'rights', 'choices' and 'freedom'.

It is all the more striking then, that although these authors avoid the worst excesses of mainstream psychology, the ways in which they define the 'problem' for survivors and the 'solutions' that they propose are often similar to those of psychology. Interwoven with the rhetoric and the political analysis, they reiterate traditional psychological concepts disguised in a more palatable and user-friendly (and therefore more insidious) style.

The rhetoric of 'legitimating women's feelings' is used simply to avoid analysis of the processes which shape everyday understandings of the world. The slogan 'validating women's experiences' disguises a covert process of discrimination whereby, under the pretence of a non-judgemental approach, some of women's experiences are accorded higher status than others.[2]

The style of these books deserves close examination. The authors often rely on quotations from survivors rather than making statements about their own opinion. They make suggestions rather than 'laying down the law'. They raise questions rather than providing answers. Such devices can make it hard to pin down the ideological content of what is being said. However, the manner in which interviewees' experiences are presented, the suggestions that are made and the 'questions' that are raised (or *not* raised) often reveal an agenda that, in many ways, is closer to traditional psychology than to feminism.

Without needing to resort to the language of sickness, these writers refer to some perceptions, specifically those involving anger towards men or fear of heterosex, as 'jaundiced', 'exaggerated' or 'unjustifiable'; they say that the survivor 'experiences' or 'relates' to sex in a certain kind of way; or they present her perceptions as true 'for her' or 'in her mind'. Where, on the other hand, the authors *agree* with women — notably where their interviewees report feeling that sex is 'really' about love and pleasure — then a different set of words come into play: these feelings are elevated to the status of knowledge and referred to as 'recognizing', 'realizing' and 'understanding', and the intervention of the woman's subjectivity between experience and 'reality' is less likely to be mentioned. Poston and Lison, for example, write that 'Sex, *in Marianna's mind*, blasts beauty and makes the fair ugly. Little wonder, of course, that she *finds* sex in marriage, which she *recognizes* as normal and desirable, to be a destructive and belittling experience' (Poston and Lison, 1989: 82, emphases added).

My criticism is *not* that such terms are used at all (language is never value-free and we all use rhetoric) but that the authors often claim to be 'neutral' in presenting women's experiences and do not debate the validity of their assumptions. Through such techniques they legitimate one way of thinking about sex and men and discredit another, and yet their preference for one kind of reading of reality is almost invisible because it accords so closely with dominant assumptions.

The common themes running through most of the books which I examined were:

1. An emphasis on the importance of being able to have sex;
2. The assertion that sex is basically 'good';
3. The assertion that most men are trustworthy (or if they are not you can tell the difference);
4. The assumption that sexual violence should not put women off sex with men; and
5. The belief that each individual woman can 'reclaim her right to a healthy sexuality' here and now.

Of course, these authors rarely refer to women's reactions as 'sexual dysfunction'. They rarely talk of 'restoring sexual adaptation'. Nor do they usually say that 'you owe it to your man' to learn how to do sex properly. Instead they talk of 'reclaiming your sexuality' and tell women to change because 'you owe it to yourself'. Any doubts a woman might harbour are soothed away: 'Reclaiming your sexuality is slow and painstaking work . . . you may question your own wisdom in trying to heal . . . but you deserve better' (Bass and Davis, 1988: 240). In the best books of this genre women are reassured that 'If and when to address sexuality is an individual decision and should not be forced' (Maltz and Holman, 1986: 8). Usually, however, sex is assumed to be a non-optional part of life. Women may be advised to be gentle with themselves, to 'give your Inner Child time to be a child and not sexualise her' until you feel ready to 'enter into an adult relationship'; but the assumption is that, eventually, they will be ready for that 'adult relationship' (McClure, 1990: 192). We may be 'given permission' to 'take a break' from sex, but this is only suggested as a temporary, and very brief, stop-gap measure: 'take some weeks — or even months if you need them' (Kunzman, 1990: 106). The issue is not whether a woman wants to 'reclaim her sexuality', but *when*.

Most of these 'How to heal yourself' books pay lip-service to women's 'right to choose' not to have sex. However, while they are full of techniques about 'how to' have sex they seldom offer any advice about 'how to' maintain celibacy within a sex-obsessed culture that links sex with love and being 'a complete woman'. Instead women are advised to 'expand the acceptable reasons for getting into sex'. Bass and Davis, in *The Courage to Heal*, suggest that women should consider starting to engage in sexual activity 'even if you're not feeling physical longing, emotional excitement or desire of any kind'. This approach, they claim, makes sex more 'accessible' to women and is a 'radical and liberating approach to female sexuality' (Bass and Davis, 1988: 254).

These authors insist that sex is healthy and fun. In the midst of documenting women's experiences of sex as degrading and terrifying, we are constantly reassured that sexuality is 'really' a source of intimacy and joy, an expression of respect and caring. The therapists do not debate this point. It is simply assumed in the voice of 'common sense' and often reasserted in the form of chants, 'affirmations' or personal messages to 'the child within'. One book, for example, urges survivors to write letters to their 'inner child' informing her that 'sex is good, it really is' (Parks, 1990: 145). Another advocates standing naked in front of a full-length mirror and repeating 'affirmations' such as: 'It's totally safe to be in my body and to be a sexual being'; 'I enjoy feeling aroused'; 'It's safe for me to be a beautiful woman' (McClure, 1990: 188).[3]

Many authors of these 'self-help' books would no doubt protest that they are not just concerned to help women 'reclaim' their heterosexuality, but are equally concerned to help women to enjoy sex with themselves, or, if they wish, with other women. This is quite true. Indeed, these books often include lesbian experiences alongside women's sexual experiences with men. Sometimes the gender of the partner is not even mentioned so that we cannot tell which is which. The authors adopt this approach as part of their belief that lesbianism is just as valid as heterosexuality. Yet, such an approach precludes any recognition that lesbian sex may have a different sociopolitical, as well as personal, meaning that is quite distinct from sex with a man. It sets up a basically gender-neutral analysis of male violence and assumes that it has no particular implications for heterosexuality or our relations with men in general.[4]

All the psychological texts that I have examined — whether they were published in 1940 or in 1990 — take it for granted that there is nothing in child sexual abuse that *should* put women off sex with men. The only difference between the approach adopted by the more 'progressive' self-help literature and early psychological theorizing is that where the psychologists of the 1940s and 1950s blamed the inappropriate reactions of children's *mothers* if sexual assaults 'ruined' girls for sex with men, these modern liberal theorists blame the inappropriate reactions of the survivors themselves. Or rather, they don't 'blame' women for feeling this way, instead they reassure them that their reactions to sex were appropriate at the time of the abuse, but are no longer a 'useful' or 'realistic' ways of responding to the world. These books repeatedly urge women to distinguish between their childhood and their adult experiences and to discriminate between the abusers and the men who are currently in their lives: 'your abuser is an aberration, a sick and unhappy person who does not represent the majority of people in your world and is a relic of the past' (Finney, 1990: 42); 'men are not the enemy . . . and it is not helpful for you to see them as such' (Kunzman, 1990: 100).[5]

Unlike much of the mainstream psychological literature, these writers agree that sometimes sex and violence might be associated, not just in women's minds or in their pasts, but out there in the here-and-now, real world. However, they are very selective in how they interpret this. If women experience repeated abuse, then this, they tell us, does not only reflect on many *men's* willingness to take advantage of 'vulnerable' women but tells us more about the woman herself. Survivors 'find a string of men who dominate and hurt them' because we are all 'destined to repeat the patterns of our most painful experiences' (Finney, 1990: 39). These are not justifiable grounds for avoiding men. Instead women should be taught to distinguish between 'safe' and 'dangerous' men and, with help, 'finally they can accept the fact [*sic*] that whereas people and situations can be safe or unsafe, trustworthy or not, they have the power within themselves to distinguish confidently which is which' (Poston and Lison, 1989: 82).

These authors describe male power as 'real' and 'a fact of life' — but only for certain women under certain circumstances. One book informs readers that: 'Barbara's fear of men is real' because: 'She was deprived of positive female role models as a child and did not learn to cultivate, as a young woman, those social skills that make a relationship with a man easier' (Poston and Lison, 1989: 80).

Another book declares that, 'To the girl who has been sexually victimized by a male, male privilege is experienced [*sic*] as a fact of life'; the authors contrast this with the 'facts' for a girl who has not been sexually victimized: for whom, they say, 'male privilege may be an irritating nuisance to be overcome, one that requires her to be assertive' (Maltz and Holman, 1986: 57).

The underlying concept is that the threat of male violence can be transcended by the woman who has the correct attitude, good role models or effective assertiveness techniques; and these authors often conclude with rousing proclamations telling survivors that they can claim their 'right' to sexual health and happiness: 'Sexual healing is a beautiful gift a survivor can give herself . . . . A survivor *can* claim her identity as a healthy, sexual person. The choice is hers' (Maltz and Holman, 1986: 138). To make this choice a woman only needs to realize her own power and to distinguish between what happened to her as a child and her present situation: 'In childhood her choices were limited, but there is no end to what she can choose for herself *right now*' (Poston and Lison, 1989: 82).

In this brave new world of positive thinking, feminist concerns about the social, legal and economic constraints on our 'freedom of choice' are minimized and the women's liberation movement's demands for control over our own bodies, our lives, our sexuality are magically disentangled from the struggles over abortion laws, compulsory sterilization, economic oppression, violence and discrimination. Instead of talking of 'demands' which are the focus for *collective* struggle, many women now talk of 'rights' as if each individual already has them and need only lay claim to them here and now. Instead of discussing sexual desire and identity as social constructions, inextricably intertwined with economic and social pressures, we are encouraged to talk only of 'choice' and finding our authentic selves. Writing letters to our 'inner child' or gazing at our own reflections and chanting 'It's safe for me to be a beautiful woman' is what seems to pass as feminism these days. Some people seem to think that we live in a post-feminist era in which the individual woman can struggle for and achieve sexual autonomy if only she is brave enough, courageous enough, strong enough, determined enough — and perseveres for long enough.

RECLAIMING OUR FEMINISM: THE POLITICAL WAY

'Sex is good', 'we can tell the difference between safe and dangerous men', 'it is safe to be a (beautiful) woman' — these are ideological declarations, not statements of uncontested fact. Statistics which reveal widespread male abuse of women and children suggest that these assertions may be true for only a minority of women. These assertions are contested by many women's day-to-day experiences of sex with men and betrayal by them. They are, or *should* be, challenged every time a woman or girl is raped by her husband, father, brother or friend; whenever a woman is beaten up in her own home; whenever a woman is murdered for 'nagging' or for 'tempting' a man, or for being in the wrong place at the wrong time, or just for being female.

The authors of the therapeutic/self-help literature, however, write as if we cannot afford to take their ideological statements — such as 'it's safe to be a woman' — as anything other than true. They present a utopian vision of a 'post-feminist' society. Their aim appears to be to replace the unpredictable and painful world that so many of us inhabit with the predictable and safe world recognized by the therapist. The success of therapy/self-help is measured in the extent to which fear gives way to inner confidence and despair to hope. This, perhaps, explains the unrelenting optimism of these books. Just as child sexual abuse 'prevention' programmes teach children that 'You can say no', so adult survivors are told that we all have the power within us to take control of our lives. This desire to help women and children to claim our 'rights' and find 'the power within' often conflicts with acknowledgement of the social, economic and political conditions under which we live — and the extent to which these delimit our possibilities (Kitzinger, 1990).

We would all prefer to feel empowered rather than powerless. Sometimes we need to develop techniques to protect ourselves from fear and despair. These techniques can often be found in the self-help literature. But there is a problem when survival strategies are presented as 'the answer' while avoiding crucial questions such as 'Why are they necessary?' and 'What are the pressures which make this "choice" the only option?'

The emphasis on personal adaptation within the self-help literature systematically eradicates other ways of coping with, or challenging, society. Women are encouraged to perceive their reactions as irrational, instead of transforming their anger into activism; they are encouraged to believe that their ways of seeing the world are inappropriate instead of insightful; they are encouraged to overcome fear of men, instead of setting up networks which make it easier to live and work in women-only space. The therapeutic/self-help literature does not just offer techniques, it often covertly insists on an entire worldview and presents survival tactics as if they were the ultimate in revolutionary strategy. When this happens therapeutic/self-help literature not only obscures, but is in opposition to, radical feminist analysis.

Radical feminist practice is concerned with recognizing our fear, and anger, and refusing to dismiss those reactions as simply 'dysfunctional'. It is about organizing collectively to challenge the institutions that deny women's rage and pain. It is also about questioning 'common-sense' understandings of the world. Radical feminists have examined the institution of heterosexuality, the social construction of desire and the links between rape and 'consensual' sex. These analyses question the existence of 'truly chosen' and 'egalitarian' heterosexual relations by focusing on the compulsory enforcement of heterosexuality (Rich, 1980); they are suspicious of appeals to some 'authentic female sexuality', hidden deep within ourselves and uncontaminated by the rule of heteropatriarchy (Jeffreys, 1990). They challenge the equation of heterosex with 'goodness', 'wholesomeness' and 'health':

> Current dogma is to teach by rote that sex is 'healthy' as if it existed outside social relations, as if it had no ties to anything mean or lowdown, to history, to power, to the dispossession of women from freedom. But for sex not to mean

dirt — for sex not to *be* dirty — the status of women would have to change radically . . . (Dworkin, 1987: 173).

Once this is accepted, there is the possibility that survivors may, after all, be 'right' in the way that they see the world. This radical feminist vision is not 'distorted'. Rather, it is free of the rose-tinted glasses of romance. Seeing relationships with men in terms of violation and exploitation may be painful, and even 'maladaptive' — but this does not make it any less accurate.

Feminist theory permits us to 'make sense' of these reactions and to see close encounters with male violence as a source of possible insight, rather than solely as a source of 'confusion'. Andrea Dworkin, who spent three years studying pornography, eloquently describes her own reactions to constant exposure to these violent images:

> The photographs I had to study changed my whole relationship to the physical world in which I live. For me, a telephone became a dildo, the telephone wire an instrument of bondage, . . . scissors were no longer associated with cutting paper but were poised at the vagina's opening (Dworkin, 1981: 303).

This changed perception left Dworkin feeling isolated: 'I retreated into silence. I felt that I could not make myself understood, that no one would know or care, and that I could not risk being considered ridiculous.' However, instead of diagnosing herself as suffering from 'delusions', 'obsession' or 'contact victimization', Dworkin identifies her reactions as a form of bilingualism: 'I developed a new visual vocabulary', she writes, 'one that few women have at all, one that male consumers of pornography carry with them all the time' (Dworkin, 1981: 303). Such analysis is completely alien to psychology. According to psychology, the Andrea Dworkins of this world are badly in need of therapy.

However, there is no simple dichotomy between feminism and psychology. The two ways of seeing the world are increasingly often intertwined. This is particularly true within the self-help literature concerning violence against women and children. Many of these books are written by feminists who are struggling with the tensions between feminist politics and psychology and, sometimes, the authors do actively engage with women's negative experiences of sex instead of dismissing, medicalizing or marginalizing them.

For example, feminist theorists have analysed the threat of the male gaze, exploring the objectification of women as meat, women as animals, as receptacles for male sexuality. Suzanne Kappeler, in *The Pornography of Representation*, discusses the portrayal of women and of animals in pornography, in zoos, in peep-shows, on the public stage, in the home and in the wild. She argues that the power relations between men and women mean that inequality extends beyond the blatant exploitations of pornography and violence into everyday ways of seeing and receiving the male gaze:

> The look between man and woman — both looking as active subjects — has been extinguished. The woman zoo extends beyond the metal slot and shutters of the peep-show. The cultural space of women, captured and framed in images, is one big Show World. There remains but one kind of look: looking *at*. Man gazing at woman, one-way (Kappeler, 1986: 81).

It is this type of analysis that is addressed in one of the most interesting sections in Carol Poston and Karen Lison's book *Reclaiming Our Lives*: a section where the voices of the two authors diverge and they engage in political debate. One author, Karen Lison, describes how much she enjoys it when a man looks at her with desire in his eyes. However, the other author, Carol Poston, describes how such a look frightens her: 'it's a look I saw a million times, and it always meant rape'. Her colleague argues this is a 'misreading' of the situation, but Poston maintains that her reactions are valid given the existing power relations between men and women. Picking up on her colleague's description of how excited she is by 'the look', 'like the look Rhett Butler gives Scarlett', Poston writes:

> Scarlett O'Hara, assertive as she is, cannot disregard Rhett Butler's sexual power; she must give in. 'The look' communicates this power imbalance, and the incest survivors are just more canny than other women in sensing it because they have, in fact, been victims of male patriarchal power. They *know* what the look means, and it threatens them (Poston and Lison, 1989: 182).

This is politics, not psychology. It is glimpses of this sort of debate within some self-help books which, perhaps more than anything else, highlight the contradictions between psychological and feminist ways of understanding the world. Where feminism draws connections between individual women's suffering and our collective experience, psychology fragments and isolates our lives. Where feminism questions the 'traditional' and 'common-sense' ways of viewing the world, psychology takes such ways of seeing for granted and reinforces them. Where feminism links personal experiences to power structures in the world, psychology focuses on the 'little world' inside our heads. Where feminism demands social transformation, psychology prioritizes personal salvation. From this perspective it becomes very hard to believe the 'up the mountain' story of psychology's roles in combating sexual violence. The growth of professional concern about sexual violence over the last 20 years is not a sign of the success of feminist demands, but of the co-option of these demands by psychologists. Sexual assault victims are now urged to submit their experiences to the professionals to be dismembered and re-membered in accordance with reality as it is defined by psychology. The medicalization of sexual abuse has reduced 'a social and political issue into a matter of "diagnosis"' (Kelly, 1988: 14). The experts have transformed the *political* timebomb of women's growing awareness of the many forms of male violence into what they call a *'psychological* timebomb' where the woman is portrayed as the threat. It is the victims who are presented as dangerous. They threaten themselves, their children, their partners and even other women's sexual fulfilment and happiness. Instead of focusing on the problem of male violence, the focus has shifted to the maladjustment of the victims.

Women's naming of male violence and demands for change have been translated into a different language by the 'incest industry':

> We spoke of male violence and deliberate socially accepted violation. They spoke of family dysfunction. . . We spoke of social change. They spoke of personal healing. We spoke of political battle. They spoke of our need to hug the child within (Armstrong, 1991: 30).

The ways in which psychology insists on sexual 'restoration' for survivors is only one part of this process of co-option, a process concerned with helping women to accommodate to living under heteropatriarchy and ensuring that male access to women's bodies continues unimpeded. Psychology is consolidating its monopoly of defining both the 'problem' of and the 'solution' to sexual violence.

The challenge now is to reclaim feminist perspectives and to retain and develop ways of supporting each other which draw on these political insights. We need to discuss and write about the contradictions and complexities of trying to achieve this in our day-to-day lives and within feminist organizations such as rape crisis lines and refuges. How do we respond to women's distress about 'failure' to achieve heterosexual functioning? How do we work with women's pain when it is increasingly articulated through individualized, medicalized perspectives? How do we recognize each of our individual concerns at the same time as offering each other different frameworks for thinking about the world? We need accounts which document and explore the nature of feminist practice in action. Above all, we need to wrest women's pain and oppression away from the experts and to question the implications of sexual violence for *everyone's* sexual experience and for all our futures. A survivor writes:

> No one can tell me that my politics are the hysterical over-reaction of a paranoid rape victim who has been pushed over the edge by a bad experience. I see reality. I have no distance from it, no more rationalizations to protect me . . . please value us, the survivors, because . . . we have seen the scary truth about our world, and we will let you know when the terror is over. We will feel it when the knot within us loosens and we know that we are finally safe in a world that really loves women and children (Placier, 1987: 193).

ACKNOWLEDGEMENTS

I am grateful to all the women who agreed to be interviewed during the course of my research. I would also like to thank Celia Kitzinger and Sheila Kitzinger for comments on an earlier draft of this paper, and Diana Mutimer for helping me to finally finish it! Thanks also to the reviewers, Marny Hall and Liz Kelly, and to the Editor, Sue Wilkinson, for useful feedback; and to the Glasgow Women's Support project for access to books and articles.

NOTES

1. Unless otherwise specified quotations come from interviews I conducted with women who had been sexually assaulted during childhood or whose own children had been abused.
2. In exploring the common psychological themes in these books I am, of course, ignoring the variation in their sophistication and political content. I am *not* looking at the feminist statements contained in some of the books, although these are sometimes powerful. Nor am I examining the specific strengths and weaknesses of each text. It is important to acknowledge that while some of these books simply use the rhetoric of 'liberated womanhood', others genuinely engage with feminist explanations of sexual violence. Indeed, some of the books from which I quote are attempting to synthesize psychology and feminism, or at least to exist in that dangerous place of tension between the two. From my reading of the psychological content of these books, however, this is a task fraught with contradictions.
3. Ironically, many therapists find that constant exposure to women's accounts of sexual violence can undermine their own faith in the innate joys of sex. Their own allegiance to the dominant version of 'reality' weakens as, through constantly working with survivors, they *too* become distrustful of men and even develop their own 'sexual dysfunctions'. Instead of considering the implications of such treacherous conversion, however, the psychological literature simply defines this as yet another 'syndrome': they call it 'contact victimization'. When therapists experience such 'symptoms' they are urged to seek the help of their supervisors in order to avoid further 'victimization' by their clients (Courtois, 1988: 236). It is clear from such diagnoses that psychology is only prepared to 'validate women's experiences' up to a certain point. If women who have personal experience of male sexual violence begin to convince others of the justice in their way of seeing the world then this must be guarded against at all costs.
4. Even sex with women can be affected by memories of abuse by men, and lesbians too come under pressure to 'heal' sexually. Recent writing exploring the specific impact of sexual assault (by men and by women) for lesbians is particularly to be welcomed (Kelly, 1991; *Lesbian Ethics*, 1992). We need to develop theory about the connections between violence and adult sexuality in which sexual identity is taken as a key difference between women and which address the specific issues around sexual experience and identity for lesbian survivors of sexual violence.
5. For some women refusing to allow the abuser to 'contaminate' their view of men in general is an act of resistance, and loving women may be seen as a 'consequence' of assault — a sort of 'failed heterosexuality'. One woman spoke to me about her concern that her abused daughter might grow up to be lesbian. She described the relief she would experience if her daughter got a boyfriend because this would 'prove' that the 'healing process' had worked, and: 'It would be one in the eye for her abuser . . . she could say to him "Fuck you. I don't care what you did to me, I can find happiness with a man and you are not going to be all men to me".'

REFERENCES

Angelou, M. (1983) *I Know Why the Caged Bird Sings*. London: Virago.

Armstrong, L. (1987) *Kiss Daddy Goodnight*. New York: Pocket Books. (Originally published 1977.)

Armstrong, L. (1991) 'Surviving the Incest Industry', *Trouble and Strife* 21: 29–32.

Bagley, C. and Macdonald, M. (1984) 'Adult Mental Health Sequels of Child Sexual Abuse and Neglect in Maternally Separated Children', *Canadian Journal of Community Mental Health* 3(1): 15–26.

Bass, E. and Davis, L. (1988) *The Courage to Heal: A Guide for Women Survivors of Child Sexual Abuse*. New York: Harper and Row.

Bass, E. and Thornton, L., eds (1983) *I Never Told Anyone: Writings by Women Survivors of Child Sexual Abuse*. New York: Harper and Row.

Becker, J., Skinner, L., Abel, G., Axelrod, R. and Cichon, J. (1984) 'Sexual Problems of Sexual Assault Survivors', *Women and Health* 9(4): 5–20.

Brady, K. (1979) *Father's Days: A True Story of Incest*. New York: Dell.

Burgess, A. and Hartman, C., eds (1986) *Sexual Exploitation of Patients by Health Professionals*. New York: Praeger.

Butler Tompkins, J. (1940) 'Penis Envy and Incest: A Case Report', *Psychoanalytic Review* 27: 219–325.

Cole, M. (1988) 'Normal and Dysfunctional Sexual Behaviour: Frequencies and Incidences', in M. Cole and W. Dryden (eds) *Sex Therapy in Britain*. Milton Keynes: Open University Press.

Courtois, C. (1988) *Healing the Incest Wound*. New York: W.W. Norton.

Crown, S., ed. (1976) *Psychosexual Problems: Psychotherapy, Counselling and Behavioural Modification*. London: Academic Press.

Dworkin, A. (1981) *Pornography: Men Possessing Women*. London: The Women's Press.

Dworkin, A. (1987) *Intercourse*. London: Secker and Warburg.

Finney, L. (1990) *Reach for the Rainbow: Advanced Healing for Survivors of Sexual Abuse*. Malibu, CA: Changes Publishing.

Giaretto, H. (1976) 'Humanistic Treatment of Father–Daughter Incest', in R. Helper, and H. Kempe (eds) *Child and Neglect: The Family and the Community*. East Lansing: Michigan State University Press.

Gieser, R. (1979) *Hidden Victims: The Sexual Abuse of Children*. Boston, MA: Beacon Press.

Goodwin, J., Cheeves, K. and Connell, V. (1987) 'Defining a Syndrome of Severe Symptoms in Survivors of Extreme Incestous Abuse', based on a paper presented at the Fourth Annual Meeting of the International Society for the Study of Multiple Personality and Dissociative Disorders, Chicago, IL.

Gundlach, R. (1977) 'Sexual Molestation and Rape Reported by Homosexual and Heterosexual Women', *Journal of Homosexuality* 2(4): 367–84.

Hancock, M. and Burton Mains, K. (1987) *Child Sexual Abuse: A Hope for Healing*. Wheaton, IL: Harold Shaw.

Haugard, J. and Reppucci, N. (1988) *The Sexual Abuse of Children: A Comprehensive Guide to Current Knowledge and Intervention Strategies*. San Francisco, CA: Jossey-Bass.

Hoon, E., Hoon, P. and Wincze, J. (1976) 'An Inventory for the Measurement of Female

Sexual Arousability', *Archives of Sexual Behaviour* 5: 291–300.

Jeffreys, S. (1990) *Anticlimax: A Feminist Perspective on the Sexual Revolution*. London: The Women's Press.

Jehu, D., in association with Gazan, M. and Klassen, C. (1988) *Beyond Sexual Abuse: Therapy with Women who were Childhood Victims*. New York: Wiley.

Kappeler, S. (1986) *The Pornography of Representation*. Cambridge: Polity Press.

Katz, S. and Mazur, M. (1979) *Understanding the Rape Victim: A Synthesis of Research Findings*. New York: Wiley.

Kelly, L. (1988) 'From Politics to Pathology: The Medicalisation of the Impact of Rape and Child Sexual Abuse', *Radical Community Medicine* 36: 14–18.

Kelly, L. (1991) 'Unspeakable Acts', *Trouble and Strife* 21 (Summer): 13–20.

Kitzinger, C. (1987) *The Social Construction of Lesbianism*. London: Sage.

Kitzinger, J. (1990) '"Who Are You Kidding?" Children, Power and Sexual Assault', in A. James and A. Prout (eds) *Constructing and Reconstructing Childhood*. London: Falmer Press.

Kunzman, K. (1990) *The Healing Way: Adult Recovery from Childhood Sexual Abuse*. Centre City, MN: Hazelden.

Lesbian Ethics (1992) Special Issue, 4(3).

Lukianowitz, N. (1972) 'Incest', *British Journal of Psychiatry* 120: 301–13.

Lustig, N., Dresser, J., Spellman, S. and Murray, T. (1966) 'Incest: A Family Group Survival Pattern', *Archives of General Psychiatry* 14: 31–40.

Lutz, S. and Medway, J. (1984) 'Contextual Family Therapy with the Victims of Incest', *Journal of Adolescence* 7: 319–27.

McClure, M. (1990) *Reclaiming the Heart: A Handbook of Help and Hope for Survivors of Incest*. New York: Warner Books.

McGuire, L. and Wagner, N. (1978) 'Sexual Dysfunction in Women Who Were Molested as Children', *Journal of Sex and Marital Therapy* 4(1): 11–15.

Maltz, W. and Holman, B. (1986) *Incest and Sexuality: A Guide to Understanding and Healing*. Lexington, MA: Lexington Books.

Medlicott, R. (1967) 'Parent–Child Incest', *Australian and New Zealand Psychiatry* 1: 180–7.

Meiselman, K. (1978) *Incest: A Psychological Study of Causes and Effects with Treatment Recommendations*. San Francisco, CA: Jossey-Bass.

Parks, P. (1990) *Rescuing the Inner Child: Therapy for Adults Sexually Abused as Children*. London: Souvenir Press.

Placier, P. (1987) 'Speaking Out as a Survivor', in P. Portwood, M. Gorcey, and P. Saunders (eds) *Rebirth of Power: Overcoming the Effects of Sexual Abuse through the Experiences of Others*. Racine, WI: Mother Courage Press.

Poston, C. and Lison, K. (1989) *Reclaiming Our Lives: Adult Survivors of Incest*. Boston, MA: Little, Brown.

Raphling, E., Carpenter, B. and Davis, A. (1967) 'Incest: A Genealogical Study', *Archives of General Psychiatry* 16: 505–11.

Rich, A. (1980) 'Compulsory Heterosexuality and Lesbian Existence', in C. Stimpson and E. Person (eds) *Women: Sex and Sexuality*. Chicago, IL: University of Chicago Press.

Search, G. (1988) *The Last Taboo — Sexual Abuse of Children*. Harmondsworth: Penguin.

Steele, B. and Alexander, H. (1981) 'Long-term Effects of Sexual Abuse in Childhood', in P. Beesely Mrazek, and H. Kempe (eds) *Sexually Abused Children and Their Families*. Oxford: Pergamon Press.

Walker, A. (1983) *The Colour Purple*. London: The Women's Press.

Ward, E. (1984) *Father–Daughter Rape*. London: The Women's Press.

Woodbury, J. and Schwartz, E. (1971) *The Silent Sin: A Case History of Incest*. New York: Signet Books.

Jenny KITZINGER is currently based at the MRC medical sociology unit in Glasgow where she is carrying out a study of how young (heterosexual) women 'manage' sexual reputation. She is about to start a new project based at Glasgow University Media Group which will examine media representations and public understandings of sexual assaults on children. ADDRESS: Glasgow University Media Group, 61 Southpark Avenue, Glasgow G12 8LF, Scotland.

OBSERVATIONS & COMMENTARIES

I

Fear of a Black (and Working-class) Planet: Young Women and the Racialization of Reproductive Politics

Christine GRIFFIN

While heterosexuality is compulsory for young women, this process is racialized and class specific as well as gendered. This is particularly clear when heterosexuality is related to reproduction, as in the panic over 'teenage pregnancy' in the USA (Phoenix, 1991; Griffin, in press). There is a considerable academic literature which is addressed to the incidence and antecedents of 'premarital adolescent heterosexual intercourse' (PAHI), paying particular attention to the activities of young working-class women and (especially in the USA) to young women of colour (Hofferth et al., 1987).

During the 1980s, the pages of news journals and academic texts in the USA reverberated with debates over the so-called 'Black underclass'. Concern over the high unemployment rates among young African-American men and other young men of colour coincided with discussions about the demise of 'the Black family' (Hare and Hare, 1984). Many radical Black scholars argued that the 'Black underclass' debate shifted attention away from the disastrous effects of Reaganomics: increasing poverty, homelessness, ill health and unemployment, which affected young African-Americans to a disproportionate extent. Some exponents of the 'Black underclass' theory, however, laid the blame for these harsh economic and social conditions at the door of young working-class women and men of colour, especially young African-American women. Apparently, the ravages of Reagan's economic policies can be attributed to the incidence of 'unplanned teenage pregnancies' among this group of young women (see Malveux, 1988 for a critique).

From a traditional (hetero)patriarchal standpoint, *any* 'teenage pregnancy' is constructed as a problem, especially if the young woman is not married. Some 'teenage pregnancies' are less acceptable than others, regardless of whether they are 'unplanned'. Hence the emphasis on the need for educational initiatives on 'pregnancy avoidance' and 'planned parenthood' which focus on young working-class women and young women of colour, since these are the groups which are presumed to constitute 'the problem of the (hetero)sexually active teenager' (Neinstein and Shapiro, 1986).

One recent US study examined the medical records of 60 young women for evidence that paediatricians had asked questions (or at least recorded information) about these young women's sexual histories during medical consultations (Hunt et al., 1988). All of these young women (aged between 12 and 20) had been admitted to emergency or casualty departments with acute abdominal pains. Paediatricians were far more likely to ask working-class African-American and Chicana young women questions about heterosexual experiences, contraceptive use and possible pregnancy compared to their white and middle-class peers. This study exemplifies the practical implications of the racialized, class-specific and gendered nature of heterosexuality for young women within the clinical domain.

The panic over 'unplanned teenage pregnancy' addresses itself to the heterosexual and reproductive activities of young women. In the USA, these debates have long moved past the point of crisis, with arson attacks, bombings, burglaries, hate mail and vandalistic attacks on abortion providers, laws demanding parental consent for young women seeking abortions in some US states and national cutbacks of Medicaid funding for abortion (Petchesky, 1990; Fried, 1990). Women of all ages are increasingly likely to be constructed as baby receptacles through the ideology of foetal rights, which anti-abortion campaigners have mobilized to present their position as a 'pro-life' stance.

Such developments reinforce a set of assumptions which construct women as responsible for the health of their offspring, conveniently obscuring the potential effects of poverty and oppression (Phoenix, 1991). The ideology of foetal rights as used in anti-abortion arguments represents the life of a pregnant woman as in direct opposition to that of her foetus (usually represented as male) in a sort of competition for 'life' and 'rights' (Petchesky, 1990). Assumptions about women's 'responsibility' for the health and well-being of their offspring are brought forward to the moment of conception. The ideology of adolescence constructs all young people as inherently prone to 'irresponsibility', especially if they are female, working-class and Black. There are no prizes for guessing which group of young women is particularly likely to be positioned as 'irresponsible mothers' in this ideological arena.

In a recent review essay on the politics of abortion and reproductive freedom in the US feminist news journal *off our backs*, Felicia Kornbluh identified 'teen sexuality' as one of six key areas for feminist activism in this domain (Kornbluh, 1991). By 'teen sexuality', of course, she was referring to *hetero*sexuality. Debates over 'unplanned teenage pregnancy' are not only concerned with the availability of abortion: they are fundamentally about power and control in the politics of heterosexuality and reproduction. While access to abortion is becoming increasingly restricted *for young women who demand one*, the picture can be very different for young women to *want* to give birth, especially if they are living outside, or on the margins of, the affluent 'First World', and if they are likely to be constructed as 'irresponsible mothers'. The main problem for the latter groups is more likely to be enforced sterilization than access to abortion, but these different positions are part of the same political equation. Enforced sterilization may appear in the guise of 'genetic counselling' for young women with disabilities; sterilization without the woman's explicit consent during other gynaecological operations; or the various 'family planning' initiatives carried out by the World Health Organization which offer financial or other incentives to 'Third World' men (or women) who 'consent' to be sterilized. In the latter case, the pressures of poverty undermine any notion of 'free choice'. The key issue in all of these different contexts is *control* and who must be given the power to make decisions about young women's heterosexual relations and reproductive activities.

The case of the first young woman in Alabama, USA, to seek a 'judicial bypass' around the parental consent required before she could have an abortion exemplifies the powerful juxtaposition of ideologies around femininity, adolescence and heterosexuality in this area. The judge found that 'Kathy' was not mature enough to make her own decision about abortion, and in an interview four months after the court hearing, he described the criteria on which he based this decision as follows: 'I based it on her looks . . . just something that comes across when you talk to her . . . her credibility' (Fried, 1990: 101). As Felicity Kornbluh argued in her review of Margaret Gerber Fried's book, if a young white woman seeking an abortion without parental consent can be treated in this way 'then none of us is safe' (Kornbluh, 1991: 13). If you are reading this and asking yourself what age the young woman was, perhaps you need to consider what criteria *you* are using with reference to this case.

Feminists involved in reproductive politics from a disability rights perspective have set debates about abortion and sterilization in a broader context, and demanded a reassessment of the ideology of foetal rights. As they point out, access to abortion and the ideology of foetal rights are used selectively: under current legislation in England and Wales, foetuses defined by the medical profession as 'seriously handicapped' can be aborted at any time up to the moment of birth (Morris, 1991). Reproductive politics can then be set in the context of the ideological framework that informed the Nazi euthanasia programme, in which the murder of thousands of adults and children with disabilities was justified with recourse to arguments about 'mercy killing'.

Where the 'rights' of young women with disabilities who are, or who wish to become, pregnant are concerned, the arguments are somewhat different, but the effects can be all too familiar. In this context, eugenicist ideas about perfecting the population are mobilized alongside the assumption that *all* people with disabilities suffer an existence of unrelieved misery and inadequacy. While radical researchers and practitioners have developed more sophisticated understandings of the complex issues raised by debates over disability, heterosexuality and reproduction (e.g. Perkins, 1991), these analyses have as yet had little impact on mainstream arguments (Morris, 1991).

The legacy of eugenicist ideas lives on in assumptions about the inherent deficiencies of young working-class women, young women of colour and young women with disabilities as potential mothers. 'Race' and class are now more likely than in the early part of this century, to be represented as cultural, rather than as biological categories in western societies, but the prevailing definition of disability still revolves around physiological, hormonal or genetic 'deficiency'. Young women with disabilities — whatever their disabilities — are constructed as 'imperfect' examples of flawed femininity to whom the heterosexual dilemma should never apply. They are definitely not encouraged to have children.

All young women face pressures to move down the 'straight and narrow' path of heterosexuality, marriage and motherhood (in that order), but such pressures are experienced and negotiated in racialized and class-specific ways which also use notions of 'normality' and 'disability' to police the transition of adulthood. The voices of young women are seldom heard within the academic, clinical or judicio-legal literatures on 'premarital adolescent heterosexual intercourse', especially if they are working-class, Black and/or young women with disabilities. The voyeuristic gaze of the adult researcher or clinician defines the boundaries of 'appropriate' heterosexual and reproductive activity. Yet despite the institutional, cultural and ideological force of such definitions, young women continue to 'deviate' from that straight and narrow path, to forge their own routes through the traps laid by heterosexuality, marriage and motherhood, to challenge and subvert 'common-sense' definitions of 'normality' and 'deviance'.

REFERENCES

Fried, M.G. (1990) *From Abortion to Reproductive Freedom: Transforming a Movement*. Boston, MA: South End Press.
Griffin, C. (in press) *Representations of Youth: British and American Youth Research during the 1980s*. Cambridge: Polity Press.
Hare, N. and Hare, J. (1984) *The Endangered Black Family*. San Francisco, CA: Black Think Tank.
Hofferth, S., Kahn, J. and Baldwin, W. (1987) 'Pre-Marital Sexual Activity among US Teenage Women over the Past Three Decades', *Family Planning Perspectives* 19(2): 46–53.
Hunt, A., Litt, I. and Loebner, M. (1988) 'Obtaining a Sexual History from Adolescent Girls: A Preliminary Report of the Influence of Age and Ethnicity', *Journal of Adolescent Health Care* 9: 52–4.
Kornbluh, F. (1991) 'The Movement for Reproductive Freedom: Is There Something for Everyone?', *off our backs* 21(10): 12–13.
Malveux, J. (1988) 'Race, Class and Black Poverty', *The Black Scholar* May/June: 18–21.
Morris, J. (1991) *Pride Against Prejudice: Transforming Attitudes to Disability*. London: The Women's Press.
Neinstein, L.S. and Shapiro, J.R. (1986) 'Pediatricians' Self-Evaluation of Adolescent Health Care Training, Skills and Interest', *Journal of Adolescent Health Care* 7(1): 18–21.
Perkins, R. (1991) 'Women with Long-term Mental Health Problems: Issues of Power and Powerlessness', *Feminism & Psychology* 1(1): 131–40.
Petchesky, R.P. (1990) *Abortion and Women's Choice: The State, Sexuality and Reproductive Freedom*. Boston, MA: Northeastern University Press.
Phoenix, A. (1991) *Young Mothers?* Cambridge: Polity Press.

Christine GRIFFIN is the author of *Typical Girls? Young Women from School to the Job Market* (Routledge, 1985) and the forthcoming *Representations of Youth: British and American Youth Research During the 1980s* (Polity). She is based in the School of Psychology, University of Birmingham, B15 2TT, UK.

II

Sleeping with the Enemy:
Mothers in Heterosexual Relationships

Rose CROGHAN

Both lesbian and heterosexual feminists are currently engaged in reinterpreting and remaking their sexual relationships. Heterosexual women are forced to do this in the context of a great deal of male-defined ideological baggage. The experience of motherhood is closely bound up with the construction of heterosexuality and of heterosexual marriage as the norm, and of the designation of motherhood either without men or outside marriage as deviant (Leonard and Speakman, 1986). Women who mother within heterosexual relationships find themselves at the intersection of two powerful ideological constructions of their experience. On the one hand, they are bound by an ideology which characterizes the sexual relationship between men and women as necessarily equal and mutually rewarding while, on the other hand, they are bound by an ideological construction of motherhood which casts the mother in the role of primary caretaker and which characterizes the participation of the father in parenting as optional. Mothers in heterosexual relationships therefore have to come to terms with the lack of fit between this ideological construction of marriage and motherhood as mutually beneficial and rewarding, and their experience of the stress which arises from coping with the work of parenting in the absence of effective support from their male sexual partner (Connell, 1987).

My own research into motherhood arose from a personal need to understand the stress I experienced as a mother within a heterosexual relationship, and to resolve the question of how far my parenting stress could be interpreted as a personal failure and how far it could be construed as the result of a particular male construction of motherhood and of gender relationships. The mothers I spoke to in the course of my research were also struggling to make sense of their distress both at their partner's failure to share the work of parenting and at what they perceived to be their own personal failure to live up to the ideal of 'good motherhood'. The increased workload which mothering brought with it forced the mothers to attempt to increase the paternal contribution by negotiating for a more equitable division of labour within their relationships. However, they typically encountered resistance to any increase in the paternal contribution from men who, because of their access to external sources of social and economic power, were unlikely to relinquish their unequal share of power and resources.

The romantic discourse of mutuality surrounding heterosexual relationships obscured both the stress which the mothers experienced, and the power basis underlying sexual relationships. Such a discourse hampered mothers in their attempts to make sense of their experience and left them without any legitimate recourse to effective relief from their distress. The simultaneous definition of paternal support as optional, and of fathers as the main source of support, invalidated mothers' sense of grievance, and forced them to see themselves, rather than their partner, as responsible for their parenting stress. Because of this, mothers within heterosexual relationships continued to accept the primary responsibility for both the physical and the emotional work of the relationship, and struggled to account for their partner's refusal to contribute equally in personal rather than in structural terms (Croghan and Miell, 1991; Croghan, 1991).

In the face of their partner's unwillingness to change, the options open to women in heterosexual relationships are limited. They can either accept inequality and look for alternative ways in which to meet their increased workload (either by working harder and reducing leisure time, or by obtaining support *outside* the relationship), or they can refuse to accept inequality and continue to press for change, thus prolonging conflict within the relationship. While there were differences in the style of negotiation (traditional women adopting more deferential strategies, and feminist women more confrontational strategies), *all* the women in heterosexual relationships were ultimately bound by their commitment to their relationship, and were reluctant to put that relationship in jeopardy through prolonged conflict. While the stress of parenting may make women aware of the discrepancy between the heterosexual ideal of mutuality and their experience of support, there can be no solution to this dilemma within the confines of heterosexual relationships as they are currently constructed. Women who abandon their inequitable partnerships but still remain committed to the ideal of mutuality within heterosexual relationships are likely to encounter the same problems of inequity and lack of access to support when they trade one male partner for another (Wilson, 1987).

Mothering is not a task which can be carried out without considerable emotional and practical support. However, heterosexual sexual relationships as they are currently constructed appear to be singularly unlikely to provide the support that women need. Women in heterosexual relationships are cut off, not only from support within their sexual relationship, but from alternative sources of support, by an ideology which reinforces women's isolation within the nuclear family, and which designates the male sexual partner as the main source of support, while severely limiting the amount of support which can be derived from this bond. The ideology of motherhood thus forces women back on their investment in unequal and unsupportive heterosexual relationships.

The problem of inequalities in power within relationships is not one which besets heterosexual relationships alone. However, for heterosexual women, personal imbalances in power and levels of emotional commitment are compounded by the structural basis of men's power, which underlines their privileged access to resources both inside and outside the relationship.

Women who parent within heterosexual relationships are struggling to understand and to challenge male definitions of their experience. Such women can at present only imagine what it might be like to parent in conditions in which one partner's unequal access to power and resources is not socially and economically sanctioned, and in which attempts to negotiate for shared parenting are not mediated through complex discourses of appropriate gender behaviour and social roles. Lesbian mothers and heterosexual women who choose to mother without men can be a source of strength to women in heterosexual relationships, since they represent an alternative to current constructions of motherhood. It is to these relationships that heterosexual feminists look in the hope of finding a model of equality, which can eventually be applied to our relationships with men.

REFERENCES

Connell, R.W. (1987) *Gender and Power*. Cambridge: Polity Press.
Croghan, R. and Miell, D. (1991) 'Accounts of Intimate Support Relationships in the early Months of Mothering', in J. Harvey, T. Orbuch and M. Weber (eds) *Attributions, Accounts and Close Relationships*. New York: Springer-Verlag.
Croghan, R. (1991) 'The Experience of Stress and Support amongst First Time Mothers', unpublished PhD thesis.
Leonard, D. and Speakman, M.A. (1986) 'Women in the Family: Companions or Caretakers?', in Veronica Beechy and Elizabeth Whitelegg (eds) *Women in Britain Today*, pp. 8–76. Milton Keynes: Open University Press.
Wilson, G. (1987) 'Money: Patterns of Responsibility and Irresponsibility in Marriage', in J. Brannen and G. Wilson (eds) *Give and Take in Families*, pp. 136–54. London: Allen and Unwin.

Rose CROGHAN works in the Psychology Department at the Open University, Milton Keynes MK7 6AA, UK.

Protean Woman: The Liquidity of Female Sexuality and the Tenaciousness of Lesbian Identity

Pauline B. BART

Alix Dobkin sings 'Any woman can/ Be a lesbian', but she doesn't say for how long. Many women previously sexually involved with women and identified as lesbian or gay, both privately and publicly (e.g. Holly Near, 1990, and Jan Clausen, 1990), are now living with men. Dr Benway, the mythical psychiatrist in William Burroughs' *Naked Lunch*, presaged this behavior when he said that all his heterosexual patients were latently homosexual and all his homosexual patients were latently heterosexual: 'It makes the head whirl' (Burroughs, 1966). What is going on when lesbians enter sexual relationships with men? This article begins to address this topic with reference to three interviews with such women.

It was apparent to those following the women's movement in the 1970s that women, from the Weather Underground to the National Organization for Women, were *choosing* women as sexual partners, including women who had been exclusively heterosexual. In recent years there has been what in some circles is considered backsliding. I have already commented (Bart, 1990) on the plasticity of female sexuality (and the sexuality of female plasticity), described here as 'protean woman'. The current debate about whether people were born 'gay', based on anatomical study of the brains of some men who died of AIDS, makes the protean woman smile. Maybe *men* were born that way and were therefore 'without sin' for having that 'lifestyle', since it hadn't been a matter of choice, but we knew many *women* who chose to belong to a stigmatized oppressed group because their lives were more integrated, their personal was their political and, while there was still housework, there was no *politics* of housework. It never occurred to those in the lesbian feminist vanguard that women, other than those who simply wanted a lesbian 'experience' or 'experiment', would go back. In fact, many 'political lesbians' reconstructed their pasts to demonstrate that they had been lesbians all along, and it was only a matter of time before their mothers, sisters and best friends would discover that truth about themselves also. But many women also learned that they could be as (or more) hurt by women than by men (see, for example, Clausen, 1990), albeit usually not physically. And some lesbians slept with men, but it was occasional: they frequently did not contracept, possibly to make it seem less real. There is a feminist support group at a major university called 'Lesbians Who just Happen to Be in Relationships with Politically Correct Men' (Taylor and Whittier, 1992).

As the USA becomes more conservative, there has been pressure to react by engaging in feminist coalition politics, which leads to a lot of politics and little feminism. This problem is most severe on issues of male violence against women, where frequently the perpetrator is a member of one of the groups in the coalition, at least symbolically. Once working with men in coalitions, unsurprisingly some women (e.g. Jan Clausen) fall in love with men, who, after all, share some common goals. When one's interactions are all female, such alleged opportunities are diminished. At the same time a libertarian laissez-faire attitude about sexuality has been promulgated by the sex 'radicals', whom radical feminists consider sex liberals.[1] 'Gender fucking' (i.e. combining various gender styles in a highly sexualized way) is an alternative to the feminist axiom that the personal is the political. In the latter perspective, with whom you sleep is *not* nobody's business but your own — to change the key word in a blues lyric.

In addition to the nature–nurture discussions (I refuse to say 'discourses') another issue raised by protean women is the relationship between identity and behavior, reminiscent of the classic social-psychological issue of the relationship between attitudes and behavior (LaPiere, 1934). For example, I started off calling this study 'hasbians', a term used in an article in *off our backs* (Schwartz, 1989) and (spelt 'hasbean') by Julia Penelope (1992: 32), but found that people to whom I thought the term applied were startled because they still clung to their prior identities or did not want to be the Other — heterosexual. Perhaps, just as it takes a while to construct a lesbian identity (or most identities for that matter), it takes a while to give it up (if one ever does) and to put on a new one. Does one give up one's lesbian friends? How many routine activities are changed? Holly Near and Jan Clausen still march in lesbian and gay parades.

None of the women I interviewed accepted the label 'heterosexual'. The four political women who had lived as lesbian feminists dealt with real or anticipated rejection from their friends for 'sleeping with the enemy'. One woman was taken aback by the phrase 'the social construction of heterosexuality', while another was insulted by being asked to write about being a heterosexual feminist, even though two of these women have been living with a man for more than 5 years and two have one or more children with the man. Nor do Holly Near, Jan Clausen, nor four of the five women I interviewed, accept the label 'bisexual'.

INTERVIEW ONE: ALICE

Alice[2] is a feminist attorney who 'came out' as lesbian after being raped, although that was not the only reason. She had attended a woman's college during the women's movement days, and choosing to become a lesbian was a much discussed topic. Her background was New England middle class and her mother was a social worker.

Although she has been involved sexually first with men, then with women, and now with a man, she refuses to identify as bisexual, saying 'I don't feel bisexual. My identity isn't wrapped up in my sexuality.' She was with men until her early 20s, with women for about 10 years after that, participating in a women's newspaper, cutting off her waist-length hair to participate. She didn't mind the 'orthodoxy' because 'it fit with my other sense of things. I liked looking like a boy. I felt androgynous.' She believes her rape helped shape her relatively separatist consciousness. She became resocialized when she was in a women's community in which they couldn't be dependent on men for traditional male skills such as fixing a car, and learned to do it themselves. She states that being with a woman is part of a range of experience that 'gives you more openness to women'. For the last 10 years, she has been with a man.

She quit law school after a particularly horrendous semester during which she was surrounded by men who sexually harassed her. She took a traditionally male job for a few months before returning to school. She remembers arguing with a male professor that women didn't need men for anything. The professor said, 'For anything?', and she realized that she had to be careful.

She was friends with her current male lover for a few years, but when their relationship became sexual she was embarrassed to be seen with him. He finally said, 'I'm not going to turn into a woman', so she 'came out' (my words). 'He's very nonintrusive and non-demanding. He felt very familiar.'

She was offended when asked to write about being a heterosexual feminist. 'How dare they make that assumption! I don't feel that I'm straight. I don't fit. I have a gay consciousness.' She is aware of a difference between herself and 'straight' women — something is missing. There is some distancing. She noted that most of the women she was with were abused, as most women are. This abuse, of which, as yet, they had no memories, made the relationship difficult. Women bond around the experience of abuse and oppression, she stated. When I asked about the gender of her next lover, if she had one, she said, 'It could be a woman'.

She is not married, and associates marriage with 'a slow death'. Furthermore, she doesn't want heterosexual privilege as long as her gay friends cannot marry. She never wanted to be a wife: 'If I had kids, maybe'.

The man she lives with, in what she terms 'a comfortable relationship', cooks and does the laundry. She does the gardening. They go out together with a lesbian couple. She needs lots of space and finds it with this man. He is 'nurturant but not demanding — not pulling at me'. He has no 'male energy' — meaning the male sense of entitlement, taking space, being disrespectful and inconsiderate. However, she said she missed the engagement and shared understanding of the world she had with her woman lovers, because while her current lover shares her politics, he is not engaged with the world as much and is less political than she is. Her best friends are still her former woman lovers, and she feels a connection she doesn't either with men or with heterosexual women, although she can't verbalize it (and she is very verbal).

INTERVIEW TWO: BARBARA

She is a white, 50-year-old Jewish middle-class woman with a PhD. Her husband is an MS, and she has three children. Her mother was a teacher and her father a self-educated chemist. Before she moved to the Midwest, she taught at a college but has been unable to settle into any occupation since. She is primarily interested in the arts and identifies as an artist. Like Alice, first she was heterosexual, then lesbian, in 'the women's community', but unlike Alice she identifies as bisexual, even though she has been married for 12 years and had an affair with a man. She doesn't know what the sex of her next partner will be.

Being a mother is very important to her. 'I wanted to have children and I did and it was a wonderful wonderful thing and I'm very blessed. I didn't know how I could take care of children and make money' [without a partner]. Having children has given her a great deal of pleasure, though her marriage is not satisfactory. However, an advantage of being with a man for her is the lack of intensity and being loved just by being. With women she had to be exquisitely sensitive all the time, especially sexually, and she didn't like the intensity. I asked if she meant that it was possible to have alienated sex with men but not women, and she immediately agreed.

She admits she has problems with intimacy, so her relationships with women were not good, and the last one had completely deteriorated. Her mother, with whom she had a close relationship, had died. 'I realized I was alone in the world. I didn't have a very clear livelihood . . . I guess I sort of got scared and I felt here was someone who was offering me security in many ways. The heterosexual marriage represents security.' She had met him 2 years before that, when she was with a woman lover. He had two very bright personable sons with him who impressed her greatly. He called her 2 years later and told her he was looking for a wife and had her in mind. Six months later they went away for a week or two after having spoken on the phone several times. Her job was unstable: 'I faced the existential openness and it was very scary.' He was offering her structure and security if she would come to Cleveland. Her women friends were very angry with her and used terms such as 'betrayal'.

She became pregnant and she realized she couldn't take care of the child by herself unless she went on welfare. She knew the relationship with the man was not good, but the baby made the difference. She feels isolated and lonely, which she didn't in the lesbian community in New York, where she had a good time, even though she rejected the 'orthodoxy'. She believes part of her problems in the marriage stem from her leaving New York, her friends, her community and the talks about issues in which they constantly engaged. She could not persuade her husband to live in New York. Currently, she is very afraid of getting old.

She feels she is moving away from marginality. The Jewish community is more central to her life, particularly the Russian Jews. The central problem is that she cannot connect with her husband — the loneliness. She thinks heterosexual women are lonely.

INTERVIEW THREE: CAROL

She is a 32-year-old white union machinist, as is her husband, and lives in the Chicago suburbs, although she grew up in various army camps, where her father was a sergeant. Her mother was a housewife and a clerk. This woman was a jock through high school and after graduating was able to enter the apprenticeship program to be a machinist. Her husband is a 'farm boy', a high school graduate and a machinist.

She has a 20-month-old daughter. She expected a boy, called the fetus by a boy's name, but is now happy she has a girl, because she can teach her to be strong. She drank three cans of beer during the interview, which took place outside her rented house, under an awning.

Unlike the other women, she always knew she was a lesbian but waited until she was 18 to become involved with a woman. She had relationships with women for about 8 years. When a particular relationship turned bad and violent, she started slowly to become involved with one of the male machinists who was her drinking buddy. It took him 6 months to be allowed to kiss her on the lips. They lived together for 5 years until they decided to have a baby. Then they married. She insists on defining herself as a 'person' rather than in any category. When asked about her next partner, she said: 'It definitely would be with a woman. It would be like a fantasy come true. I've dreamt about it all my life. Those are my feelings.' But she is sexually 'faithful' to her husband because she wants to be honest.

She participates in lesbian culture to some extent. After her child was born, her lesbian friends had a fairy godmother party and gave the baby certain qualities as gifts. Furthermore, she is spending a week without her child at the Michigan Womyn's Music Festival, a gathering of lesbians and their female friends, with a heavy lesbian ambience. Last year she took the baby. I asked her how she was going to manage being around all those nude and topless women. She said they were going to have to tie her to a tree and that she'd probably have an orgasm every hour. She goes out 'with the girls' about twice a year and her husband doesn't object. When I asked her what kind of woman she liked she said 'feminine women — not football players like me', but she also said that her husband got her in touch with her feminine side.

When she was a lesbian, she became involved in 'lesbianism' but not political activities. 'I stay away from politics', she said, but she believes in America and in buying American. She is not religious and was married by a judge in a garden in which they played softball after the ceremony. She was never 'straight'.

She told me that her friends completely accepted her choice to be with a man, unlike Barbara's friends, and she reported no embarrassment such as Alice experienced.

CONCLUSION[3]

None of the women I have interviewed so far has internalized a heterosexual identity: a lesbian identity is clearly tenacious. While four were what could be called 'political lesbians', none left relationships with women for political reasons. If one were to hypothesize about the kind of woman who would be likely to go from women to men, one would never think of a woman such as Carol. And, rather than (re)turning to men in anger at the lack of radical feminist politics, Barbara resented lesbian feminist politics, although she 'did' the bar scene and went to conferences. The women all appear to be involved with men who leave them alone, and/or respect their independence. Four of the five men did some or all of the cooking. Sexuality does not appear to be crucial to any of the women. A protean woman, Ruth Colker, wrote (1991): 'I don't know what the word "sexual" means in the context of an intimate relationship with a woman. My use of the word "sexual" is not intended to suggest any particular activities; it is only intended to indicate the high degree of intimacy in the relationship.' Having children, rather than having sex or a desire for commitment, leads to marriage, but neither heterosexual motherhood, nor sex with men, nor marriage, leads necessarily to the adoption of a heterosexual (or even bisexual) identity.

The apparent tenaciousness of a lesbian identity contrasts with the fluidity of female sexuality: even Carol, who until her current relationship, fit the paradigm of the woman who was 'born lesbian', could change her behavior (if not her identity). Why would women who were lesbian or 'gay' (and who still do not identify as heterosexual) choose men as their primary or only sex partners? Heterosexual privilege or 'normality', especially economic security for women who want children, seems part of the motivation. This was true for Barbara, and I expect such structural factors will be present in future interviews. Disappointment with lesbian relationships was mentioned by both Barbara and Carol (whose last lesbian relationship became violent); and the women speak of some degree of comfort with men:

Alice's partner is 'nurturant but not demanding' and has no 'male energy'; Barbara appreciates the lack of intensity and feels loved just by being. There are some men who, in spite of societal permission to be oppressive, do not use that privilege — at least in their current relationship. And it is not surprising that women's relationships with women were not as perfect as they expected, especially given the continuing effects of the pervasive violence, particularly child rape, in women's backgrounds. Lesbians are increasingly documenting the damage we inflict on each other — and evidence of the hurt and pain inflicted within lesbian communities is sometimes used to justify protean woman's turn to sex with men. Everything men do to women, women do to women. But the differences are still statistically significant.

NOTES

1. I have never completely recovered from the 'sex wars' when so many lesbians signed the Feminist Anti-Censorship Task (FACT) Force brief, against the MacKinnon–Dworkin anti-pornography ordinance, which made statements such as women don't need protection. Tell that to the half of my class that was raped. When the Commission on the Status of Women in Los Angeles proposed a version of the ordinance, and MacKinnon discussed it, the first question from the audience was always from some lesbian who would ask, 'What is that going to do to our pornography/erotica/S&M/*On Our Backs*?' with no reference to what this ordinance was going to do for the majority of women, including lesbians. Bringing Adam Smith into the bedroom was not my idea of feminism. As I stated to Kitty MacKinnon in 1985, 'Being a lesbian for political reasons after the FACT brief is like being a Stalinist after the 1936 Purge Trials'.

2. All names given are, of course, pseudonyms. I decided not to interview some of the more well-known women or women who were my friends' former lovers because I knew that readers would be picking over the manuscript of this article to try to find them. Some items in the interview descriptions, in particular demographics, have been changed to preserve anonymity. My questions were minimal and I added questions as women brought up various topics or as they were grounded in the material. This is preliminary research and obviously my conclusions will be stronger after completing more interviews — especially with women of color.

3. An additional two interviews were conducted after this paper was written. Both women had married men they called 'gentle', who had no problems with their past lesbian relationships and were not intrusive. One said he was so gentle it was like going back to a woman (she had had another affair with a man). Neither woman identified as hetero or bisexual, and both were involved with women's culture and feminism. Both women had been married before being lesbian. One considered the core of her relationship a life immersed in feminist spirituality. The first woman, in a manner reminiscent of Barbara (p. 249), is relived by the absence of constant relationship talk in interaction with a man. The second woman, again like Barbara, is married to a man raised outside the USA. It is possible that women who become involved with men after relationships with women are those who prefer partners they do not have to 'process' with, and who prefer less intense and intimate interaction with their partners.

REFERENCES

Bart, Pauline B. (1990) 'Feminist Theories', in Henry Etzkowitz and Ronald M. Glassman (eds) *The Renaissance of Sociological Theory: Classical and Contemporary*. Itasca, IL: Peacock Press.
Burroughs, William S. (1966) *Naked Lunch*. New York: Grove Press.
Clausen, J. (1990) 'My Interesting Condition', *Out/Look* 2: 11–21.
Colker, Ruth (1991) 'Marriage', *Yale Journal of Law and Feminism* 3: 321–6.
LaPiere, R.T. (1934) 'Attitudes vs. Action', *Social Forces* 13: 230–7.
Near, Holly (1990) *Fire in The Rain, Singer in The Storm*. New York: William Morrow.
Penelope, Julia (1992) *Call Me Lesbian: Lesbian Lives, Lesbian Theory*. Freedom, CA: Crossing Press.
Schwartz, P. (1989) 'On the Hasbian Phenomenon', *off our backs* 19(6): 11.
Taylor, Verta and Whittier, Nancy (1992) 'Collective Identity in Social Movement Communities: Lesbian Feminist Mobilization', in Alden Morris and Carol Mueller (eds) *Frontiers in Social Movement Theory*. New Haven, CT: Yale University Press.

Pauline B. BART is Professor of Sociology in the Department of Psychiatry at the University of Illinois at Chicago. She has published extensively — mainly on issues of violence against women, and on women's physical and mental health issues — and also writes poetry. Her books include *Stopping Rape: Successful Survival Strategies* (with Patricia O'Brien, New York: Teachers College Press, 1985; formerly Pergamon Press, 1985); and *Violence Against Women: The Bloody Footprints* (with Eileen Moran, Newbury Park, CA: Sage, 1993).

IV

Feminist Therapy with Heterosexual Couples:
The Ultimate Issue is Domination

Doris C. DeHARDT

In 1985, my article 'Can Feminist Therapists Facilitate Clients' Heterosexual Relationships?' appeared in the *Handbook of Feminist Therapy*. In that chapter I discussed my deep ethical concerns regarding therapeutic facilitation of heterosexual relationships: 'If my observations are correct that women often become less rather than more the persons they are capable of becoming when struggling to develop or maintain a relationship with a man, how can I, a feminist therapist, committed to empowering women, facilitate my clients' heterosexual relationships?' (DeHardt, 1985: 170–1. In this chapter I outlined a method of analysis for women clients to use in assessing the integrity of their (intimate) heterosexual relationship(s). Implicit in my discussion of this analysis was that feminist marriages (feminist heterosexual relationships which are sexually intimate and formally committed) are possible. Now I believe that feminist marriage is, like military intelligence, an oxymoron.

By feminist relationship I mean *truly mutual sharing* of responsibility for the relationship and any children, commitment, respect, trust, affection, intellectual stimulation, empathy, spontaneity, desire for intimacy, desire for and support of partner's development as a whole person, and of resources: material, emotional, political and social. I say 'truly mutual sharing' because lots of 'New Age' men say they do these things, but their stated attitudes are not congruent with their behaviors (Bergman, 1991).

The social construction of heterosexuality is embedded in the social construction of gender (Lorber and Farrell, 1991). Heterosexuality for males is fundamental to the 'real men' ('masculine') paradigm, along with domination and eroticization of domination (Bartky, 1990; Jeffreys, 1990). Other central themes in male heterosexuality are: not being like women, violence, competition and emotional, political and social control, particularly of children and women's bodies, minds, souls, options and material and emotional safety. (Author bell hooks points out how, for example, black men choosing to enact this pattern of behavior do so at life-threatening risk in patriarchy [hooks, 1990].) Yet, given a chance, no man is exempt from the 'masculine' paradigm. How does a woman partner find safety and celebration with a person so constructed?

My research on how much and how little men and women like and dislike each other (DeHardt, 1988) suggests that the structure of gender, which includes not liking and respecting persons of the other gender, renders substantial improvement in female–male relationships impossible. Structural changes must be made in the larger framework of domination — a framework in which gender, along with class, ablement, religion, age, race, ethnic identity, sexual orientation, geographic region and language, is embedded.

To begin to do this we need first to examine impulses towards domination and elitism in ourselves. Each one of us has been reinforced in certain ways for dominating others. (Most) all of us see ourselves as special cases, too — exceptions to the harmful situations described earlier. Yet, like our male and female clients who say they have or want an egalitarian relationship, we deny and mystify how our own lives represent the structures we most decry. Without looking at our own impulses to domination, it is harder to move away from our focus on oppression; without focusing on our own internalized domination, we cannot effectively posit theory, do research or be therapeutically liberatory. It is necessary to acknowledge how our own experiences both facilitate and impede our visions and actions of resistance. The difficulty of this task cannot be minimized.

I discuss three group (collective) methods for us in working on *shared and reciprocal internalization of oppression and domination*. Briefly defined, these are internalized prejudice against the self and against others, respectively.

1. The first was developed by Gail Pheterson, in her article 'Alliances between Women Overcoming Internalized Oppression and Internalized Domination' (Pheterson, 1990). The goal of Pheterson's groups is to produce alliances, that is 'knowledge of, respect for, and commitment between persons who are in essential ways different but whose interests are in essential ways akin' (Pheterson, 1990: 36). The commonality of interest I construe to be 'commitment to eradicating the ideology of domination' (hooks, 1984).

Over 100 Dutch women met during a period of some months and were instructed by facilitators to talk about how they felt about themselves in the form of life stories, and in terms of what experiences they had had with solidarity (understanding, respect and unity among similar persons), and in making alliances. The women were Jewish and non-Jewish, black and white, lesbians and non-lesbians, mothers and non-mothers. Pheterson's conclusion is crucial to our understanding of power and domination:

> It is important to note that internalized oppression and internalized domination interact not only between different persons but also intraphysically within one person. Oppression and domination are experienced as a mutually reinforcing web of insecurities and rigidities. Although the political consequences of oppression are opposite to those of domination (e.g. powerlessness vs power), the psychological consequences are surprisingly alike. The fear of violence one feels as a victim of oppression reinforces the fear of revenge she feels as an agent of oppression. The isolation resulting from feelings of inferiority reinforces the isolation resulting from feelings of superiority. The guilt felt for dominating others likewise reinforces the guilt felt for one's own victimization. Since maintaining a posture of dominance is often tenuously balanced upon denying inferior status, the individual suppresses and conceals characteristics which reveal social powerlessness (Pheterson, 1990: 45).

If women are to achieve liberatory relationships with men, at some point the men in question must be included in such a process. My own clinical experience working with heterosexual men in counseling situations makes me dubious that this can succeed.

2. The feminist philosopher Ann Ferguson (1991) describes a global plan for connecting with others in liberatory ways, while dealing with oppressions and

various forms of domination. She conceptualizes a global feminist ethic in which women like us and not like us, and men who are 'gender deviates', join together to work on normative goals (visions). Ferguson (1991) envisions pluralism in the form of feminism and cites the work of eco-feminists as an example of struggle with dominance. The central basis of commitment to such work she defines as revolutionary love — empathic identification with those both like and unlike ourselves. Again, the question of male participation is problematic. Who decides who 'gender deviates' are? Men who call themselves feminists may claim membership, but as noted earlier, men may self-identify in merely self-serving ways, without exhibiting congruent behavior.

3. I have developed a micro-level group activity which expands on Pheterson's (1990) program. I ask women to look in a mirror and describe themselves, writing down for their own use what they see. This information is used after the telling of life stories and experiences with oppressions and dominations. (The stories can take several sessions.)

After the life stories, group participants are then asked to read their 'face in the mirror' descriptions and to rate themselves privately on a dominator scale which looks like this:

1	2	3	4	5	6	7
littler dominator			average dominator			bigger dominator

Important things left out of the 'face in the mirror' descriptions help placement on this scale. My use of this exercise has revealed that white women seldom say 'white' or words to that effect, and wealthy women seldom say 'privileged' or words to that effect, and so on. The surest sign of privilege is not recognizing it.

The facilitator(s) answers questions about what being a dominator means (e.g. benefiting from skin color in selection for a teaching assistantship). But each woman selects her own number, and when these are shared, criticisms and judgments are disallowed. The purpose of the exercise is to learn — from women who are different — how one sees oneself in contrast.

Women are again asked to look in the mirror: this time to describe how they feel they have been oppressed. What shame and anger do they see and why? Scores are individually selected on the oppression scale, and sharing proceeds as previously.

1	2	3	4	5	6	7
littler oppression			average oppression			bigger oppression

After all women have shared their scores on both scales, a general discussion is held regarding similarities and differences in oppression and dominance. Participants are asked to identify how they themselves use strategies (denial, anger, other-blame, poor me) to keep from owning their own 'stuff'. Facilitator(s) disallow (hierarchical) comparisons and judgments of another woman's work, but encourage self-awareness.

I find this exercise, or the thought of doing this exercise, helpful to women working on heterosexual partnerships. By doing or thinking about the exercise, women naturally explore for themselves whether their men partners are willing and able to do this work. For some, it is a liberatory exploration.

We feminist therapists must do this kind of dominance work and we must be aware of dominance-reinforcing aspects of clinical theory and research. Since, overall, most of our clients are heterosexual women, we merely further subjugate women working on themselves and in relationships with men if we are unable to achieve considerable self-awareness and ownership of our own privilege and/or striving to maintain dominance systems. Reinforcing heterosexual relationships is bound to subjugate women — unless real dominance analyses are presented.

Heterosexual psychologists, psychiatrists, social workers and counselors have struggled to 'fix' heterosexual relationships for themselves and for their clients. The typical result is co-optation of women's anger, sexual and physical abuse, and the perpetuation of women's powerlessness.

REFERENCES

Bartky, Sandra L. (1990) *Femininity and Domination: Studies in the Phenomenology of Oppression*. New York and London: Routledge.
Bergman, S.J. (1991) 'Men's Psychological Development: A Relational Perspective', *Work in Progress*, No. 48. Wellesley, MA: Stone Center Workshop Paper Series.
DeHardt, Doris C. (1985) 'Can a Feminist Therapist Facilitate Clients' Heterosexual Relationships?', in L.B. Rosewater and L.E.A. Walker (eds) *Handbook of Feminist Therapy: Women's Issues in Psychotherapy*. New York: Springer.
DeHardt, Doris C. (1988) 'Gender Opposite Dislike as a Therapeutic Issue', paper for XXIV International Congress of Psychology, Sydney, Australia. (Reprints from D. DeHardt.)
Ferguson, A. (1991) 'Constructing Ourselves through Community', paper for the Philosophy and Women's Studies Symposium, Boulder, CO, USA.
hooks, bell (1984) *Feminist Theory: From Margin to Center*. Boston, MA: South End Press.
hooks, b. (1990) *Yearning: Race, Gender, and Cultural Politics*. Boston: South End Press.
Jeffreys, Sheila (1990) *Anticlimax: A Feminist Perspective on the Sexual Revolution*. London: The Women's Press.
Lorber, J. and Farrell, S.A. (1991) *The Social Construction of Gender*. London: Sage.
Pheterson, Gail (1990) 'Alliances Between Women Overcoming Internalized Oppression and Internalized Domination', in L. Albrecht and R.M. Brewer (eds) *Bridges of Power: Women's Multicultural Alliances*. Philadelphia, PA: New Society Publishers.

Doris DeHARDT is Psychology Professor Emeritus at California State University, Long Beach, now residing in Boulder, Colorado, USA.

V

'Safe by Nature': Reconstructing Heterosexual Identity Under the Sign of AIDS[1]

Cindy PATTON

I recently delivered as a lecture a version of the text which follows. During the question period, a man of about 35 said he did not believe that he, personally, should have to wear a condom. He had never 'been at risk' and while he believed other men should wear condoms he could see no reason why he should. I suggested that being fluent with condom use was a gift to himself and his women partners, since he and they might in the future decide they ought to use them. 'They are uncomfortable', he said. 'Practice makes perfect', I said. 'Better to start now when the immediate need is perhaps less urgent.' He was unconvinced. Why should he have to wear them, when he had never 'done anything wrong'?

There is, at the very core of heterosexual identity, an apparent incapacity to understand what is being said about safe sex — why? I find it baffling that a relatively small change — use of a condom or, at most, shifting to non-intercourse forms of sexual pleasure — is greeted, especially by heterosexual men, as if it were tantamount to castration. Heterosexuals seem to view homosexual personhood, homosexual activities of any sort, even homosexual 'safe sex', as at least partially risky. And yet, heterosexuals accept that only particular *heterosexual individuals* are risky — that is, an act of 'ordinary' heterosexual intercourse is never risky; but having any form of contact with certain heterosexuals — drug users, sex workers, people of color — is risky. While the logic promoted within gay male culture views particular *acts* as risky and to be modified or avoided, the logic within heterosexual culture remains one that views certain *individuals* as risky and to be avoided.

Within gay male culture, there has been a massive effort to reinvent homosexuality and homosexual identity as 'safe sex' while retaining long-standing gay culture values, like the acceptance of promiscuity and experimental sex. The campy button which reads 'safe sex slut' is not viewed as contradictory within gay male culture. This effort ideologically to reconstruct gay sex as safe sex seems to have partially succeeded; and for heterosexuals, too, since 'safe sex' is now interpreted by many to apply largely to 'kinky', that is 'gay', 'bisexual' or 'promiscuous' sex. By sharp contrast, heterosexuals seem to have gone to great lengths to deny a place for safe sex within heterosexual identity. The very sexual techniques which make *queer sex safe* seem to ruin heterosexual sex: 'real sex' is that which does not require any of the techniques or latex accoutrements of 'safe sex'. There is a dichotomy between 'normal' heterosexual sex and 'safe sex', at least conceptually. Heterosexuals routinely invoke HIV antibody testing as a mechanism to determine when to use a condom, and this misperception of testing, promoted by the media and public-health system alike, is tragic and fatal for women. In addition, heterosexuals who initially use condoms with a partner seem to abandon them when a 'relationship' — however defined — is established. Studies suggest that there are important disparities between heterosexuals' willingness to use condoms with new or 'suspect' partners versus using condoms in primary or long-term relationships. Ironically, *ceasing to use condoms* may signal trust and commitment for heterosexuals (Gallois et al., 1990).

Of course, I'm not the first person to criticize heterosexual ideology — feminists have long made similar claims about how it prevents women from controlling their bodies and lives. And I want to be clear that I am not suggesting that anyone abandon their cross-gender sexual relations. The typical rebuttal to criticism of heterosexual relations, and especially heterosexual intercourse, is that if men and women stopped 'doing it' it would be the end of the human race. The far right has capitalized on just this argument, but with an interesting twist: Gene Antonio, author of perhaps the best-known right-wing book on AIDS, argues that homosexuals should be quarantined because 'safe sex' is a plot not only to allow homosexuals to 'continue their filthy practices' but to cause 'self-extinction of mankind' (Antonio, 1986: 148). To counter arguments that he might be homophobic, Antonio argues that gay people, and the (US) Centers for Disease Control, which the 'homosexual lobby' mysteriously controls, are heterophobic and attempting, through promoting safe sex for everyone, to cause dissent between men and women and aversion toward heterosexual intercourse. This seems paranoid and silly, but only displays in relief a much more pervasive but less articulated fear which undercuts the efficacy of risk reduction education. Pop sexology gurus Masters and Johnson pulled out all the stops when they wrote their *Crisis: Heterosexual Behavior in the Age of AIDS* (Masters et al., 1988). The fundamental difference between gay sexuality and heterosexuality lies not in the gender of object choice, but in attitudes toward the meaning of safe sex. Instead of safe sex being a form of liberation from fears of infection, a practice of pleasure, safe sex is presented as something to be dreaded, which turns sex into a confrontation with danger. It turns out that safe sex = queer sex, and the fear of perversion is transformed into a fear of safe sex. This queer calculus allows the sexologists to conclude with a bizarre formulation that opposes *safe* and *natural* sex. They are particularly disgusted by the technical implications of safe sex, and never even consider the non-intercourse practices which might constitute safe sex as potentially satisfying elements in the heterosexual repertoire. The following section from their book reveals the deep-seated fear of the *cultural* danger of safe sex:

> Sex partners of uncertain [HIV antibody] testing status could . . . wear disposable plastic gloves during all intimate moments. These gloves, after all, aren't too different from condoms. Yet we are unwilling to seriously entertain such an outlandish notion — right now, it seems so unnatural and artificial as to violate the essential dignity of humanity (Masters et al., 1988: 118).

Pretty strong objections to a little latex. And doubly ironic given that Masters and Johnson have long preached the malleability of human sexual behavior. Why is a latex glove any more unnatural or undignified than performing daily exercises to tighten vaginal muscles, or step-by-step exercises to help men learn to delay ejaculation? Masters and Johnson propose that heterosexuals do any act they choose, so long as they have gotten three (yes, specifically three) negative HIV antibody tests, spaced 3 months apart. Of course, they note, heterosexuals must abstain from sexual intercourse during this time in order for the test results to be valid. For Masters and

Johnson, safe sex is a kind of punishment for those who 'fail' or refuse to take the test, or who can't abstain for the 9 months which they view as sufficient to eliminate the possibility of test errors. This none-too-subtly redraws the line between a homosexuality which they themselves once studied and deemed normal, and a heterosexuality which they now want to preserve as natural. Even condoms are unacceptable, not only because they are not 100 percent 'safe', but because while 'many couples find the post-orgasmic glow a time of tenderness in which they want to lie quietly together with their genitals still in union, they run a distinct risk of having just such spillage [of the semen from around the now "receded" penis] occur' (Masters et al., 1988: 116).

On one side we have a 'natural' heterosexuality which has no limits, but can accept no latex. On the other side, we have all those people who, because they are truly queer or merely nominally queer, are condemned to safe sex, that latex-ridden set of activities which dehumanizes its practitioners. This barely concealed homophobia sweeps even aberrant heterosexuals under the banner of perversion, and naturalizes the condomless heterosexual intercourse which women need to challenge. Masters and Johnson invoke precisely the terms which have always been used to describe both non-submissive women and homosexual sex: dehumanized, unnatural, artificial, not to be taken seriously.

The heterosexuality which I am invoking here is, I think, recognizable to all of us — either because it is the beacon by which we gauge our inadequacies, or because it is the monument against which we define our difference. It is a heterosexuality that is not new, but is newly dangerous for women. After a two-decade attempt to wrest control over our own bodies by fighting *for* legalized birth control and abortion, organizing *against* sexist violence and sexual harassment, and working to achieve women's agency and freedom to seek sexual pleasure, all this is in jeopardy again because the logic of safe sex under the sign of AIDS has once again constituted heteromasculinity as exempt from change. The terror at the heart of men's willingness to wear a condom is equaled only by the power heterosexual men have to make someone else — usually a woman — protect them from themselves. But while we may all feel sympathy toward the men who have fallen victim to that trap called heterosexual masculinity, the fact is that while men fear for their sexual identity, their women partners need to fear contracting HIV.

It is easy to find fault with men who lie about their past to their wives and girlfriends, but it is not just a few unredeemed men who are the problem. At fault is the continuing construction of heterosexuality and specifically heterosexual intercourse as 'safe by nature' which prevents women from protecting themselves. Until heterosexuality means more than intercourse, and can always accommodate a condom, women will be forced to make case-by-case, situational demands on men. The paradox is this: heterosexual identity can only be reconstructed as truly 'safe sex' when heterosexual men are just *queer enough* to wear a condom.

NOTE

1. This paper is drawn from Cindy Patton (1993) '"With Champagne and Roses": Women at Risk from/in AIDS Discourse', in Corinne Squire (ed.) *Women and AIDS: Psychological Perspectives*. London: Sage.

REFERENCES

Antonio, G. (1986) *The AIDS Cover Up? The Real and Alarming Facts about AIDS*. San Francisco, CA: Ignatius Press.

Gallois, C., et al. (1990) 'Preferred Strategies for Safe Sex: Relation to Past and Actual Behavior among Sexually Active Men and Women', paper presented to International AIDS Conference, San Francisco, CA.

Masters, W.H., Johnson, V. and Kolodny, R.C. (1988) *Crisis: Heterosexual Behavior in the Age of AIDS*. London: Weidenfeld and Nicolson.

Cindy PATTON is a writer and activist, and Assistant Professor of Rhetoric and Communication at Temple University, Philadelphia, PA, USA. She is author of *Sex and Germs: The Politics of AIDS* (Boston: South End Press, 1985); *Making It: A Woman's Guide to Sex in the Age of AIDS* (with Janis Kelly; Ithaca: Firebrand, 1987); *Inventing AIDS* (New York: Routledge, 1990); and a forthcoming book on women and AIDS (Falmer, 1993).

VI

Heterosexual Identity: Out of the Closets

Julia PENELOPE

WAS THERE HETEROSEXUALITY BEFORE 1901?

Like the terms that refer to other sexualities, such as 'lesbian' and 'homosexual', which were first used at the end of the nineteenth century, the word 'heterosexual' is a relative newcomer to the English vocabulary. Interestingly, 'heterosexual', as an identifying label for individuals who are attracted to a sex opposite from their own, was not coined until 1901, when W.A. Newman Dorland used it in *The Illustrated Medical Dictionary*, where it referred to an 'abnormal or perverted sexual appetite toward the opposite sex' (*Oxford English Dictionary*, Supplement: 3987). The concept of 'heterosexuality' is, then, a late development in western societies, and we owe much to Dorland's scientific foresight in perceiving the need for such a term and providing one. Yet, no one has thought it noteworthy that 'heterosexual' postdates terms like 'lesbian', 'homosexual', 'invert' and 'Sapphist', nor has anyone commented on the fact that it entered our vocabulary as a stigmatizing label. The single exception to my first generalization is Christine Downing (1991), who has only the following to say:

> Obviously this [the late coining of terms for sexuality] does not mean that there was no same-sex or contra-sex loving until then; . . . The new language may not have created the new identities, but it certainly validated and substantiated them.

Slight as her words of caution are, however, Downing is correct in asserting that sexualities clearly exist prior to, and whether or not, we have specific labels for them. Social constructionists, for example, have been quick to assert that the sexualities of lesbians and gay men could not have existed *as we know them* prior to the coining of the labels that denote them. By analogy, if this were true, it would also have to be true of heterosexuality.

Was there heterosexuality prior to 1901? This is a difficult question to answer. Unlike artifacts connected with work, hunting and eating, sexual identities do not, cannot, leave behind evidence of their existence for the anthropological record, and much of our knowledge about human sexuality is inferred from the behavior of other animals, such as rats and gorillas. We may, of course, deduce that certain sexualities have persisted through time by examining pictographs and petroglyphs, the rock paintings that have survived into this century.

While we have numerous pictographs illustrating men engaged in intercourse with various other animals, one, in particular, recorded at Site 35, Hook, in Gilliam County, Oregon (Loring, 1982: 197), indicates that some concept of heterosexuality existed on the North American continent prior to Contact (before Native American tribal cultures had come into contact with the white, European invaders).

This pictograph is both suggestive and troubling. For one thing, the figures of the women and man aren't engaged in copulation. They're not even touching, although the male figure is clearly holding out his arms toward the female figure, as though to embrace her. The female figure, however, with her arms raised and stretched above the height of her shoulders, appears to be reacting with fright or disgust, and the position of her feet suggests that she is quickly back-pedalling away from the male. Of course, it is prudent not to read too much into pictographs, but readers should also note that, even though no physical contact has been made, the male figure is ejaculating. That single drop of ejaculate indicates that the male figure may have had an intuitive concept of heterosex, and this pictograph may be our earliest evidence of the phenomenon of premature ejaculation. But we should not make too much of such evidence.

Indeed, it is unlikely that we will find satisfactory prehistoric evidence of heterosexuality. Instead, I turn now to the invisibility of heterosexuals and how this has deformed their efforts to forge an identity for themselves.

THE STAGES OF HETEROSEXUAL IDENTITY

After 1901, heterosexuals had to struggle briefly with the burden of disapproval carried by the term 'heterosexual'. How long this must have gone on remains unclear, but I presume that the experience of being 'outed' in a medical dictionary must have taken some time to recover from. Say, a few weeks. We cannot, nevertheless, make light of the effects of stigmatization on heterosexuals, because the results, though borne largely in silence, remain. How else are we to account for the fact that a majority of heterosexuals are still in the closet, and remain so for most of their lives? In fact, most of them, when asked to list the terms they use to describe their identity, list terms that label their social and economic, or religious and ethnic roles, omitting entirely any label that can be construed as referring to a *sexual* identity.

They simply do not think of themselves as 'heterosexual', a phenomenon one can account for in several ways. There is, to begin with, the lingering stigmatization of perversion left over from the turn of the century, now complicated by an understandable ambivalence. How is an individual to embrace her (or his) heterosexuality, as they are constantly being exhorted to do by the mass media, when s/he must somehow negotiate the treacherous middle ground between 'normality' and 'perversion' without much that counts for reliable guidance? On the other hand, heterosexuals, being an insecure lot, turn most often to the popular media for reassurance and for role models. Indeed, those economic resources and technologies not geared specifically to war and the making of war are wholly devoted to describing, portraying, promulgating, ridiculing and otherwise promoting heterosexuality as a way of life.

Psychological studies of the past 20 years describe and document a series of 'phases' in the lives of heterosexuals, what I call here 'identity crises': that is, specific points in their lives at which heterosexuals are known to stop and wonder exactly *who* they are (or might be) and *what* their lives mean (or might mean) (e.g. Erikson, 1968, 1982; Gould, 1978; Levinson, 1978).

The first identity crisis occurs when an individual enters puberty, and experiences a variety of covert threats, bribes and commands to behave in an acceptably heterosexual manner. It is at this point that many individuals realize consciously that the external pressures to conform from parents, teachers, ministers and peers — a combination of institutional and private leverage which Adrienne Rich (1986) has called 'compulsory heterosexuality' — have become coercive, developing a desperate urgency. A majority decide to go along with the social program, at least superficially, and declare themselves 'heterosexual'. Even women who know or suspect they are lesbians often force themselves into heterosexual relationships.

The second identity crisis occurs between the late teens and early 20s, depending upon the age at which the individual must figure out how s/he is going to survive or earn a living. In western societies, it is assumed that males have to work, regardless of their sexual identity; the economic class of their parents determines, to a large extent, which occupations are open to them. Females, however, must now decide whether to choose an occupation or a career or find a male whose career options indicate that he will be able to support her. A woman who has decided to defy social pressures to declare herself a lesbian knows, of course, that she must find a way to support herself. In contrast, the woman who has declared herself heterosexual now has the option of becoming a 'homemaker', if she can find a man to support her. In either case, women discover that their options for self-support are significantly less remunerative than those available to men, a realization that enhances the attractiveness of heterosexual behavior for women because they may be able to forego working for wages. Unfortunately, too many discover too late that this 'choice' has confined them to wageless work in the service of a man, a servitude often made worse by male violence acted out in the relationship as battering or child rape (cf. Kelly, 1992; J. Kitzinger, this volume; Schacht and Atchison, this volume).

In spite of media portrayals of the fun and romance of heterosexual behaviors, women understand perfectly well that choosing between heterosexuality and lesbianism is a practical, economic decision, not an emotional one. Because the chances of a woman's making a decent living for herself are severely limited, many 'choose' heterosexuality and marriage, perceiving heterosexuality as a 'better' choice among several bad options. Of course, we must also take into consideration that a majority of women simply do not conceive of themselves as having choices about whom they are supposed to love, because lesbianism and celibacy (except within the confines of a religious order) are seldom visible as options at the time that most women must choose how they are going to live. It is possible that the political and economic functions of marriage can be traced directly to the fragility of heterosexual identity itself, since, without enforced (or heavily encouraged) marriage and the various other props that portray marriage as the 'ideal' lifestyle, it is probable that heterosexuality would not occur to women as a viable way of living.

Heterosex and marriage are both male imperatives, because men are dependent on women for all of life's basic needs: food, shelter, hygiene, and other forms of domestic care. Hetero men seem incapable of surviving on their own, although no one has yet determined whether this incapacity is genetically or socially determined. When women finally realize that there is nothing endearingly human about the man they've married, they 'come to' during the third identity crisis wondering exactly what they have been doing with their lives during the past few years, and angry with themselves for having been so duped.

If the first identity crisis focused on asking 'Who am I?', the third one, which usually occurs in the late 20s, is concentrated on trying to figure out what one is *doing* with her life. Many heterosexual women suddenly raise up their heads from the dishes, the diapers, the grocery list, the washing, to wonder: 'Why am I spending my life this way?' This is a critical identity crisis, for it is now, at a point well into her life, that each woman evaluates her past and imagines what her future might be like. At this age, many women have discovered, from any one of a number of talk shows (e.g. in the US: Geraldo Rivera, Sally Jesse Rafael, Oprah Winfrey, Phil Donahue) that there are, indeed, other ways to define one's sexual identity, and they frequently undertake a series of experiments to determine which of the possibilities is most comfortable for them. If, after trying lesbianism, bisexuality or celibacy, a woman decides that heterosexuality is a dead-end career, she will likely begin the necessary procedures to remove herself from the roles forced upon her.

Some women, however, wait until the fourth heterosexual identity crisis. Many women, as they approach menopause in their 40s, realize that the most significant role available to them — bearing and raising children — is no longer a viable identity. Having accepted the heteropatriarchal definition of themselves as wives and mothers for so long, they find themselves adrift, without an identity. Postmenopausal women have a number of choices. For example, they can, of course, continue to take care of one or more 'men'. Or, they can, if the opportunity exists, continue their role as 'mothers' in a less stressful fashion, and learn to function as grandmothers to their children's children. Many middle- and upper-class women turn to volunteer work, taking care of other people's needs. A considerable number, however, reasoning that 'the children are grown' and knowing that their husband is unlikely to grow up if he hasn't by this time, elect to leap for their freedom and become, finally, lesbians, leaving husbands, children and grandchildren to fend for themselves.

Heterosexuality qualifies only as a prefabricated way of living that one slips into anonymously, just as one puts on a hotel bathrobe of the 'one size fits all' variety. It appears to be a rather superficial overlay of social conditioning, not an inherent or integral part of a woman's make-up. Remove the social institutions which support it, and the whole fragile edifice will collapse.

REFERENCES

Downing, Christine (1991) *Myths and Mysteries of Same-Sex Love*. New York: Continuum.

Erikson, Erik H. (1968) *Identity: Youth and Crisis*. New York: W.W. Norton.

Erikson, Erik H. (1982) *The Life Cycle Completed*. New York: W.W. Norton.

Gould, Roger L. (1978) *Transformations: Growth and Change in Adult Life*. New York: Simon and Schuster.

Kelly, Liz (1992) 'Review of Tilman Furniss: *The Multi-Professional Handbook of Child Sexual Abuse*', *Feminism & Psychology* 2(3): 473–6.

Levinson, Daniel J., et al. (1978) *The Seasons of a Man's Life*. New York: Knopf.

Loring, J. Malcolm (1982) *Pictographs and Petroglyphs of the Oregon Country*. Los Angeles, CA: Institute of Archaeology, University of California.

Rich, Adrienne (1986) 'Compulsory Heterosexuality and Lesbian Existence', in *Blood, Bread, and Poetry: Selected Prose 1979–1985*, pp. 23–68. New York: W.W. Norton.

Julia PENELOPE lives and works in Athol, MA, USA. She is a well-known lesbian and feminist writer, and her most recent book is *Call Me Lesbian: Lesbian Lives, Lesbian Theory* (Freedom, CA: The Crossing Press, 1992).

VII

Disability and 'Compulsory Heterosexuality'

Yvon APPLEBY

In suggesting that heterosexual feminists need to examine 'compulsory heterosexuality' as an institution, Adrienne Rich (1989: 129) omits to include the different experiences of disabled women, whose reality is in many ways external to that of 'compulsory heterosexuality'. I use the term 'disabled' to describe the fact that some people are disabled by a society which organizes to exclude, separate and disempower some of its members. Being disabled, then, is a statement about a power relationship that is socially constructed and socially maintained. It is a form of apartheid. This segregation is maintained by the organization of space and transport solely around the needs of ablebodied people; the lack of understanding and acceptance of mental illness or learning difficulties; and the general social invisibility that is a result of being excluded from the major dialogues that take place within society.

Ablebodied feminists have a responsibility actively to ensure that they do not block or prevent the access of disabled women's experience within feminist theory and practice. This responsibility should be undertaken with vigour, courage and honesty — questioning, perhaps painfully, our ablebodied assumptions and privileges. Simply leaving a space for disabled women to fill themselves is not facing up to this responsibility and places all the responsibility and work upon disabled women themselves. This actively ignores the real differences in power, access and income that exist between disabled and ablebodied women. It is also essential that ablebodied feminists do not speak on 'behalf' of disabled women as this would further the power imbalance that exists and in any case disabled women are more than 'able' to speak with knowledge and clarity on their own behalf and construct their own agenda for us to follow. Jenny Morris writes about the importance of integrating disabled women's experience into feminist theory:

> This does not mean that the experience of disability and old age should be 'added on' to existing feminist theory. Integrating these two aspects of identity into feminist thought will be just as revolutionary as feminism's political and theoretical challenge to the way that the experience of the white male was taken as representative of general human experience. Indeed feminism's challenge must remain incomplete while it excludes two such important aspects of human experience and modes of social and economic oppression (Morris, 1991: 8).

Here I point to the exclusion of disabled women from Adrienne Rich's (1989) theory of 'compulsory heterosexuality'.

Adrienne Rich argues that heterosexuality is heavily promoted. The pressures on disabled women to engage in heterosexual practice operate differently from those to which ablebodied women are subjected. Disabled women are particularly at risk of (hetero)sexual abuse and rape, while they are generally not considered to have any sexual feelings or functions (motherhood) and are therefore considered to be less than female (Campling, 1981; Morris, 1989). Indeed for many disabled women the right to bear and raise their children is denied them and if they do then it is monitored and controlled by external forces (Griffin, this issue; Perkins, 1992). It is therefore inappropriate for Rich to suggest that disabled women have the same option to 'escape such causal violations along with economic disadvantages [and] may well turn to marriage as a hoped for protection . . .' (Rich, 1989: 126). In reality this does not appear to be a 'choice' that many disabled women feel that they have. Rich also talks of women responding to the New Right's oppression of difference by using a strategy of 'assimilation' and 'retreat into the sameness' (Rich, 1989: 120). Again, these are perhaps not 'choices' that disabled women have as their reality is of invisibility and exclusion. The assumption of asexuality, and the *denial* of disabled women's sexuality means that heterosexuality can seem far less 'compulsory', and this can facilitate the acceptance of a lesbian identity, as in Kate's experience:

> I have a strong sense of my accident having liberated me when it comes to relationships. I was 19 when I had my accident and I'd grown up with an unthinking expectation of getting married and having numerous children. My immediate reaction in hospital, and for months and years afterwards, was of feeling neutered and completely rejected as a sexual being by men. But I also remember the glimmers of feeling real freedom from Society's expectations of me. Society had rejected me, but that also meant it didn't have any power over me, either. I didn't have to achieve the role of wife and mother any more. . . . Eventually I was able to have my first relationship with a woman without any of the traumas that many of my gay women friends have gone through. I haven't had to face family reactions of 'Why haven't you got married?' or Society's reaction of 'Why haven't you got a man?' because I'm not expected to have one! (quoted in Morris, 1989: 98–9).

In my own research into the invisibility of disabled lesbians within the lesbian community (Appleby, 1990) many of the women I interviewed described similar experiences. 'Lucy' came out at the age of 22 and found her sexuality easier to accept than her identity as a disabled woman: 'There was no model of sexuality pushed at me'. At that time she says that she found it hard to look at her own reflection as her visible difference from the ablebodied norm was more difficult for her to accept than the invisible difference of being a lesbian, as she was considered to be asexual. For some women, though, exclusion from heterosexuality can make the choice of a lesbian identity or celibacy seem less positive a choice because of the implication that they could not get a man anyway. Moreover, the assumed asexuality of disabled women means that a *lesbian* sexuality is equally denied. The father of Sharon Kowalski, disabled in a car crash, is reported to have said 'What the hell difference does it make if she's gay or lesbian or straight because she's laying there in diapers?. . . Let the poor kid rest in peace' (cited in Thompson and Andrzejewski, 1988: 226). In this case, Sharon Kowalski's expressed wish to continue her chosen relationship with her lesbian lover Karen Thompson was for many years denied her.

Adrienne Rich also points to the oppression and denial of lesbianism as a feature of *all* women's lives. This is especially the case for disabled women. Although freer from heterosexual surveillance and control, many obstacles prevent free entry into lesbian community and lesbian culture. Lack of access to information, ramps, signers and braille material, together with a lack of awareness of the needs of women deemed to have mental illness or learning difficulties are some of the factors that work to exclude disabled lesbians. Unfortunately ablebodied lesbians are not free from the prevailing dominant ideas that disabled women are somehow 'other' and nothing to do with them. Organizations 'for' disabled people tend to provide insufficient information about lesbianism, and lesbian groups are ill prepared to deal with disability issues.

I contacted a range of charitable organizations which maintain a high profile on disability issues to ask what they offered lesbians. Some were able to reference useful material (e.g. The Disabled Living Foundation) while others expressed a broad support for an individual's right to choose her own sexuality (Campaign for Valued Futures for People Who Have a Learning Difficulty). Mencap (Royal Society for Mentally Handicapped Children and Adults) replied that if the issue of lesbianism arose their first obligation would be 'to ensure that this was not environmental or other pressures that was leading someone to misinterpret their own situation'. SPOD (Association to Aid Sexual and Personal Relationships of Disabled People) showed a more vigorous and active response and anticipates publishing a booklet on disability and homosexuality. The lack of access to information can make contact with the lesbian community very difficult. 'Pat' describes the process:

> I heard a public announcement for [a lesbian and gay befriending service] on the television. I couldn't ask anyone to tape it for me so for months I sat with my tape recorder at 10.39 each evening when I thought that it might be on. Sure enough it was, literally months later that I was able to tape the telephone number.

Access to information does not guarantee entry into the lesbian community. I contacted six lesbian lines to find out what was wheelchair accessible in their area. Wheelchair accessibility is only one area of access that would prevent a disabled woman's entry into the lesbian community but I used this as a comparison as most people have some understanding of physical access. Of the six lines that were contacted only one was able to offer a partially accessible venue. All the women I spoke to were concerned and explained that it was very difficult to find somewhere that accepted lesbian bookings at affordable prices and those that did were often in basement or in upstairs rooms and not accessible.

Adrienne Rich's analysis of compulsory heterosexuality is both an important milestone in the development of feminist theory and provides a clear example of where the experiences of disabled women are external to the analysis of 'all women'. This is perhaps a reflection of its time of writing, where disabled women were at best 'added on' and at worst totally ignored. Rich (1989: 129) speaks of the 'special quality of courage' which is necessary when we question the shaping of identity, power, preference and desire. As feminists we must use this courage to question our collusion with 'ablebodiedism' and must seek continually to develop feminist theories and practice which integrate the experiences of disabled women from the outset.

REFERENCES

Appleby, Yvon (1990) 'Access Limited: An Exploration into Why Disabled Lesbians are so Invisible within the Lesbian Community', unpublished dissertation, Staffordshire Polytechnic.

Campling, J. (1981) *Images of Ourselves: Women with Disabilities Talking*. London: Routledge and Kegan Paul.

Morris, Jenny, ed. (1989) *Able Lives*. London: The Women's Press.

Morris, Jenny (1991) *Pride Against Prejudice*. London: The Women's Press.

Perkins, Rachel (1992) 'Catherine is Having a Baby', *Feminism & Psychology* 2(1): 110–12.

Rich, Adrienne (1989) 'Compulsory Heterosexuality and Lesbian Existence', in Laurel Richardson and Veta Taylor (eds) *Feminist Frontiers II: Rethinking Sex, Gender and Society*. New York: Random House.

Thompson, Karen and Andrzejewski, Julie (1988) *Why Can't Sharon Kowalski Come Home?* San Francisco, CA: Spinsters.

Yvon APPLEBY is currently researching lesbians in education and is based at the Division of Education, University of Sheffield, The Arts Tower, Floor 9, Western Bank, Sheffield, UK.

VIII

A Homogeneous Habit?
Heterosexual Display in the English Holiday Camp

Helen (charles)

How has an increased awareness and presence of lesbian, gay and now bisexual identities affected heterosexuals? Does the adoption of the dyke crew-cut by straight women signal an appraisal of lesbianism? Does the wearing of cowrie-studded dreadlocks or Doc Martens by straight Black women point to a potential zami or khush? And the question foremost in my mind: now that the stability of heterosexuality (in the long-term monogamous sense) is being challenged, will there be an increase in the number of people who consider the existence of 'choice' in sexual identity?

Actively turning heterosexuality into a habit, rather than a chosen sexual identity, might well throw up some interesting developments in terms of the differences within heterosexuality per se. For not all heterosexuals can be said to have had no choice in the sexuality they enjoy. Ex-lesbians and gay men choose to be straight (see Bart, this volume). Het friends and family of lesbians and gays choose to be straight. But it is food for thought that these particular choices become necessarily based on and constructed around a binary opposition: are these decisions to be heterosexual dependent on the knowledge of the oppositional 'non-heterosexual'? And if that knowledge did not exist, or was not appropriate, would 'heterosexuality' be just a habit?

But, heterosexuality is not composed of heterosexual couples as homogeneous units. In fact, heterogeneity may be a more useful description in this so-called multicultural society. For the heterosexual model may be reproduced across cultures and interculturally, but it is merely a template for the diversity of practices within heterosexuality. The shape may be the same but the materials, arrangement and colour will always be different. Having said this, however, it is possible to see an element of such homogeneity in heterosexual display — particularly in the English holiday camp.

Last year, I had the rare opportunity to observe heterosexuality as a 'postmodern' lifestyle — that is, a portrayal of (family) life which attempts to delete the internal concerns of a 'class-less' society and results in the formulation of a stereotype akin to those pumped out in postwar Britain. As home care support workers, two of us were accompanying a resident on her annual holiday. The setting was the new-style holiday camp, CenterParcs, situated in Elvedon Forest, Suffolk, and boasting almost 900 villas, a tropical swimming complex (complete with Tarzan calls every 20 minutes), fitness and health studios, restaurants, bars and the indispensable shopping mall. On arriving at reception, as part of a new week's worth of holiday-makers, we harboured individual first impressions of what was to be a kind of anthropological journey into the realm of what constitutes Normal Life in England. For us, the spectacle of hundreds of white, 'ablebodied', co-residential (nuclear) units comprising two or more children was a culture shock. My co-worker's exclamation: 'It's *so* heterosexual!' paralleled the thoughts I was having about it being *so* 'white' and heterosexual. The CenterParcs ethos was such that it embodied distinct codes of heterosexual conduct, which were stereotypes in themselves: respectability in the production and exposure of non-'pretended', always-happy couples and their families; protected by their able bodies and whiteness. But it was all contained in the confined space of a man-made village-camp.

What we were seeing was a large dose of a standardized image. The holiday village attracted *us* primarily because of its reputed wheelchair accessibility. Why did it attract so many stereotypical heterosexuals, I wondered. The answer, of course, lay in the advertising: a powerful, propagating medium, controlled by a dominant culture which sees itself as the norm.

An article by Amanda Mitchison (1992) describes how the myth of the American Wild West was adopted to 'almost fetishistic ends' within the camp walls of Fred Pontin's Country and Western Venture weeks of the mid-1970s. She tells us about 'fully grown men and women dressed up as cowboys, Indians, gamblers, saloon hussies, Mexicans . . . and other loosely associated historical archetypes', and goes on to say how:

> . . . the success of these holidays demonstrates not only how total has been the American conquest of British culture, but also just how inclined we are to behave eccentrically if brought together in a confined space (Mitchison, 1992: 38).

Could this eccentricity have something to do with heterosexuality? Or is it connected to being white (cf. [charles], 1992) and British? Or all of these? Perhaps these were insights into how (one form of) white British heterosexual identity operates. Having been heterosexual myself, the family images that were projected in and around the purpose-built CenterParcs village highlighted the necessity to understand the heterogeneity of heterosexuality. For I certainly could not identify my previous heterosexual self with the images around me. I had not seen or been part of the ideology of these 'fully grown men and women' who seemed to be dressed up as heterosexual stereotypes.

Perhaps it is the annual need to see or maintain reflections of 'real' heterosexuality, in its most stereotypical state, that draws these people together. A week of mingling with a miniature version of the dominant culture gave us withdrawal symptoms and sent our ever ready eyes in search of concrete images of the differences we were accustomed to in our respective communities: mobility, lesbianism and Blackness. If we had been able to retain the act of the traditional anthropologist, we would have left CenterParcs with our anecdotes and memories, confident of our existences as part of a dominant culture. As it was, the peculiar institution of a stereotypical heterosexuality made its contemporary imprint and forced us to concede that we had been ever so gently pushed into the interstice of the 'subcultural'.

As we drove away from the glossy package that was our holiday, I wondered if the three of us would have become our own stereotypes, if our self-images had not refused the seemingly desperate economy of 'heterosexual' life in Britain.

REFERENCES

(charles), Helen (1992) 'Whiteness — The Relevance of Politically Colouring the "Non"', in H. Hinds et al. (eds) *Working Out: New Directions for Women's Studies*. London: Falmer.

Mitchison, A. (1992) *The Independent Magazine* 23 July: 38.

Helen (charles) likes the shape of her name to be respected. The fact that the 'family' names of many black people originate in the nomenclature of slave-owners means that naming has not been a matter of free choice for centuries. She is an active member of the Brighton and Hove Black Women's Group, and is currently researching Black, lesbian and 'white' identities.

IX

Sisterhood in the Service of Patriarchy: Heterosexual Women's Friendships and Male Power

Tamsin WILTON

Until the age of 29 I was happily, enthusiastically and actively heterosexual. Between 29 and 35 I was still officially a 'practising' heterosexual, but was increasingly struggling with the difficulties of reconciling my heterosexuality (and by then my marriage) with my emotional, intellectual and political life. Then, in the best (and most ideologically unsound) tradition of romantic narrative, I fell in love with a lesbian, and on Hallowe'en 1987, at the age of 35, I 'came out'.

What follows is not, I must stress, simply a case of the new convert evangelizing, nor of the released convict advocating prison reform. I do not believe that lesbianism holds the high moral ground of feminism, nor do I want to disavow my heterosexual past as mistaken, unhappy, abusive or somehow less 'real' than my lesbian present. On the contrary, I believe that some of my heterosexual relationships were as egalitarian, politically radical and emotionally intimate as it is possible for a heterosexual relationship to be. What is important, for women and for feminism, is to critique and to problematize the institution of heterosexuality and to examine the implications of heterosexual identity for feminist practice, and I want to use my particular history to contribute to this enterprise.

My own heterosexual experience is the familiar stuff of feminist research findings (Gavey, 1992; Hite, 1987) and hence of little interest here. Suffice it to say that I found myself in an emotional and sexual trap, obliged to turn for comfort, warmth, closeness intimacy and sexual pleasure to members of a social group whose interests directly and in every way conflicted with mine. Women's sexual and intimate relationships with men, however consensual and egalitarian on an individual level, are de facto acted upon by, and obliged to engage with, the hegemonic construction of heterosexuality which assigns power, autonomy and subject-hood differentially to men and to women. Thus, for the great majority of the world's women, the very notion of 'consent' in relation to sexual activities with men is problematic (Gavey, 1992; Jeffreys, 1990).

Heterosexuality then, emotionally and sexually, was for me largely characterized by a continual struggle to assert my autonomy, get my needs met and have my subjective experience recognized. This never-ending process ranged from the painful attempt to argue with one lover who flatly refused to accept that I had any sensation whatsoever inside my vagina (because a male doctor had told him that the vagina has 'no nerve endings', he insisted that my physical sensations were the result of hysterical delusion), to the recognition that I would have to train myself to reach orgasm as rapidly as possible, because 'sex' ended with male ejaculation. This is nothing new. We have known for decades that men generally have little to offer women, emotionally or sexually (Hite, 1987; Greer, 1970; Gavey, 1992). What I now recognize as important is that what I have called 'a continual struggle' was a process *entirely unrecognized* by me as such. Additionally, what I want to focus on here is the role played by heterosexual female culture, sisterhood, solidarity, woman-bonding, call it what you will, in *supporting and sustaining* the power differential between heterosexual women and men.

The mutual support which women, as oppressed groups (I use the plural to indicate that the oppression of women takes different forms in different cultures and at different historical times), have offered each other is traditionally seen within feminisms as a feminist phenomenon, pro-woman and potentially radical and subversive (Rich, 1986; Jeffreys, 1985; Raymond, 1986). Adrienne Rich, indeed, sees such bonding as part of a 'lesbian continuum', no less. This is something which has been taken up readily by heterosexual feminists in order to negate the difference between lesbian feminism and heterosexual feminism. How often do we hear heterosexual feminists assert that 'we are all women-loving women, what you do in bed is immaterial'? I suggest that this identification of women's friendships as intrinsically 'feminist' is politically very dangerous for two reasons. Firstly, because it acts to make lesbianism 'invisible' — exactly as patriarchy has always done — and to diffuse the threat posed by lesbian feminists to heterosexual supremacy, and hence to male supremacy. Secondly, because, in my experience, as a heterosexual woman, bonding between heterosexual women acts to shore up the heteropatriarchy.

Woman-bonding within heterosexuality operates within a set of contradictions. On the one hand, it functions as 'consciousness raising', as a forum for recognizing that our problems with heterosexual relationships are not individual and unique to us, but shared by many women. The consensus is not that each individual woman is struggling in isolation with purely personal problems, but that it is the nature of men in general which causes difficulty: 'men are like that!' On the other hand, my long experience of heterosexual female friendships reflects an essentialist tendency — a tendency to regard men as 'naturally' flawed, in the way that children are held to be 'naturally' immature (indeed, men are often characterized in heterosexual women's talk as childish or child-like, as 'great babies' or 'big children'). Men come in for much criticism, and sympathetic sisterly reassurance when a particular man has treated a particular woman badly typically depicts the man as an unfeeling or selfish bastard, and as representative of his sex. What conspicuously does *not* come in for criticism, true to its ubiquitous 'elemental' status, is heterosexuality. The motivation for heterosexual woman-bonding is analogous to that of a battlefield hospital: to get the casualties fit and well so that they may be sent straight back to fight — not to rescue combatants from the horrors of war or to protest at war itself. The contradiction at the heart of heterosexual woman-bonding is that, however clearly it is reiterated that 'all men are like that' or 'all men are bastards', women suffering at the hands of men are only ever advised to leave *him*, never to leave *them*. Heterosexuality as the institution which oppresses women is never challenged: the possibility on offer is never to break out of jail, merely to institute a change of jailer. Thus the oppressed collude with the oppressor, patching up the harm done by him, and keeping it secret, private, 'women's business'. The irony of it all is that such support, involving as it does slagging off men, disloyalty to male partners and secret insubordination, can be experienced as subversive, as challenging to male dominance, whereas in reality it is no different from what goes on among groups of heterosexual men complaining about their womenfolk.

This process of collusion was not available to my conscious scrutiny until after

I became a lesbian. It was only when I recognized a new (and distressing) shallowness in my relationships with long-standing heterosexual women friends that I began to analyse what was happening now and what had been happening 'then' (i.e. when I shared a heterosexual identity with them). Some, made defensive by my lesbianism, refused to talk about their intimate relationships with men. They suspected (quite rightly) that I now had a new piece of advice to offer, 'leave them', and it was not something which they were prepared to hear. Nor were they prepared to hear anything about my lesbian relationship, silencing me time after time with loudly voiced assertions that it simply wasn't important, it didn't matter to them that I was a lesbian, it didn't change the way they felt about me. Beneath this anxious mask of tolerant liberalism was a plea that I should refrain from saying anything which would oblige them to perceive themselves as heterosexual rather than as simply female. Leaving our sexual relationships out of the conversation left us with very little to talk about. To my initial surprise, women with whom I had previously enjoyed many animated and affectionate evenings, talking deep into the night and sharing what had seemed at the time witty and perceptive feminist insights into 'the man problem', became diffident and inarticulate. Conversation became embarrassing and stilted, full of uncomfortable pregnant silences. Once or twice I have attempted to address what I felt was probably going on beneath the surface, but this has always resulted in strenuous denial and, all too often, in the subsequent mysterious death of the friendship.

Others have chosen to continue sharing the narratives of their heterosexual relationships with me, leaving me biting my tongue in frustration. It is no longer easy for me to understand why women put up with men, no longer easy to listen to a dear friend repeat for the Nth time the same old story of abuse, betrayal, neglect and misery and merely nod my head in sympathy. I want to shake them, to cry, 'get out! escape! find yourself a good woman!' What I have to keep reminding myself is that they are still stuck on Planet Hetero, still breathing its air, still weighed down by its gravity, still regarding me as a creature from another planet.

This is more than merely a personal dilemma for individual heterosexual women: it is a political problem for feminism. While heterosexual woman-bonding functions so efficiently to support patriarchal power relations, and while heterosexual women think in terms of 'men' or even 'masculinity', without at the same time recognizing the institutional nature of heterosexuality, there is no chance of developing a sustainable and credible critique of heteropatriarchy. We need to develop new and radical critiques of female friendship that go beyond mere sentimentality if we are to dig out the roots of patriarchal power from down among the women.

REFERENCES

Gavey, Nicola (1992) 'Technologies and Effects of Heterosexual Coercion', *Feminism & Psychology* 2(3): 325–51.
Greer, Germaine (1970) 'The Politics of Female Sexuality' in *OZ* May.
Hite, Shere (1987) *Women and Love: A Cultural Revolution in Progress*. Harmondsworth: Penguin.
Jeffreys, Sheila (1985) *The Spinster and Her Enemies*. London: Pandora.

Jeffreys, Sheila (1990) *Anticlimax: A Feminist Perspective on the Sexual Revolution*. London: The Women's Press.

Radicalesbians (1970) cited in Lisa Tuttle (1986) *Encyclopedia of Feminism*. London: Arrow.

Raymond, Janice (1986) *A Passion for Friends*. London: The Women's Press.

Rich, Adrienne (1986) 'Compulsory Heterosexuality and Lesbian Existence', in Adrienne Rich, *Blood, Bread and Poetry*. London: Virago.

Tamsin WILTON is author of the forthcoming *Lesbian Studies Primer* (Routledge) and teaches in the Faculty of Health and Community Studies, New University of the West of England, St Matthias, Oldbury Court Road, Fishponds, Bristol, UK.

INDEX